Computing and Informatio y

Eric Deeson

Blackwell Education

First published 1988

Basil Blackwell Ltd
108 Cowley Road
Oxford OX4 1JF
UK

British Library Cataloguing in Publication Data
Deeson, Eric
  Computing and information technology.
  1. Computer sciences—Questions & answers—For schools
  I. Title
  004′.076

  ISBN 0–631–90168–X

Illustrated by Anne Langford
Typeset in 10/12 Garamond and Optima by Columns of Reading
Printed and bound in Great Britain by Butler & Tanner Ltd,
Frome, Somerset

Cover A computer graphics display of a VLSI spatial light
modulator chip designed by Douglas McKnight.
© Department of Physics, University of Edinburgh.
Reproduced by permission; photograph courtesy of Peter
Tuffy.

Contents

Hallo and welcome

Read me

I hope you enjoy reading and working with this book as much as I enjoyed writing it. To make that possible, it will help if you read this introduction quickly; it includes details about how to use the book, and points to save you time and trouble.

Information technology (of which computing is a crucial part) is very important as the basis of many aspects of modern life. It's an exciting subject to explore—not just because of its importance, but because it's changing very fast: it's an area in which science fiction very quickly turns into fact. Every week, there are new developments; many of these are likely to affect the lives of most people in a short time.

The biggest problem with this rapid rate of change is that it's hard for learners, teachers, and exam boards to keep up. It's hard, too, to know what's important now, let alone what will be important in a couple of years' time. In the context of the course you're following, this means public exam syllabuses differ quite a lot from each other; they're also likely to change quite fast. That caused me a problem. Though I wrote this after the first AS students started their courses, not all the exam boards had published even draft syllabuses.

All the same, I believe this book adequately covers your needs. I've used all available information on AS level syllabuses to prepare it, and I include various methods of helping you study further. (I'll come back to those shortly.)

This book's too fat

However, for two reasons there's more in this book than you need for your course. First, each exam board includes topics others omit, so there's material here you don't want but others do. Second, I've tried to look forward, so I include quite a lot no exam board yet asks for.

There are three ways you can find out what you need to study and what you can skip. The first is to rely on your teacher to tell you: you can assume that he or she has carried out the research needed to know your syllabus in some detail.

The second is for you to study the syllabus. However, syllabuses are often rather vague, and reading yours may not help you as much as you'd like. Don't forget that exam boards provide syllabuses for the teachers—who know what all the terms mean and have a feeling for required level of detail—rather than for the learners.

The third approach is to look at, and to try working with, actual exam papers. In this book, with many thanks to the exam boards for the permission, I include a number of 'real' questions. For this first edition (written early in 1988), there isn't a huge bank of questions I can call on; also, all those available are sample ones—open to change, and perhaps devised more quickly than would be the case with questions for actual papers.

However you go about that research, you may perhaps find areas in your course *not* treated in this book. That's because some boards offer choice between areas covered in great depth. You may need supplementary reading in that case—check Appendix C for some ideas (well, check that appendix in *any* case).

The exam boards vary, too, in their methods of assessing students. You may, or may not, have some kind of case study to explore; if you do, the depth of study required will depend on the board. You may, or may not, have to produce course work or carry out some kind of project; if you do, the details will depend on your board.

I've included ten case studies in this book, one at the start of each chapter. I know they're short, and simpler than 'real life', but I hope you find them interesting reading, whatever your needs; you may also wish to use them for case study practice, but I don't ask many direct questions about them. Most of the case studies, by the way, don't link very closely with the content of the chapters in which they appear; don't let that worry you.

Exam questions

The questions I *do* ask come in two blocks at the end of each chapter. The second block contains relevant sample questions from the exam boards, and there are more of those in Appendix A. I give in round brackets—(n)—the mark for each question or part question as stated by the boards; square brackets—[n]—contain the marks I've guessed where the board doesn't supply the information.

In an exam you'll need to spend something like a minute and a half per mark. Again that depends on the board. I give the name of the board after each question, so you can particularly look out for ones like those you may meet yourself. If you do that, work out more closely how many minutes you'll need to spend per mark.

The boards who kindly allowed me to use their questions are (with my codes):

- The Associated Examining Board (AEB)
- The University of London School Examinations Board (London)
- The Joint Matriculation Board (JMB)
- The Cambridge, Oxford and Southern School Examinations Council (COSSEC)
- University of Oxford Delegacy of Local Examinations (Oxford)

Here's how best to use a 'real' exam question like those. Read quickly through it, then do as much work as you think you need to be able to write a good answer. That work may include study of your notes, and of this and other books; talk with fellow students on the course, your teachers, and others; thought; and planning.

Then leave the question, for as much as a day if you can. When you come to attempt it for real, do so under exam conditions—with no help, no TV or music, no interruptions, and in the correct time for the question. (Take the time to be at the rate of a minute and a half per mark unless you've found out otherwise.) Only then, look at the my notes in Appendix B.

Where they relate to exam board questions, the notes have neither been provided nor approved by the boards. They're brief anyway—not even summary answers. However, some exam boards publish guide answers and marking schemes for their sample exam questions. As with syllabuses, these are to aid the teachers—but if you're working without a teacher, these notes (if you can get them) may provide some extra help.

In the Appendix A questions I include some that concern case studies. While you won't be able to do much with these without the case studies they relate to, the questions will give you some idea of what to expect in this context.

Self-development questions

The first block of questions at the end of each chapter goes by the name of self-development. I made these questions up. I did so, thinking of use in two ways—for you to attempt as your teacher suggests, or for you to think about (alone or in a group) if you're interested.

I don't give marks for these questions (though again there are brief notes in Appendix B) as most are open-ended. By this I mean you can spend almost any amount of time on each one, from perhaps a few minutes up to (in some cases) several weeks. There are plenty of ideas here for class activity, research projects, and coursework assignments; some could even lead to hobby tasks or business opportunities. They are to help you develop yourself as a person with interest in and understanding of information technology, rather than as a store of facts.

There's a couple of hundred of these self-development questions in this book. Clearly you won't have time to go far with more than a small fraction of them. Please don't try to prove me wrong: you'll end up with a nervous breakdown if you do. Too many questions can damage your health.

MORE questions?

Even so, there's another source of questions in this book. Near the start of each chapter I've put a list of objectives; the list begins 'When you have worked through this chapter you should be able to . . .'. Each objective in the list is written as a question you can set yourself as a quick revision test.

That's not the real reason I've put in those lists of objectives, though. They are, perhaps, the best way for you to relate this book to your syllabus and to your progress through the course.

I've therefore also collected all ten lists of objectives together as Appendix D. You have my permission to put a copy of that appendix into your notes file, and—with your teacher's help—to delete the objectives that don't apply to your exam board. As you work through the course, you can then tick off the objectives met, and also note by them the date and the page numbers in your notes.

Appended

There's one last appendix to draw to your attention: in Appendix C I list some resource items that may help with your study. You should read this list quite early in your course, and refer to it again and again as you need.

Finally, just before the index is a glossary. This is a sort of little IT dictionary. Despite what I said above, there *is* a factual aspect to this course, and you *do* have to know the meanings of quite a lot of words, phrases and abbreviations. Though my glossary doesn't provide all the answers, you should find it easy to refer to quickly, and you should find it of value for revision.

Thanks and such

By such means, I've done all I can to make this book interesting and of use to you. If you think I could have done more, please let me know your views. Then I'll be happy to acknowledge your help when I set to work on the next edition. Meanwhile, I now gladly note my appreciation of aid given me already, by:

- the exam boards who let me use their questions;
- the people and firms who supplied photographs (acknowledged after each caption);
- people who've supplied useful thoughts in discussion: fellow IT teachers at Joseph Chamberlain College, Birmingham (in particular Flick Blewitt, Chris Field, Mike Greaves, John Morris, Charley Munden, Bridget

Parsons, Mary Phillips, and Eileen Young) and others (in particular Doug Brown, John Foster, Richard Fothergill, Jacquetta Megarry, Pam New, Tim Reeve, Brian Samways, and Kathy Streddar);

- the many—far too many to count, let alone name—who've supplied useful thoughts in their writings, talks, phone calls, and electronic mail messages, or during the hectic 24-hours-a-day interactions at conferences;
- the members of my family, for their well-practised patience as I so often vanish into my study;
- Jenny Healey, who had a huge number of words to process from scribbled sheets and gabbled tapes;
- Don Manley, my persuasive Blackwell editor and Diyan Leake, the best copy editor I've ever encountered;
- Alan Hunter, who read the draft manuscript in incredible detail and fed back many very useful comments, and
- the past and present students who, knowingly or not, have been the testbed for much material in this book.

Even my present students were born too early to work at AS level computing: they'll just have got their Advanced level results by the time this book comes out. So I'm glad to dedicate the work to them, my 1986–88 Advanced Level Computer Science class:

Jawaid Akhtar	Ebrahim Mohamed
Mohammed Ajmal	Tunu Miah
Barry Benn	Latika Parekh
George Ellis	Tajinder Sagoo
Amjad Hussain	Mohammed Shafique
Ahmed Kasu	Jason Southall
Sajad Khan	Sanjeev Sudera
Arshad Mahmood	Mark West

And I dedicate it to you—in a sense my future students—and to your success in the IT-based twenty-first century!

Eric Deeson
Harborne
Birmingham

January 1988

1 Information technology and computers

Figure 1.1 *This communications satellite under test shows links between telecommunications, video, computing and electronics, major threads of information technology* (British Aerospace)

Case study 1—Esther Boswell processes words

Esther Boswell owns a small computer consultancy company; both she and her colleague Keith Starsky use word processor systems for the preparation of correspondence, guide booklets and reports. A typical simple session runs like this.

After ensuring that the computer system's properly connected and switched on, Esther inserts her working disc into the drive and 'boots' it to start things moving. Booting involves getting the system automatically to set up the word processor function and to carry out two or three introductory tasks. The word processor's main menu appears on screen, followed by a list of all the text documents stored on the disc.

Some of these 'texts' are standard layouts that Esther uses to give a uniform look to her various kinds of work. Pressing a couple of keys causes the system to transfer a copy of the layout she needs for writing reports into the computer's memory. All this takes just a few seconds.

The next stage involves typing in the actual text of the report; Esther has prepared this mentally and has rough notes on paper, so she knows pretty well what she wants to say. So she types with fair confidence, despite using only two or three fingers.

Editing is a fairly straightforward task too. A quick key-press lets Esther jump back to the start of the document; she works through it on the screen, inserting extra material, deleting stray characters as required, and laying it out better. Sometimes she moves a whole paragraph from one part of the text to another. Sometimes she uses special keys to call up task-oriented screen menus to help her choose the effects she wants. Sometimes she even transfers to her new document material from others she and Keith have written in the past. She can also call on a spelling checker program to tell her about words that could be wrongly spelt.

The word processor is a WYSIWYG one—'what you see is what you get'. This means that at all times the text appears on screen much as it would be printed out on paper. Esther's current document is, however, to be produced in two columns and the WYSIWYG screen doesn't show that. After a while, therefore, Esther turns back to the main menu and asks the system—with another key-press—to 'preview' the text, to show it on screen properly laid out in double column format. This allows

Figure 1.2   *Esther Boswell's word processor hardware is a standard micro system* (International Computers Ltd)

electric typewriter quality. At this stage, Esther is interested only in seeing a rough draft, so she chooses the first option. The text transfers to the printer's own store (buffer), thus freeing the computer for other tasks while the printout is being made.

The author checks the paper draft carefully for final errors and possible opportunities for further polish. After a bit more editing, Esther is satisfied and saves her text as a file on disc for use in the future. This requires a few more simple operations from the word processor's main menu, but takes only seconds. Finally she 'locks' the file to make it fairly safe from accidental erasure and instructs the system to print out a high-quality copy for their client.

All that work took no more than a couple of hours. During it Esther typed in and carefully edited a seven-page document. Since she learned how to use the word processor, she's put all her reports and a number of fairly standard letters on to disc. This is because she realises that she can quickly print any of them out at any time in the future, with or without change. Already she's had some proof of this: they've been able to produce updated copies of some reports at great speed for other clients.

Another major benefit of this aspect of the system is not so obvious. It's that, even after a few more years, Esther and Keith could carry the saved masters of all their reports and other such documents around on no more than two or three floppy discs that cost less and take up less space than a small paperback book. The benefits as regards office organisation will be enormous, they are sure.

The way the office computer system is organised allows other benefits. Esther and Keith both use their microcomputers a lot, and not just for word processing. The machines are linked together to form a simple network; each user can easily access the other's files, and they share a hard disc drive (as well as having their own floppies) to make that access straightforward. Because they do not work in the same room, they have a dot matrix printer each; however, they plan to buy and share a fast, high-quality page printer as soon as the prices drop enough.

her to take a close look at the overall final appearance of the document. One or two more errors come to light and Esther quickly edits those as before.

The main menu also provides her with the option of pressing a key to tell the system to print a copy of the text in the computer's memory. The printer is a common dot matrix machine that either churns out text in 'draft mode' at impressive speed or prints rather more slowly with

Introduction

For many people now, the process of transferring thoughts to paper is no longer inhibited by the problems of control of pen or old-fashioned typewriter—word processing makes the task much more like fun.

Indeed in almost all contexts the word processor is showing its potential of becoming a powerful liberating force. If you have not yet experienced that liberation with your work, I urge you to try it as soon as you can.

The computer is the basis of modern information technology (IT), and in this book I shall be looking specifically at its uses and its links to other equipment. The

computer, or at least its main component, the microprocessor, is also the most obvious part of the majority of IT systems; we therefore need to understand it to the extent of seeing its relevance to the wealth of practical applications and implications. It is also important to accept that computers can, and often do, stand alone as useful total systems in their own right.

For all these reasons, this chapter provides an overview of the use and nature of computers. The technical content won't be heavy; however, I am taking the chance to provide a vehicle for bringing together a lot of the basic jargon that you're bound to come across in your reading and discussions.

There's a good deal more jargon that I shan't mention here—this chapter covers what I feel is indispensable to a proper understanding of how computers can help people work with greater efficiency and more enjoyment. As far as concerns technical terms, however, note that the book closes with a detailed glossary of relevant terms that I hope you'll refer to whenever you need.

Objectives

When you have worked through this chapter, you should be able to

1 state what information technology is and explain its importance
2 discuss briefly the significance of information technology to the financial world
3 describe briefly some of the uses of Prestel
4 comment on the benefits of information technology to public and private transport
5 define 'computer' and explain the terms used in your definition
6 state the difference between analog and digital signals
7 define 'computer program' and explain why people need programs
8 state, with examples, the difference between data and information
9 draw a block diagram of a standard computer, showing the directions of data flow; explain the function of and need for each block; and give examples of each type of peripheral
10 define 'bit' and 'byte' and discuss the use of bytes as a measure of computer memory size
11 distinguish between ROM and RAM
12 discuss the nature and uses of a mainframe, mini-computer, micro-computer and network
13 define 'hardware', 'software' and 'firmware'
14 discuss the basics of internal and external computer communications
15 describe the features and use of a typical word processor

1.1 IT is the basis of modern society

Information technology (IT) concerns the uses of systems that allow the transfer, storage, processing and presentation of information; its interest should be the benefit of society and of its individual members. In that computers are information processors and very efficient devices for controlling information storage and transfer, it is a fair claim that information technology as we know it depends on them.

It is also a fair claim that society as we know it depends on information for its efficient running. We can define 'information' as that which adds to human knowledge—and knowing what is going on is essential for societies to survive and for individuals to be effective members of them.

Indeed, it is hardly possible to think of any human activity which cannot and does not already benefit from the availability of information, and therefore cannot or will not gain from developments in IT. The computer has never been an invention looking for an application (as has been the case with some other inventions); its progress has always been demand-led, in that people have at all times been able to say 'wouldn't it be nice if we could . . .'.

Computers have therefore developed very rapidly. They have also already become essential tools in most (if not all) large organisations, and grown in importance in smaller firms and the home. Both trends continue without any sign of slowing down.

The case studies which you'll find in this book, like the one that opened this chapter, will give some idea of how computer-based systems are being used already. Let me now take a quick look at some more general areas of application.

1.2 IT at work

In the financial world there has been tremendous change in the past decade or so. Before IT became common in the clearing (High Street) banks, most customers were resigned to spending lengthy periods in queues to cash cheques, to carry out transfers, or even just to enquire about the status of their accounts. Transfers could take up to a week to pass through the system, and errors were not uncommon.

Now the queues in bank branches are much reduced by the ubiquitous 'hole in the wall', the 24-hours-a-day **autoteller** (Figure 1.3). This can provide cash on demand and a display of current balance as well as offer more and more other information and services. Indeed, a growing number of customers can obtain such information and services without going out—they can use their personal computers through the medium of 'home and office' banking, for example on Prestel (Figure 1.4). In that case, of course, cash withdrawals are not available, but because of so many spinoffs of IT in banking, the personal need for cash is falling fast anyway. (I'm not sure, though, whether we'll ever reach a true cashless society, though many people predict that that will come about.)

Money transfers now take place much more quickly, too, and with somewhat less error, cutting costs in various ways. Indeed, a growing number of people and organisations are able to leave a proportion of those transfers entirely to the computers, letting them buy and sell goods, stocks, shares and currencies automatically and instantaneously on the basis of continuously updated details of market prices. Money is information, after all, as you'll agree if you think about it.

I mentioned Prestel in that account. Prestel—the world's first public viewdata service—is a splendid example of IT, with its tight relationship between computers, video and telecommunications. By linking your TV set or computer

Figure 1.3   *The autoteller can make bank and building society usage much less trouble* (Barclays)

Figure 1.4   *Telebanking is even more comfortable and offers more features than the autoteller, though it can't give you cash* (Royal Bank of Scotland)

and the telephone network with a modem, you can rapidly access a huge bank of information interactively. Thus, after looking at travel timetables on Prestel, you can book seats and holiday packages. You can make hotel and theatre bookings in the same way, and order deliveries of groceries, flowers and other gifts. You can send messages to Prestel users elsewhere with the system's electronic mail facility, and to non-users by linking to the world-wide telex and mail networks. News; local and world weather; educational, financial and geographical data—all these and many more areas of information (as well as games) are available to Prestel users at any time of day or night, often at little more than the cost of a local phone call (Figure 1.5). Prestel is the subject of the case study in Chapter 2.

IT also helps public transport to provide a better and more efficient service. It allows management to have a clear,

Figure 1.5   *Prestel users have a huge range of services at their finger tips* (Telefocus)

Figure 1.6 *Telecommunications allows bus and train drivers to keep in touch with their control centres* (British Railways Board)

Figure 1.7 *The mobile phone can save some people hours of trouble each day* (British Telecom)

up-to-date picture of the position and status of each vehicle (whether plane, train or bus) and to keep in touch with the crew (Figure 1.6). As an appreciation of this continuous knowledge grows, maybe there is hope that public transport delays will become a dim memory of the past!

At the same time, private transport is not being left behind by the IT revolution. The number of car drivers able to remain attached to their office by the invisible umbilical cord of a radio link to the telephone system is growing (Figure 1.7), while their journey times are falling because of linked traffic-control systems, more quickly and efficiently operated road works, and warning messages from the in-car computer. Indeed, London has started a route-finder system which gives each subscribing driver full information about the best way to any destination, taking account of one-way streets, likely temporary delays, road closures and traffic jams.

At work, IT-based information transfers (including word processing and electronic mail) can markedly increase efficiency and job satisfaction. At leisure, Prestel-style sports bookings and details of entertainment programmes and restaurant menus help people lead fuller lives. At home, the personal computer is starting to take up an essential role outside of playing games—the home is in transition to a unit integrated into society rather than being a traditional castle with closed drawbridge. Prestel-style information communications is linking with cable and satellite television and video phones so much that there is a marked growth in the number of people working with IT from home—telecommuters, people call them. Indeed, IT *is* the basis of our modern society. There are dangers in that as well as huge benefits, but it is a fact.

Just as IT is the basis of our society, so the computer is the central focus of IT. So let me turn now to considering the computer itself.

1.3 The computer—basis of IT

What is a computer (Figure 1.8)? That question has many answers, because computers are different things to different people. Indeed, some might say that it doesn't matter at all what a computer actually is, for our concern should be simply its place in society and its usage in specific situations. While there is truth in that comment as far as the uninterested user may be concerned, I think it is important for you to have some kind of clear view. Here then is a definition that can get us started.

A computer is a modern, high-speed, general purpose, digital electronic, stored program data processor.

I agree this definition is far from perfect in that it tends to raise more questions than it answers. Indeed, there are plenty of computers nowadays that don't fully meet the definition, but as far as concerns machines like those we shall concentrate on in this book, it'll do very well.

Let's look at that sentence term by term.

Modern

The computer as we know it, and as typified by office, school and personal micros (for instance), goes back in

Figure 1.8   *The modern micro is a high-speed, general purpose, digital electronic, stored program data processor* (InterTan UK Ltd)

Figure 1.9   *The computer of over three decades ago does not differ in principle from a modern micro* (IBM)

essential concepts only a few decades. Authors who write histories of computing tend to start with people, ideas, and dreams in the sixteenth and seventeenth centuries and onwards. The stories that they can tell are interesting ones, but this isn't the place for them. I shall concentrate on the computers of today and tomorrow.

In fact, today's machines are not essentially different from those developed by the end of the Second World War (Figure 1.9). In other words, our office and personal computer systems aren't really different from those early electronic calculating machines used for research, ballistics, code-breaking and so on. In various countries, a great deal of effort is now currently being put in to develop the next so-called generation of computers—but pretty well all I say about computers in this book will apply to them too.

High-speed

The central processor of even a cheap home computer can carry out millions of operations in a second—and does so all the time it is switched on. The most powerful of modern machines may work a thousand times faster, but for most normal purposes such speed is unnecessary, especially in view of the fact that the price of a fast computer is far more than a thousand times greater than the price of one that is not so fast.

General purpose

With suitable equipment attached to it, and with suitable instructions to guide it, the modern computer could do almost anything one could want. Agreed, in very many cases the trouble and cost would not be worth the results, but

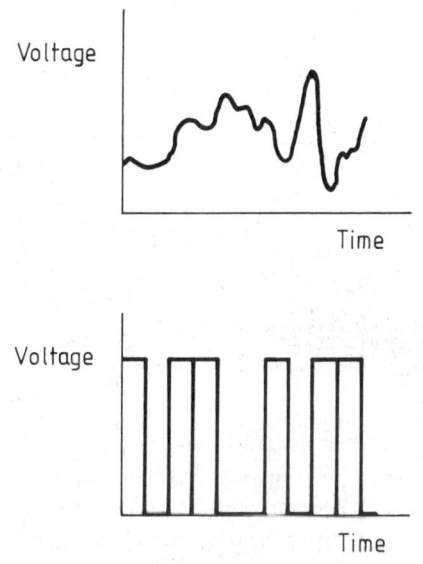

Figure 1.10 *Single purpose computers appear in many common contexts* (Timex; Canon (UK) Ltd; Philips)

almost anything *is* possible. However, this phrase—general purpose—makes the distinction, explored further in a moment, between the 'programmable' computers of home and office and the single-purpose devices used in a wide range of equipment such as digital watches, calculators, video equipment and cars (Figure 1.10).

Digital electronic

The tasks of any item of microelectronic equipment such as a computer are carried out by small electric currents, thousands or even millions of times smaller than those through a lamp or speaker. In the case of lamp and speaker, however, the current can take any value between zero and a maximum—but the current in a digital system such as a computer comes in pulses of a restricted number of different sizes. When one is concerned with complex situations, digital systems are far easier to design and work with than the others, the so-called analog ones.

Figure 1.11 shows the difference between analog signals (as in a lamp or conventional phone system) and digital ones (such as those involved in data transfers in some telecommunications units). Crudely, we can say that **analog** signals are wavy, whereas **digital** ones are pulsed. Figure 1.11 in fact shows the simplest form of digital signal: the current can be either high or low—almost all computers carry 'binary' digital signals like this.

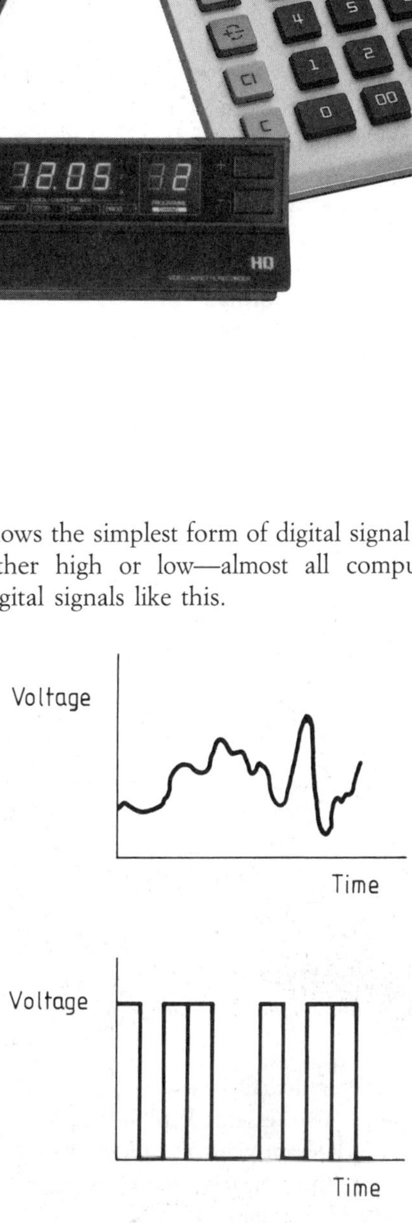

Figure 1.11 *Analog signals are wavy, whereas digital ones involve pulses*

Stored program

A **program** is a set of instructions which the computer can follow, in order, to carry out a given task. Because the machine works so fast, to be efficient it *must* be able to store the instructions it has to follow. The resulting stored program concept is one of the most crucial aspects of the computer. This point links with the one made earlier about general purpose as opposed to single purpose. A single-purpose device such as the one at the heart of a pocket calculator has a fixed, factory-set program to carry out just a small range of tasks; those devices too must have their programs stored. However, in the case of general purpose systems the programs can be changed—these systems are 'programmable'.

Data processor

In the same way as a food processor processes food—with the output material in a different form from that input—so a data processor processes data. **Data** describes the way computers and similar devices handle what humans would call information. However, because the equipment has no intelligence in any human sense, it cannot understand the information that is fed into it, so we use the word data instead. In brief, then, data is information without meaning. All information fed into a computer becomes data in the form of binary digital electronic signals—those pulses of electric current I mentioned above.

It is worth saying a little more about information and data. The torn piece of paper shown in Figure 1.12a tells you nothing. The characters on it have the power to carry meaning, but because they do not do so, the paper bears data rather than information. If a matching piece of paper now turns up saying, 'Meet J at map ref', SPO284 would become meaningful—no longer data, but now information. Thus, the work of a computer is information processing—but it actually processes data.

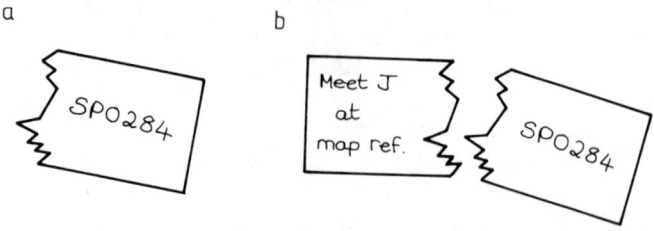

Figure 1.12 *Data and information are not quite the same*

How does the computer actually carry out its work of information processing? The essential points appear in Figure 1.13. This block diagram gives the functions of the main sections of any computer; it also shows how the sections link to carry flows of data.

Let's go through those blocks one by one.

The part of the system concerned with data processing

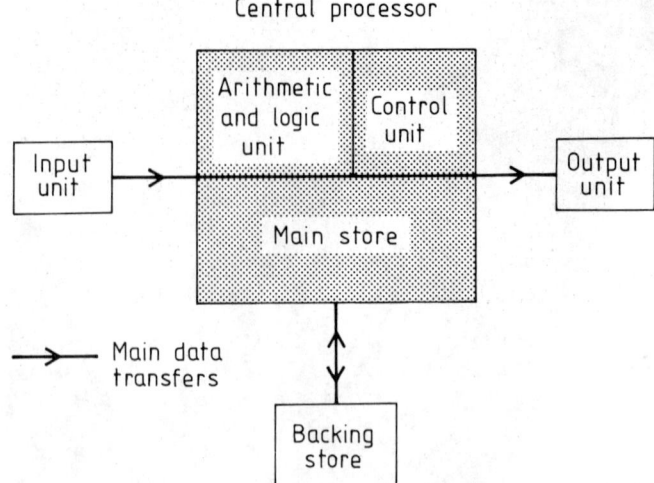

Figure 1.13 *There are five main parts to a computer*

itself—the actual handling of data in binary form—is shaded in the sketch. It is the central processor, or **central processing unit** (CPU), and we can think of it as the main unchanging part of the system as a whole. Each step of the processing is carried out by the **arithmetic and logic unit** (ALU) in the central processor; it does so under the guidance of the **control unit** (which includes a sort of clock to keep all the system's activities in step), following the instructions held in the program in the memory (main store).

Because of the fairly small size and high cost of a computer's main store, and our need to get our programmable computer to carry out an unpredictable but enormous range of tasks, the system needs back up (secondary) memory, or backing store. This is a peripheral device (being outside the shaded area of the central processor in Figure 1.13); its job is to hold currently unwanted data and program instructions.

People have devised a number of different systems for holding data in backing store (Figure 1.14). Currently, the most popular systems involve the use of magnetic media; these can hold large quantities of data tightly packed on to a magnetic surface like that of audio cassette tape. Indeed, the backing storage device used often with the cheapest home and portable computers is actually a simple audio cassette recorder, with the data kept on a standard or miniature cassette.

Magnetic discs, of which there is a huge range of types, have a major advantage in that they are two-dimensional, whereas tape is in effect one-dimensional. This means that you can access any package of data on a disc far more quickly. Very high capacity hard discs are growing rapidly in popularity as backing store for small computer systems; the price of these is falling extremely quickly. At the moment, however, the lower capacity 'floppy' (i.e. flexible) discs are more common; being replaceable in the drive, these at least offer a theoretically unlimited library of programs and data.

Figure 1.14 *There are various ways to use magnetism to hold data in backing store for future use* (3M)

Note though, that replaceable hard disc units now exist.

We use bits and bytes to measure memory sizes and related matters. As I've said, a computer must be able to store the program instructions and data it's currently working with. It must also be able to store the so-called operating software instructions—all the details of how the computer is to carry out the tasks you may give it. All these things are data as far as the computer is concerned, electronic representations in some form or another of binary numbers. The computer's circuits, chips and memory devices handle strings of binary numbers following certain rules.

A binary number goes under the name **'bit'** (= binary digit); it can take the value 1 or 0 only (high and low in Figure 1.11).

A **byte**—the unit of data that can carry a single character—is a set of 8 bits, so its value can range from 0 (0000 0000) to 255 (1111 1111). In the case of most traditional cheap home and school micros, the byte is the same as a word, the set of bits the system can process as a single unit. Of increasing importance in the office, in education, and in the home are 16-bit micros, machines working on data whose unit (word) is 2 bytes long. Sixteen-bit machines, and even more so the 32-bit ones that are starting to appear, can deal with more data more quickly;

they are also less restricted in the size of main store they can access.

Memory size is normally measured in bytes, to indicate how much data can be stored. The maximum size of a home micro's memory is usually 65 536 bytes. We call this 64K for short. Here K stands for kilobyte; one **kilobyte** is 1024 bytes. This is close to 1000; the special use of the capital letter is to remind us that the figure is a bit bigger than that. Quite often we need even larger units than the K. The principal ones are the **megabyte** (MB)—just over a million bytes (1 048 576 to be precise)—and **gigabyte** (GB)—just over a thousand million.

The main store of a micro is commonly in two parts (Figure 1.15). The operating software is permanently fixed in what we call ROM, read-only memory. This stores data so the system can access (read) it but not change it. The contents of ROM are truly fixed, even when the power is off. Unchanging and unchangeable ROM is clearly no use for storing your programs and data. We must be able to alter these, so have RAM for this purpose. The system can access (read) the contents of RAM and also change (write to) it. Both RAM and ROM come on special microelectronic chips (integrated circuits), though other techniques are under development.

In discussing the concept of backing store, I introduced

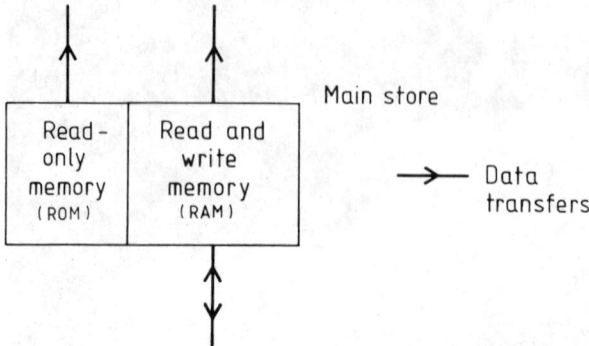

Figure 1.15 . *ROM chips are read-only—you can access their data but not change it; RAM chips provide read and write memory—you can change their contents as well as get at it*

the term 'peripheral', to describe a piece of equipment you can link to the central processor. Figure 1.13 shows two other crucial peripherals, the input and output units which respectively allow data to enter and leave the system. In particular, a computer must be able to communicate with the people who use it and with other machines. Communication is of course a two-way process that applies as much to the communication between two machines, and between people and computers, as to that between two humans. We need to pass information, queries, commands and instructions (all becoming forms of data) into the computer through some kind of input device; it does the reverse for us by way of an output device.

A standard personal computer provides direct input from the keyboard and supplies direct output to some kind of visual display (monitor, TV set, or flat liquid crystal display—LCD—unit). Without an input device and an output device, no computer is much use—it won't be able to obtain data for processing nor will it be able to do anything with the results of that processing. In fact there are many different ways of getting data into and out of a computer processor; in other words, many input and output devices are available for use. We'll look more fully at all this in Chapter 3.

1.4   There are various kinds of computer

What I described in the last section, and showed in Figure 1.13, is a typical small personal computer, or micro (short for microcomputer). There are various definitions of the term 'microcomputer', but I can best describe it as one normally used by only one person at a time.

Groups of micros linked together as a network are becoming very common in education and offices. Each unit in the network (in other words each work station at which someone can sit) most of the time acts as a simple stand-alone micro. However, the use of the network can also allow at least a certain level of inter-communication; for instance, one user can send messages to a second, and all can share data and other scarce resources.

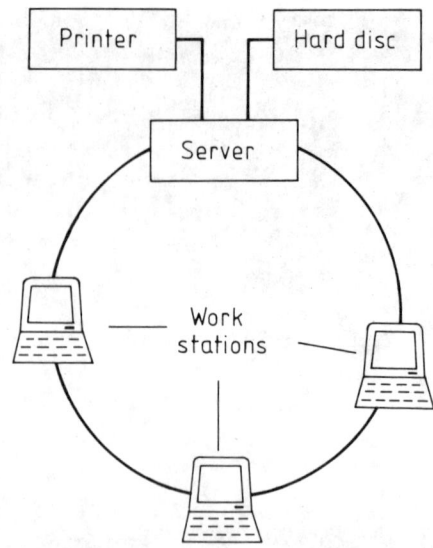

Figure 1.16   *There is much of value to working on a network instead of with isolated micros*

The sharing of scarce resources by the work stations of a network (Figure 1.16) is of obvious value. Thus, a high-capacity hard disc is preferable to a number of separate floppy disc drives if there is a frequent need to access complex and/or costly programs and large quantities of common data. Again, it is usually better to share one or two high-quality printers between the users of a network than to provide a cheap one for each; after all, most people normally require printing to be carried out no more than about 10% of the time. Networks come in various styles as discussed in Chapter 3; each has its own advantages and disadvantages.

Networks are fairly new. The more traditional solution to the problems of sharing data and scarce resources between work stations is the mini (minicomputer—Figure 1.17).

Figure 1.17   *A minicomputer can handle the needs of a number of users during the same working session* (Wang (UK) Ltd)

While in layout a minicomputer system may look much like a network, a mini is in fact a single processing system able to run a number of terminals at the same time. In turn, a terminal may look much like a microcomputer work station on a network; however, it will normally comprise little more than an input device and an output device (such as a keyboard and display). Such a terminal is called dumb; in contrast, an intelligent terminal is one that also incorporates a degree of local processing power.

The physical area over which a network can extend is fairly limited at the moment. Few systems operate well if a work station is more than about half a kilometre from the centre. As the rate of data transfer between work station and centre is much lower in the case of a mini, the links can be a lot longer. Thus, it is fairly common to join terminals in different buildings or even on different sites using a simple cable or a microwave link.

The limit on the size of a minicomputer system is in fact the number of terminals it can handle. The mini's central operating software must continually scan all the terminal cable links for incoming data and keep control of the needs of the various users. Most current minis are powerful enough to handle no more than about a dozen terminals—but they can do so efficiently and cheaply.

Where a large number of geographically separate users need to access a single central computer through terminals, they must turn to a mainframe computer in order to cope. Mainframe describes the largest types of computer, ones that offer great computing power and processing speed as well as the ability to look after a large number of terminals. Large central processors used to be made up of banks of circuit boards and valves; these, in turn, were mounted on steel racks or frames—hence the word 'mainframe'.

We now use the word 'mainframe' to describe the large computers used in the data processing departments of major companies such as banks, insurance companies and government departments (Figure 1.18). Often, as well as having a lot of terminals linked to them, such systems may handle dozens of other peripherals such as disc drives and printers. A major difference between any kind of mainframe computer and the others is that it needs permanent staff to keep it working.

For completeness, I also ought to mention the term 'super-computer', sometimes applied to the very largest and most modern mainframes. Super-computers characteristically offer extremely high processing speed, so they can handle the huge quantities of data involved in the work of, for instance, a meteorological office and spacecraft control. However, all this terminology is now in the melting pot as the marketing people invent new names—like mini-micro and super-mini—in an attempt to imply that their products are truly new.

1.5   Computer warehouse

When talking about computers and other IT systems, people often use the terms 'hardware' and 'software'.

By 'hardware' we mean all the physical equipment within a system. Thus, it includes a micro's central processor and its various parts as described above, plus the peripherals that the particular user will need to be able to work with it. In effect, then, it is what comes in the boxes when you decide to purchase a 'computer'.

A 'computer', however, is no use until it has instructions to follow and data to work on. You can buy the programs—sets of instructions—you need to turn an empty and ineffective machine into a useful working system on tape or disc (for instance) as you wish. Thus, people buy games on cassette for a cheap home computer or such things as data bases and graphics programs on disc for an office machine.

The programs a computer uses to carry out a given task are software. Software, consisting as it does of programs, is in fact something you can't touch; however, it must be carried in some form of touchable medium readable by a backing storage device—a disc or cassette, for instance. Note that those discs and cassettes are not the software itself; they simply carry the software the computer uses.

In fact few (if any) computers nowadays are completely empty when viewed as a set of hardware—they are all able to do something when you switch on, even if it's only to look for software on disc. This means that certain programs must reside permanently inside the hardware. Those programs are software (by the above definition) but are an inherent crucial part of the hardware. In fact, they will often be in chips (integrated circuits) plugged permanently into the computer's main circuit board. In that these chips which carry programs are neither software nor hardware, we use the word 'firmware' for them. Firmware is software held on chips (ROM chips, in fact—Figure 1.19); the name also includes programs that the user may later decide to add to the system if those programs are on chip and if the chips can be accepted by the particular hardware.

Figure 1.18   *A mainframe system is very powerful and can support a large number of users in any session* (International Computers Ltd)

Figure 1.19   *Among a computer's storage chips are some ROMs that carry software* (Acorn Computers Ltd)

Figure 1.20   *You need a modem to link a computer with the phone network* (Apple Computers UK Ltd)

1.6   No computer is an island

I've already made clear that the central processor, the main part of any computer system, is entirely useless without peripherals; it therefore must have the ability to transfer data outside itself. A stand-alone micro involves data transfers between the peripherals and the central processor, but in many contexts you can much enhance its usage by allowing communication with systems elsewhere.

Unless we're dealing here simply with data transfers between the different parts of a local area network (or even using a long lead between a stand-alone micro and a printer in the next room), we at last return to telecommunications and IT in general. Indeed, in so far as the remote terminals of a mini or mainframe involve links to the centre in which the data transfer is through phone cable or radio links, I've hinted at that already.

However, to see the true value of communications between separate computers, we need to recall some of the ideas raised in the general descriptions of IT systems early in this chapter. Thus, when computer users access a viewdata system like Prestel to explore public transport timetables and make bookings, they're explicitly using IT by integrating computer systems and a telecommunications network (the phone system in this case).

We'll come back to Prestel in Chapter 3, but now it's worth noting that at the moment you need a special piece of equipment called a modem (Figure 1.20) to link the computer with the phone line. The main reason for this is that, as we have seen, computers are digital devices that transfer data in the form of pulses of electric current. Phone exchange lines can't handle digital signals effectively—the prime task of a modem is to convert the digital output of a computer to the analog form needed by the phone line and to do the reverse for incoming data.

If you work from home as an employee of a large company, or have other reasons to transfer data more effectively than by traditional mail, the use of communications links and communications software in the computer is very exciting and can be very cost-effective. I'll return to this theme later in the book, but feel that it is worth noting now that this important aspect of IT is certain to become an integral part of all computer systems within only a very few years.

1.7   Looking forward

It's worth repeating that the description of computer hardware and software given in this chapter isn't likely to date very fast. Though the papers announce significant advances in IT and computer technology almost daily, the basic principles are fairly fixed. The cost and complexity of computer systems have fallen fast over the last few decades and will continue to do so. Progress in microelectronics is the reason for this, as chips become more complex yet cheaper. We can see just the same rate of advance in the case of electronic calculators, digital watches, and broadcast receivers. Credit-card sized computers are beginning to appear, as are a variety of systems fixed to a watch-strap.

Miniaturisation is not, however, the only objective of the computer industry. As far as peripherals are concerned, people expect voice input and output to be crucial features of the new computers of the 1990s, while in the case of the central processor, we can look forward to systems which involve a number of processors working as a team in a range of different tasks at the same time.

It won't be so long, therefore, before the traditional picture of a computer as keyboard, screen, and various hidden electronic bits and pieces disappears. We'll consider later what types of system may replace this, but you can be sure that the basic concept of Figure 1.13 will still be able to describe them.

SELF-DEVELOPMENT QUESTIONS

You'll need to do some research, other than working your way through the chapter, to answer these questions adequately. You won't have time to do all the questions, though in some cases it's a good idea to work in a small group. *After* you've done the work, check the notes in Appendix B (page 134).

S1.1 How has IT changed the ways banks operate? Note some drawbacks to these changes.

S1.2 Survey users of different banks' autotellers; find out the services on offer and used, and the advantages and disadvantages people see in these machines. If possible, use or observe an autoteller to check for yourself.

S1.3 Survey the needs of people in a post office queue; how could IT improve the service? Report on this.

S1.4 Use Prestel for *two* of the tasks below; make brief notes on your actions and their effects. Compare the methods, and the costs, with those of traditional ways of meeting the same needs.

    a How can you go by train from Glasgow to Gatwick in order to check in at about 1400 next Saturday?

    b Obtain a list of the contents of the latest issue of *Information Technology and Learning*, a magazine published by MUSE (an educational IT association).

    c Send a message to the author of this book. (I guarantee no answer, though!)

    d What was the weather like in Copenhagen yesterday?

    e Order a gift for someone you like (but don't send the order unless you can pay for it!).

S1.5 Explain how a computer differs from a cheap calculator. And from an expensive one.

S1.6 Draw a block diagram of a computer, showing the directions of data flow; explain the function of and need for each part; sketch and name examples of each type of peripheral.

S1.7 Give examples of five types each of hardware, software and firmware available for a micro used in your school or college.

S1.8 How many bytes of storage are available on each model of micro and each type of disc used in your school or college? Make a list worth putting up in the staffroom.

S1.9 If you can look at a network, decide what the arrangement used is, and what problems that arrangement may cause.

S1.10 Use a word processor to prepare brief notes for a beginner on how to use the word processor.

S1.11 Make a table comparing the features of a word processor with those of an electric and an electronic typewriter.

S1.12 Discuss the nature and uses of a mainframe, minicomputer, microcomputer and network.

S1.13 'Money is information.' Discuss this statement from Section 1.2—and the converse: 'Information is money.'

EXAMINATION QUESTIONS

Note what I say at the start of the previous section. Note, too, that you should be able to do each question, once prepared, under exam conditions in about as many minutes as there are marks for it. There are brief notes at the end of the book on these questions, too, in Appendix B—but you shouldn't refer to those till you've tried the questions.

Q1.1 **a** Explain what word processing is and describe briefly the software facilities a word processing system might provide.　　　　[5]

    b Give an example of one organisation in which the introduction of a word processing system would be beneficial. Explain what the benefits might be.

(COSSEC)　　　　[5]

Q1.2 Discuss briefly some of the developments in computing that have led to the widespread use of computers in homes, offices and factories.

(COSSEC)　　　　[10]

2 IT at work

Figure 2.1 *The beautiful robots that replace so many people in the modern factory are only one aspect of information technology at work* (Austin Rover)

Case study 2—On the shop floor

Counter-Fate is a fairly small forging firm. Its work is to forge machine parts from hot metal; there's also a certain amount of assembly. Life in a forging mill has always been unpleasant and dangerous. The work is quite easy to automate, so Counter-Fate has been using robots for more and more tasks since the early 1950s. Figure 2.2 outlines their current system. I'll run through it from the start, using the names the few factory workers have given to the robots.

Pal is an automated pallet, a trolley that shuttles to and fro between the store and the start of the line. It brings a load of half a dozen heavy (75 kg) steel billets (blocks) every minute and a half. Pal is a line-following electric

trolley: it follows a line painted on the floor (so it's easy to change the route); sensors round Pal's edge make it stop at once if it feels an impact. When it's tipped its load into the billet bin, Pal follows the line back to the store.

Pal carries its own small processor and memory. Its inputs—information about the environment—come from the touch sensors round its edge and also from the line-following system. Here a light shines onto the ground and a set of photocells measures how much bounces back. The processor outputs are control signals for the motors that drive its wheels and tip the tray that carries the billets. (See Section 2.1 for details.)

Like most factory robots, Robert is a general purpose pick-and-place machine. Every 15 seconds it must take a steel billet from the jumble in the bin and place it neatly

Figure 2.2 *Robots play various parts in a forging mill*

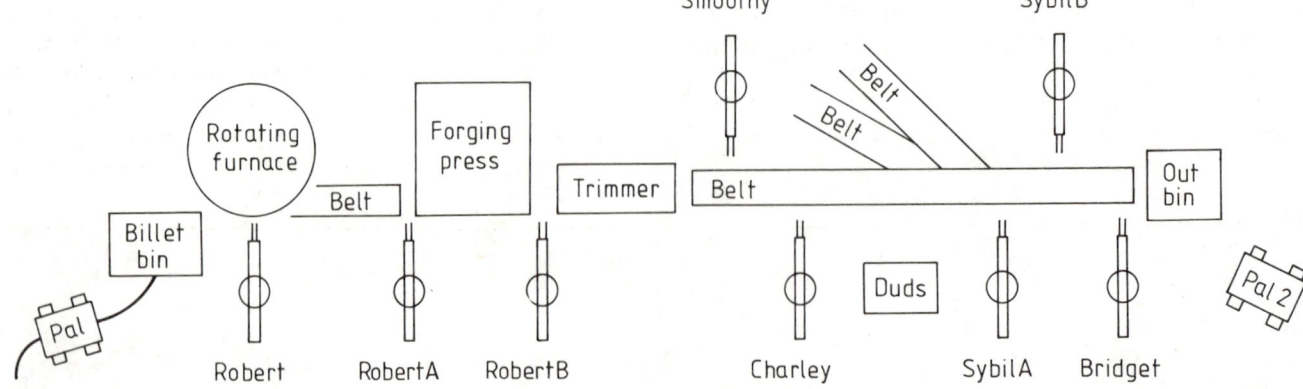

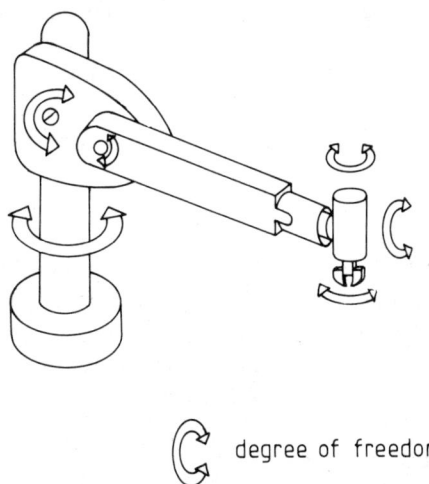

C degree of freedom

Figure 2.3 *This typical static programmable pick-and-place robot has six degrees of freedom and a claw (gripper)*

in the furnace—which has a temperature of 1200 °C. No mistakes allowed! Two aspects of Robert's work need special care—that high temperature and the random placing of the billets in the bin. Otherwise this is a standard static robot; it has six degrees of freedom (axes round which it can move), as shown in Figure 2.3.

RobertA and RobertB have much the same task as Robert, and are in fact identical machines—they are just programmed differently. RobertA takes a hot steel billet off the belt leading from the furnace and places it in a die (mould) inside the forging press as the 2500 tonne upper part moves up. When the press closes, it squeezes the billet into the shape of the die. RobertB moves the billet into a second die for the next forging action and, after that, takes it out and puts it in the trimmer.

Counter-Fate's staff program robots like these by example—'follow me' is the phrase used. When a robot has to learn a new cycle of actions, someone guides it through them with care, moving the claw directly or with a keypad from point to point. The computer works out the quickest, smoothest and safest route between each pair of points and makes that the next step in the program stored. It's easy to add details of timing—this is important, because all the machines on the line must work in step. (It's no good if Robert tries to put a billet in the furnace when the door's closed or if RobertA or RobertB don't move their claws away before the 2500 tonne weight of the press comes down.)

You can also program the steps of a robot's cycle by keyboard, or even have a computer-aided design system work out what the machine has to do. However, that latter method (a technique of integrated manufacture, or computer-aided design and manufacture—CADCAM) is something Counter-Fate hasn't tried yet.

The forged steel objects leave the trimmer with the waste bits of metal (flash) taken off the edges. They still need polishing, and Smoothy, a finishing robot, runs over each one with a sander before Charley, at the checkpoint, decides whether it's good enough to go on down the line.

Charley is the firm's most advanced robot—it can see. A TV camera scans the object and the processor compares the image with the 'perfect' data in its store. Counter-Fate is still experimenting with Charley, and someone stands by the line to give a proper visual check. If human or robot decides there's a fault, Charley swings the heavy block of metal into the duds bin. Otherwise, the blocks move onto the assembly line, to be joined by parts from elsewhere. The two Sybils are assembly robots—the same machines as the Roberts and Smoothy, but programmed to fit the parts together as required.

Last on the line is Bridget the painter, yet another static robot of the same type. Bridget is programmed to spray paint over the assembled metal forgings as they come past at 15-second intervals. Bridget has no claw; there's a spray gun fixed at the wrist and the machine moves this round the object, coating every nook and cranny, as programmed by a follow-me routine.

This is rather a simplified account of some of the robots' work at Counter-Fate. All the same, it should be clear that robots have replaced people for good reasons. For sure, they are cheap, and reliable, too—but check the list:

Pal and Pal2, the automated pallets, effortlessly move sharp, heavy lumps of metal around. People here no longer have to do backbreaking and dangerous work. Robert puts a 75 kg block into a 1200 °C furnace every 15 seconds—people don't long survive conditions like that. RobertA and RobertB have their claws under a 2500 tonne forging press—often people used to lose their hands or arms doing that job. Smoothy and Bridget carry out dirty tasks in a toxic atmosphere.

Counter-Fate has steadily increased its business in the decades since their first robot (a mechanical device whose program was on a belt like that of a music box). To them the benefits have been reduced overheads—the robots do the hard and dangerous work, leaving the staff to concentrate on supervision, maintenance and sales. The firm's output is more than twice what it was thirty years ago; they employ 10% fewer people, but those people are far better paid and enjoy their work much more.

Introduction

Assembly line robots and other aspects of industrial automation perhaps form the most public face of modern IT. A robot *is* an IT system—Figure 1.13 describes it just as it shows the main parts of a 'normal' computer. A robot, though, gathers its own input data, using sensors; its output consists of signals that control electric circuits. This is still IT—the robot depends on 'knowing' about its environment before it can react properly.

Most uses of IT noted in this chapter offer far less glamour. However, all follow the definition at the start of Section 1.1. Also, all the main systems relate clearly to Figure 1.13.

There are many, many thousand uses of computers and of new IT in general. In the surveys in this chapter I shall pick out broad applications areas. The chapter will thus give you an overview of the field, to which you should be able to link any specific application. Each of the book's ten case studies will also help you gain a broad picture, for I haven't made them too specific either.

Objectives

When you have worked through this chapter, you should be able to

1. give an account of the principles of robotics using automated pallets and static general purpose arms as examples
2. discuss the nature and advantages of automation
3. state what feedback is, and discuss examples
4. write simple control program outlines
5. give examples to show why people prefer a robot to a human worker
6. describe how a typical user works with a computer-aided design (CAD) package and the hardware that might be involved
7. distinguish between paint software, business graphics, and CAD
8. outline how advanced CAD software can simulate the testing of a design
9. state the principles of computer-aided design and manufacture (CADCAM)
10. state the nature of an office and outline typical information flows
11. compare traditional and electronic methods of office information handling
12. discuss the five main business software programs and list five others
13. describe how to use a spreadsheet
14. describe how to use a business graphics program
15. list the advantages and disadvantages of integrated business software and give examples of its use
16. describe the use of a critical path analysis program (scheduler)
17. outline the value and use of electronic organisers (hardware or software)
18. outline the value and use of a stock control package
19. outline the value and use of accounts software
20. outline the value and use of payroll programs
21. list the main uses of IT in education
22. list uses of business software by tutors and learners
23. outline the value and use of computer-managed learning (CML)
24. discuss examples of computer-aided learning (CAL) software and place them on a spectrum of 'intelligence'
25. outline the value and use of CAL authoring systems

2.1 Computers in control

It's a good idea first to go on with the theme of the case study—automation. We'll see more about the hardware side of this in Section 3.6, but here I need to introduce the concept of feedback.

Automation involves giving machines control over their action so they can carry out tasks without human presence. Feedback is crucial to this, as only with feedback can a system react correctly to the environment. We'll discuss it in the context of a line-following system as used by the Pal robots in the case study. As we saw there, a light shines down and photocells detect how much light the ground reflects. Figure 2.4 shows the arrangement (viewed from inside the pallet).

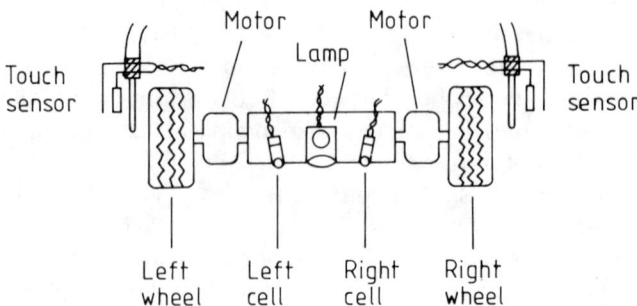

Figure 2.4 *A line-following wheeled robot detects the track by an arrangement of lamp and photocells*

When the machine is on the line, both cells detect a lot of reflected light. If it wanders off one will report less light. The system speeds up the motor driving the wheel on that side to turn the trolley back onto the line. The output thus affects the input, and vice versa; this is feedback. The line-following program might be something like this

```
drive both motors at set speed
repeat
  if left-sensor output falls raise
  left-motor speed
  if left-sensor output rises lower
```

```
left-motor speed
  if right-sensor output falls raise
  right-motor speed
  if right-sensor output rises lower
  left-motor speed
until touch-sensor output rises
stop both motors
```

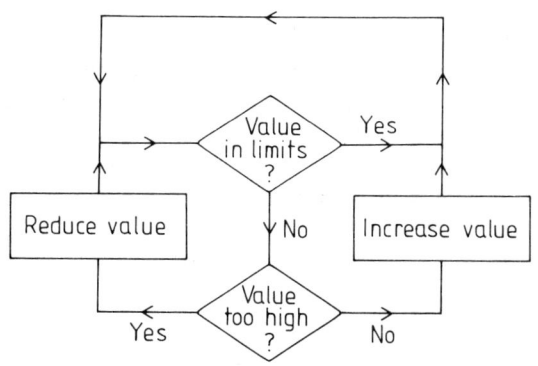

Figure 2.5 *The concept of feedback is crucial to automation*

Figure 2.5 shows this feedback loop; the system can cycle through it every few thousandths of a second.

Here are some more examples of feedback in use in automation and robotics:

- A robot claw will close until touch sensors on the inner surface tell it to stop.
- The rollers of a sheet metal mill move apart or together to keep the thickness in the pre-set range (Figure 2.6).
- The energy output level of a heater in a furnace will adjust so the temperature sensed matches that set on a thermostat.
- The rate of input of chemicals to a continuous flow process changes until the concentration and acidity sensors' outputs are correct.

What is a robot then? With a microprocessor at its core, it is programmable (single-purpose robots are now rare). The program provides a system with feedback between

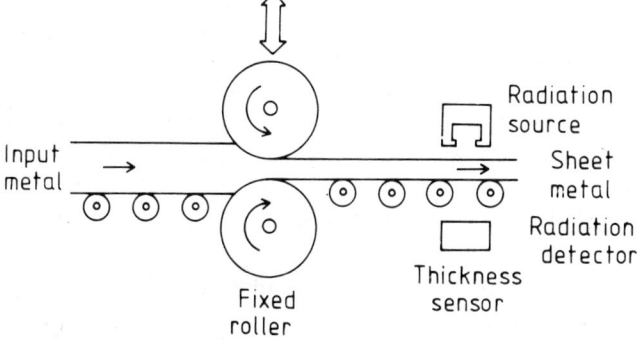

Figure 2.6 *Metal sheet thickness control is an example of automation*

input sensors and output electric control units. The output signals control movement in one or more degrees of freedom (axes of rotation or linear motion). The actual motion may involve electric motors, or hydraulic (pressure in liquid circuits) or pneumatic (pressure in gas circuits) units.

The most common sensors for a 'traditional' robot are strain gauges which detect how much motion in a given axis there has been. In effect, therefore, they measure the position of each moving part. Chemical sensors (acidity, ionisation, concentration) appear in special automated control systems. Machine vision is much more complex: the central processor must analyse the image in a video camera. Robots that can see are still rare and experimental.

Programmable moving robots come in a number of groups. (Few look much like people—the robots, or androids, of fiction—they don't need to.) We can class robots by their local 'intelligence' or autonomy. They range from remotely controlled trucks (which need a distant full-time human 'driver') to the robots of industry and space probes. In between are toy robots and robot pets, the floor robots you may have used at school or college, and simple robot arms. Programmable home machines (like washing machines and video recorders) are in there too.

We'll come back to this subject in Section 3.6; also in that section is something on interfacing—the links between the analog sensors and output units of an automated system and the digital central processor. A micro is a purely digital device; systems with a mix of analog and digital parts are hybrid. (Purely analog computers exist too, though few are general purpose. An airline's flight simulator is an example; hybrid forms cannot work fast enough.)

2.2 A matter of design

Computer-aided design (CAD) has long been a major area of IT; we came across it in the case study in the context of **computer-aided design and manufacture** (CADCAM). However, it isn't just industrial designers who use CAD—it's of value to people working on circuits, civil engineering projects (bridges, road systems and such), office and kitchen planning, and making maps and charts. Engineers, planners and architects, as well as designers, use CAD, therefore. They may, however, use versions in which CAD stands for computer-aided drawing (or draughting) rather than design; the simpler versions offer less processing power as far as concerns the drawn object.

A CAD hardware/software system has a number of parts. This is so whether it's a cheap micro-based package or one for aircraft design costing hundreds of thousands of pounds. The parts are

- central processor with main and backing store
- control and design software
- a library of designs for use in the grand plan
- graphics input units as well as keyboard

- high-resolution (high detail) output monitor and plotter

The special input units may include a graphics pad on which you can draw with a special pen and/or a mouse to control the movement of a dot (cursor or pointer) on screen. (Section 3.5 gives more details of these, and of others that may be of use.) The output plotter (also detailed in Section 3.6) is for drawing on paper in high detail.

The user builds up the design on screen, as Figure 2.7 outlines. The software will allow

- freehand lines to be made straight
- circles, ellipses, curves, triangles and rectangles to appear from simple codes
- zooming in on any section to enable high detail
- the use of a library of standard shapes you can add at any point in any size and style (e.g. nuts and bolts, transistors, windows, motors, kitchen units)
- shading, 'air brushing', and line or solid colour
- text (titles, labels, dimensions, remarks) in a wide range

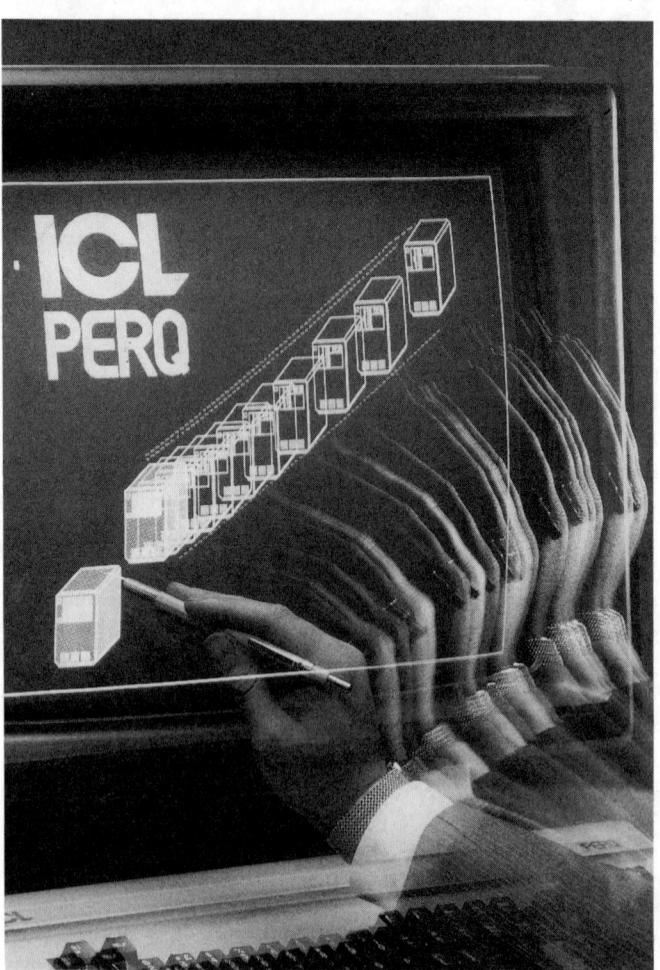

Figure 2.7 *Building up even a complex design is not too hard a task with a CAD system (ICL)*

of directions, sizes and styles
- scaling
- transfer of a section from one place to another

At any stage the user can save the design (or part of it) to disc for later, and send it to the plotter to get a copy on paper. Also, if the design is of a three-dimensional object or structure, you can view it from different angles and even tour round it and send the result to videotape.

It's useful to think what you can do with a word processor to produce a text. A full CAD system is a picture processor and must offer the same range of techniques and features. It deals with graphics to produce a two- or three-dimensional drawing.

We use the word 'graphics' in IT in three ways; don't be confused. One group of graphics programs is designed to produce two-dimensional pictures for pleasure or profit as art, or to support other activities—in advertising, TV graphics and presentations, for instance, as industrial or commercial art. At the lowest levels, we can call these programs painting software. However, that term hardly covers the work done for film and video.

The next meaning of 'graphics' appears in office software. Business graphics involves making line graphs, bar charts and pie diagrams to represent statistical data. We'll look at this more fully in Section 2.3 under IT in the office (though there are many uses outside the office).

Thirdly, 'graphics' covers CAD, as described here: two- and three-dimensional designs for an industrial purpose. There are several styles of three-dimensional design graphics. The simplest product is a wire-frame model; this consists just of lines to show all edges between surfaces. A wire-frame model looks rather like a bird cage. Next is the surface model—the surfaces between the wires are filled with colour or shading to give a solid look, but there's no internal detail. Most complex is the solid model which *does* have an internal structure. In Figure 2.8 are (a) a wire-frame model of a simple house, (b) a wire-frame model with hidden lines removed, and (c) a surface model. A solid model would let you enter and study the layout of each room.

As well as let you build up, study, save and plot your design, some advanced computer-aided design systems will let you test it. This means you can check how good the design is without going to the trouble and cost of making a real model (to try in a wind tunnel, for instance). Testing depends on the system concerned; here are some examples where software analysis of a design is common. You can

- simulate wind tunnel tests on a car, plane, bridge, block of flats, or power station
- carry out time and motion studies within a kitchen to see if the layout is efficient
- analyse energy losses from a building to check the insulation
- apply various input signals to a circuit to see if you get

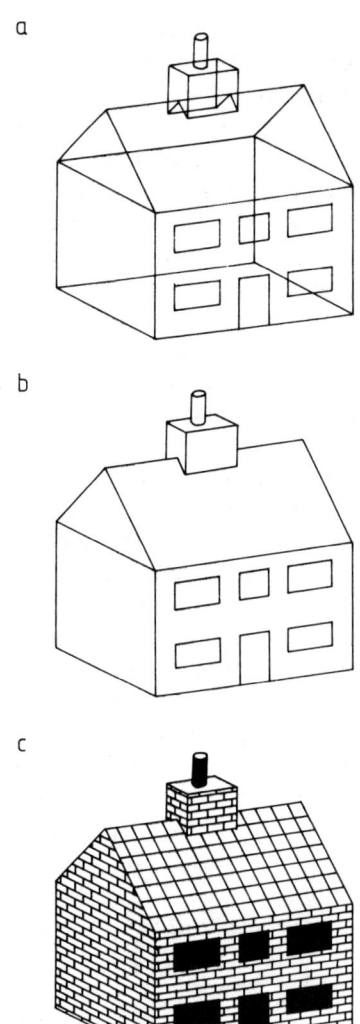

Figure 2.8 *Wire-frame and surface models are the two simplest forms of three-dimensional design*

the right outputs
- load a bridge with various volumes and types of traffic in different wind conditions to find out if it is strong enough

The output of an advanced CAD package need not be just to paper in a plotter. The software may let you use a mouse or joystick to move round inside a complex structure so you can look at it from all viewpoints, perhaps sending the result to video tape for later study. Much the same approach is to record all possible views on a video disc. Then you can work with an interactive video package to tour the structure as you please.

The final form of output brings us back to CADCAM—computer-aided design and manufacture. The right kind of CAD software will record on disc or tape (or send along a direct line) the instructions an automatic machine tool or robot needs to build a model or full-scale version of your design. People use this so far only for metal parts, such as gear wheels; maybe one day we'll be able to design a house

on screen and have robots build it on a patch of land when the plans are approved.

2.3 The electronic office

Here we'll look at the main types of business software needed by an office, whatever its size and function.

What is an office?

Any office has always embodied the basic features of IT, as it explicitly handles information. Any office takes in information and puts it out; it will also store, access, and process information. Figure 2.9 shows that: it's much like Figure 1.13, which shows what a computer does with data.

The only real difference between the two diagrams is the new 'access' feature. Here I think of the need for the people who use the office to lay their hands on—access—information stored there. Think of even a very simple task, like dealing with a phone call—information access is crucial.

IT concerns the analysis and improvement of any information handling system. Though offices have evolved over hundreds of years, huge improvements follow modern IT. That's because the traditional office depends on information on paper (the phone doesn't change that much). Paper is bulky, messy, open to loss, abuse and damage, and very costly, both in itself and as far as concerns associated working time, equipment and furniture.

IT doesn't rely on paper, though it links with paper-based systems as need be. Instead, IT is electronic—it offers an office the chance to input, output, process, store, and access

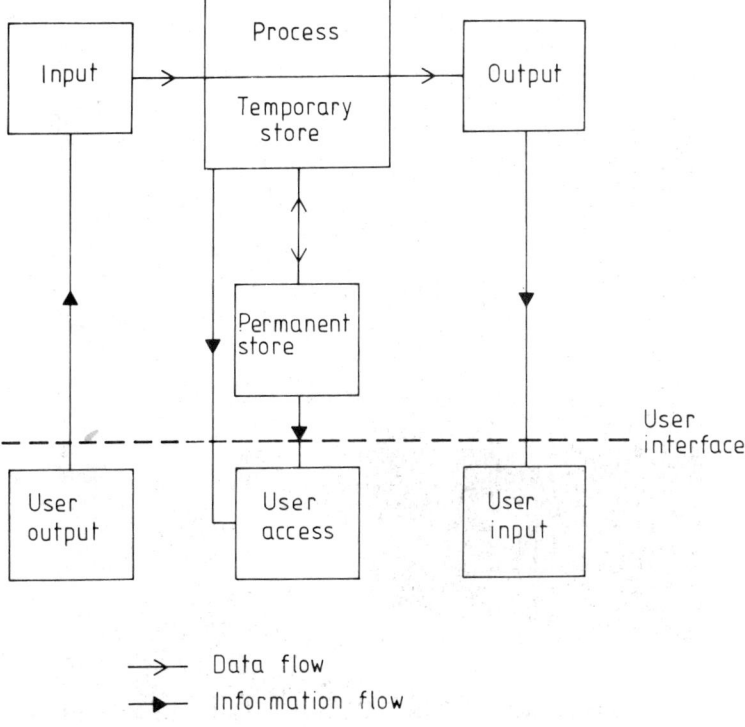

Figure 2.9 *An office is an information handling system*

information electronically all the time. This leads to great savings in costs of all kinds, including those that relate to storage space, security and the time spent on individual tasks.

As compared to games or robot control programs, for instance, office software directly concerns handling information in its own right. There are five main categories of business software. Here's a summary.

Word processing can make a typist's task much simpler. A word processor allows the entry and easy editing (amendment) of text in a computer's main store on its screen rather than just out to paper. It lets the user code the stored material for layout and for special effects such as highlighting certain sections. It lets you get a printout (hard copy) at any stage. And, most important of all, a word processor can save the text on disc any time you wish, for access, amendment and further use in the future.

Data base software gives particularly flexible access to the user's files of data stored in suitable electronic form. It offers all the features—and more—of a sophisticated paper-based filing system or card index, but does so

electronically. As a result, a computer-managed data base can be very speedy and versatile in use, as well as saving a huge amount of space.

Communications software is designed to let the user get information from, and send information to, a second, distant, computer. It involves joining the two via a tele-communication network. Thus you can link your micro by phone with a public data base, such as Prestel or Telecom Gold, or send data to a second private computer in much the same way.

Spreadsheet software at its simplest level of usage is for dealing with accounts. A spreadsheet is a grid of small screen cells (boxes) in which labels, numbers and formulas can go. The formulas relate to the numbers in other cells, so as soon as you add or change one, the whole of the grid follows suit as appropriate.

At the level of the simplest balance sheet, you can use a spreadsheet to keep automatic totals in the various rows and columns. However, it's also easy to devise grids to let you see the effect of possible, rather than actual, changes. In this way, spreadsheets offer great predictive and planning power.

Figure 2.10 *There's a pattern to how information and goods move round a company*

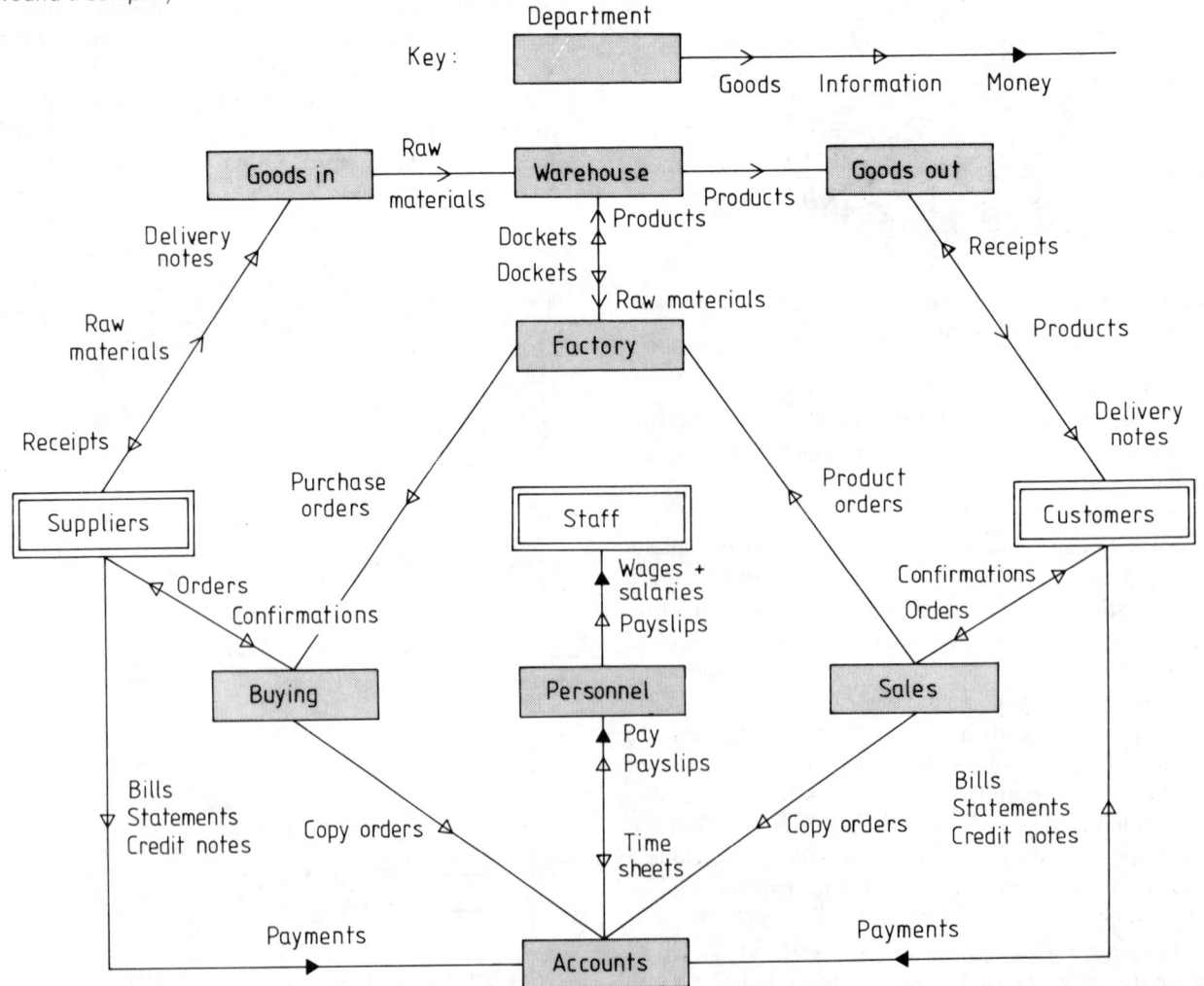

Business graphics programs work on sets of data to produce line graphs, bar charts, and pie diagrams. It's straightforward, for instance, to obtain graphs showing how sales vary from month to month or how they split into different categories.

Figure 2.10 shows all the flows between the functional areas of a firm. Apart from the factory itself (the production sections) and the warehouse, all the departments shown—personnel, accounts, purchasing, sales, goods in, and goods out—are offices as we've thought of them. Indeed, in a small firm, one person may carry all these roles.

The firm's actual function is to obtain raw materials and process them into finished goods; the goods then pass out to the customers. These movements are the firm's various flows of materials. However, you can see that, in order to support that movement of physical items, there are far more flows of information—which, in the traditional office, would be in paper form. In the modern office, each such flow can be an electronic data transfer; as we've seen, that offers many advantages for efficient and cost-effective working.

The information flows include three cash flows—payments to suppliers, payments from customers, and wages and salaries to staff. As far as office working is concerned, and indeed that of the economy as a whole, money is information. Because of this, financial movements are open to handling by IT just as much as the other types of information transfer in the diagram.

Of the five main types of office software, we've already studied word processing and communications software; the third—data base working—comes up in Chapter 6. Now we'll look at spreadsheet and business graphics programs. The first is a lovely example of how computers can lead to almost totally new kinds of activity. (The only other I can think of at the moment are the 'arcade' games, like Space Invaders and Defender!)

On a very simple level, a spreadsheet is a two-dimensional table (Figure 2.11).

Each box in the table is a cell. The one shaded in the table is in column C and row 4—it's cell C4. So each cell has its own reference. When you start the spreadsheet up, it highlights the top left cell, A1 (in colour, perhaps); you can move to any other cell by pressing special keys. The highlighted cell at a given moment is the one where your next typed data will go.

Spreadsheets vary greatly in size. Some have hundreds of rows and columns, giving you many thousand cells to work with. The display can show only part of this great grid, but as you move the highlight the screen 'window' will move to suit.

Each cell starts off empty; in use it can hold a number, a word or two (such as a row or column title, or a short message), or a formula. It's this formula feature that gives real power to spreadsheets. For instance, you may want your spreadsheet to hold the sales, outgoings and profit for each of the last three months. You'll start your grid by putting titles for the rows and columns, moving the highlight from cell to cell as required. Next is to enter the sales and outgoings figures for each of the three months. Figure 2.12 shows the sort of result you'll get.

On paper, you'd now subtract the figures in each column to get the monthly profits in row 4 and add the figures in each row to get the totals in column E. With a computer spreadsheet's formula feature, things are much simpler—you just insert formulas into the cells concerned and let the software do the work. In this case you'd put in cell B4 the formula B2 − B3 (i.e. the profit for October is that month's income minus its outgoings). Instead of seeing the formula on screen, you get the answer. See Figure 2.13, which shows the effects of a similar formula in E2 and of copying that down the column and the one in B4 along the row.

The main office use of spreadsheets is in financial costings and estimates. For instance, it is very easy to change one figure (such as the cost of packaging) and see the effect of that change on all dependent values. This forecasting aspect is crucial for planning. We call it carrying out a 'what if' exercise—'What if the price of balsa dropped 6%?' or 'What if we give the workforce a 10% rise?' All the same, it's important to realise that spreadsheets have very many other uses. They can be of value wherever there's a need for tables of data; for instance, market researchers use them for the results of surveys and teachers for marks and registers.

Figure 2.11   *A spreadsheet is a two-dimensional array of a number of cells*

	A	B	C	D	E
1					
2					
3					
4					
5					

	A	B	C	D	E	
1		September	October	November	Total	
2	Sales	111.11	222.22	333.33		
3	Outgoings	99.99	188.88	277.77		
4	Profit					
5						

Figure 2.12   *You start a spreadsheet with row and column titles and main data*

	A	B	C	D	E	
1		September	October	November	Total	
2	Sales	111.11	222.22	333.33	666.66	
3	Outgoings	99.99	188.88	277.77	566.64	
4	Profit	11.12	33.34	55.56	100.02	
5						

Figure 2.13   *The spreadsheet completes the balance sheet automatically: it uses the formulas in the shaded boxes to put values there*

Information output by a word processor or a spreadsheet is strictly to inform—information for presentation (to others or perhaps to the originator at some later time). Graphics also presents information in this way. Rather than doing so in text (as does a word processor) or as tables of figures (like a spreadsheet), it's now in picture form. Information as graphics is a very powerful method of communication—there's much truth in the old saying that a picture is worth a thousand words (even if that saying is itself in words).

Traditional graphic forms of representing information are the line graph, bar chart (or histogram), pictogram (a form of bar chart), and pie diagram. Such graphics, suitably selected and prepared, aid communication in such contexts as reports to management, share holders, staff and public; advertisements and sales literature; handbooks and manuals. In the last context in particular there's also a place for line diagrams, with or without shading—of buildings and other structures, equipment and parts; it's straightforward to prepare pictures like these using special artwork software (Section 2.2).

Figure 2.14 plots the data from the spreadsheet of Figure 2.13; most people prefer data in graphic form. These graphs are two-dimensional; three-dimensional graphing is common too, and colour often adds even more information.

When you note the splendour of these effects, it's amazing how easy most business graphics software packages are to use. In essence, all you have to do is enter the data, and choose the type of display. Data entry is, I admit, tedious, but most graphics packages let you select the display type from a visual menu, so at least that part of the work needs only a few moments.

Integrated business software suites avoid the problem of entering data more than once: they can automatically pass data between tasks. In other words, integration lets you share common sets of data between different programs. It also allows

- switching between programs without loss of data
- the same style of operation, screen layout, and key sequences in each program so you don't have to learn how to do the same things in different ways when on different tasks

In Figure 2.15 are some common questions that arise in this context.

In the case of a report, processed text is the backbone; codes in it call on spreadsheet tables, data base records and graphic representations where appropriate. The report may also include pictures from other sources (see Case Study 7). Communications routines could also be involved if any of the authors are working from home, if the firm sends the prepared material direct to the print shop, or if it's put in viewdata form for people outside to access by phone.

Integrated software packages offer massive advantages. However, they do cause some problems. The main one is the cost of coming to terms with them. Although purchase is not costly, the staff must work hard at familiarisation. The so-called user interface is the major problem, that being

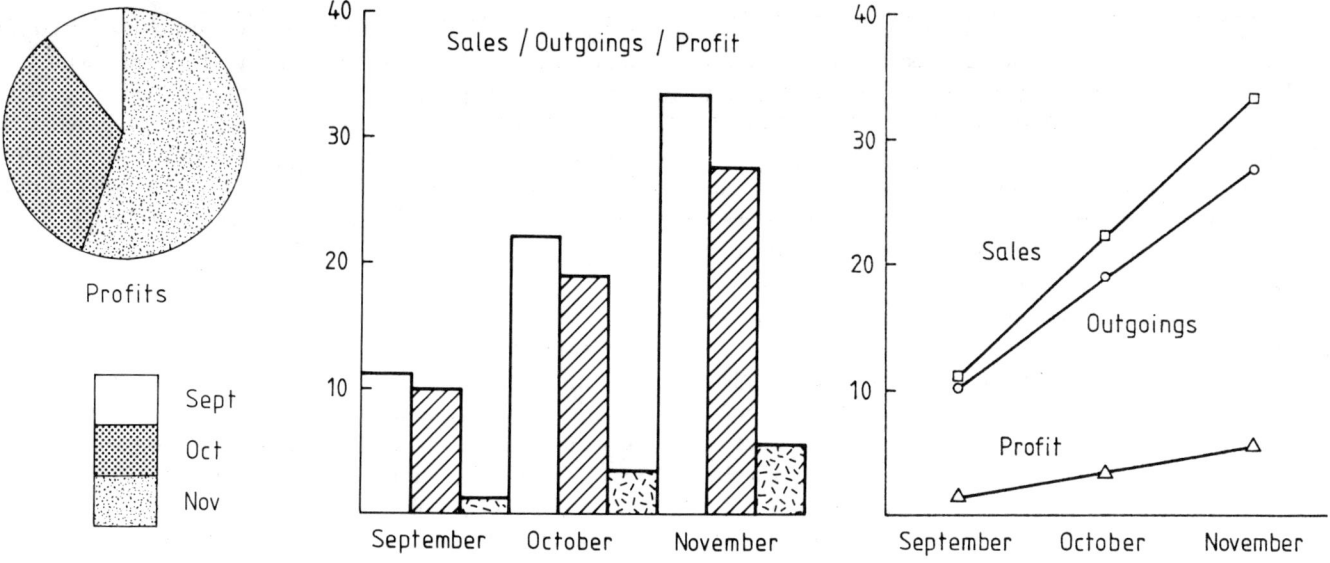

Figure 2.14   *Graphic data can be very easy to follow*

jargon for how (easily) the user can interact with the package by way of keyboard and/or mouse and screen.

Figure 2.15 includes, for simplicity, only the five main program functions I covered above. There are other types of software used in the office, however, and some degree of integration appears here too.

2.4 Other kinds of office software

Those other business programs include packages to handle payroll, stock control, accounts, appointment diary and task lists.

Critical path analysis (CPA) allows the efficient planning of a project over time. The technique isn't new, but computers have made a tremendous difference, as they can carry out so well and fast the complex tasks involved.

Figure 2.15   *How far can one combine the function of the various types of business software?*

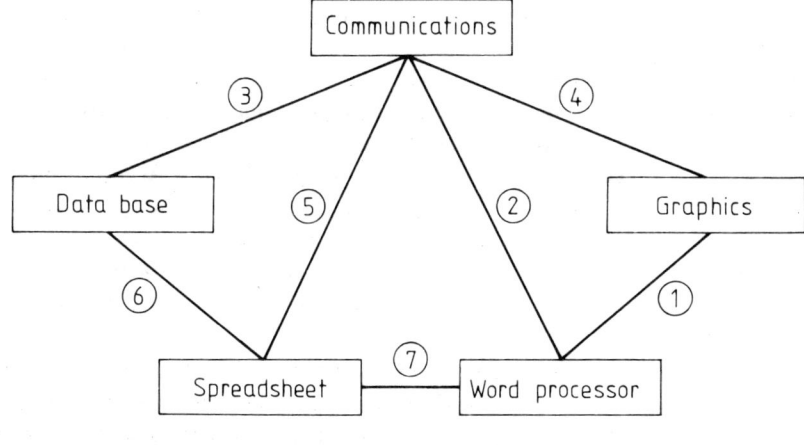

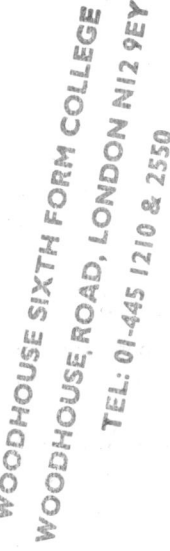

1. Can I put graphics into a word processed report ?
2. Can I word process material from a remote data base ?
3. Can I send data from a data base through the phone system ?
4. or pictures produced by a graphics package ?
5. or a spreadsheet grid ?
6. Can I use a spreadsheet to analyse data extracted from a file ?
7. Can I put sub spreadsheet grids into a word processed report ?

A typical project handled well by CPA is a large construction job, such as building a new warehouse. To complete such a project means undertaking a large number of separate tasks. Each requires certain materials, labour, and length of time; also, it cannot start till certain other tasks are finished. Thus, plastering needs certain raw materials and specialist labour to be on site and may take two weeks. The task can't begin, however, until the walls are up and someone's installed the electrics and other services. On the other hand, the decorators can't move in till the plaster's on and dry.

Using a CPA program lets the builder produce a complete list of all tasks and their needs in terms of materials, labour, completed tasks, and time. The program will also want to know how long materials take to be delivered once ordered, and such restrictions as the use of the plasterers on other sites. In some cases, too, weather conditions will be relevant.

Once all this information is in, the program will build up a master plan for the project. An outline for a simple case is in Figure 2.16; it shows a small number of tasks, each part of an overall project. The tasks are in 'boxes', and the line coming out of each gives the number of days it needs to complete. The diagram also shows the sequences: thus, we can't start Task E until both B and D are done.

The program works out and shows the critical path for the project. The critical path—the heavy line in the figure—defines the overall timetable the project must keep to if it isn't to fall behind schedule. By adding up the times required for each task along that particular path from start to end, it obtains the number of days to finish the project. Only by cutting times along the critical path can the project finish sooner (and cutting times may change the path itself as other tasks become critical).

Hard copy of the chart, best made on a large plotter (Figure 3.18b) is of great help to project management. If things go wrong on site, it's then easy to see what to do to keep the project on schedule. Things that go wrong could include incorrect or late deliveries of supplies, bad weather, sickness, and errors in the plans.

Organisers include various types of battery driven electronic diary (Figure 3.12a)—including wrist watch and 'credit card' types—as well as software designed to run on an office micro or network. Organiser software is meant to provide the flexibility of combined diary, appointments system, address and telephone record, and 'things to do' book—almost to be, in effect, a computer-based personal assistant. People find of value a package of this nature if

- they spend a lot of time at a desk with a computer available,
- the computer is left on all the time (or keeps accurate time when switched off), and
- the package concerned is easy to access, whatever else they're doing with the computer at the time.

Stock control packages became popular and important early in the history of business computing. As long as they're updated properly, they keep accurate records of stock levels. However, a typical inventory program (as it is sometimes called) can do more than just monitor the stores situation and give reports on the need to re-order certain items. A good system should aid management in all sorts of related decision-making exercises. For instance, it should be able to recommend re-order levels on the basis of supply and demand, display storage costs (including capital tied up), and note the effects of delivery delays, depreciation, deterioration, and relationships between items. A program in this field should also be able to put a value on stock held at any moment.

Accounting is the reason for that last sentence. Any firm must be able to keep track of the money flowing through it (as in Figure 2.10). At the crudest level, this means keeping accounts (lists) of all incoming and outgoing sums of money; the difference between these credits and debits during a period gives the firm's financial balance. In practice there are different kinds of credits to think about and to take account of, and different types of debit too. Accounts based on more detailed categories provide further information about the firm's position. Then there are tax (including VAT) and other such things to include in practice.

Figure 2.16   *A project control program shows the critical path you must follow to complete the project on time*

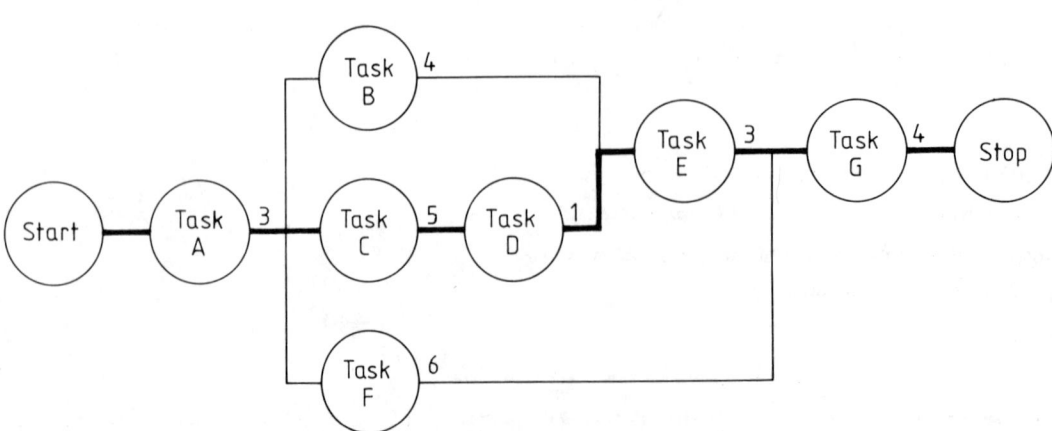

In the days of information based on paper, companies used three main books to hold the details of their accounts. In the sales ledger went notes about each invoice, including receipt of payment. The purchase ledger carried similar details about outgoings. The third, the normal ledger, was to hold both these sets of details in various categories, so as to make fairly straightforward the end of period accounting—statement of position, balance sheets, profit and loss accounts, list of debtors, and details of how long each bill has been left unpaid.

Most computer accounting software packages follow the same structure and principle, and allow the same well-tried approach. Much of the work to be done could involve the spreadsheet, however, so people wanting to computerise their accounts think of that approach, too. A major problem, all the same, is keeping such programs up to date in the light of changing Government requirements.

Payroll software, in much the same way, is like a data base (Chapter 6). This is because a firm has more to do with its staff than just pay them. Personnel administration would be a better description of a suitable program—can it list all the staff on a certain grade, say, who live in a certain road, and tell you their National Insurance numbers, for instance?

A simple payroll program will do the following for each member of staff:

- work out gross pay, including overtime, commission and bonus;
- deal with the various deductions (such as tax, union dues, pension fund and so on);
- provide a statement of gross and net pay and deductions (the pay slip);
- pay out; and
- keep an up-to-date record of total gross pay, tax and so on, as the law demands.

By 'pay out' I mean that where a firm pays in cash, the software should also analyse the numbers of each note and coin to put in each wage packet. If cheques are the means of payment, it should print those out ready for signature. If, instead, there's direct transfer between bank accounts, the file needed by the firm's bank should be prepared. The wider type of personnel administration software would cover these needs, of course, but these also involve a staff data base.

Of course, there are implications here for the accountants. Thus all the tax deducted from gross wages and salaries has to be paid to the Inland Revenue, with a proper statement. What we need is to integrate the payroll and the accounts software to automate this task, too. As I noted above, integration is important in these software areas as well.

2.5 Learning with IT

Many people expect conversations between young learners and their home tutor computers to replace human teachers in a few decades. Children would then go to school to play, to gain social skills, join in sports, go on trips, explore machines, carry out experiments, work in dance and drama, and so on. Open learning, the predecessor of computer-based study at home, is certainly growing fast in Britain and elsewhere.

Where are we at the moment? IT hasn't yet much affected learning in schools, colleges, and universities. Only a minority of places expect all learners to use computers as a matter of course.

The main current uses of IT in schools and colleges are:

- awareness—allowing learners to gain familiarity with the field
- IT/computer studies/science—learning about IT and its uses as a subject of study in its own right, rather than as a tool in other areas
- management and administration—IT as a tool for support work in offices, libraries and departments
- using 'business' software—word processing and such in its own right
- computer-aided learning (CAL)—where IT systems add to other learning resources in any subject area
- control—using a computer to capture data from its environment and to control other equipment

I'll say nothing about arcade gaming, working with school computers within private enterprise, or the use of posh modern equipment to impress visitors during Open Days!

Management/administration and using 'business' software are basically the same in that both involve the same hardware and software. The difference is that in the former case it's the staff who use the systems, while in the latter it's the learners.

The most important types of business software here handle word processing, graphics (picture processing), data base work (information storage and access), communications (information transfer), and the use of spreadsheets (tables processing). Staff also find uses for stock control packages and critical path analysis software (for course design and scheduling).

Each of these types of software has many possible uses for school and college staff and learners. Here are some:

Word processing

Staff—worksheets, handouts, notes, question banks, stock lists, notices
Learners—essays and other assignments, projects, reports, magazine items

Graphics

Staff—graphing many relationships in theoretical and practical contexts; producing quality illustrations for overhead projection, notices or distribution; clearly showing expenditure and assessment breakdowns

Learners—graphing experimental results; producing quality illustrations for projects, assignments, and reports

Data base

Staff—student records; orders, suppliers, and stock records; reference files; glossaries; question banks; class registers

Learners—reference and revision notes; glossaries

Communications

Staff—access to public data bases (such as Prestel, the National Educational Resources Information Service (NERIS), and The Times Network System (TTNS)); electronic mail; electronic communication with different areas or even different countries

Learners—reference to remote public data bases for project work and other research; electronic publishing to the community and elsewhere (and reading electronic magazines from other schools); finding out about jobs and places in further and higher education

Spreadsheets

Staff—budgeting and accounting; analysis of assessments and examination results; processing and analysis of experimental results; registers and mark books

Learners—tabulation and analysis of experimental results; tuck shop accounts

Computer-aided learning (CAL) is the most obvious use of micros in education. By computer-aided learning I mean *all* study situations in which computers join other resources (books, projectors, video, special equipment, and so on). In each case the computer with associated software has some role in the learning of subtopic, topic, area or field. All learning resources are seen, at least by the authors of the individual software packs, to be of potential value if called on to assist. Although no single resource is *essential*, any formal education course (in any subject) is made or broken, in practice, by the resources the tutor calls on and by the effectiveness with which s/he uses them. All that applies to the computer—it is not essential for any subject but there is no subject to which it can't add something.

However, there's one type of CAL approach where the computer is, by definition, essential. That is computer-managed learning (CML). In a full-fledged CML course the

computer guides each learner through a branching individualised scheme toward the distant goal. The guidance includes setting and marking assignments, diagnosis, remedial advice and specifying the next stage. The system may even control audio-visual and related software resources (such as slides, worksheet printing or on-screen administration, and interactive video); some go the further step of monitoring the learner's practical work (for example, in electronics). Full CML systems are becoming common in vocational training but remain rare in schools. For sure, we're still a long way from having an IT system which can remotely approach the intelligence, flexibility, power, speed and humour of a human tutor.

Most CAL programs are still very restricted, but comprise a vast range of potential uses of the computer as a resource for learning. They include what most often carry the name of educational software—packages such as:

- revision drills and objective test programs
- so-called page-turning—non-interactive—routines that present screen after screen of text, perhaps with a few simple diagrams and/or questions
- simple games based, say, on using a second language in a strange city or building up electric circuits
- graphic introductions to certain areas, maybe with animation and maybe with interaction
- computerised teaching machine programs with perhaps a certain degree of branching
- interactive simulations, e.g. of a science experiment or running a shop

Figure 2.17 sets these out on a spectrum of 'intelligence'; this relates to how interactive a program is, how much it is content-free, and how flexible it is in use. As you pass along the spectrum, the programs become harder to design too.

There's a major problem with 'traditional' CAL. Only the most superficial drill and practice program can hope to cover a large area of our giant syllabuses and be at all complete. The more thoroughly a program explores an area, the smaller the area must become. To provide a comprehensive bank of resources over the whole formal school curriculum for 5- to 16-year-olds, we need a million learning software packs of this traditional type. We shall never get them.

What tutors are starting to use instead with their learners are what we can broadly call tools—business software without specific content (word processors, graphics, statistical analysis, data bases and such). Here, as we've seen, the

Figure 2.17 *There's a spectrum of 'intelligence' for computer-aided learning software*

Pure test	Crude drill	Text + drill	Text + drill + graphics	Authored suite + graphics	Simulation
Corrected test	Helpful drill	Text + helpful drill	Authored suite	Super authored suite	Complex simulation

computer is a general background aid rather than a learning resource tied to small areas.

Another way forward for tutors is to use authoring systems such as *Microtext*, *Top Class*, or *Pilot*. Such software is designed to make it fairly simple to transfer teaching sequences to computer (or to computer-based interactive video). Simple they may be, but a great deal of work is still needed on the part of the tutors to produce effective material, and it isn't likely that such approaches will become common soon. All the same, it's the authoring approach that we'll need to enable the computer–learner 'conversations' mentioned at the start of this section.

The most important questions that follow introducing IT into education concern how much the curriculum should change. Will the current approach suit the learners of the early twenty-first century? Will society need *them* to be able to reel off a load of definitions and formulas? Will society need *them* to know how to build a mortice joint, use a Geiger-Müller tube, or know the French pluperfect? Will society need *them* to be literate and numerate in the senses we now use the words?

SELF-DEVELOPMENT QUESTIONS

See Pages 134–135 for notes on these questions.

S2.1 Discuss why we class a robot or other automation system as IT.

S2.2 Visit a local firm that uses robots and write an essay about one of them. Include notes on its degrees of freedom, sensors, and method of programming.

S2.3 Totally automated factories will soon exist. Choose a field of industry that appeals to you (manufacture or mining) and design fully automated plant in as much detail as you like. Discuss the advantages and disadvantages compared to the approach of the past.

S2.4 What is automation? If it contributes to lower employment, is it a good thing?

S2.5 Outline the control program for a metal sheet thickness system (Figure 2.6). Express it in flowchart form as in Figure 2.5.

S2.6 Outline the control program for RobertA (Figure 2.2).

S2.7 Program a floor robot (turtle or buggy) to carry out some simple tasks. How much is it autonomous?

S2.8 Program a robot arm to take an egg from an eggbox and place it in a saucepan or beaker of boiling water.

S2.9 Use a suitable CAD system to output and study one of these:

a a planned modern kitchen layout
b plan of a five-unit industrial estate
c a circuit using one or more transistors or chips for a stated purpose
d the layout of a Georgian-style front door
e a modern phone handset design

S2.10 Explore an interactive video system that lets you tour round and study a place or a map. How flexible is it in practice?

S2.11 Some people call the modern IT-based office 'the paperless office'. Is it possible to work entirely without paper?

S2.12 Describe with care two minor office tasks and relate each to Figure 2.9.

S2.13 An IT alternative to paper storage of information involves microform. Find out about this; compare it to paper and electronic storage.

S2.14 Use a spreadsheet for one of the following.

a tuckshop accounts (or similar) for a week
b your own accounts for a week
c analysis of the results of a science experiment
d analysis of the results of a survey (e.g. market research)
e producing multiplication tables
f holding a page of a teacher's mark book

S2.15 Use a business graphics program to display data from S2.14 or elsewhere in different forms. When is it best to use each of line graph, bar chart and pie diagram?

S2.16 Produce a version of Figure 2.15 that covers your own likely needs.

S2.17 Use a critical path analysis program for planning one of the following, or an activity of your own.

a a holiday
b a disco
c a sports event
d bringing a new product to market

S2.18 Use an electronic organiser and compare it to a paper-based approach.

S2.19 Do the same for an electronic store of phone numbers.

S2.20 Set up a stock control system for a school or college subject department.

S2.21 Investigate the use in a local firm of one of these software suites:

a stock control (inventory)
b accounts
c payroll (personnel)

S2.22 Write an essay based on your view of the first and last paragraphs of Section 2.5.

S2.23 Choose half a dozen CAL programs in a subject area you know about. Quickly assess the practical value of each. Write a report that would be of use to a teacher of the subject. Introduce this with a couple of paragraphs of general points leading to Figure 2.17; place the programs on the spectrum and give a brief assessment of each one.

S2.24 Use a CAL authoring package to produce a short learning unit in a topic you know about. Assess the result in the hands of typical learners. Present the unit, with any necessary notes, to a teacher of the subject and assess the comments.

S2.25   NERIS is a viewdata base for teachers. Use it, if you can, to find out about resources to aid learning some of the concepts in this chapter.

EXAMINATION QUESTIONS

Q2.1   A small manufacturing business requires software to help perform budgetary control and financial modelling. There is a need to study the effects on overall profitability of changes in hourly paid wage rates, costs of materials, prices of products, and units sold.

What type of software package should the company investigate? Explain the advantage of using such a package compared with using a computer program specially written for the company using a conventional programming language.

(AEB specimen paper)   (5)

Q2.2   A company is engaged in the manufacture and marketing of buttons of various designs. Included amongst its activities are the following:

i   ordering and maintaining a stock of raw materials
ii   scheduling production according to known requirements and forecasts for orders, the existing stock of buttons, and the availability of materials, labour, and machinery
iii   marketing the company's products, receiving orders, and making sales forecasts
iv   maintaining a stock of buttons and fulfilling orders for them
v   handling all of the company's financial transactions
vi   providing overall management of the company and planning for the future

These six fields of activity are broadly the responsibility of six departments in the company, respectively known as Raw materials (R), Production scheduling (P), Sales and marketing (S), Button despatch (B), Accounts (A), and Management (M).

Describe, by means of an outline flow diagram with notes, the flow of data between these departments within the company. Identify the activities in which a computer system might be involved, and in each case explain how it would be used.

(COSSEC)   (25)

Q2.3   In an office environment, what is meant by the term 'integrated package'?

(4)

A large retail firm classifies its customers into ten different types; it also deals with eight different categories of supplier. For each item passing through the retailer, the purchase and sale values are known, as are the customer type and the supplier category. This information is held in a data base on the firm's mainframe computer.

The chief accountant, who has a personal computer with an integrated package, wishes to present as part of his year-end figures a glossy brochure. This brochure traditionally shows (i) a breakdown of the purchases, (ii) a breakdown of the sales, (iii) comparisons of these with the previous year's figures, (iv) some indication of trends.

a   What information will the chief accountant require on his personal computer from the mainframe?

(3)

b   How will he get this information onto his PC?

(3)

c   Suggest some presentations of the data that he might wish to use in the brochure.

(10)

d   What hardware devices might he use for output?

(Oxford)   (3)

3 Computer hardware

Figure 3.1 *A mainframe computer processor can handle the needs of many users, many tasks, and many peripherals at the same time, but there has to be a permanent staff to help* (IBM)

Case study 3—Keith Starsky logs on

Keith Starsky works with Esther Boswell in CompAid, a small computer consultancy (Case study 1). They subscribe to the British public viewdata system Prestel for three main reasons.

- Prestel provides a useful form of electronic communication as well as links to full electronic mail and to telex.
- Prestel carries a large data base of helpful information.
- Prestel's home and office banking service assists the efficient management of the bank accounts.

Figure 3.2 *A modern office phone system is flexible enough to allow machine communication as well as human communication*

CompAid's computer network includes the communications software needed for access to Prestel (and to other viewdata systems). Figure 3.2 shows how it links to the phone service. Two of the three exchange phone lines carry splitters to allow dual use—one for the office fax machine (a sort of communicating copier—Section 3.6) and the other for computer communications. A modem joins the computer network to the exchange line. This device (Sections 1.6 and 3.6) allows data transfers between a digital computer and the analog phone network.

Keith has gained the task of dealing with most of CompAid's electronic communication simply because he reaches the office well before eight in the morning. Phone usage then is charged at the cheapest rate. When he arrives each day, therefore, he settles at a work station with a cup of coffee and logs on (connects) to Prestel. When the computer network is running, he needs just a few key-presses to access the communications software and one more to instruct the computer to ring Prestel. The system has the phone number in store, so sends the digits automatically; if it can't get through, it keeps trying, while Keith looks through the post or admires the fine view of distant Sheffield across the Derbyshire countryside.

To log on to Prestel once you've made the link, you need to prove you're allowed in by sending a ten-digit identification code and a four-character password. Keith's software knows the identification code too, but for security reasons it does not send the password: Keith does that himself from his keyboard.

Most days there are three or four electronic mail messages waiting for when Keith logs on—a message on Prestel's welcome screen tells him of this. He presses key

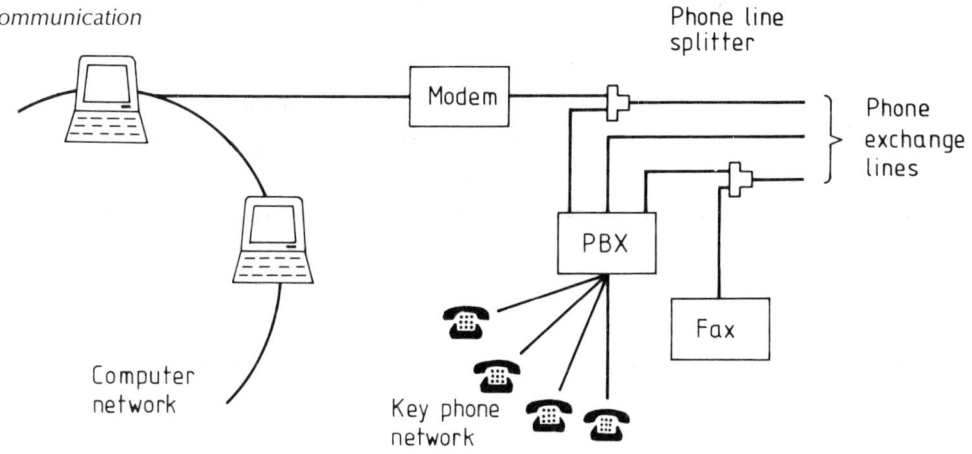

0 to look through them. Today there are a couple of messages from the consultant in Edinburgh with whom Esther and Keith work on a major project; an order from a client in Bristol for some manuals; a telex from a firm in London asking for details of their services; a query from a teacher in a nearby college; and a couple of messages from friends. Keith prints out a copy of each message ready for action later in the day.

Yesterday, as is normal, people in the CompAid office prepared several messages for sending out on Prestel; they stored them on the network's hard disc ready for Keith to deal with. Now he presses another key to send mail, and transmits these messages and acknowledgements of those just received.

There is another special task for Keith to do on Prestel today. In a few weeks Esther is going to a meeting in Canada; she wants to get things moving on travel arrangements, hotels and so on. He therefore types ***canada** to obtain the menu shown in Figure 3.3.

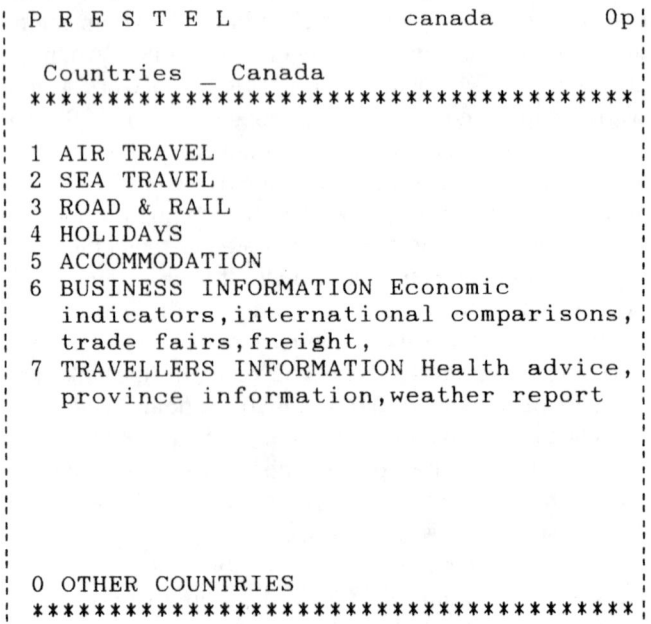

Figure 3.3 *You can access material from Prestel's huge bank of information through a large number of menu pages*

As you can see, this menu will let Keith quickly get at the information he needs. He works through the sections of interest, and prepares a file of screen printouts for Esther on such things as

- air schedules and prices
- tourist office details
- hotel information for Toronto, the city where the meeting is
- weather and climate summary

Maybe during the day Esther will have time to decide on her plans in more detail. She can then give Keith a list of bookings to make and information to ask for the next time he logs on to Prestel.

Here are some other things Keith has used viewdata for:

- obtain details for new staff of local IT courses
- book a temporary secretary when their own had an accident
- find out about life assurance
- sort out how to send a computer to Nigeria
- order some official publications
- get copies of useful computer programs
- check local unemployment figures
- get weather forecasts and road reports ready for meetings round the country
- transfer funds from one CompAid account to another
- hire a car when his own was away for service
- have a present sent to Esther on her birthday
- order groceries for a sudden office party
- book lunch for a working meal with a client
- publish a request for software information on a public 'notice board'

Keith uses Prestel's home and office banking to transfer funds between CompAid's main and savings accounts. Electronic banking, with its 24-hours-a-day access, is a lot quicker and simpler than standing in a High Street queue or working by mail. As well as letting him transfer funds, the system can also

- show each account's statement whenever they want,
- add to or delete from the list of standing orders,
- arrange payments of many of the firm's bills,
- order cheque books and printed statements, and
- enquire about individual payments in and out.

Unlike an autoteller machine ('hole in the bank's wall') a home and office banking system terminal like this can't pay out cash, of course. Otherwise it's much more flexible and easier to use.

Introduction

Still, people use cash a lot less now than they used to. If you view money as information, you can see that IT has much to offer the world of banking and finance. It is not hard to view money as information—just think of the immense amount of paperwork associated with much of its use. Many trees die each year to feed those paper needs—cheques, paying-in slips, ledger (account book) entries, standing order forms, paper statements, letters from banks to overdrawn customers, credit card slips (three copies each plus carbon sheets), and so on.

Handling information electronically is far cheaper and quicker than working with dirty, bulky paper that is easy to damage and lose. Banks have long realised this and have already replaced a large proportion of paper-based transactions with electronic ones. Also autotellers, home and office banking and smart cards (credit-card sized money-handling computers) are starting to have an impact on the lives of the banks' customers and replace *their* paperwork with electronic IT.

Modern IT concerns the handling of information in electronic form by machines—that is the storage, processing and transfer of information as data. In this chapter we look at computer hardware—but never forget that the task of computer hardware is to handle data that is information for its human users.

Objectives

When you have worked through this chapter, you should be able to

1 list ten or more uses of Prestel, describe several in detail, and comment on their advantages compared to traditional methods of handling the same tasks
2 discuss the significance of IT in the current financial world and in the future
3 list the parts of a computer's central processor and explain their functions
4 distinguish between ROM and RAM, and note typical sizes
5 comment on a central processor as an electric circuit
6 explain the difference between an integrated circuit and a chip
7 draw and explain a simple sketch of the structure of a computer processor
8 state what a register is, and explain two examples
9 outline what happens during a computer's fetch–execute–reset cycle
10 note the nature and advantages of a RISC machine
11 distinguish between an instruction's opcode and address part
12 describe how a processor carries out simple assembly language instructions

13 state the three main levels of computer memory and briefly explain the working of each
14 outline the nature of bubble and CCD memory and compare these to traditional microelectronic devices
15 describe the nature and value of cache storage
16 list several input and output devices and describe their action and use
17 discuss the nature and value of a WIMP (desktop) environment
18 compare dumb and intelligent terminals
19 write brief notes on character, line and page printers
20 compare bed and drum plotters
21 discuss the value of computer output on microform (COM)
22 comment on speech recognition and synthesis
23 compare optical mark reading and optical character reading
24 compare magnetic and optical stripe cards
25 discuss the use of bar codes in shops and libraries
26 outline the nature of fax
27 list some sensors and describe the use of one
28 explain the need for analog-to-digital and digital-to-analog converters
29 describe briefly the concept of automation, with an example
30 list the functions of a peripheral interface
31 compare serial and parallel data transfer

3.1 Computer architecture

Here again is Figure 1.13, the basic outline of any digital computer system. In this chapter we look in more detail at the parts of the system and at how they work together to process input data.

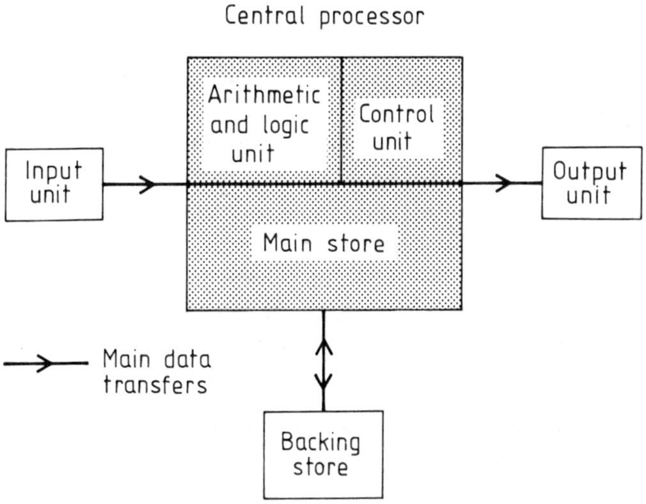

Figure 3.4 *The five main parts of a computer work together to process data efficiently*

The functions of the five parts are as follows; look back at Section 1.3 if you need.

Processor

This consists of the **arithmetic and logic unit,** the **control unit** and clock, and the **store.** The control unit contains a number of small special stores called **registers.** Their tasks are to control

- the order in which the system carries out instructions,
- data transfers to and from the store, and
- data transfers to and from peripherals.

The clock sends out pulses at regular intervals (millions per second, in fact) so that all control operations keep in step.

The arithmetic and logic unit works with registers too. It also contains a number of electrical subcircuits called **logic units;** their task is to operate on items of data, to do the actual processing.

In many modern micros, a single chip carries all these parts, so handles all these tasks. We call such a chip a **microprocessor.** Whether a single chip or not, a computer's central processor links very closely to the main store, as Figure 3.4 shows.

Store

Being so close to the processor, the 'immediate access store' contains data needed for current tasks. (Data includes program instructions.) The store consists of a number of cells (or locations); each can hold a byte of data (an 8-bit binary number of a value between 0000 0000 and 1111 1111). The system refers to each cell by a unique number or address. Many older micros cannot have more than 65 536 address numbers, so their main store size has an upper limit of 64 K. Modern micros can address quite a lot more memory, while mainframes may be able to handle hundreds of megabytes.

As we found in Chapter 1, a computer needs permanent operating software to keep it working. Many or all of the operating software instructions must be in the main stores; we use **read-only memory** (ROM) chips to carry them. The rest of the available memory is for current data; such data can and will change from time to time, so it goes into **read and write memory** (RAM).

A small micro may have 16 K ROM and 16 K RAM when purchased; the user can add up to 32 K extra RAM later to let it handle more data (for instance, larger programs).

Backing store

With backing store, typically one or more disc drives, we turn to the computer's **peripherals,** the variable hardware we can add to the fixed central unit. A backing storage unit allows the computer to access the data it holds, for transfer to main store or into registers for immediate processing. The computer can also save data in the backing store for the future.

Input units

The function of an input unit is the transfer of data into the system from outside. It may be a device like a keyboard that lets a human user interact with the computer; it may be a link to the output of a second remote computer (as when your micro gathers data from Prestel); it may be a sensor that passes details of air pressure into the system; or it may be a reader which can automatically transfer data held in such forms as bar codes, the magnetic ink characters at the bottom of a cheque, or printed text.

Output units

These are the reverse of input units—their task is to convert data output by the system into some useful form. Examples are the screens, printers and speakers needed by humans; a telecommunication link to a remote machine; or the switches and motors of a robot machine tool.

A real computer needs all five of these sections in its hardware. It needs a program (instructions viewed as data) in store, perhaps copied from backing store. It can then accept data from an input unit, work on the data in the processor on the basis of the instructions as decoded by the control unit while the clock sends out its control pulses, and send the results to the output unit.

The data involved when in transit, the control signals sent out by the control unit, and the pulses broadcast by the clock all involve digital electric currents. A computer is therefore a huge and almost unimaginably complex electric circuit. What you see inside a computer (Figure 3.5) will not

Figure 3.5   *Even a small section of a computer's circuitry is very complex* (John Why)

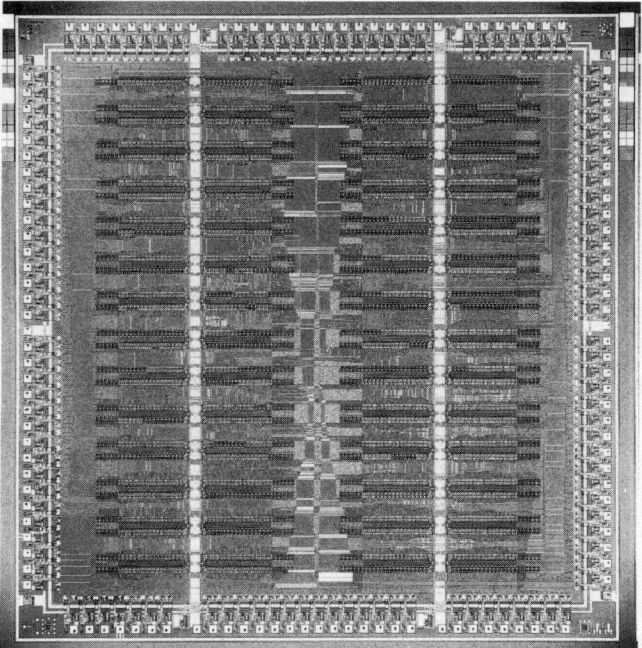

electronic elements and the links between them. These sit in a slice of silicon only a few millimetres square—the integrated circuit; the edges of the slice connect to the pins (legs) of the chip (Figure 3.6b) before the whole thing is packed in plastics for protection (Figure 3.6c). You need a powerful microscope to see the details of the integrated circuit in that slice of silicon—Figure 3.6c provides a view, but don't forget that the circuit is three-dimensional; this is just the topmost of ten or more layers.

3.2 Inside the central processor

Bearing in mind how complex the central processor's circuitry really is, you'll realise that the layout of Figure 3.7 is much simplified. It shows in more detail the central block of Figure 3.4, with the most important registers and subcircuits. (**Registers** are small stores able to carry no more than a few bytes of data for use during processing.)

This plan of the central processor needs some explanation. It shows in some more detail three parts of the processor—the store with its cells at the bottom, the arithmetic unit upper left, and the control unit upper right. There are storage cells in the arithmetic and control units too, but these are the special registers I mentioned already; some can carry a byte of data (or less), while others carry 2 bytes. The most important register is the **accumulator**; its function is to hold the results of processing data. However, all the registers are temporary stores of data during processing.

The plan also shows the central processor's links to two peripherals—an input unit off to the left and an output device to the right. In outline, therefore, the picture is much the same as that of Figure 3.4. Note, however, that I now

Figure 3.6 *A chip is a marvel of miniaturisation, its scrap of silicon (integrated circuit) containing a three-dimensional array of many thousand elements and the links between them* (Plessy Semiconductors Ltd; IBM)

look simple. There's a large number of chips planted over the surface of a **printed circuit board** (a plastics sheet with metal tracks formed on both sides to reduce the number of wires you'd otherwise need).

A **chip** itself (Figure 3.6a) is also an enormously complex electric circuit; it may contain hundreds of thousands of

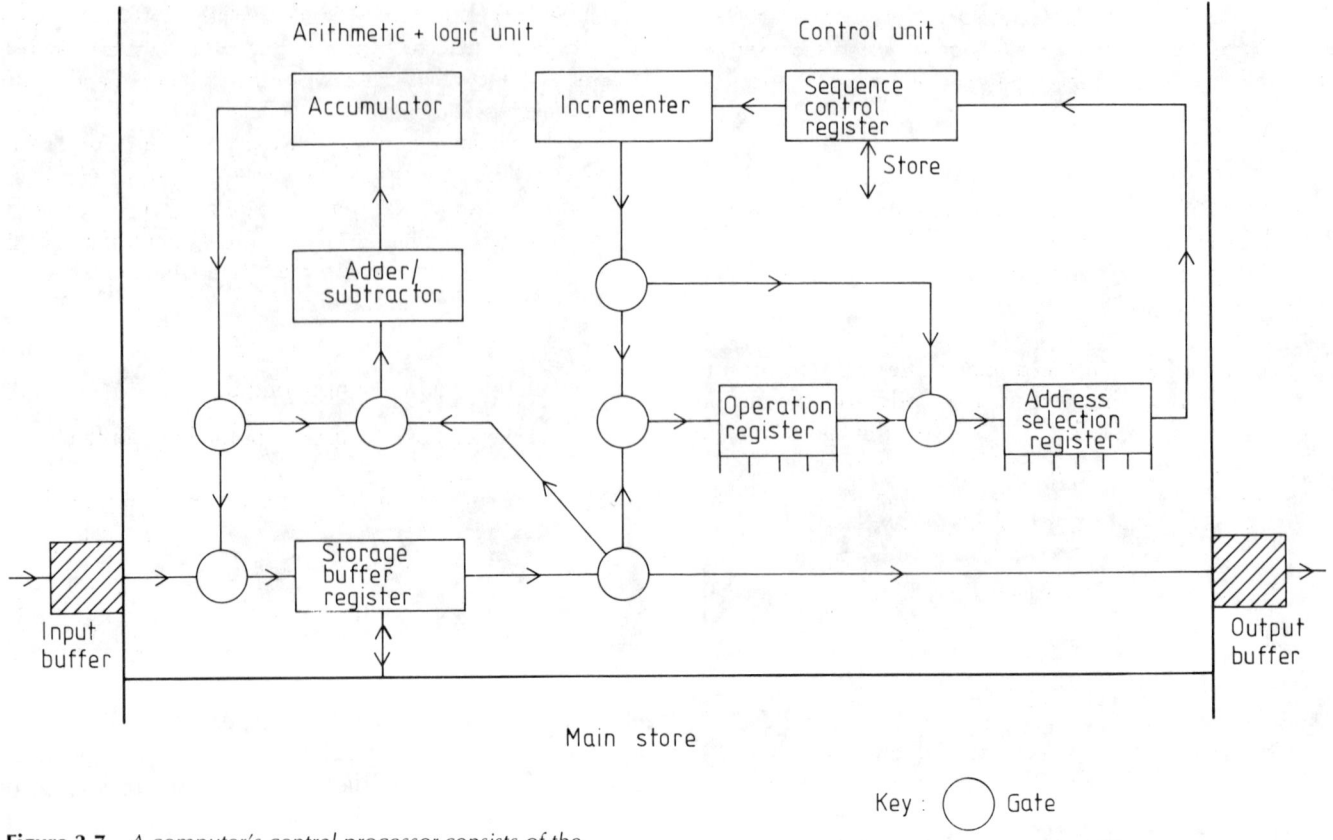

Figure 3.7 *A computer's central processor consists of the store, a number of registers and various special circuits*

Key : ◯ Gate

→ Data flow

show a buffer between each peripheral and the processor.

A **buffer** is another type of temporary storage unit; it is larger than a register (able to carry perhaps hundreds or even thousands of bytes)—its job is to hold data in transfer between processor and peripheral so that the processor doesn't have to take so much care of it. By this I mean the buffer can allow for the very different speeds of working of a processor and a peripheral, and for the needs of co-processors, for instance. Most interfaces (Section 3.6) between a processor and peripherals contain buffers to smooth the transfer of data.

The small circles in Figure 3.7 are special switches called **gates;** their task is to route bytes of data the right way through the system. Each gate has its own data input and output lines, as shown in the plan. It also has a control line (not shown) to link it to the control unit. A pulse of electricity along a control line will tell the gate concerned when to open to let data through. In reality, a processor contains many thousand gates—there are several, for instance, between each cell in the store and the registers outside.

3.3   The processor at work

The account that follows is in two parts. First, I describe a single cycle of action in the processor. During any one such

cycle, the processor fetches an instruction from the store and carries it out ('executes' it). This is the work of the control unit. Second, I briefly discuss a few typical instructions, mainly to show something of how the arithmetic and logic unit works. (I'll call it simply the arithmetic unit from now on.)

In both cases units of data move from one storage site (cell, buffer, or register) to a second. In a transfer from a memory cell or register, it's a *copy* of the data that moves—the contents of cell or register do not change. In a transfer from a buffer, on the other hand, the data actually leaves, and the rest shuffles along one place. A buffer, therefore, is like a queue.

In a transfer *to* a cell or register, the new data will replace what was there before. Designers and programmers must therefore ensure that a copy of the previous contents is stored somewhere else first if they will need it later. On the other hand, in a transfer to a buffer, the new data joins the end of the queue.

A single cycle of action in the processor consists of

a *fetch* the next instruction to carry out, from the store;
b *execute* (carry out) the instruction; and
c *reset*—get ready for the next cycle.

We call this the fetch–execute–reset cycle. At its start the address selection register contains the storage address—I'll call it *n*—of the next instruction the system must access. Here is what then happens during one cycle. This is a simple account, but it is in principle much like what happens in most CPUs.

a During **fetch** the control unit opens the right switches (gates) to allow a copy of the content of cell *n* to transfer to the storage buffer register.

A copy of the content of the address selection register—the value *n*—goes to the sequence control register.

The instruction in the storage buffer register consists of two parts. The first is the code for the action required—the **opcode.** A copy of this goes to the operation register. The rest of the instruction is the **address** of the cell to be used when the system carries out the instruction. A copy of this 'address part' goes to the address selection register.

At the end of this stage, then, the address of the current instruction is in the sequence control register, the opcode is in the operation register, and the address used for the operation is in the address selection register.

b In the **execution** stage, gates open in the control circuits depending on the opcode in the operation register. Thus, the system sets itself up to carry out that particular instruction.

At the same time, gates open between the storage buffer register and the store, to allow access to the cell whose address is in the address selection register.

Thus, at the end of this stage, the control unit is able to carry out the current instruction by doing the right thing to the right chunk of data. That is likely to involve the arithmetic unit (the circuits on the left in Figure 3.7); I'll come back to that shortly.

c To **reset** ready for the next cycle, the address selection register must carry the address of the cell that contains the next instruction. The address *n* of the current instruction is at the moment in the sequence control register. Unless the opcode tells the system otherwise, the next instruction is in cell *n* + 1. Switches open to allow the content of the sequence control register to pass through the incrementer—which just adds 1 to the value—to the address selection register.

If the opcode dictates otherwise, however, the address selection register must already carry the address of the next instruction, so the incrementer action is not needed. I'll explain that more fully later.

At the end of this stage all is ready for the next cycle—the address selection register carries the address of the cell which contains the next instruction to use.

A modern microprocessor can carry out any of a hundred or two instructions. (Even an efficient **'reduced instruction set computer'**—RISC machine—is likely to have dozens.) A computer program consists of a sequence of instructions to carry out a given task.

Broadly speaking, the instructions fall into three groups—they may concern input/output data transfers, involve the arithmetic unit, or control the way the system works through the program.

I'll give some examples of each. For this purpose I'll use typical three-letter assembly language instruction codes. We'll look at assembly programming languages in more detail in Chapter 5, but the examples should be clear enough for our purpose now. Follow each one through on the plan of Figure 3.7.

Peripheral data transfers (input/output)

INP *n* = transfer a byte of data from the input buffer and store it in cell *n*

The data leaves the buffer and passes to the storage buffer register. From there a copy passes to the right cell.

OUP *n* = copy a byte of data from cell *n* to the output buffer

Again the data passes through the storage buffer register.

Arithmetic unit transfers (process)

LDA *n* = copy ('load') a byte of data from cell *n* to the accumulator

The data passes from the storage buffer register through the ADD/SUB unit (which has no effect on it) to the accumulator.

STA *n* = copy ('store') a byte of data from the accumulator in cell *n*

The data passes from the accumulator through the storage buffer register.

ADD *n* = add a copy of the content of cell *n* to that of the accumulator

Gates open to store a copy of the accumulator contents in the ADD/SUB register; a copy of the content of cell *n* passes from the storage buffer register to ADD/SUB; this adds the byte to the one it already holds and passes the result to the accumulator.

SUB *n* = subtract the value in cell *n* from that in the accumulator

This is just the same as ADD *n*, except this time the ADD/SUB unit is switched to allow subtraction; again the result goes to the accumulator.

Program control

As we've seen, after the control unit has carried out the instruction in cell *n*, it normally turns to the next instruction in the store. One of the strengths of programming is to allow control to jump to a different instruction from the next. This allows the program to loop through a series of instructions a number of times, or to jump to a special sequence for some reason. There must, therefore, be various jump (or branch) instructions. Here are some.

BIZ n = branch to the instruction in cell n if the accumulator
        contains a zero value

BIN n = branch to the instruction in cell n if the accumulator
        contains a negative value

BRA n = branch to the instruction in cell n unconditionally
        (no 'if' in this case—just do it)

Finally there must be an instruction to stop working with the program—

HLT n = halt

The value of n doesn't matter in this case; people often therefore use 0.

As I have said, a real computer can act on dozens or hundreds of different instructions. The ten here are enough to allow quite useful programs, however. This is the philosophy behind the RISC concept, the reduced instruction set computer—most of the many standard instructions are not often used, so a non-RISC machine is unnecessarily complex, and unnecessarily slow.

3.4 How a computer remembers

We've now seen in some detail that a computer stores data in the processor in three levels. The lowest level, the one very close to the action of the control and arithmetic units, consists of a number of registers, each able to carry no more than a few bytes. The contents of the registers will change almost every time the computer goes through a cycle. That is why the registers are close to where things happen—to speed up the computer's work.

The next level in the computer's memory ladder is the **main store.** As its alternative name **'immediate access memory'** implies, this too is quite close to the action. However, while in most cycles data will transfer into and/or out of the main store, this must be able to carry a large number of bytes (or words). The main store is quite compact and works fast; all the same, data transfers that involve it can't be as speedy as those using registers. The main store carries the current program instructions and the data the program needs and produces—I mentioned before that this may need 64 K or much more.

Although in the past people used various methods of building a computer's main store, the integrated circuits in chips are now universal. Chips are cheap, compact, reliable, and very fast in action; they also use very little power. These features explain their wide use in audio, radio, video, and other IT equipment as well as in computers.

People are now working on other main storage techniques. Most advanced is bubble memory. **Bubble memory** chips store data bits in the form of very small magnetic domains (the bubbles); these stream around tracks in a thin magnetic film. The bubbles reflect light differently from the film around them, so a **light-emitting diode** (LED) and a photocell make up the mechanism for reading the data.

Bubble storage is costly and quite a lot slower in action than modern electronic chips. It is, however, very robust, so it is of value in high vibration and other unusual environments. A second advantage is that bubble RAM is non-volatile: the data stored remains when the power is switched off.

Storage in a **charge-coupled device** (CCD) is much like bubble memory as far as concerns those comments. A CCD chip is, however, made from semiconductor material like ordinary chips, and the bubbles this time are little domains of electric charge.

Before I turn to a computer's third level of storage—backing store—I must mention **cache memory.** This is becoming common in large machines. Such machines have—and need—very large main stores; the problem with these is that it takes time to transfer data to and from the individual cells. Cache memory is front-line main store—it may contain just a few thousand bytes, so it is fast-acting. The computer's operating software has the task of moving from main store to cache the instructions and data it expects the program to need during the next few cycles. A cache store is therefore like a block of registers as regards access, and like a section of main store as regards function.

Data storage also takes place at a third level. This is even further from the centre and slower in action than main store; in fact I am now talking about the **backing** (or **secondary) store,** a peripheral rather than part of the central unit. See Figure 3.8 for the levels of computer storage.

A computer is a general purpose device. Each user will want to apply it to different needs in different ways. We've already discussed a good number of applications for computers—but there are very many more. A computer *must* have a backing store, therefore, to let each user work with the system on his/her own particular library of programs and collections of information.

Backing store (or secondary or auxiliary store) can hold data in very large amounts for long periods of time. In this case there are many techniques we can call on. We can't use these techniques for main storage because the data transfer rates are far too low—taking milliseconds (thousandths of a second) rather than microseconds (millionths). In choosing between the various backing storage techniques, we need to bear in mind

- the speed of action (which depends on the time to find the right place as well as on data transfer rate),
- the capacity (how much data a backing storage system can hold at one time), and
- the cost (both that of the storage unit itself and that per byte of storage medium).

It is useful to class on the basis of access method the different techniques that support backing store. While each

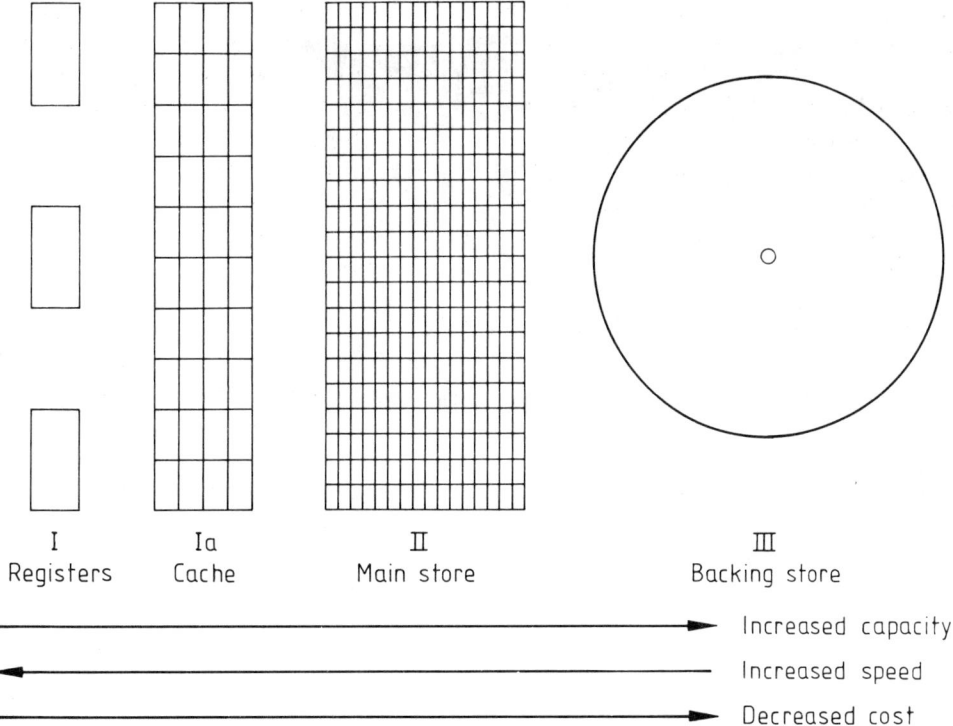

I	Ia	II	III
Registers	Cache	Main store	Backing store

Increased capacity

Increased speed

Decreased cost

Figure 3.8   *All computers have several levels of storage for data (not drawn to scale)*

can access one data item from a large number, a **serial** system can do so only by starting at the beginning and working through till it finds it. A **direct access system**, on the other hand, can go straight to the right place. The standard examples in the case of computer storage are magnetic tape and magnetic disc respectively. Audio tape and disc provide a fairly close analogy—if you want a certain piece of music on a cassette, you must spool through until you reach it; you can move the stylus straight to the right part of a disc (if you know where it is).

Direct access (sometimes called **random access**) is clearly faster when you need to find data records from a file in any order. However, it is more costly than serial access and, in many cases, serial access is all you need; the latter is, in any case, faster if the records are in order and you want to process most of them in one run.

Figure 3.9a shows a typical mainframe computer tape drive; the sketch of Figure 3.9b, of a typical layout, shows there's not much difference from an audio tape system in essence.

A typical full roll of (12.5 mm wide) computer tape is 1100 m long and can store about 100 megabytes (MB) of data. However, the way the system works with tape means that it stores data in blocks with empty spaces between rather than continuously: in fact the storage density within the blocks may be as high as 300 bytes per millimetre. In use, the tape moves at around 3 m/s past the 'heads' that erase, write and read the data. As we shall see, however, the tape does not run smoothly. Rather, all the time in use, it

stops and re-starts in each inter-block gap. It is the high acceleration involved that makes the two tape loop reservoirs necessary—without them, the tape would snap when starting or stopping.

The tape is a plastics film coated with magnetic material (as with audio). The system records data in nine parallel tracks across it, so each 8-bit byte runs across the tape; the ninth track provides space for a parity bit (see below) for each byte. Refer to Figure 3.10. In the write head is a set of nine tiny electromagnets. As the tape passes the head, pulses in the electromagnets form the dots in the magnetic coating. The erase head's job is to jumble up the surface magnetism to let the two types of dot show up. Sometimes, however, there could be an error, and the parity bit is there to help the system detect this.

Various codes exist to represent characters. In any case, the 256 values allowed by an 8-bit byte (0000 0000 to 1111 1111) are plenty enough for the alphabet (upper and lower case), digits, punctuation marks and other symbols. Different computers use the many values left over in different ways.

A common character coding system is **ASCII**, the American Symbolic Code for Information Interchange. Another is **EBCDIC**—say it ebb-sea-dick—Extended Binary Coded Decimal Interchange Code. I used ASCII in Figure 3.10—each character appears as a sequence of 0s and 1s in tracks 1–8. Thus the character T has ASCII code 84, and in binary this is 0101 0100. On the tape each 1 is a dot (domain) of north–south magnetism, with a 0 being

Figure 3.9 *A computer's tape drive is much the same in principle as an audio system* (IBM)

b

south–north. However, I haven't tried to show that in the sketch.

If you look at the 0s and 1s of Figure 3.10, you'll see that in each row of dots across the tape there's an odd number of 1s. In the case of T—0101 0100—there already is an odd number of 1s. As the system writes T to the tape then, it puts a 0 in the parity track. The ASCII code for e, however—0110 0101—has an even number of 1s; in putting that on tape, therefore, the system adds a 1 parity bit, to keep an odd total of 1s. We call this approach odd parity (some computers use even parity).

The point of **parity checking** becomes clear when we look at the reading process. This involves the read head (Figure 3.9b); it works the opposite way to the write head. As the tape passes below the read head, the magnetic dots in the

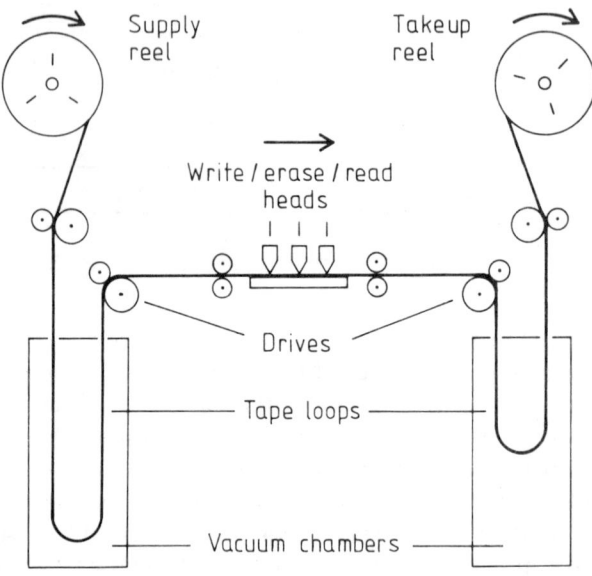

Figure 3.10 *Each byte of data runs across the width of the tape, with a parity check bit in the ninth track (not drawn to scale)*

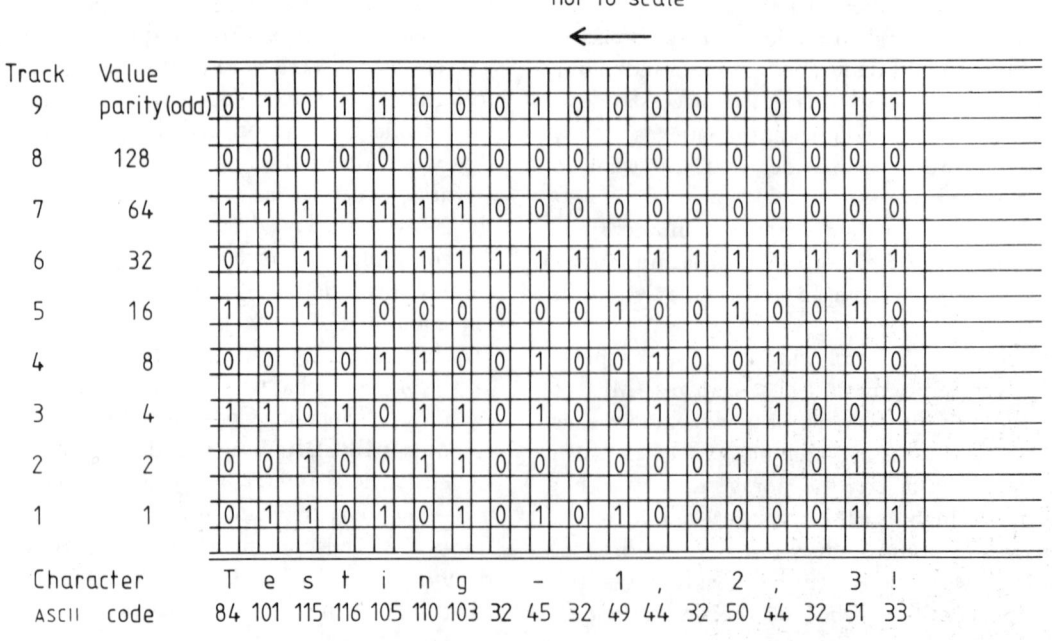

Track	Value																			
9	parity(odd)	0	1	0	1	1	0	0	0	1	0	0	0	0	0	0	0	1	1
8	128	0	0	0	0	0	0	0	0	0	0	0	0	0	0	0	0	0	0
7	64	1	1	1	1	1	1	1	0	0	0	0	0	0	0	0	0	0	0
6	32	0	1	1	1	1	1	1	1	1	1	1	1	1	1	1	1	1	1
5	16	1	0	1	1	0	0	0	0	0	0	1	0	0	1	0	0	1	0
4	8	0	0	0	0	1	1	0	0	1	0	0	1	0	0	1	0	0	0
3	4	1	1	0	1	0	1	1	0	1	0	0	1	0	0	1	0	0	0
2	2	0	0	1	0	0	1	1	0	0	0	0	0	0	1	0	0	1	0
1	1	0	1	1	0	1	0	1	0	1	0	1	0	0	0	0	0	1	1
Character		T	e	s	t	i	n	g	–	1	,	2	,	3	!				
ASCII code		84	101	115	116	105	110	103	32	45	32	49	44	32	50	44	32	51	33

surface cause pulses of current in each of the nine detectors. (The process is electromagnetic induction.) A series of nine 1s and 0s (current pulse or no current pulse) pass into the computer for each byte read. The system checks the parity—and if it finds an even number of 1s in any set, it reports an error. Parity checking is normal with data transfer. It's not just for tape.

What about the data blocking and inter-block gaps mentioned above? Tape is a serial access backing storage medium. With data stored at several hundred bytes per millimetre there's no way you could spool the tape to the site of the item you want. Thus to search a taped personnel file for the details (record) of Abdul Bloggs, you have to start the tape at the beginning and read each record into the processor until it recognises the right one.

What's done is this. The system reads a data block into a special buffer and stops the tape while it works through the buffer contents, processing the data as required. Then it starts the tape again to take the next bufferful (block). As the tape is zooming past the read head at several metres a second, without inter-block gaps the system would miss some records. Even using two buffers alternately—the technique called double buffering—the problem remains. Typically, one block will hold 2 K, and the tape will use 10 mm inter-block gaps.

Let's now turn to magnetic disc, the main direct access backing storage medium. At the back of the photograph in Figure 3.11 there is a drive, as used with a pack of ten hard discs for a mainframe. There's also a sketch of the system involved, with just five discs in the pack.

A **disc** is a sheet of material—metal if hard, plastics if floppy (as with many micros)—coated with a magnetic layer like that of tape. In use, the disc pack spins, while the head unit can move in and out along a radius. The radial movement allows the heads to access any of the 200 or so cylinders made up of the 200 or so concentric tracks on each surface. The discs spin at around sixty revolutions a second. Thus, within a short time the system can access any block of data on any surface. There is therefore direct access: no need to read through the data until the right block appears. Typically it takes a mainframe disc drive only a few tens of milliseconds to reach the data needed; the transfer rate may be as much as 2 MB/s.

Each block of data stored on a disc is in a **sector**; there are perhaps ten sectors in a track, with inter-block gaps between them. To find a given record, then, the software must know the cylinder, surface and sector (block). Then the head assembly will move in or out, the right head will be made ready to pick up data, and the system then just has to wait till the sector concerned comes round.

To allow for direct access like this to the hundred or so megabytes a disc pack can handle, one or more indexes are stored in the pack. To find the record for Abdul Bloggs this time means looking in the index to find the cylinder, surface and sector that contains it. This extra step doubles the access time; all the same, using discs remains very fast.

The principles above apply to such discs as the floppy used with smaller computers. While the details vary, in all cases the disc spins a tiny distance away from the head, so that specks of dust and finger prints on the disc surface can cause major damage. Because of this danger, many types of disc are sealed into the drive—you can't change them, so you must back your data up with some other form of store.

There has been great progress in backing storage technology in recent years. Holes punched in cards or paper tapes were the main early method, but punched media are now of historical interest only. Progress with magnetic media has led to more compact backing stores; in the case of laptop and other portable systems, very small tapes and discs are now common. However, there has been much progress in chip technology too—removable memory chips provide the backing store in the two small British micros shown in Figure 3.12.

Video technology has also made much progress in the 1980s. Not only is high-density video tape used for some compact computer tapes, but laser (including compact) and other forms of video disc are showing more and more promise. These can all store huge amounts of data in a small space, even hundreds of megabytes in a square centimetre.

Figure 3.11 *Mainframe disc drives use packs of hard discs* (International Computers Ltd)

b

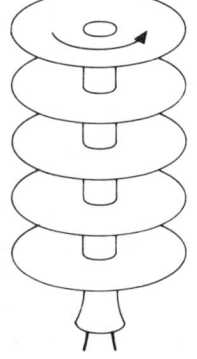
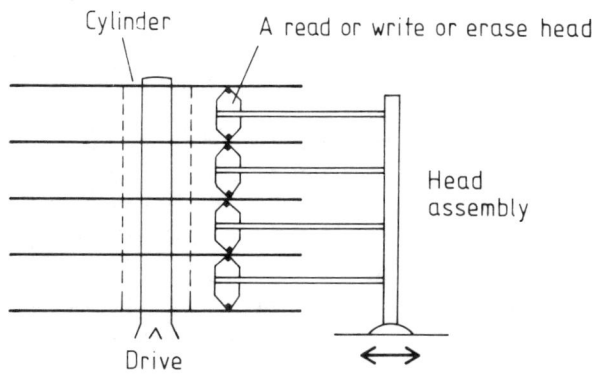

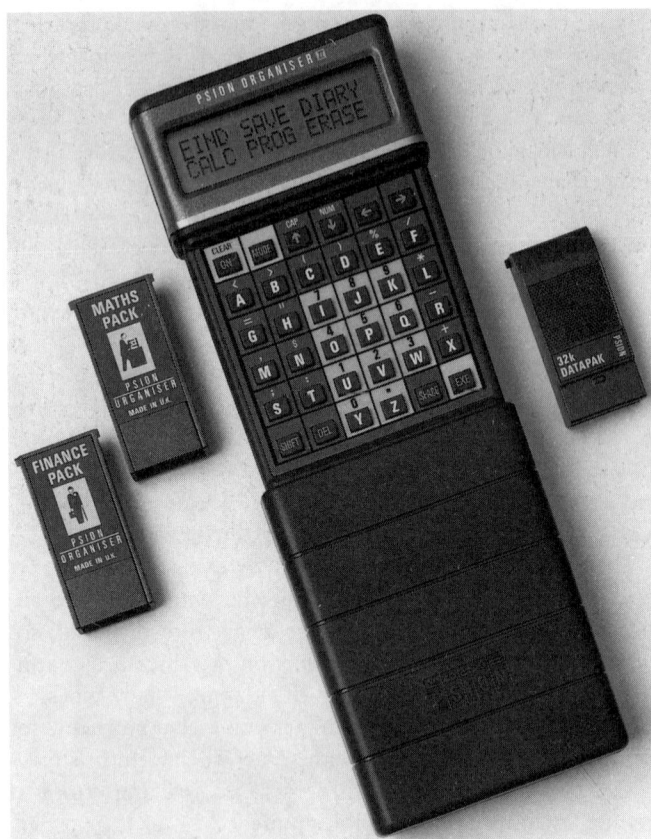

Figure 3.12   *The Psion Organiser pocket computer and the Cambridge Z88 laptop both use removable memory chips as backing store* (Psion plc; Cambridge Computers Ltd)

Most 'traditional' in style is the **CD-ROM,** read-only backing store on compact disc. People now widely use this to hold large data bases (encyclopedia text, directories, and so on) for fast access by micro.

Less 'traditional' is supplying video sequences as well as other data on a video disc backing store. This is also read-only, the technique used in interactive (user-computer-controlled) video. Such techniques as these are an interesting information technology convergence between two fields. Their importance will accelerate as it becomes simpler to write data to an optical surface as well as to read from it.

3.5   Input and output units

There are many ways to get data into a computer for processing, and out again after. It is useful, therefore, to group input and output units on the basis of context. See Table 3.1. The biggest group is clearly that for communication with a live user, though the others are growing as computer usage widens. We'll look at input units first.

Table 3.1

Input	Input and output	Output
Communication with user		
Keyboard	Light pen	Screen
Microphone	Terminal	Printer
Mouse, etc.	Touch screen	Speaker
Graphics pad		Plotter
Microform unit		
For machine-readable data		
Bar code reader		Bar code printer
Magnetic ink reader		etc.
Mark reader		
Communication with machines		
Scanner	Modem	
Stripe reader		
Cauzin strip reader		

A **keyboard** is a set of switches; touching each switch sends a unique code to the input buffer. There are many kinds, from a simple numeric keypad like a video remote control to a full typewriter-style system with tens of extra keys. There are designs such as the Maltron, with layout designed for comfort and ease of use, and the six-button Quinkey (Microwriter) which allows effective one-handed use. All the same, the ancient QWERTY layout (AZERTY in some countries) lives on, with either real moving keys or flat switches set in a sealed surface.

Although the use of a keyboard buffer means that input characters can queue up before the processor deals with them a block at a time, this is not always efficient. In particular, a common use of keyed data entry is for such things as personal information to go into a data base for later access. In such cases, key-to-store systems allow the much more efficient transfer of fresh data direct to backing store. A large number of data entry keyboards may link to several disc drives via an encoder, a special small computer. The main computer can get on with its work, as data entry is off line rather than on line (under main computer control). Later on, the system can merge the fresh data with the old in a batch (see Section 5.3).

Each day people enter many, many millions of bytes into computer storage using keyboards. In most cases they read the information from paper. Machine-reading techniques like those I'll come to shortly are likely to lead to a big change in this field soon. So too is voice recognition. The input device here is a microphone; this sensor (Section 3.6) converts sound waves into electrical signals the system can handle. However, sound waves are very complex, especially where speech is concerned. When voice recognition techniques are powerful enough to work with dictation with few errors, people will be able to talk freely with their computers. This is likely by the mid-1990s.

People communicating with each other do so most easily by speech; typing is the least simple. In between come drawing and writing, and the graphics pad input device lets you communicate this way with a computer. The system senses where the tip of a special pen is on the pad's surface, so as you draw or write, signals pass to the processor. Graphics pads play their main role in work such as computer-aided design, but a version appears in banks for signature checking.

A mouse is of no use for actual data entry. However, it can control a pointer on screen and thus let you choose from a menu (for instance) without using the keyboard. A **mouse** (Figure 3.13a) is a small box with a large ball underneath and a couple of buttons on top for you to press. As you roll the mouse over your worktop, sensors measure the movement of the ball and tell the computer. Suitable software moves the pointer to suit. Figure 3.13 also shows a tracker ball (an upside-down mouse you control with the palm of your hand) and a joystick, or paddle, as you may have used with video games. All three, if the software suits, can control movement on screen.

A **WIMP** environment is a common way for a micro user to interact with the system; the letters in the name stand for windows, icons, mouse and pointer. The software involved with this input and output technique of human–computer communication allows you to

- have a split-screen display with different tasks in the different windows—to word process a text while looking at a second and referring to graphic data, for instance;
- control what you want done by referring to icons—little graphic blocks on screen that represent different tasks or parts of the system—rather than by typing in commands or referring to entries in a text menu;
- work with a mouse rather than, or as well as, a keyboard; and
- to control a screen pointer to effect what you want.

Figure 3.14 shows some aspects of work in a WIMP environment. Relate it to the above list. Some people call this working in a **desktop environment.** That is because what the screen shows is rather like a desktop—working documents in the centre with access to nearby clock, calendar, calculator, notepad, waste bin, and other documents and files.

I call the use of a WIMP environment an input/output system as input of data to the computer and output from it

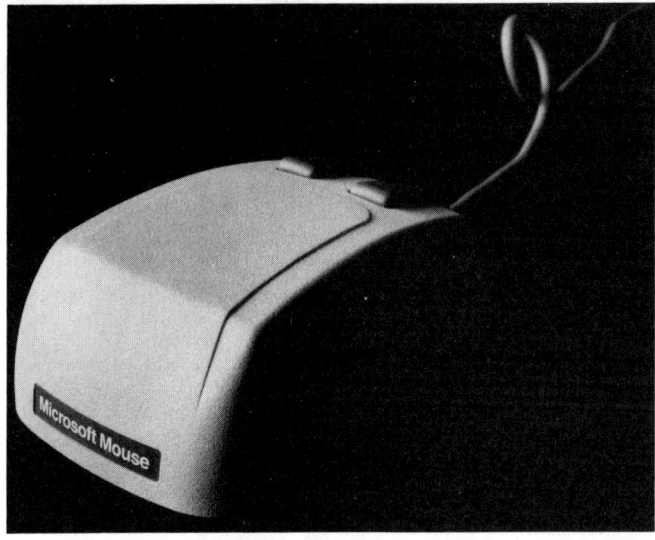

Figure 3.13 *The user moves a mouse, tracker ball or joystick (paddle) to control movement on screen* (Microsoft; Marconic Electronic Devices; Wang)

link very closely. It is really the mouse that has that effect, for the mouse closely controls what happens on screen.

Two other ways for the user to interact closely with screen output involve use of a light pen and a touch screen. A **light pen** has a photocell in the tip and a lead to the computer. As you move the tip round the screen the system can work out where you are pointing from moment to moment. With suitable software you can therefore draw directly on screen,

Figure 3.14   *A WIMP environment can be very friendly*
(Apple Computers UK Ltd)

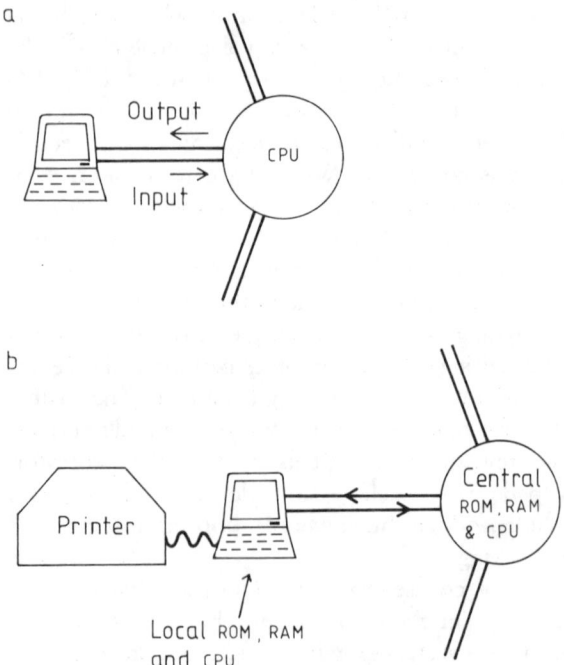

Figure 3.15   *Terminals link a number of users to a single central processor so they all think no one else is using it*

using the keyboard only for such things as colour control and to smooth freehand lines and curves. Light pens are common in computer-aided design packages.

A **touch screen** is much the same in effect. Along the top of the screen and down one side is a row of closely spaced infra-red lamps; their beams shine onto a row of photocells along the bottom and down the other side. Thus in front of the screen is a grid of invisible beams—when you touch the surface the system can work out where your finger is. The touch screen is not of wide use in computer-aided design; it is of value for interaction in public information displays and with people lacking keyboard skills.

The **terminal** is the most important combined input/output unit. A terminal lets one of a number of users interact with a mini or mainframe; the computer shares its time between the users so all think no one else is working with it. Each therefore needs an input unit (keyboard) and an output unit (screen and/or printer); the terminal links to the central processor as in Figure 3.15a. This shows a 'dumb' terminal, one whose every action involves the central processor and which may thus suffer problems of slow speed when the system is busy. An 'intelligent' terminal has some memory and processing power of its own, so it can handle at least simple tasks itself. Such a terminal (Figure 3.15b) may even have its own backing store, to make it still less dependent on the system. (Note that you use a fully intelligent terminal each time you use a micro to log on to Prestel.)

The ultimate in this direction is the network—comparatively little central power and lots of linked autonomous work stations (see Chapter 8).

Now I'll turn to the list of output units designed for communication with a human user—screens, printers, speaker, plotter, and microform unit.

The **standard screen**—monitor display—works with a cathode ray tube much as does a TV set; indeed most home micros feed a TV set rather than a monitor. Displays differ in being monochrome (black and white, perhaps with a green or amber filter to make the image more restful) or colour, and in their resolution. A display's resolution concerns the closeness of dots it can show as separate—the

higher the resolution, the more detail it can show and the smoother lines and curves will be.

Liquid crystal displays (LCDs) are fast becoming common, mainly (so far) in battery-powered units. An LCD uses little current; just as important, it's flat, so it takes up far less space than the bulky cathode ray tube. There is rapid progress in raising the size of LCDs at the same time as cutting their cost. Newer models offer high contrast, and colour systems won't be far behind.

Though computers have long been acclaimed as leading to a paperless society, most users at least sometimes want a permanent record—hard copy—of their system's output. Many types of printer exist to provide that; they vary enormously in price, speed, output, quality and versatility. We can group them on the basis of whether they in effect print a character, a line, or a page at a time.

Cheapest—and slowest—are the character printers. Most common in this group are (impact) **dot-matrix** machines; they form each character from a set of vertical lines of dots, each dot made by a tiny pin pushing ink from the ribbon onto the paper. The more pins the better the characters; modern 24-pin dot printers can give high quality at speeds up to a few lines a second. The major advantage of the approach is that a huge range of characters is possible with the dot patterns—Figure 3.16 shows this for a nine-pin print head. Thus you can switch between upright and italic, from roman letters to Greek, Arabic, Russian (and so on), and also have a good range of character sizes on offer. Dot printers can output graphics too, for instance dumping onto paper a good copy of a complex screen image, with different shadings for the different colours.

Figure 3.16 *As it forms characters from dots, a matrix printer allows a huge range of type styles (as well as graphics)*

Inkjet printers also build up characters from dots (and so offer type variety plus graphics). In this case there is no impact, so these machines are quieter. Instead of a row of pins that jump out and in, the inkjet print head has a row of tiny nozzles fed with ink; it pumps out tiny droplets of ink as it moves across the paper. You can print in colour with some dot-matrix printers, but the inkjet system is better for this.

Daisy wheel, golf ball and thimble printers work rather like typewriters; because they produce perfectly formed characters, they are still quite common in the office. At the end of the 'petals' of the daisy wheel, or over the surface of the golfball or thimble, lie raised character shapes. The system moves the right shape into place; it then bangs ink from the ribbon onto the paper. These machines are therefore slow and noisy; they can't produce graphics; and if you want to change type face (style or size) you must stop the machine and put in a new wheel, golf ball or thimble. Printers in this group are likely to vanish soon.

By some method or another, a **line printer** runs off text a line at a time, in effect first doing all As, then all the Bs, and so on. As with daisy wheel machines, pre-formed characters move into place before being hammered onto the ribbon over the paper. This time, however, the characters are on the surface of a fast rotating **drum** (barrel printer), chain or belt; the output is up to a hundred lines a second. The machines suffer all the problems of the daisy wheel group, but, being very fast, are also large and costly. Their main use is for printing large numbers of similar documents (like personalised junk mail letters, gas bills and insurance policies).

However, page printers are starting to take over. **Page printers** in effect produce a page at a time; some can output several sheets (several hundred lines) a second. The price of such machines for school, office and home is falling fast, but running costs are high. A page printer (such as the laser machine) is rather like a photocopier in appearance (Figure 3.17) and mode of action. Its print quality is very high, therefore, and it is as flexible as a dot matrix machine. Its input, however, is not the scanned image of a sheet of paper but the electronic output of a computer.

The above account of computer printers doesn't include all the types that exist; all the same, I have dealt with the most common. Now I turn to **plotters,** machines designed specifically for graphics output on paper (and of great value in computer-aided design).

A plotter has a pen (or more of different colours) able to move round a sheet of paper under computer control. In a small (flat bed) unit (Figure 3.18a) the paper lies flat and the pen moves in both the x and y directions to access any part. Larger (drum) machines (Figure 3.18b) have the paper rolling up and down while the pen moves to and fro. Both types can produce detailed graphics and lettering to a high

Figure 3.17 *A page printer looks and works rather like a photocopier* (Wang (UK) Ltd)

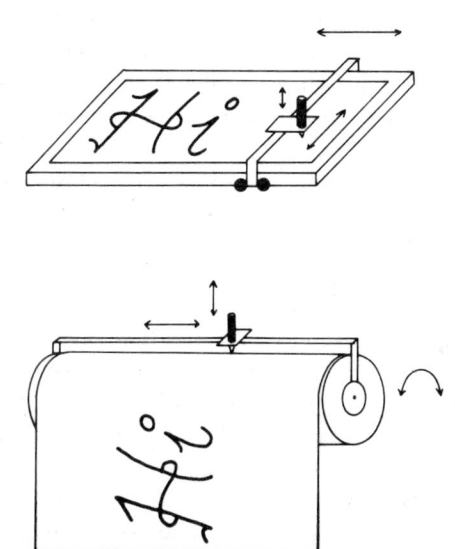

Figure 3.18 *Plotters can build up detailed graphic designs on paper*

standard—charts, maps, plans and so on for architects, designers and engineers.

Small plotters are often very slow, but the pen speed of a large machine can reach a metre a second. All types work faster than a good draughtsperson; they don't make mistakes, either.

A **microform output unit** is, in effect, yet another type of printer. This time, the output system writes the data (text and/or graphic) to microform (film or fiche) rather than to paper. The tiny images produced need special readers so people can get information from them; on the other hand, a few hundred sheets of fiche or rolls of film take up little space yet carry as much as several filing cabinet drawers. This technology—**computer output to microform** (COM)—is therefore of great value to firms like insurance companies and banks who'd otherwise have to store vast quantities of paper in their archives.

I mentioned voice recognition earlier as a likely method of data input for a few years' time. Voice recognition—microphone plus suitable software—will free people from a huge amount of computer-aided drudgery: they will be able to move away from the tyranny of the keyboard. **Speech synthesis** is the corresponding output approach—suitable software plus speaker lets a computer talk to the user. There are many situations where this is of value, when the user's eyes should be looking elsewhere than at a screen. Using tools, cooking, and driving are obvious cases.

Developments in speech synthesis are further advanced than in voice recognition. It shouldn't be too long, though, before a person can have a natural two-way conversation with a machine. There is great effort taking place toward this in a number of countries.

3.6   Non-human communication

Talking with a computer still means the user has to give full attention to a machine. Systems that let data feed automatically into store can make things even better. Every day thousands of people spend their time copying information from paper into computers. Dictating it into a microphone wouldn't be much more fun—but if the computer can read, that *is* be an advance.

There are several ways to produce machine-readable data. In view of the last paragraph, the most important are those that let the system access material written or printed on paper. **Optical mark reading** (OMR) is one such you may have come across—it is widely used with answer sheets for objective test papers in public exams (Figure 3.19), but has value in market research, stock taking and other areas where people fill in multi-choice forms.

In use, each sheet (source document) passes through the reader. A row of lamps and photocells checks for light reflection at each point on the paper. A place with a mark reflects light differently from one without, so the software can access the data.

Optical character reading (OCR) is more advanced but less reliable. The source document passes through a scanner which again contains a row of lamps and photocells—but now these are much smaller and closer. The software's task is not just to note where the marks are, but to process the reflected data in an attempt to recognise printed, typed or hand-blocked characters from their shapes. Clearly this is much harder, but there's such a huge demand for scanners able to read forms, letters and other text that progress is fast. Users of desktop publishing (DTP—Case study 7) often have scanners to make their work easier, for instance.

An older form of character recognition is **magnetic ink character reading** (MICR). The reader works with material printed in magnetic ink; it can accept only digits and four other special shapes. The main use of MICR is at the bottom of cheques. Each cheque carries three numbers—for the bank branch, the account, and the cheque itself. A clerk uses a magnetic ink typewriter to add the cheque's value. Now the piece of paper is fully machine-readable, and the bank's computers can process it at speed.

Bank users also know another machine-readable magnetic data input system—the stripes on cheque and credit cards. The stripe carries various identification numbers that, when accessed by a credit card reader or autoteller (Section 1.1), let the computer check whether the card is valid for the person who carries it. A magnetic stripe can carry about 2 K of data. **Optical stripe cards** are now starting to appear. These stripes carry several megabytes of laser-readable data; they are much the same as the surface of a compact disc. An optical stripe card could carry its owner's complete personal and health record, for instance. People are also looking at its potential for data bases—one stripe could hold all the text in this book.

The last few types of machine-readable data differ from the first in that they aren't also human-readable. Sometimes this is a drawback; mostly it's not. You'll surely know a very common such form of data, the bar code that appears on many books and packaged foods. A **bar code** (Figure 3.20) holds characters each in the form of two bars and two spaces; bars and spaces come in three widths.

On a food item the bar code gives country of origin, manufacturer, type of food, and package size. It does *not* include sell-by date or price, as these aren't fixed. In use, a reader (with lamp and photocell) at the point of sale informs the processor what each item is. The computer memory contains the price details (which the shop can change at any time). The cash register can show the price, and print it on the till slip with details. It's usual for the system to keep a stock check automatically, too; then the staff can find out at any time how many 450 g tins of beans (for instance) they have sold that day and how many remain.

Many libraries use bar codes for books and for users so the computer can read the tickets automatically and keep proper records of who has what books and when they become overdue for return.

The last machine-readable data type to mention is the

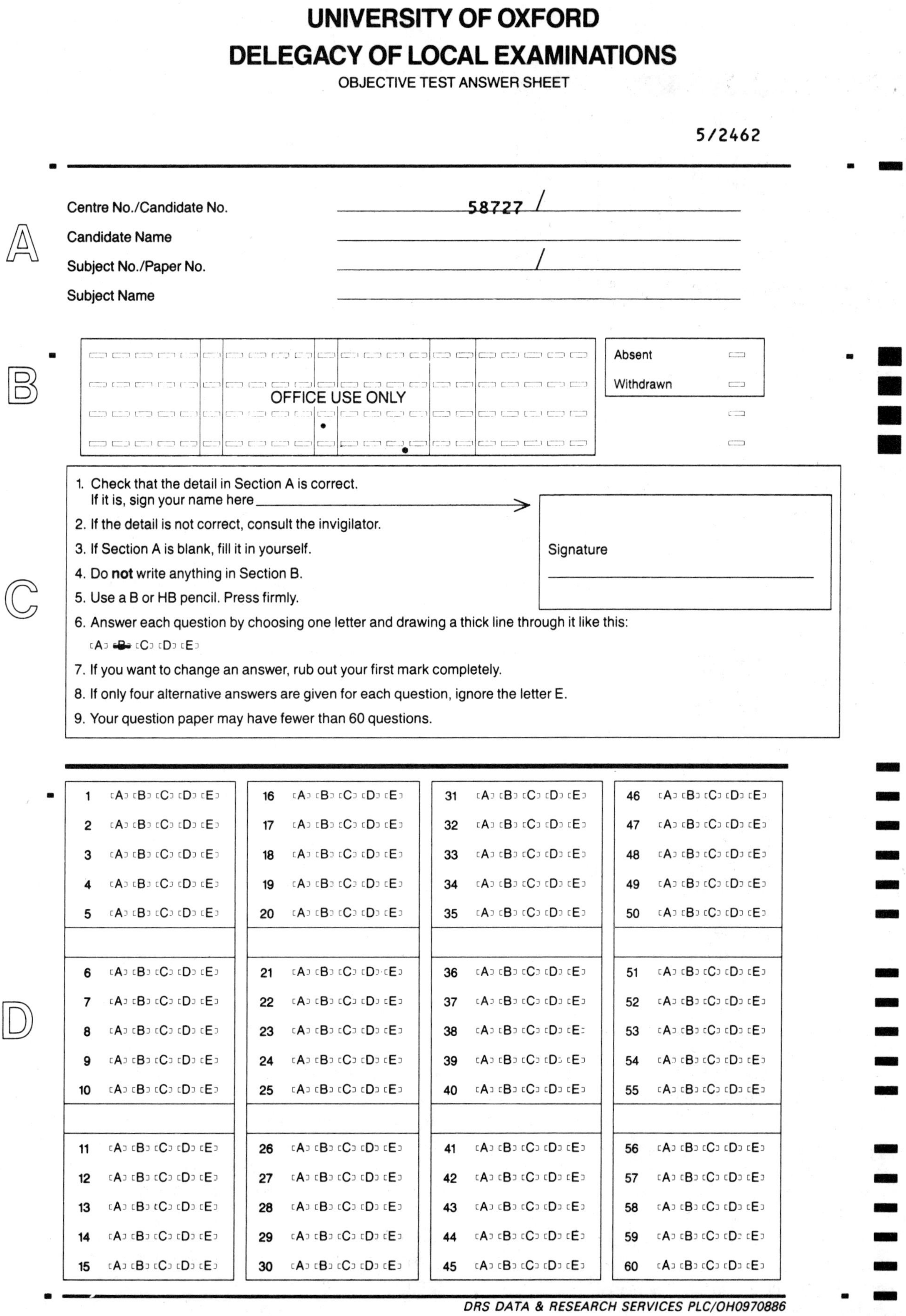

UNIVERSITY OF OXFORD
DELEGACY OF LOCAL EXAMINATIONS
OBJECTIVE TEST ANSWER SHEET

5/2462

A

Centre No./Candidate No. _____ 58727 / _____

Candidate Name _____

Subject No./Paper No. _____ / _____

Subject Name _____

B

OFFICE USE ONLY

Absent ⬜
Withdrawn ⬜

C

1. Check that the detail in Section A is correct.
   If it is, sign your name here _____

2. If the detail is not correct, consult the invigilator.

3. If Section A is blank, fill it in yourself.

4. Do **not** write anything in Section B.

5. Use a B or HB pencil. Press firmly.

6. Answer each question by choosing one letter and drawing a thick line through it like this:

   ⊏A⊐ ⊏B⊐ ⊏C⊐ ⊏D⊐ ⊏E⊐

7. If you want to change an answer, rub out your first mark completely.

8. If only four alternative answers are given for each question, ignore the letter E.

9. Your question paper may have fewer than 60 questions.

Signature

_____

D

1 ⊏A⊐ ⊏B⊐ ⊏C⊐ ⊏D⊐ ⊏E⊐	16 ⊏A⊐ ⊏B⊐ ⊏C⊐ ⊏D⊐ ⊏E⊐	31 ⊏A⊐ ⊏B⊐ ⊏C⊐ ⊏D⊐ ⊏E⊐	46 ⊏A⊐ ⊏B⊐ ⊏C⊐ ⊏D⊐ ⊏E⊐			
2 ⊏A⊐ ⊏B⊐ ⊏C⊐ ⊏D⊐ ⊏E⊐	17 ⊏A⊐ ⊏B⊐ ⊏C⊐ ⊏D⊐ ⊏E⊐	32 ⊏A⊐ ⊏B⊐ ⊏C⊐ ⊏D⊐ ⊏E⊐	47 ⊏A⊐ ⊏B⊐ ⊏C⊐ ⊏D⊐ ⊏E⊐			
3 ⊏A⊐ ⊏B⊐ ⊏C⊐ ⊏D⊐ ⊏E⊐	18 ⊏A⊐ ⊏B⊐ ⊏C⊐ ⊏D⊐ ⊏E⊐	33 ⊏A⊐ ⊏B⊐ ⊏C⊐ ⊏D⊐ ⊏E⊐	48 ⊏A⊐ ⊏B⊐ ⊏C⊐ ⊏D⊐ ⊏E⊐			
4 ⊏A⊐ ⊏B⊐ ⊏C⊐ ⊏D⊐ ⊏E⊐	19 ⊏A⊐ ⊏B⊐ ⊏C⊐ ⊏D⊐ ⊏E⊐	34 ⊏A⊐ ⊏B⊐ ⊏C⊐ ⊏D⊐ ⊏E⊐	49 ⊏A⊐ ⊏B⊐ ⊏C⊐ ⊏D⊐ ⊏E⊐			
5 ⊏A⊐ ⊏B⊐ ⊏C⊐ ⊏D⊐ ⊏E⊐	20 ⊏A⊐ ⊏B⊐ ⊏C⊐ ⊏D⊐ ⊏E⊐	35 ⊏A⊐ ⊏B⊐ ⊏C⊐ ⊏D⊐ ⊏E⊐	50 ⊏A⊐ ⊏B⊐ ⊏C⊐ ⊏D⊐ ⊏E⊐			
6 ⊏A⊐ ⊏B⊐ ⊏C⊐ ⊏D⊐ ⊏E⊐	21 ⊏A⊐ ⊏B⊐ ⊏C⊐ ⊏D⊐ ⊏E⊐	36 ⊏A⊐ ⊏B⊐ ⊏C⊐ ⊏D⊐ ⊏E⊐	51 ⊏A⊐ ⊏B⊐ ⊏C⊐ ⊏D⊐ ⊏E⊐			
7 ⊏A⊐ ⊏B⊐ ⊏C⊐ ⊏D⊐ ⊏E⊐	22 ⊏A⊐ ⊏B⊐ ⊏C⊐ ⊏D⊐ ⊏E⊐	37 ⊏A⊐ ⊏B⊐ ⊏C⊐ ⊏D⊐ ⊏E⊐	52 ⊏A⊐ ⊏B⊐ ⊏C⊐ ⊏D⊐ ⊏E⊐			
8 ⊏A⊐ ⊏B⊐ ⊏C⊐ ⊏D⊐ ⊏E⊐	23 ⊏A⊐ ⊏B⊐ ⊏C⊐ ⊏D⊐ ⊏E⊐	38 ⊏A⊐ ⊏B⊐ ⊏C⊐ ⊏D⊐ ⊏E⊏	53 ⊏A⊐ ⊏B⊐ ⊏C⊐ ⊏D⊐ ⊏E⊐			
9 ⊏A⊐ ⊏B⊐ ⊏C⊐ ⊏D⊐ ⊏E⊐	24 ⊏A⊐ ⊏B⊐ ⊏C⊐ ⊏D⊐ ⊏E⊐	39 ⊏A⊐ ⊏B⊐ ⊏C⊐ ⊏D⊐ ⊏E⊐	54 ⊏A⊐ ⊏B⊐ ⊏C⊐ ⊏D⊐ ⊏E⊐			
10 ⊏A⊐ ⊏B⊐ ⊏C⊐ ⊏D⊐ ⊏E⊐	25 ⊏A⊐ ⊏B⊐ ⊏C⊐ ⊏D⊐ ⊏E⊐	40 ⊏A⊐ ⊏B⊐ ⊏C⊐ ⊏D⊐ ⊏E⊐	55 ⊏A⊐ ⊏B⊐ ⊏C⊐ ⊏D⊐ ⊏E⊐			
11 ⊏A⊐ ⊏B⊐ ⊏C⊐ ⊏D⊐ ⊏E⊐	26 ⊏A⊐ ⊏B⊐ ⊏C⊐ ⊏D⊐ ⊏E⊐	41 ⊏A⊐ ⊏B⊐ ⊏C⊐ ⊏D⊐ ⊏E⊐	56 ⊏A⊐ ⊏B⊐ ⊏C⊐ ⊏D⊐ ⊏E⊐			
12 ⊏A⊐ ⊏B⊐ ⊏C⊐ ⊏D⊐ ⊏E⊐	27 ⊏A⊐ ⊏B⊐ ⊏C⊐ ⊏D⊐ ⊏E⊐	42 ⊏A⊐ ⊏B⊐ ⊏C⊐ ⊏D⊐ ⊏E⊐	57 ⊏A⊐ ⊏B⊐ ⊏C⊐ ⊏D⊐ ⊏E⊐			
13 ⊏A⊐ ⊏B⊐ ⊏C⊐ ⊏D⊐ ⊏E⊐	28 ⊏A⊐ ⊏B⊐ ⊏C⊐ ⊏D⊐ ⊏E⊐	43 ⊏A⊐ ⊏B⊐ ⊏C⊐ ⊏D⊐ ⊏E⊐	58 ⊏A⊐ ⊏B⊐ ⊏C⊐ ⊏D⊐ ⊏E⊐			
14 ⊏A⊐ ⊏B⊐ ⊏C⊐ ⊏D⊐ ⊏E⊐	29 ⊏A⊐ ⊏B⊐ ⊏C⊐ ⊏D⊐ ⊏E⊐	44 ⊏A⊐ ⊏B⊐ ⊏C⊐ ⊏D⊐ ⊏E⊐	59 ⊏A⊐ ⊏B⊐ ⊏C⊐ ⊏D⊐ ⊏E⊐			
15 ⊏A⊐ ⊏B⊐ ⊏C⊐ ⊏D⊐ ⊏E⊐	30 ⊏A⊐ ⊏B⊐ ⊏C⊐ ⊏D⊐ ⊏E⊐	45 ⊏A⊐ ⊏B⊐ ⊏C⊐ ⊏D⊐ ⊏E⊐	60 ⊏A⊐ ⊏B⊐ ⊏C⊐ ⊏D⊐ ⊏E⊐			

DRS DATA & RESEARCH SERVICES PLC/OH0970886

Figure 3.19 *Mark readers allow automatic data input from certain types of form*

Figure 3.20   *A bar code holds numbers in machine-readable form*

Cauzin strip. Like so many others, this is an optical system—the reader contains a row of lamps and photocells and senses the data in the strip by reflection. The strip shown in Figure 3.21 is a BBC BASIC program to display an input message as a continuously moving banner. Cauzin strips provide a compact way to carry computer data in books or through the post.
through the post.

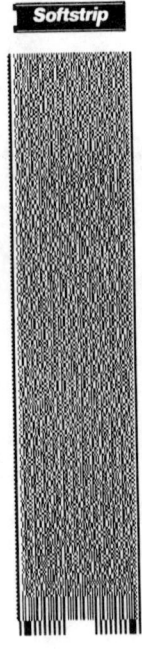

Figure 3.21   *A Cauzin strip carries computer data in a compact form*

Some of the automatic data input techniques I've mentioned above have corresponding output units. Thus you can print bar codes and Cauzin strips with a dot matrix printer for a second computer to read. As I mentioned earlier, banks use magnetic ink character printers as well as readers, and of course many optical character readers (scanners) can handle text in printout form.

All the forms of data input and output I've so far mentioned in this section involve some type of physical medium: paper or magnetic strip, for instance. Such a physical medium intrudes in the free flow of data between computers, but we need it because the contexts preclude purely electronic storage and transfer.

There are, all the same, many cases where we can use purely electronic input and output. These contexts are for communication between machines without human intervention. We've already met the **modem**—an essential hardware link between communicating computers that use the phone system. This is an input/output unit—when one machine sends (outputs) data, the other receives it (input). Figure 3.22 shows what I mean.

While you don't need a modem if your communicating machines have a direct link (as on a network—Chapter 8), using the phone network makes one essential. This is because computer data input and output has to be digital, whereas the link between you and the phone line carries only analog data. (Refer to Section 1.6 if you need to.)

Phone links between machines appear elsewhere in the IT world. A good example is fax.

A **fax** (facsimile) machine is rather like a photocopier. Its scanner prepares an image of a sheet of paper, but instead of sending that image straight to a second sheet, it pushes it down the phone line. At the other end, a second fax machine receives the data to produce a copy on paper. Modern fax machines can transfer a copy of a document across the world in only a few seconds—but, like computers, they're digital, so they need modems to interface with the phone system.

Another important area of machine communication is automation. Automation involves machines that control themselves—modern heating and security systems, robots, and automatic machine tools, for instance. We met this kind of thing in the case study at the start of Chapter 2.

The processor at the heart of all these takes, as input, data about the environment; it outputs signals to control switches, motors and other devices.

The input data comes from sensors. A **sensor** sends out an electric signal that depends on some physical feature of its environment—for instance, light level, temperature, pressure, acidity, or blood sugar level. A sensor's output is therefore almost always analog in form; thus, it doesn't suit

Figure 3.22   *A modem is an input/output device for communication between machines*

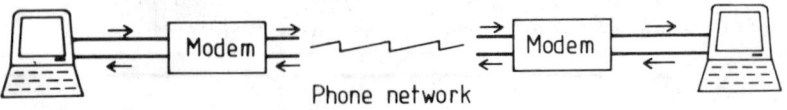

the computer's input, for that must be digital. You have to have an **analog-to-digital converter** (ADC) in the interface (link) between the two, therefore. As the ADC's analog input value changes, its output pattern of digital pulses changes to suit.

The reverse appears on the output side. Say the system is to control an electric fire to keep the room at 20 °C. A sensor on the wall will output a current which varies with temperature. The ADC in the interface that links it to the processor will input digital values that the software can check. The output, through a **digital-to-analog converter** (DAC), controls the current through the fire. The processor will also need to check the thermostat setting in case the user changes it from 20 °C.

All this needs a very simple program, something like this:

```
EVERY 10 SECONDS
READ stat
READ sensor
REPEAT
IF sensor < stat THEN INCREMENT OUTPUT
IF sensor > stat THEN DECREMENT OUTPUT
UNTIL sensor = stat
```

(Increment means increase the value by one unit; decrement means decrease it by one unit.)

Clearly even a small processor could control the temperature or air conditioning of many areas in this way, and still be able to monitor the building for intruders and fire. Environmental control systems are cheap and effective.

A **robot machine tool** (Figure 3.23) is much the same. Its inputs will be position and pressure sensors, for instance; the output signals will control a range of switches and electric motors. You may have used a mobile robot (floor turtle or buggy): it's much the same, even if far simpler. In any case, once the program is correct, the robot can repeat

Figure 3.23   *Once programmed, a robot can carry out its task exactly as often as you like* (Lamberton Robotics Ltd)

the same cycle of action for ever—cheaply and efficiently, without getting bored, tired or sick.

I've mentioned interfaces—links between a processor and peripherals—a couple of times. The function of an **interface** is to allow efficient communication between two devices. At the very least it will be a plug and socket and lead. In most cases it will contain a buffer (Section 3.2) while analog-to-digital and/or digital-to-analog converters (ADCs and DACs) go here too (see above). However, there are other functions.

Data transfer over long distances (as by phone line) is serial—the bits pass along the line one by one. Parallel transfer is quicker, however. In this case each bit in each byte (plus the parity check bit) has its own wire in a ribbon cable (Figure 3.24). This lets data pass a byte at a time—a lot faster than bit by bit. However, we can't use parallel transfer over a long distance as the bits soon get out of step (skewed).

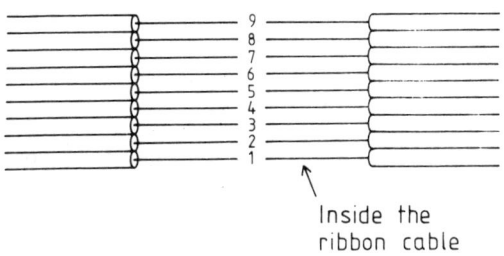

Figure 3.24   *Parallel transfer is speedy, but the bits soon go out of step*

An interface may therefore offer conversion between serial and parallel signals.

Here's a list of interface functions (I include those we've already met).

- physical link
- buffer storage
- ADC and/or DAC
- serial/parallel conversion
- transfer of control signals
- handshaking (the exchange of ready, receipt and interrupt messages)
- switching
- matching voltage levels and current strengths

SELF-DEVELOPMENT QUESTIONS

See Page 135 for notes on these questions.

S3.1   Spend a session or two with Prestel to explore *one* of the assignments below. Word process a report of 750 words on your findings, referring to an appendix of eight or ten Prestel page printouts.

   a   What information might Keith (in the case

study) present to Esther for her meeting in Toronto?

b Esther's Toronto meeting will last three days, starting at 2pm on the third Monday next month. She lives near Sheffield. Prepare a travel and accommodation schedule for her. How much of this could Keith book on her behalf using Prestel?

c Choose one of the IT application areas discussed in Chapter 2 and inform a manager in that area what Prestel can offer.

d If you think you know what your job may be in a few years' time, do assignment S3.1c in that area instead.

e Instead of a computer, you can use a TV set and a special keypad and phone line link to access Prestel. Would it be worth getting Prestel at home?

S3.2 Word process a 750-word comparison between interactive viewdata (of which Prestel is an example) and broadcast teletext (like Ceefax and Oracle). Include a summary of what the latter offers.

S3.3 What are the advantages and disadvantages of home and office banking on Prestel?

S3.4 Will we ever have a cashless society?

S3.5 Log on to a scrolling viewdata service, such as Telecom Gold or TTNS. Briefly explore the main options on offer and take notes (or add notes to a printout of your session).

S3.6 Look inside a computer and identify the main printed circuit board and as many types of chip as you can. Find out the function of each type of chip and identify it as (for instance) processor, ROM, RAM, input/output control. If you can obtain a circuit diagram for the system, try to relate it to what you see and to Figure 3.7.

S3.7 Make a copy of Figure 3.7 and study it. Study too the description (Section 3.3) of the functions of the different parts and of the fetch–execute–reset cycle. Then test yourself (or, better, a friend).

S3.8 For each of the following assembly language instructions describe fully what happens during the corresponding cycle of action in the processor. In each case, assume that the address selection register contains the value 3000, and the instruction is held in cell 3000.

> INP 4000
> LDA 4000
> SUB 4001
> BIN 3020

S3.9 Write an assembly language program to take two numbers from the input and send the larger value to the output. Store the instructions from cell 3001 and the data from cell 4001. Explain what your program does, and how.

S3.10 Write a brief account of the three main levels of computer data storage. Include notes on cache.

S3.11 Find out what you can about bubble memory—its nature, and how it can store data (write and erase) and be read. Write a short illustrated essay on what you have learned.

S3.12 As Question S3.11, but for CCD (charge coupled device) memory.

S3.13 Use the data for a typical magnetic tape to answer these questions:

a What is the mean data storage density (bytes per millimetre)?

b What is the proportion of data blocks to inter-block gaps?

c What are the maximum and mean data transfer rates?

d How long would it take to scan through a whole tape?

S3.14 How many codes do you need for all computer keyboard characters? Find out how the ASCII and EBCDIC code systems deal with these. Write your name in ASCII and in EBCDIC codes, in decimal and in binary each time. In the binary case, add parity bits on an even parity system. How do different computers make use of the 'spare' codes?

S3.15 Sketch a floppy disc in its protective case; find out the functions of the various parts. Compare a floppy disc with a mainframe disc pack.

S3.16 Find out about CD-ROM technology and uses, and write a short essay on the subject.

S3.17 People are exploring various kinds of optical media for backing storage. Make notes on them.

S3.18 Obtain a circuit diagram of a keyboard. Can you work out how different key-presses send different codes?

S3.19 Try as many different keyboards and keypads as you can. Compare them on the grounds of ease of use, comfort, efficiency and cost.

S3.20 Research the current status of speech input techniques. What are the likely advantages and disadvantages compared to keying?

S3.21 Find out about WIMP working environments and (if you can) try one.

a How many windows can you have at once? What can you show in them?

b Sketch some typical icons, giving what each stands for.

c What can you do with mouse movement? What do the mouse's buttons do?

d Describe the use of a screen pointer.

S3.22 Make notes on the nature of liquid crystals, and their use in displays (with digital thermometers and calculators, for instance).

S3.23 Build up a reference table to compare the various

types of printer mentioned in Section 3.5.

S3.24 Compare a dot printer and a plotter used to produce the same graphic image.

S3.25 Visit a bank and ask someone to show you the hardware used with magnetic ink characters and stripe cards.

S3.26 Find out the data written into a product bar code and how the coding works. Visit a library or supermarket to discuss the values of—and problems with—bar code-based stock control.

S3.27 Visit a copy shop or office to see fax in action. Do they also use electronic mail? If so, with which system and for what tasks?

S3.28 Use a mobile robot (turtle or buggy) and learn how to program it. Write notes on the inputs and outputs concerned.

S3.29 Write notes on interfacing, with examples from hardware you use.

EXAMINATION QUESTIONS

Q3.1 Teletext and viewdata systems are generally available. Services provided by these systems are specifically aimed at home users, business users and educational users. For each category of user, describe *two* distinct services which are particularly relevant. (JMB) (9)

Q3.2 State why program instructions which are being executed need to be in the immediate access store. (London) (1)

Q3.3 A football club is to issue passes to members. These will be checked at the entry turnstile against a computer file of members. Describe briefly two alternative types of pass that might be used and the associated equipment needed; comment on the suitability of each system. (London) (6)

Q3.4 **a** Explain why printers usually contain a buffer store. (2)

b Explain why it is necessary to have two-way communication between a printer and the central processor. (London) (2)

Q3.5 A particular plotter is controlled by numeric instructions (0–3) which cause the pen to move from its current position in one of four directions in units of 0.1 mm as shown in Figure 3.25a. For example, 2,1000 means move left 100 mm from the current position. Assuming the pen is initially at the point 0,0, write a sequence of instructions to draw the rectangle of Figure 3.25b, indicating any additional types of instruction needed. (London) (5)

Q3.6 Most computer systems have both an immediate

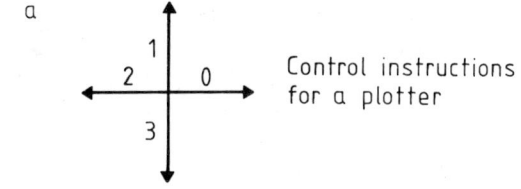
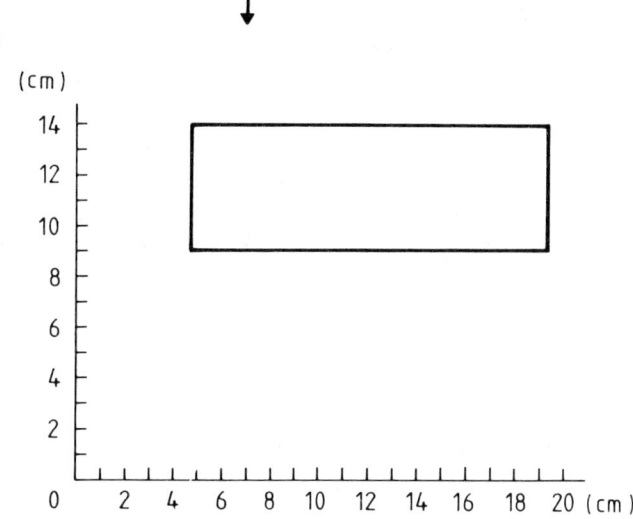

Figure 3.25 *How can you control a plotter (Question Q3.5)?*

access store and a backing store. List **two** characteristics of **each** type of store which together show why this is desirable. (JMB) (4)

Q3.7 The computing department in a school was asked to investigate the use of a computer to control the stage lighting. Their report pointed out that a special interface would have to be constructed. What is meant by an interface, and why is it necessary? (JMB) (2)

Q3.8 Figure 3.26 represents a robot arm. The arm has a claw at the end. The arm may be raised or lowered by a motor. The claw may be opened or closed by a motor. Both motors are controlled by the same computer.

Sensors mounted on the arm and claw are

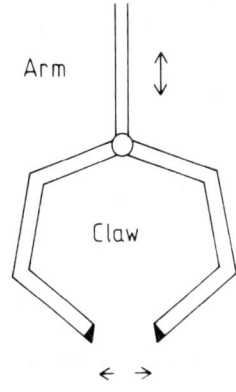

Figure 3.26 *Get a hold of this (Question Q3.8)!*

connected to the computer via a special 4-bit store called SENSOR-PORT. The bits in SENSOR-PORT are allocated as shown.

bit number	SENSOR-PORT
3	arm low enough for claw to touch object
2	claw gripping
1	claw fully closed
0	claw fully open

Each sensor signals that it has detected the condition by setting its bit in the store SENSOR-PORT to 1. Otherwise that bit is reset to 0.

The computer gives instructions to the robot arm by 'storing' numbers in a special 4-bit store called ACTIVATOR-PORT. The bits in ACTIVATOR-PORT are allocated as shown.

bit number	ACTIVATOR-PORT
3	arm direction up/down
2	arm motor on/off
1	claw direction close/open
0	claw motor on/off

The codes used are

1   arm direction up; claw direction close; motor on
0   arm direction down; claw direction open; motor off

a   Given that the robot arm starts at its highest position with the claw fully open, what is intended to be achieved by the following sequence of operations?

1   Set ACTIVATOR-PORT to 0100
2   If bit 3 of SENSOR-PORT is 0 go to step 1
3   Set ACTIVATOR-PORT to 0000
4   Set ACTIVATOR-PORT to 0011
5   If bit 2 of SENSOR-PORT is 0 go to step 4
6   Set ACTIVATOR-PORT to 0000
7   Set ACTIVATOR-PORT to 1100

b   What would be indicated if the setting of SENSOR-PORT after step 6 were 1110?

c   What should be the setting of SENSOR-PORT after step 6 if the above sequence of operations has been successful?

(JMB)   (6)

Q3.9   Microcomputers often store system software in read only storage, whereas large computers normally use backing store for the purpose. State an advantage of each method for storing system software.

(COSSEC)   (2)

Q3.10   **a**   Draw a diagram showing how a magnetic disc is organised into blocks, tracks and cylinders.

(4)

b   What is the purpose of organising the disc in blocks?

(2)

c   If the file stored on a moving head disc extends over more than one track, suggest why it might be preferable to store the next part of the file on the same track of another surface rather than on a different track of the same surface.

(COSSEC)   (2)

Q3.11   A tumble dryer is a machine which dries clothes after they have been washed. It consists of a rotating drum in which the clothes are tumbled, a fan which blows air through the drum, and a heater which heats the air as it enters the drum. The user of the tumble dryer may switch it on or off, and may set a dial which indicates the maximum temperature for the air entering the drum. Apart from this the machine is controlled by a microprocessor.

The machine has two sensors which provide data to the microprocessor. There is a temperature sensor where the air enters the drum and there is a humidity ('wetness') sensor where the air leaves the drum. When the machine is switched on, the drum rotates, the fan blows, and the heater is adjusted so that the air entering the drum is maintained at about the temperature indicated by the setting of the dial (TMAX). This continues until the humidity of the air leaving the drum is below a pre-set level (HMIN). At this point the heater is switched off, but the drum and fan continue to run for another ten minutes.

a   The signals from the two sensors need to be converted for use by the microprocessor. Explain what this means.

b   Illustrate the control process for the tumble dryer, by means of a flow diagram or otherwise, and describe the algorithm followed by the microprocessor, making clear any assumptions you consider appropriate.

(COSSEC)   [25]

Q3.12   Figure 3.27 shows a section of road, with road works causing a single track section.

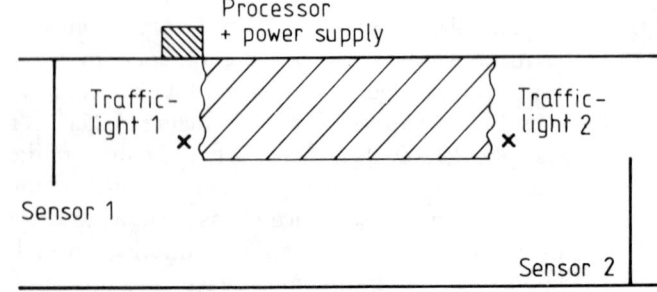

Figure 3.27   *A traffic-light system is an example of process control (Question Q3.12)*

Each vehicle sensor is activated by the wheel of a vehicle pressing on it. The sensor and the traffic-lights are linked to and controlled by a micro-processor, which is located by one of the traffic-lights, together with a battery to provide the required power supply.

a Describe the activities which need to be performed by the microprocessor and its associated interfaces.

b What problems may arise in practice and how can the system be designed to minimise the adverse effects of such problems?

c Would a more sophisticated system, possibly with more vehicle sensors (or more advanced ones), be more effective?

(COSSEC) [25]

Q3.13 There are about fifty busy road junctions in the centre of a city. Each is controlled by a set of traffic-lights connected to its own microcomputer. It has been proposed that all the traffic-light micro-computers should be linked to a central computer which would carry out two tasks:

a collect data relating to traffic flow in the city centre, to help in the design of future road improvements and traffic control;

b co-ordinate the changing of the traffic lights by providing advance warning of traffic leaving one junction bound for the next.

Describe briefly the hardware requirements for such a system.

Failure in one or more parts of the system is likely to occur from time to time. What features should be built into the various parts of the system so that in the event of a failure most of the system can still perform adequately?

(COSSEC) (25)

4 Handling information

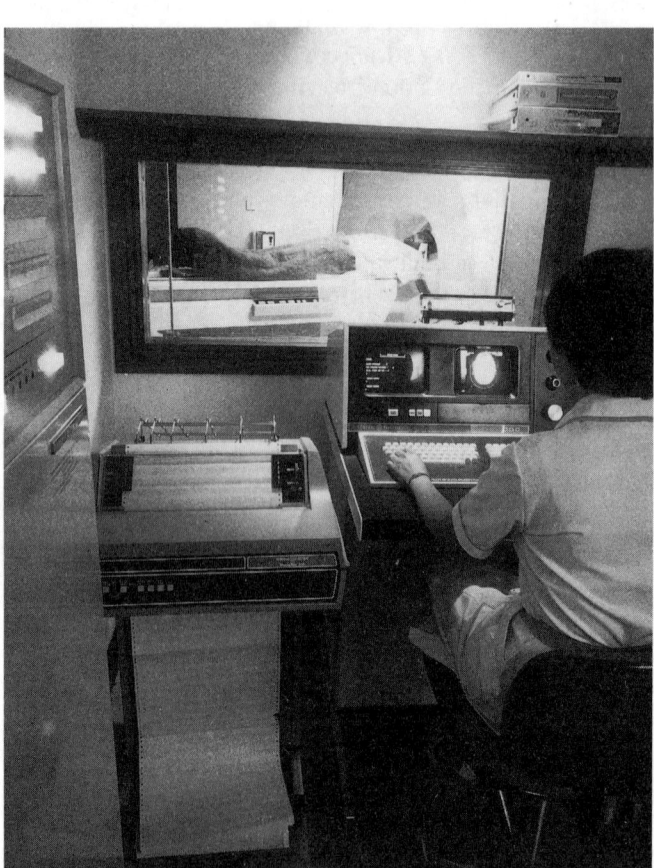

Figure 4.1 *Information technology is essential for running a modern health service* (International General Electric Co. of New York)

Case study 4—Information is good for your health!

Kuldip Singh is a nurse in a fairly small rural general hospital. He works in a surgical ward and, with his colleagues, uses IT a great deal. In the ward office is a terminal link to the hospital's mainframe computer. This provides ready access to records about current (and past) patients. Each time Kuldip uses the system, he has to enter his name and secret password. This lets him see current details only of patients in the ward at the moment. The staff nurse in charge can find out more about more patients than this, while doctors and senior staff can work with all patient records in store.

The mainframe holds several hundred thousand patients' records. This is far better than the old paper-based approach, as it avoids there being more than one record for a given person; allows rapid access and amendment;

and is easy to use for research. Thus it's simple to obtain details of all people who've broken an arm—to look for relationships with gender and age, or to list the kinds of accident involved. In much the same way, a doctor can very quickly check all people who've had a certain drug in case of any pattern of side effects. Kuldip, who's working hard for a degree, has sometimes helped with searches like these.

One of Kuldip's patients at the moment is a woman in intensive care. Sensors measure her pulse, breathing, blood sugar level, and brain waves all the time and feed the data to a processor in a box by her bed. The makers programmed the unit to sound an alarm if any of these measures strays outside a pre-set range. Every so often, Kuldip has to check the readings displayed on the unit's flat screen and mark them on the woman's chart.

He's heard of more modern systems that store all the data on a small cassette tape for later input to a computer for automatic graphing and analysis. While the hospital doesn't use these, one of Kuldip's recent patients wears a rather similar device all the time; each week this young man visits the clinic and has his tape checked by the main computer. Local and remote monitoring, as these two units provide, make life much safer for many people—they don't need to be troubled by having frequent manual checks made, and of course a nurse can now look after more than one or two intensive care patients at a time.

Sensing units like those described also offer a great deal to diagnosis (trying to find what's wrong with a patient). For this purpose, Kuldip's hospital computer links to all the surgeries and clinics in the area. A patient works through a set of questions on screen to provide the personal details for the record (if he or she is new) or to let the computer access the existing record. Further questions explore the current symptoms so the machine can suggest the most likely causes and the treatment the doctors could try. It uses an 'expert system' package, a system showing 'machine intelligence'. As we'll see in Section 9.1, an expert system stores the knowledge of a number of experts and provides a framework for applying it in given cases.

The wide area network just described is part of the Healthnet system used in many parts of Britain. It links hospitals, surgeries, clinics, labs, pharmacies and suppliers, not just for the kind of use mentioned above but for the rapid transfer of memos, reports, notes, orders, and so on. Each terminal is a micro (with printer and modem), so it is of use for all kinds of local tasks; those include work with the local records, word processing, and calling up the various Prestel-style viewdata bases that serve health care.

IT offers much to another important area of health care—aiding the disabled. Physically disabled people can now control wheelchairs, robot arms and other such machines that carry out the tasks of wasted muscles and paralysed limbs. Talking word processors (and other units fitted with speech synthesisers) are of much value to the blind and partially sighted, as are Braille readers and OCR units (Section 3.6) that scan printed text. Disabled people at home, and others at risk, carry alarm units to call automatically for help (by radio or through the phone network) if, for instance, they fall.

Kuldip finds the many uses of IT for health care of great interest. He has a number of ideas for new ways that processor-based units can help the sick and disabled, and hopes to do research in the field when he's got his degree.

Introduction

Case study 4 concentrates quite a lot on automation and communication areas of IT in health care. The more conventional uses of computers are highly important—and not just the great data base of patient records. Hospitals and health workers find of value almost all the kinds of office software looked at in Chapter 2. Accounts, payroll, and stock control suites are crucial in an industry where one site can employ thousands of staff and spend many million pounds a year. The scheduling of in-patients—to beds, to surgeons, to theatres—and running appointments for thousands of out-patients are tasks that gain from computers. So too are research and the daily work of the labs and pharmacies.

Computers handle the data that represents information in a number of ways. While with small tasks the data handling structures and methods don't matter much, with large amounts of data they become very important. In this chapter we'll look at ways computers represent data and hold it ready for processing. In practice the main way involves holding data in files in backing store; I'll open the subject in this chapter, but leave its main study to Chapter 6.

Objectives

When you have worked through this chapter, you should be able to

1 list the main uses of IT in health care
2 give an account of local and remote patient monitoring
3 outline some ways modern technology can help the disabled
4 define binary and hexadecimal systems and convert numbers between binary and denary and binary and hex (both ways)
5 add, subtract, multiply and divide binary numbers, including use of the binary point
6 obtain the 2s complement of a number and use it in subtraction
7 explain and use the sign and magnitude method of floating point number representation, and work with it in fixed word length contexts
8 state the nature and cause of rounding error, overflow and underflow
9 state the need for programmers to work with different data types
10 give examples of three common data types and list three less common ones
11 explain, with examples, the need for special data structures for processing
12 give examples of the use of linear lists and multi-dimensional arrays
13 explain, with an example, the nature and use of a last in, first out stack
14 explain, with an example, the nature and use of a first in, first out queue
15 explain, with an example, the nature and use of a linked list
16 state, with examples, what a pointer is and does
17 define a tree and the terms node, parent, child, leaf, root, sub-tree
18 enter random string or numeric data into a small binary tree and access it in order

4.1　Computers count

In a digital device such as a computer, each current and voltage it works with doesn't vary smoothly from lowest to highest value, but can be at one of only a few levels. The simplest digital system has only two levels; we call these 0 and 1, for low and high. This binary logic, as it is called, is almost universal in IT systems based on microelectronic circuits.

The rules of binary arithmetic, and the structure of the binary numbers that represent data units, are just like those of the denary (base ten) system we're used to. A binary number is a set of binary digits (bits), each either 0 or 1. Counting in binary is easy then: 0, 1, 10 ($= 2$), 11 ($= 3$), 100 ($= 4$), 101 ($= 5$), and so on. Starting at the right-hand end of a binary number, the place values are 1 (2^0), 2 (2^1), 4 (2^2), 8 (2^3), etc. It's dreary, but not hard, to translate between binary and denary (either way). Here's an example of each.

To convert 1010 1010 into denary, add the place values where a 1 appears, starting from the right—that is, 2 + 8 + 32 + 128, or 170.

To convert 209 into binary,

a write down binary place values from the right till the leftmost is larger than the denary number, and

b take away place values in turn, starting with the highest you can—put a 1 in that column if you can do it and 0 otherwise. Like this:

```
a   256  128  64  32  16  8  4  2  1
b     0    1                           209 − 128 = 81
           1                            81 −  64 = 17
                0   1                   17 −  16 =  1
                   0   0   0  1   1 −   1 =  0
```

So $209_{10} = 1101\ 0001_2$.

Note how we write binary numbers—grouped in fours. Some people call each such group a nibble (or nybble), as it's half a byte. (A byte is a group of 8 bits.) Grouping in fours is useful as we can replace each nibble by a single hexadecimal (hex) digit. Hexadecimal is base 16 counting; we use A–F for the values 11–15, then 16_{10} is 10_{16}. Table 4.1 relates the denary values 0–15 to binary and hex; it may help to learn it.

Table 4.1

Denary (base 10)	Binary (base 2)	Hex (base 16)
0	0	0
1	1	1
2	10	2
3	11	3
4	100	4
5	101	5
6	110	6
7	111	7
8	1000	8
9	1001	9
10	1010	A
11	1011	B
12	1100	C
13	1101	D
14	1110	E
15	1111	F

Because IT systems, in effect, handle, process, store and transfer numbers in binary, you may need to be able to work with these numbers yourself. Skill in handling them doesn't relate to using computers, however, so don't feel you *have* to know them for your work with IT.

Adding and taking away binary numbers follow the denary rules. When adding, you need to carry excess values to the next column left—as here, with 101 + 1011 + 10111 + 101111.

```
        1 0 1
      1 0 1 1
    1 0 1 1 1
  1 0 1 1 1 1 +
  ─────────────
  1 0 1 0 1 1 0    Answer: 101 0110
  ─────────────
    1 2 2 2
```

What you carry is the *number* of groups of 2 in each case (here mostly 2, as 2 × 2 = 4).

Taking away involves borrowing from the column on the left if necessary. Again a group of 2 is involved—if you borrow 1 from a column, that gives you 2 extra in the column to the right of it. Work through this one, starting at the right as usual.

```
      0 2 2
  1 1 0 0 1 1
  1 1 0 1 0 −
  ───────────
    1 1 0 0 1
  ───────────
```

To multiply two binary numbers, you need to know your 1 times tables: 0 × 1 = 0, 1 × 1 = 1! As before, work just as in denary. Follow this through. (But I leave you to finish by adding the three results rows. . . .)

```
      1 0 1 0 1 0 1
          1 0 1 1 ×
  ─────────────────
      1 0 1 0 1 0 1   ⎫ multiplying
    1 0 1 0 1 0 1 0   ⎬ involves
  1 0 1 0 1 0 1 0 0 0 ⎭ left shift
  ─────────────────
  =
```

Finally comes division. Do this in the standard long division way; the only parts that aren't very easy are the little subtraction sums. Here's an example, dividing 101 0101 by 1011.

```
                  1  1  1 remainder 1000
  ┌──────────────────────
1 0 1 1 ) 1 0 1 0 1 0 1
          1 0 1 1
  ──────────────────────
            1 0 1 0 0
            1 0 1 1
  ──────────────────────
              1 0 0 1 1
              1 0 1 1
  ──────────────────────
                1 0 0 0
```

We could go on with that last one, past the binary point. Binary fractions (still going by the denary rules) have place values 1/2, 1/4, 1/8, 1/16, ... (0.5, 0.25, 0.125, 0.0625, ...). Using binary fractions, the answer to that division is 111.10111 .... (It goes on, and you'd better check it!) You may need to be able to add, subtract and multiply numbers with fractions, as well as dividing them.

Computers must handle negative numbers as well as fractions. There are various methods. First, though, recall that computers work with data in chunks of fixed length. The chunks are 8-bit bytes in the case of older micros; I'll stick with that example to keep things simple.

The value of a byte can range from 0000 0000 to 1111 1111 (in denary from 0 to 255, and in hex from 0 to FF). That's a total of 256 values. If half of those stand for negative numbers, then there's only half left for positive ones—the range, -128 to $+127$, must still have 256 values.

As 0000 0000 follows 1111 1111, we could take 1111 1111 as -1; then -2 would be 1111 1110, with -3 as 1111 1101, and so on down to 1000 0000 for -128. We call this method of representing numbers the 2s complement form; the negative numbers have 1 for the leftmost bit, with 0 and the positive values having 0. The value of this form is to make subtraction simpler for machines.

Say you have to take number y from number x. You can instead add the 2s complement of y to x—it gives the same result and is not so hard.

First, though, you need to obtain the 2s complement of y. This is straightforward; there are two steps. I'll illustrate with $y = 101\ 0101$ (really 0101 0101, note).

First, switch each 0 in y to 1, and each 1 to 0. This gives 1010 1010 (it's called the 1s complement). Second, add 1 to the 1s complement to obtain the 2s complement: 1010 1011. Add that to x, and ignore any carry at the left end, and you get the value of $x - y$.

Another important method for handling negative numbers is 'sign and magnitude'. Here the value of the leftmost bit in the byte shows the sign; again 1 is for negative numbers and 0 for positive ones. The remaining 7 bits give the value. This time, counting down from 0000 0000, we have 1000 0001 (-1), 1000 0010 (-2), and so on. Again, because there can still be only 256 numbers in all, the values have a smaller range. In fact 1111 1111 is -127 and 0111 1111 is $+127$ (1000 0000 has no meaning).

So far I've looked at whole numbers only, but we know we can have binary fractions too. The computer's registers and storage cells that hold numbers are fixed in size—what *can* we do to increase the range of numbers they can handle? Floating the point is the answer.

Floating point representation is much like the standard form of numbers used in maths and science. There we write 1 560 000 as 1.56×10^6, for instance. This number form consists of a value between 1 and 9.99 ... (the mantissa) and the power of 10 (the exponent) by which you must multiply it. In that example, 1.56 is the mantissa and 6 is the exponent. In denary then, four digits (here 156 and 6) can express values between 0.000 000 001 (1, 0, 0, and -9 for 1.00×10^{-9}) and 999 000 000 (9, 9, 9, and 8). To do this, however, we have to accept precision of no more than three significant figures—we couldn't fully show 1 567 000 this way, for instance, let alone 1 567 892.

Floating point binary numbers involve just the same approach. We set aside some of the bits in the register for the mantissa and some for the (binary) exponent; each will be in 2s complement form to allow negative values. Here's an example of a common approach, with double-byte registers giving us 16 bits to play with.

Perhaps 10 of those bits are for the mantissa—1 for the sign and 9 for the value; that leaves 6 for the exponent (again 1 for the sign, and 5 for the value). The number is 'normalised' (put in standard form) so the binary point is at the left of the mantissa. Figure 4.2 shows the 16-bit register content.

The largest positive number this can hold is 0111 1111 1101 1111—that is, $+0.1111\ 1111\ 1 \times 2^{+1\ 1111}$. The smallest is 0100 0000 0010 0000. Similar thinking applies to the negative range. I leave you to work out all four values in full! You'll find the range is still not very exciting. You should also realise you can't store 0 in floating point form (why not?) and the nearest allowed value to it isn't really very near.

In practice, even cheap old micros that can hold fractional numbers use a lot more than 2 bytes in their registers, so both problems are reduced. This is multi-precision, my 2-byte example being double precision. Even so, no digital system can offer perfect precision (any more than *you* can be perfectly precise when you measure something, whatever help you have).

Lack of precision can lead to errors in number crunching. Thus, some older calculators would give, for instance, 1.9999999 when you divide 6 by 3. Such things can occur when several numbers lose least significant figures by a

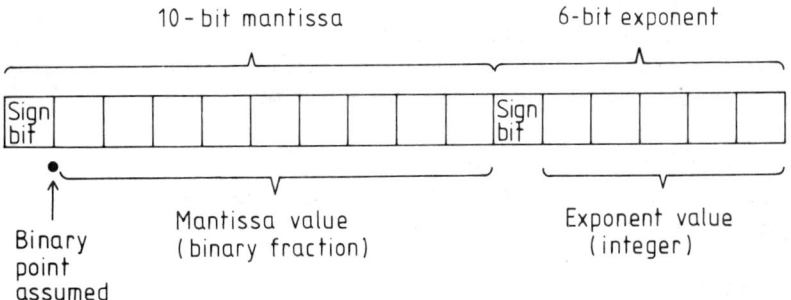

10-bit mantissa   6-bit exponent

Figure 4.2 *Storing binary numbers in a fixed length register involves normalised binary fraction and exponent, both in 2s complement form; this is one possible arrangement*

Binary point assumed

Mantissa value (binary fraction)   Exponent value (integer)

rounding process—we call them rounding errors.

It's also the case that no computer can handle numbers larger or smaller than certain values. If a sum leads to a result larger than the system can cope with, overflow occurs. This would happen in single precision positive integer work with 150 + 150, for instance, because the top limit is 255. Underflow, on the other hand, occurs if a result is smaller (closer to zero) than the system can handle.

4.2   Characters, strings and data types

Computers aren't just number crunchers; indeed processing numeric information is only a small part of their work. Most business software deals with non-numeric material—for instance, strings of characters. By character I mean anything you can obtain from the keyboard—not just the letters of the alphabet (capitals and lower case), but also the various punctuation marks and symbols, the digits 0–9 (which do *not* themselves have numeric values), the effects of the SPACE bar, and the RETURN (or ENTER) key. You may use all of these when entering text into a word processor, say; the system must allow the storage, processing and transfer of any character just as much as a pure number.

As we have seen, ASCII is a widely used method of handling characters. Each keyboard character gets its own code (from 32 to 127). As a single byte can have 256 values, that leaves many spare codes. Manufacturers use most of these in no standard way, but common uses are parity checking in 8-bit word transfer; control of printer (e.g. new sheet, backspace) and of screen (e.g. colour, go to top left corner); and special characters (for foreign language work, italic letters, or graphics blocks perhaps).

A string is a sequence of characters, such as 'Hello!' or 'R2D2' or even ' ' (the empty, or null, string). As a string can range widely in length, storing it and moving it round the system means the computer must know how many characters it contains. Figure 4.3 shows two ways—putting the string's length (number of characters) at its head, or using a special code to mark its end.

There's more a computer needs to know in order to process data correctly under software control. This bit pattern—0011 1100—stored in an 8-bit cell or register could be an integer (whole number) of value 60, part of a floating point binary number, a character ('<' in ASCII or something else in another system), or an instruction in machine code (Section 5.4).

The computer's operating software (Section 5.2) will take care of keeping instructions away from other data. However, it's up to the programmer to make clear which of the other data types is involved at any moment. The computer holds all data in the main store; each data item has a label by which the program refers to it. The value of the data item is likely to change, so we call the data item a variable. It's sometimes of use to give labels to constants as well, to make them easier to refer to. Table 4.2 covers these points.

Table 4.2

	String	*Integer*	*Real number*
Constant	'Hi!'	2	2.0
Variable	User's name	age	height
BASIC label	**name$**	**age%**	**height**
BASIC identifier	**$**	**%**	**—**
Pascal identifier	**CHAR**	**INTEGER**	**REAL**

The table concerns three major data types—character strings, integers (whole numbers), and real numbers (non-integers). For each I give an example of a constant and a variable value. Then I show how two major program languages (Section 5.4) keep the data types distinct.

In the BASIC program language, the data item label includes an identifier to define the data type. The $ and % highlight string and integer data respectively; if there's no identifier the system assumes a real number.

Here are some BASIC instructions using the three types of label. The first set are process assignments (read the = after the keyword **LET** as 'take the value' or 'become'). Next are input assignments. These use the keyword **INPUT**; **INPUT** followed by a label tells the computer to

- put a question mark on screen to tell the user to do something,
- wait for the user to key a response and press RETURN, and
- store the entered data under the label given.

The third set of BASIC instructions concerns output. Despite its name, the **PRINT** keyword sends a copy of the data to the screen rather than to hard copy. (In the old days it really *did* mean 'print'!)

Here are the examples of these instructions.

a *Input*

INPUT title$
INPUT year%
INPUT distance

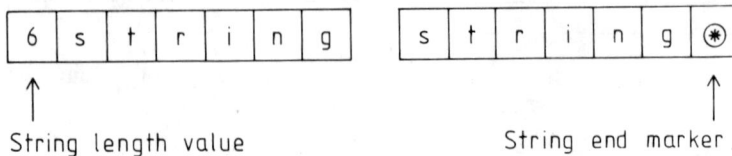

String length value   String end marker

Figure 4.3   *A computer must know how long a string is*

b *Process*

LET greeting\$ = "Hallo," + name\$ + "!"
LET perimeter% = 2 * (length% + width%) [* means multiply]
LET speed = distance/time [/ means divide]

c *Output*

PRINT "The capital of Austria is" + capital\$
PRINT product%
PRINT totaldue

The Pascal programmer must use labels too, and identify the data type of each. In this case, however, the identification is at the start of the program; after the keyword **VAR** you list and identify all labels you use. Like this:

VAR
    item: CHAR;
    cost: INTEGER;
    vatrate: REAL;
price: REAL;

The need to identify data types follows the fact that the system will process each type in its own way. There's no point in squaring the year or in taking the second pair of digits away from a real number.

In the case of numbers, processing integers is much faster than working with reals. (Maybe you can accept that after Section 4.1!) As a result it's good to use integer labels where you can. String processing isn't arithmetical, of course, for here we want to do things like changing an initial letter to upper case, or taking the characters between the first and second commas of an address to be the road name.

Some program languages allow for other data types, such as arrays (or matrices), multi-precision and complex numbers, and Booleans. A Boolean can have only two values—**true** or **false**; it's of special value in control systems. Here you could write, for instance, something like *if day and cold then increment heater-current*: *day* and *cold* can each be true or false; only if both are true should the system turn the heating up.

4.3 Data structures

As long as computer and programmer know the data type of an item, they can process it. However, if there's a lot of data to process, it helps to structure it. This means handling it in a way that leads to greatest processing speed and efficiency.

Various data structures exist; each is of value in certain contexts. For humans a list is a simple and useful data structure. It's the same in IT. Here's an example, the temperatures in a garden over half a summer's day, starting at 0100.

time/h	1	2	3	4	5	6	7	8	9	10	11	12
temperature/°C	15	14	13	13	12	14	16	17	19	21	24	23

You may need to know the times of the lowest and highest values, or to put the list in order. Computer users have such needs too; they're not easy to handle if the data items are twelve separate integers.

Instead we use the (linear) list structure, giving the set of values a single label; thus **temp%(11)** is 24. Note the use of the % identifier—these values are all integers. We can of course have lists of reals and of strings.

A list then is a linear set of a fixed number of data items (called elements); each element has a subscript to mark its place in the list. The data will take up a sequence of cells in store, but the system will use one label for the whole set, the identifier saying what kind of data is involved. In programming, it's normal to use loops (of the **FOR . . . /NEXT . . .** type—see Section 5.5) to enter the data items, to process them, and to output the processed list.

The linear list (or vector) just discussed is also worth thinking of as a one-dimensional (1D) array. A table is a 2D array; an example is a more detailed weather record:

time/h	1	2	3	4	5	6	7	8	9	10	11	12
temperature/°C	15	14	13	13	12	14	16	17	19	21	24	23
humidity/%	50	49	46	43	40	35	31	32	30	38	58	77
rainfall/mm	0	0	0	0	0	0	1	0	0	1	14	3

Now the data covers the paper in two dimensions. While the computer would still hold it in a linear sequence of storage cells, it would need to know that it's a 2D array, and also the number of rows and columns in the human mind. In BASIC, we use **DIM** as the keyword giving that information. In this case, **DIM weather%(3,12)** would tell the computer to work with a 2D integer array with three rows and twelve columns. In Pascal the declaration would be **VAR weather: array [1..3, 1..12] of integer;**.

As a linear list is in truth a 1D array you'd have to set that up in the same kind of way. On the other hand, there are plenty of cases where more than two dimensions come in handy. Thus **DIM pupil\$(30,4,7,6)** sets up a 4D string array to hold the names of the 30 pupils in each of four classes in each of seven year-groups in each of six schools. Using such an array it would be easy to find, for instance, the fourteenth person in class 3C at school 5; without a data structure the task would hardly be possible.

Be aware of one point, though. There's a huge amount of data in that array: $30 \times 4 \times 7 \times 6 = 5040$ strings, needing around a hundred kilobytes (100 K) to store. Files (Chapter 6) are better in such cases, though you still have to type the data in!

4.4 Flexible data structures

Arrays (I include 1D lists) are very useful structures indeed, and many program languages offer them. An array of numbers (real or integer) is, in mathematics, a matrix. (That's why some people call the list a vector, a 1D matrix.)

Some systems include advanced matrix handling techniques with these data structures, for they're of value in many contexts in science and engineering, for instance.

Common, easy to follow and useful as arrays are, they're fixed in size once they are set up. We sometimes need more flexibility; other data structures offer that. Most of the others are 1D; for multi-dimensional work you need to deal with two or more of them in parallel (or, again, turn to files for help).

The stack is a data structure whose length you can change by adding items to, or taking items from, its open end. It's like the stack of jobs in my in-tray—each new job goes on the top, and each time I decide to do a job I take the top one. Archaeologists face the same situation as they dig down a new site. See Figure 4.4.

Figure 4.4 *A stack has one open end; a new item goes on there, and that's the only place you can take an item from*

Like any other data structure, a stack exists in store as a sequence of cells. However, we talk of the top (open) and bottom (fixed) of a stack, so you may like to think of it as a vertical construct. In truth, a computer's stack hangs upside-down!—the fixed bottom is at the top of memory (the cell with the highest address), so the top is below it. In any event, 'last in, first out' (LIFO) describes its use. Refer, if you like, to Figure 4.4: each new data item pushes onto the stack's open end, and even newer ones bury it; each data item removed from the stack pops off the open end. Thus if you want the third data item 'down' in the stack, you'd need first to pop (remove) the two between it and the open end. This sometimes means rather tortuous programming.

On the other hand, looking after a stack is very easy for the computer. The computer has a register in which it stores the address of the data item exposed at the open end. We call this the stack pointer. The stack pointer value changes each time the system pushes a data item onto the stack or pops one from it. Stack data processing is thus very fast. One programming language, Forth, uses the stack as its only data structure. Forth programs run very quickly as a result, so Forth is of much use for control. (Indeed, the only British micro not supplied to use BASIC was set up with Forth; this was the Jupiter Ace.)

Figure 4.5 shows the result of a few stack operations based on Forth instructions.

All computers use one or more stacks for their own needs. You can't get at these yourself with most high-level program languages. If, therefore, you want to use a stack, you have to model one with a 1D array, with the subscript of the element at the open end acting as the stack pointer. This is only a model, though, so it wouldn't work as fast as a true stack.

The next data structure is the **queue.** This is like a stack but has two open ends, one for popping and one for pushing. Queue is a good name, for, as with a queue at a post office counter, the first data item that goes in is the first to come out. Hence the term **'first in, first out'** (**FIFO**). Unlike the case of a post office queue, however, popping doesn't cause all the data items to shuffle forward one place; that would make things far too slow. In Figure 4.6, I show a

Figure 4.5 *Stack-based operations are fast as there's only one pointer to use*

Keyboard command	Display	Stack pointer	Top of stack					Comment
			5	4	3	2	1	
A B	OK	2				B	A	Stack was empty
•	B OK	1					A	'•' pop & display
C D	OK	3				D	C	A	'OK' command done
• • • •	D C A 0 stack empty OK	0 0						
3	OK	1					3	
dup	OK	2				3	3	'Dup' copy top item
8 + •		3			8	3	3	'+' pop & add top
		2				11	3	two items &
	11 OK	1					3	push result

Keyboard command	Head pointer	Tail pointer	Queue 5	4	3	2	1	Comment
push T R A	3	1			A	R	T	Queue was empty
pop pop	3	3			A			
push E L	5	3	L	E	A			
push F	1	3	L	E	A		F	Head cycles round

Figure 4.6 *A queue is restricted in space and involves two pointers*

very small queue as it goes through a few operations.

As a queue's data items remain in their cells till popped, a queue moves through memory like a caterpillar. Even if it started at the top of memory, it would eventually crash into, and corrupt, the program at the bottom. A queue must therefore be restricted to a block of memory, through which it cycles, as in Figure 4.6. Programmers working with queues must arrange this; they must also check that (a) the head doesn't crash into the tail (**overflow**), and (b) there's no attempt to pop data from an empty queue (**underflow**).

These matters, plus two pointers to look after, mean that working with a queue is harder and slower than with a stack. Operating software has to do it—buffers (Section 3.0) are queues. Programmers work with data queues mainly to model real queues (important for shop design and so on); a certain splendid type of game also involves data queues. As with stacks, you have to set up any queue you need with a 1D array.

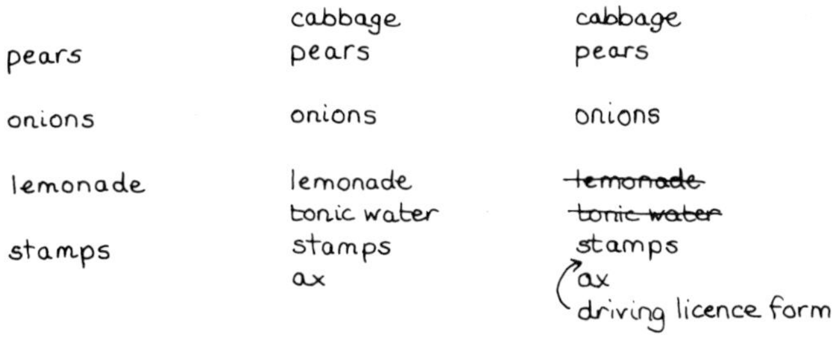

```
            cabbage           cabbage
pears       pears             pears

onions      onions            onions

lemonade    lemonade          lemonade
            tonic water       tonic water
stamps      stamps            stamps
            ax                ax
                              driving licence form
```

Figure 4.7 *A linked list is like a task list in action*

Figure 4.8 *With a linked list you can add an extra data item to, and take an item from, any point*

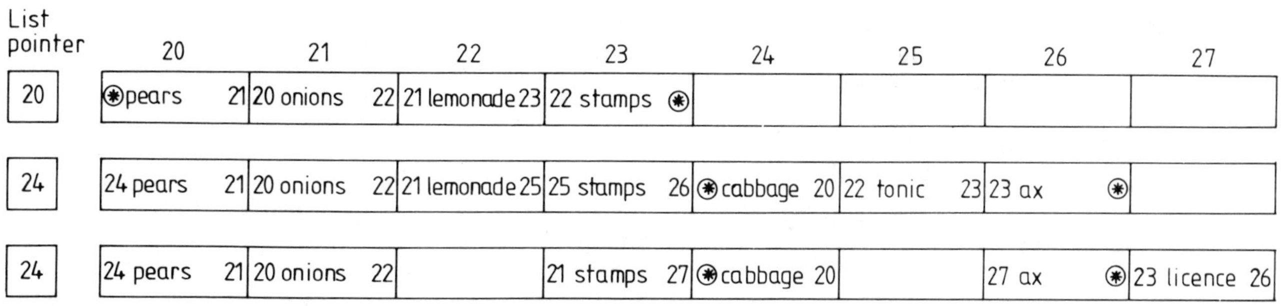

Stacks and queues are more flexible than 1D arrays used in the normal way, as they aren't fixed in length. All the same, access to them is only at an end; you can't add a data item somewhere in the middle or take one out from there. A **linked list** gives that extra power, especially a doubly linked list like the one I now describe.

Figure 4.7 shows a shopping list as you leave home and over a few stages of thinking of extra items to buy and of going into shops. See the need to insert and remove items not just at the ends but in the body of the list.

It's fairly easy for humans to use scruffy paper-based lists like that. Inside computer store, though, the structure needs rigorous organisation. The system has a pointer to the first data item in the list, that one has a pointer to the second, which points to the third, and so on. The last data item has a special ('null') pointer to show there's no more. Adding and taking away items involve changing pointers. Follow through the steps in Figure 4.8 with care.

You can no doubt see how flexible the linked list can be; each item has a pointer to the one before it in the list and a second pointer to the one after. *All* the data structures we've looked at involve pointers; each is the address of the cell pointed to, stored somewhere for ease of access. In my examples, I've used over-simple pointer values to keep things easy. In practice, each cell can store only 1 byte, and the cells used will have high addresses.

An extra complication, at least in the case of the linked list, may lead to the need for yet more pointers. Say you often wanted to be able to get a printout of the data items in alphabetical order. Rather than processing the list each time, it'd be simpler to add a second pointer at the head and tail of each data item; a second list pointer (to 22 in the case of

List pointer	20	21	22	23	24	25	26	27
20	⊛pears 21	20 onions 22	21 lemonade 23	22 stamps ⊛				
24	24 pears 21	20 onions 22	21 lemonade 25	25 stamps 26	⊛cabbage 20	22 tonic 23	23 ax ⊛	
24	24 pears 21	20 onions 22		21 stamps 27	⊛cabbage 20		27 ax ⊛	23 licence 26

the first line of Figure 4.8) would lead to the start of the alphabetic linked list. On the other hand, it's possible to manage without the head pointers.

It is clear that there are various types of linked list. Maybe I should close the linked list list by noting that it's sometimes worth joining the two ends to make a linked **ring**. This means you replace the list's null head and tail markers with pointers to tail and head. You still need the main list pointer(s) so you can get at the data, but now, if you need to process the items again and again, it's straightforward.

4.5   Up the tree

All the data structures so far (apart from the simple numeric ones) are in essence linear—they've some kind of straight line structure. This also applies to multi-dimensional arrays, for these are really just sets of lists. A tree, on the other hand, is not a linear data structure—it allows branching from one data item to more than one. Like a family tree, it has a number of levels; people therefore call it a **hierarchical structure.**

You can view the data in Prestel in this way—the main menu leads to other menus; each in turn leads to more. You can work down from the main menu (see the heavy line in the sample of Figure 4.9) to reach the page you want.

In the sketch are the terms we use in this context. Each data item is a **node**. If it leads to one or more at a lower level, it's a **parent** (or parent node); each item it leads to is a **child** (node). If a node has no children, it's a **leaf** (or **terminal node**); the **root** node, on the other hand, has no parent. Finally the lines between the nodes are the **branches** of the tree. Each non-leaf node, by the way, is the root of a **sub-tree.**

The simplest kind of branching tree is one where no parent has more than two children. We'll discuss in detail only such binary trees. Our concern is how to hold such a branching structure in the linear store of a computer.

As with the linked list (which you can view as a unary tree, with no more than one child per parent), each data item needs pointers. As well as the back pointer to the parent, there must be a pointer to each child. A binary tree needs two such pointers, to the left and right child respectively. Any pointer place can carry a code (null pointer) if there's nothing to point to.

There's a small binary tree in Figure 4.10. It's still a tree in the form humans would recognise, but I've put in the three pointers for each node. As before, I'm using simple numbers to make things less hard to follow. In practice, each pointer will carry the address of the cell holding the first byte of the data item concerned.

When I set this tree up, I entered these data items in order: mouse, dog, seal, monkey, horse, ape, rat, roe, cat, cow, human, tiger, moose. The standard rule for putting data into a tree is—lower values to the left, higher values to the right. For strings, value relates to alphabetical order. In each 'cell' appears the data item, with back pointer in front; the left and right pointers follow it. Outside is the 'cell' number. The only other thing to note is that I've slightly changed the branching shape to make the links clearer.

To access all the data we 'traverse' the tree. There are different ways to do this—they depend on the outcome wanted, on the type of tree, and on the pointers used. (Some trees use other pointers than the three discussed above, such as pointers to siblings, data items with the same parent.) The method I'll mention is the **in-order traversal.**

To traverse tree:

1 Traverse left sub-tree
2 Access root
3 Traverse right sub-tree

Figure 4.9   *A hierarchical data structure is like an upside-down tree*

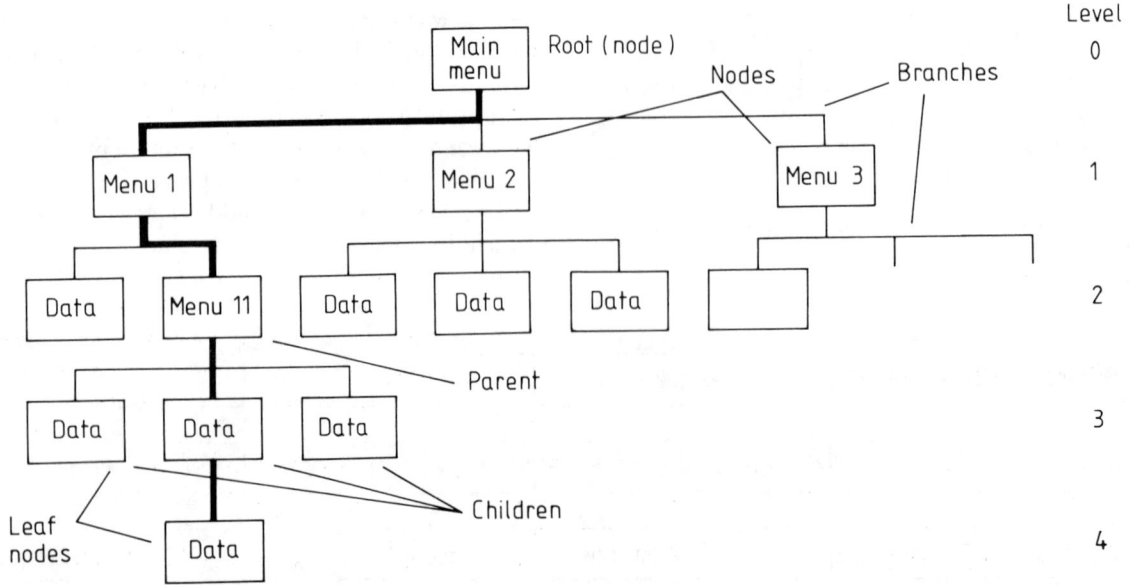

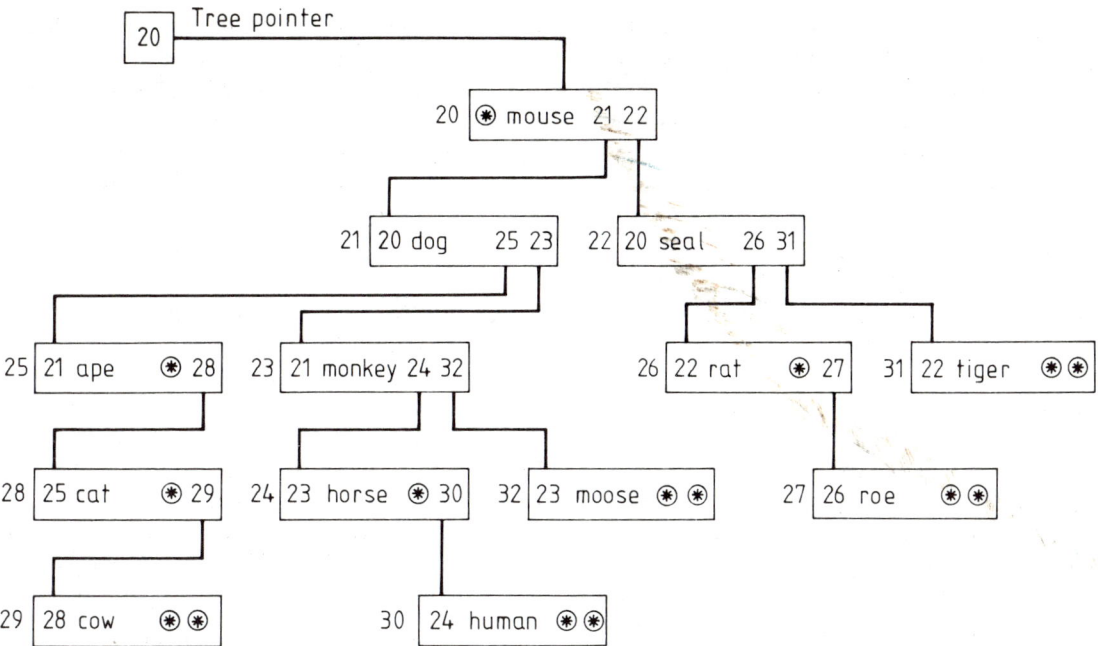

Figure 4.10 *Each data item in a binary tree comes with two child pointers and usually (as shown here) a back pointer*

Traverse means, 'Go to the child; access (display) it if it's a leaf. If the node reached isn't a leaf, traverse again.' This definition of traverse is *recursive*—it includes itself, like a nested set of Russian dolls.

Best try it, starting at the root. Take care! If you succeed, you'll find you've listed the data items in order. Hence the name of the method.

Other tasks systems need to do with trees in practice, as with linked lists, include adding and deleting data items. These are beyond the scope of this book, however—but it's all to do with pointer processing.

As I mentioned above, a Prestel-style data base carries its information in tree form. Such a data base can be very large—far too large to hold in main store. The data must then live in backing store, for access as required. This brings us to perhaps the most important data structure in practice; it involves holding data files in backing store. We'll cover it in detail in Chapter 6.

Holding data in backing store means there's no limit to the amount. On the other hand (Section 3.4), it takes longer to get at it. With a tree data base on disc, it's fairly easy to transfer a whole sub-tree into main store when the sub-tree has become small enough.

SELF-DEVELOPMENT QUESTIONS

See Page 136 for notes on these questions.

S4.1   Visit a hospital, clinic or surgery and discuss their use of IT.

S4.2   Write a short essay on IT in health care.

S4.3   Use the Healthdata viewdata base. What is the value of this kind of communication to health care workers?

S4.4   Convert these numbers (a) to binary and (b) to hex: 7, 49, 249.

S4.5   Convert these numbers (a) to hex and (b) to denary: 0000 1101, 0101 1010, 1001 1001.

S4.6   Set yourself addition, subtraction, multiplication and division sums in binary, starting with numbers between 4 and 8 bits long. Check your answers in denary.

S4.7   Carry out these sums, using 2s complementation and addition: 0101 1010 − 0000 1101,   1001 1001 − 0101 0100, 1100 0000 − 0011 1111. Check in denary.

S4.8   Convert to binary: 11.25, 123.625, 10.015625

S4.9   Express the negative values of S4.7 in normalised floating point form using sign and magnitude. Work in double precision with 9 bits for the mantissa.

S4.10   Explain what a rounding error is, with a denary and a binary example.

S4.11   Explain the difference between number overflow and underflow.

S4.12   State and explain what 0010 1010 0001 0101 could stand for when stored in two adjacent bytes.

S4.13   Devise a short program in BASIC, Pascal or Logo (or other suitable high-level language) to show the use of strings, integers and reals.

S4.14   Find out about Booleans and (if you can) devise a program that involves this data type.

S4.15   Produce a short BASIC or Pascal program using a 1D array (list).

S4.16   Discuss two cases where a 3D array would be of

value. Explain how one of them would be stored by a computer and the need for dimensioning it.

S4.17   Find out more about Forth. Use an approach like Figure 4.5 to explain some of the main words and operations.

S4.18   Model in a 1D array the use of a stack to handle a list of household tasks.

S4.19   Explore a shop queue (or similar) simulation package. Write brief notes on it. Include how the model differs from the queue data structure.

S4.20   Model in a 1D array the use of a queue to handle a list of household tasks.

S4.21   Explain how a linked list works. Use as example the development of an essay plan.

S4.22   Re-design Figure 4.8 to include alphabetical ordering of the data items.

S4.23   Use arrays to model a linked list essay plan.

S4.24   Enter these numbers into a binary tree in the order given: 48 17 9 83 19 44 75 92 9 2. Lay the tree out as in Figure 4.10. Showing your method, traverse the tree to obtain a list in number order.

S4.25   If you exchange steps 1 and 3 of the in-order traverse, do you obtain your data items in reverse order?

S4.26   Outline how to add a late entry to a binary tree, and how to delete one you no longer need.

EXAMINATION QUESTIONS

Q4.1   A certain hospital has a large computer system providing many interactive VDUs which are used in wards, consulting rooms, and by the hospital administration. Discuss, with reasons, the advantages and disadvantages of such a system compared with a manual system.
(AEB specimen paper)   (8)

Q4.2   The list of characters 170788 could represent one of: the number of milliseconds since a microcomputer has been switched on; the date when a particular file was last accessed; a file name. Describe the internal machine representation of this list of characters for each application.
(London)   (6)

Q4.3   **a**   By means of diagrams, explain how data is added to and removed from the following data structures: a queue; a push-down stack.
                                                        (4)

   b   What is a linked list? Describe in detail how you would implement such a list when it is to be stored in immediate access storage.
                                                        (6)

   c   A linked list is held in immediate access storage and each element of the list contains five fields. [A field is a space for a single data item.] The first field is the key field. [The key field contains the data item you search for.] Give an algorithm, which uses two parameters, to find an element in the list. The first parameter is the value of the key field which is to be found. The second parameter returns either the value 0 if the element is not found, or the value of the pointer to the element if it is found.
(JMB)   (6)

Q4.4   The contents of a storage location may be interpreted in a number of different ways depending on the circumstances in which it is used. For a particular computer with a 12-bit word length a certain word holds the binary pattern 1001 0110 0100.

   a   What value is represented in the above word if it is interpreted in each of the following ways? Show your working.

   (i)   an unsigned integer
   (ii)   a signed integer in 2s complement form
   (iii)   an unsigned three-digit integer in binary coded decimal
   (iv)   a signed floating point number

   The leftmost 8 bits are used for the mantissa, and represent a 2s complement binary fraction with the binary point immediately after the leftmost (sign) bit. The binary exponent is in the rightmost 4 bits and is an integer in 2s complement form.
                                                        [8]

   b   State the range of values that may be stored using each of the above representations. (Where appropriate you may express your answers in powers of 2.)
                                                        [4]

   c   Explain what is meant by 'storing floating point numbers in normalised form'. Why is it done?
                                                        [4]

   d   The decimal number 0.4 corresponds to the recurring binary fraction 0.0110 0110 0110 011 . . . Show how this number would be stored as accurately as possible using the representation described in **a iv**.
(COSSEC)   [4]

5 Software matters

Figure 5.1 *The western world of finance could hardly survive a minute without IT* (The International Stock Exchange Photo Library)

Case study 5—Topic: SEAQ

17 October 1986 was the day of the Big Bang, when the London-based stock market brought itself into the twentieth century with a vengeance. It involved de-regulation (so finance houses no longer have to specialise but can buy and sell as they wish); increased competition (more organisations are allowed to buy and sell); and 24-hour working with the stock exchanges of the rest of the world. IT is the pivot for all these changes.

IT has long been a crucial part of the lives of all organisations and people working with money. Money is information, after all (Section 1.2). The changes brought by the Big Bang needed a powerful, reliable, new integrated system. This was Topic, a superb Prestel-like viewdata service. Topic has, at its centre in the City of London, nine big mainframes. Between them they provide continuously updated prices for the vast number of stocks whose transfers involve thousands of millions of pounds a day. The public face of Topic is SEAQ, the Stock Exchange Automated Quotation system. Its viewdata frames provide information at two main levels.

Anyone who wishes to may subscribe to the lower level (or even access it through Prestel); they obtain, for each stock that interests them, current price, the recent range of price, and the day's volume of dealings.

Level Two is only for access by Stock Exchange members. These people can also obtain quotes from, and details of the amounts of stocks available at, all the dealers who have the stock on offer. The Level Two user can buy and sell direct through the system (or by phone or other methods). All the time information enters the system from the dealers (and from other sources, like stock exchanges round the world); Topic updates each SEAQ page once a minute.

Users can store pages of interest, or get printout. Most seem to leave the display on-line all the time; many use windows so they can keep an eye on several pages.

The biggest problem with Topic in the early days was that it couldn't cope with the huge demand for this cheap, up-to-date information. When they started to set the system up, the planners thought there'd be about a thousand Level Two subscribers. In fact the figure had reached 4000 by the first day. There were breakdowns in the first week as a result. (And for a few months the phone system couldn't always cope.)

Many of the problems wouldn't have appeared if the Stock Exchange had decided to put SEAQ onto teletext rather than viewdata. With teletext they could cycle through all the pages in a continuous broadcast by cable or radio; viewdata is two-way so each user can request each page of interest (getting it in a couple of seconds). However, the two-way nature of viewdata does allow those concerned to deal as well as to access the details they need.

Introduction

The Topic system as a whole consists of those nine central mainframes, linked (by direct cable or through the phone network) to nearly ten thousand remote terminals and to Prestel. As well as this hardware, much depends on the software to manage all the tasks—the continuous updating of thousands of records, each access, and all dealing interactions. There's no intrinsic problem with the hardware —but it's on the software that Topic survives.

Indeed, software matters more than hardware. As with SEAQ, any computer's software has a hierarchy, a number of levels. In this chapter, we'll take a look at those software levels.

Objectives

When you have worked through this chapter, you should be able to

1 describe the Stock Exchange Automated Quotations system, SEAQ, and comment on its features
2 discuss the layered nature of a computer's software
3 list and explain the main general tasks of a mainframe's operating software (OS)
4 describe multi-programming, multi-usage, multi-processing, batching systems, and real-time working, with examples of use, and note the main OS functions in each case
5 give examples of interrupts and outline the process of interrupt handling
6 list some tasks a micro user faces that a mini or mainframe's OS would handle
7 state what disc formatting entails
8 describe, with an example, a hierarchical (tree) directory layout and its use
9 state the need for backing up data and outline methods of doing it
10 list other disc management tasks
11 discuss the nature and advantages of spooling
12 state what a job control language is, and note some uses
13 distinguish between multi-programming and multi-user time sharing
14 outline the nature of machine code programming
15 show, and discuss, the spectrum of program languages
16 state, with examples, the use of the four fields of an assembly language instruction
17 state the functions and usage of editor and assembler programs and of directives and macros
18 outline the main addressing modes
19 compare high-level program language to human language
20 compare high- and assembly-level program language
21 list the features that describe a high-level program language, and comment
22 compare methods of program control branching and looping
23 compare compilation and interpretation
24 show some knowledge of several major high-level languages
25 comment on user interface quality

5.1 Software matters more than hardware

There's a huge variety of arrangements of IT hardware (equipment) and will be more in the future. All the same, we can describe any system in terms of central processor plus peripherals (backing store and input and output units). Whatever the structure of a given system, it needs software—sets of instructions in the form of programs—to run.

Hardware without software is no more use than a car without someone who knows how to drive. Indeed, more and more effort and cash are put into software development round the world than into hardware development.

Most people's main concern is with software used to carry out the tasks they want their IT systems to handle—**applications software**. However, applications, looked at in some detail in Chapter 2, are only the outside layer of the computer's onion-like software structure (Figure 5.2). In this chapter we concentrate on the lower levels.

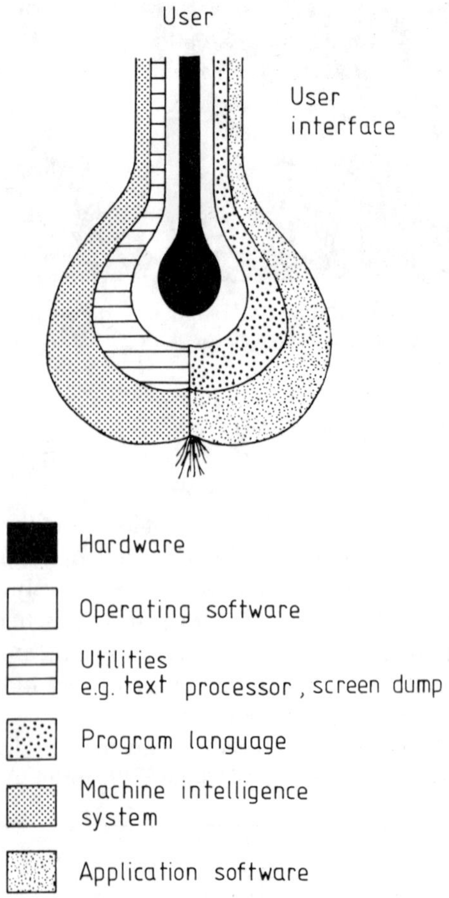

Figure 5.2 *A computer's software is in a number of layers*

The innermost layer—or set of layers, in practice—in any computer's software hierarchy is the **program** (or suite of programs) that keeps the hardware working properly. This goes by the name of **operating software** (or **control program**). A computer's operating software (OS) is the program(s) the hardware needs to carry out instructions of higher layers without too much human hassle.

The purpose of OS isn't just to give the user an easy life—after all, the designer of every aspect of a computer should have that aim in mind. It is at least as important to keep the computer working as close to full time as possible; only then can its huge power fully be realised. As every part of the whole hardware/software/liveware unit costs money, it isn't good to leave any of it idle.

In particular, the processor—which can carry out millions of actions a second—isn't used to the full when there are data transfers to peripherals. Doing no more than scanning the keyboard at which you're typing a couple of characters a second is not economic, nor is just sending text to a printer which can work at not much greater speed. Similar losses of processing time can occur during the preparation stages for any particular job, or when something goes wrong that the user must investigate. In any context, humans are far brighter than computers—but on the whole they're far, far slower.

Thus, a major task of the OS is to ensure that at any moment the tremendous power of each part of the system is being used most effectively. This task itself uses computer processing effort; it also reduces the amount of memory available for the current application. However, overall there's a huge gain in efficiency.

Here are the tasks of a mainframe computer's operating software:

- transfer of programs, sub-programs and other data to and fro between main and backing store as needed
- scheduling how the system is to carry out the various jobs in hand, with the aim of continuous processing
- control of the use of peripherals, including lines from terminals
- (if more than one program is being carried out during a period) handling the tasks of each program in turn, aiming for continuous processing and efficient data transfer to and from peripherals, all the time bearing in mind priorities
- handling problems and errors automatically as much as possible
- arranging temporary storage (e.g. spooling to disc data that's to be printed if no printer is available, and getting it back later)
- looking after backing up and security (Sections 6.3 and 10.2)
- keeping the staff informed about what's going on and what action they may need to take
- every so often (say, at the end of a shift) or on demand, printing out a log (report) of all jobs dealt with, their

progress and any problems met
- putting the cost of each job against the name of the person or department concerned

At the start of a typical session with such a mainframe, then, the chief operator will instruct the OS, using a program (set of instructions) in job control language, what tasks it's to carry out. All necessary details will be supplied, including the priority of each job—and then the system will be left to look after itself. The OS will sort out the details of the jobs and their priorities; it will also check the resource needs of each one (including the proportions of tasks that involve input, process, transfers to and from backing store, and output).

The rest of the session, the OS will carry out all the tasks described above. From moment to moment it has to try to keep the processor busy and to arrange data transfers. Sometimes it will send a message to the staff, perhaps asking for a certain disc pack to go in a certain drive, noting that a printer needs its paper changed, or indicating when a certain job is complete and what should be done with it next.

Clearly a large mainframe like this needs complex operating software. It also needs a fairly large full-time staff to look after it—the chief operator, the shift leader, the people concerned with the wants of the peripherals, a data librarian to handle the issue and return of discs, and so on. (See Section 9.3.)

All those staff are rolled into one person in the case of a stand-alone micro or network station; that one is the actual user. The user's concern is to get on with specific applications rather than to bother with operations and control. The OS of a small system must therefore be prepared for this, but even so its tasks don't differ greatly, except in scale, from those described for the mainframe. A significant difference, all the same, is that a mainframe's OS is so large that much of it stays in backing store for the 'boss', the executive (or monitor, or supervisor), to draw from only when it needs. There's no point in printer routines taking up precious main store during the run of a program that involves no printing, for instance.

5.2 Inside the operating software

In this context there's currently another significant difference between a micro and a mainframe. The latter offers **multi-programming**: it can share time between several programs in memory at the same moment. Much of the effort of a mainframe OS therefore goes to scheduling how the tasks of these programs interleave. Figure 5.3 shows how an OS may share the work of processor and peripherals between three programs in a multiprogramming context.

Multiprogramming follows the demand for continuous processing, the demand to use the CPU for as close to 100% as possible. Few programs need CPU time for more than, say, 25% of a run (most require much less); the

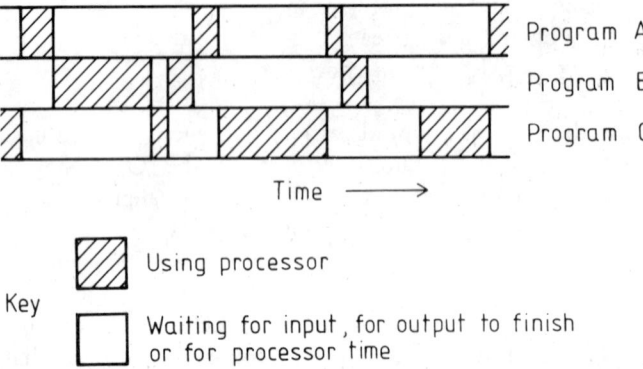

Key

▨ Using processor

☐ Waiting for input, for output to finish or for processor time

Figure 5.3 *Multiprogramming lets the parts of a computer share time between the tasks of different programs*

interleaving concept is clearly a good way to raise efficiency. It means the main store must be partitioned, to give a chunk to each program. That in turn means each program's instructions must be re-locatable, able to work wherever in store they happen to be. Producing re-locatable code is a task for programmers; however, it's the OS that manages the memory during a multiprogram run.

The main store is limited in size, so management isn't easy. To help out, some mainframes use a technique called **virtual storage**. Instead of loading all of a large program from disc, the OS takes just a block of it as required. In virtual storage, then, the OS shuttles blocks (overlays) of each program from each program disc into main store.

We can therefore expand the OS task list for a multi-program environment. The following tasks are the function of the part of the OS called the **scheduler**.

- ensure that the system carries out as many jobs as possible in a given time
- ensure that it's not always the same job that goes to the end of the queue when there's conflict
- ensure rapid responses to each interactive user
- ensure rapid response to each interrupt from some other part of the system (a hard interrupt) or from the operating staff (soft)
- ensure that no resource—processor, partition, peripheral —stays unused for very long
- work the virtual storage technique (if supplied)
- prevent any chance of overload (when one or more parts can't cope with the demand)

A hard interrupt is a signal from a peripheral that it needs the CPU to do something. For instance, an input buffer may be full or an output buffer empty. When an interrupt arrives, the CPU must be ready to drop what it's doing at that moment and deal with the problem. At the end of each fetch–execute–reset cycle (Section 3.2), the OS checks the **interrupt flag register**. This contains a bit—a flag—for each interrupt line. The bit sets to 1 (the flag waves) when there's an interrupt request; the OS resets it to 0 (stops it waving) when it's dealt with the matter.

When the CPU checks the register, a non-zero value shows there's an interrupt to handle; the actual value informs the system what the matter is. To drop what it's doing, the OS copies the contents of all the registers (Figure 3.7) to its stack; it then turns to the routine for dealing with that particular interrupt. After it's carried this out, it resets the flag, takes the old register contents back from the stack, and gets on with its interrupted task.

All that takes just a few microseconds. A CPU will have to deal with tens or hundreds of interrupts a second. Each has a priority assigned to it. This is so the system knows which to deal with if more than one appears at a given moment. It also needs to know whether to ignore an interrupt that interrupts its handling of another interrupt. Highest priority goes to a warning of a power failure. If the supply voltage starts to fall, the system must save to disc all the programs in main store and their data; it has to be able to do this within a few hundredths of a second.

Other interrupts would follow such events as in the list below. These aren't in any priority order; in any event, it's normal for priorities to change as the system's jobs change. Some events that may cause an interrupt are

- the need to update the real-time clock
- a full input buffer (including that bringing data in from backing store)
- an interactive user pressing a key
- a user pressing BREAK or ESCAPE
- the chief operator's 'hold' signal
- an empty output buffer (including that to backing store)
- when a peripheral has finished a job
- when a program needs a peripheral
- a hardware fault
- a software error (bug)
- when it's time to check a control sensor (Section 3.6)

All computer systems work with interrupts in this way—it's not just if they're multiprogramming.

Few micros yet offer much in the way of multi-programming, though progress is bound to be swift in the next few years. At the moment, however, a micro's OS (the most common standards being **control program for micros** (CP/M) for 8-bit machines and **MicroSoft Disc Operating System** (MS-DOS) for 16-bit hardware) doesn't need to be as complex as that of a mini or mainframe. Indeed, it's left to the authors of applications programs to cover such needs as messages to the user to change discs and printer paper.

Micro users need to be aware of some aspects of their OS so they can get full benefit from it. While a given application program should include OS calls as required, there are still things a user may have to do, at least sometimes. Here are some of the user's tasks:

- choosing the right OS for a given job (if there's a choice)
- setting up the system (hardware, firmware and software)

- checking the peripherals
- loading the required program into store
- disc management (including organising libraries and directories)
- memory management
- making a link to a second computer (including for viewdata)
- (re)setting date and time

Disc management is in most cases by far the most important of these. It involves jobs you have to do before you use a disc as well as meeting other needs during and after.

A disc must be formatted before you can use it with a given machine. A formatted disc carries signals in its magnetic surface to show where the tracks are and where the sectors begin (Section 3.4). It may then need a title, a datestamp and a directory tree before you can put on it the programs you need.

A **disc filing system** (DFS) that offers more than the simplest structure for holding the data has a hierarchical (tree-like—Section 4.5) plan for its directories. Figure 5.4 gives an example; it's much like the way you may arrange your books.

To access the physics programs, say, you'd change the directory from the root to **prog/bas/sci/phys**. (I use typical short directory names.) Then load and save programs in the usual way. That may seem fiddly; yet in the case of the 20 MB hard disc of a micro used by several people, such a system is essential. The same principles apply to using floppy discs. Here, however, with only perhaps 1 MB on line, you'd have one or more discs for each major activity and put on them fairly simple sub-directories.

Whether you use a hard disc or floppies, a crucial task is backing up data. We'll see how the user of a mainframe (or rather its OS) does this in Section 6.3, but backing up is just as important with a micro.

Backing up means making a copy of the data in case of problems. Each time you save a program, text file or other set of data to floppy, you should repeat with a second disc. This is so important that some micro software does it automatically or at least prompts you to do it yourself. Most people are very lazy about this (even after the experience of losing a lot of work)—if *you* aren't strict, why not back up your floppies once a week?

Most micro hard disc units are fixed—you can't change the discs for backing up. Making a safety copy of data on fixed hard disc means either backing up onto a pile of floppies (which is slow) or using a **tape streamer** (which is costly). A streamer is a special high-speed tape unit; it takes only a few minutes to copy all the contents of a hard disc.

Some other disc management techniques let you

- set up an auto-boot routine (so the disc gets things ready automatically on starting up—'pulls the system up by its boot straps')
- lock a file to prevent some kinds of accidental damage
- merge files together
- delete a file or group that's no longer needed
- compact (get rid of chunks of wasted space on disc)
- find out how much space there's left
- list the files on disc (all of them or just those in a directory sub-tree), maybe with details of length and date
- search for a given set of bytes and perhaps change or move it
- restrict file access to password holders
- change a file name

(I use the word 'file' here in its widest sense—any structured set of data in main or backing store.)

Figure 5.4 *A hierarchical disc directory layout saves a lot of time*

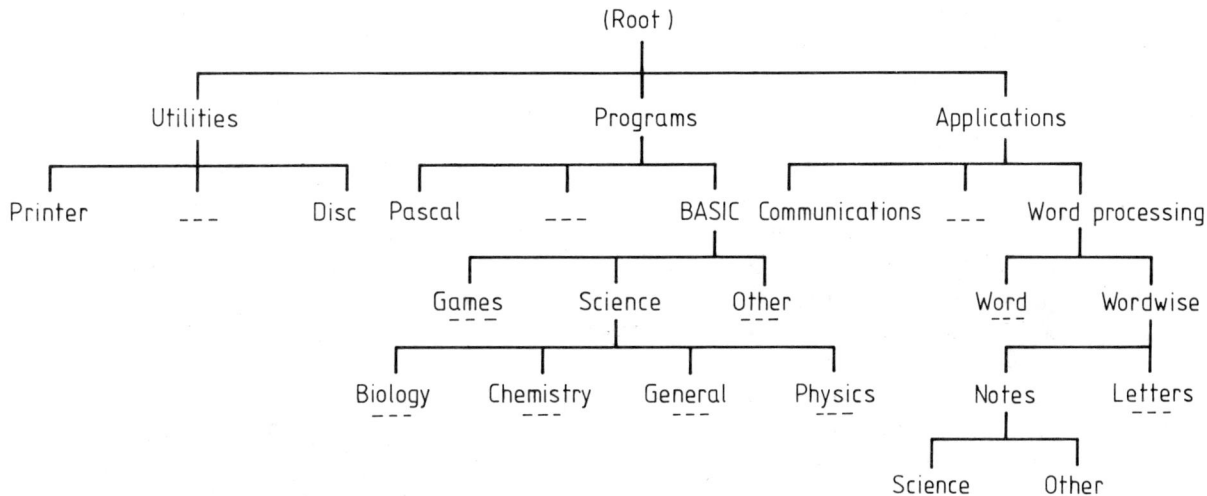

5.3   Types of operating software

Operating software used in a multiprogramming environment is probably the most complex. There are other kinds of computer system usage; each has its own type of OS.

A **batching system** handles jobs in batches (groups supplied in sequence). The computer does the first job, then the next, then the third, and so on. This can only be for non-interactive tasks. That means there's no user on line to enter data and await output—no keyboard and screen are involved. The computer expects each program, along with details for the OS of what peripherals it needs, plus all the data required. It prints out the results for the whole batch and the staff then pass these to the users.

Spooling is common with batched work. The main computer is not usually involved with preparing the data the programs work with. That data may be machine readable (Section 3.6): it's best for a separate small computer to transfer it to disc or tape. People enter input data on a key to store (disc or tape) unit (Section 9.3); again a small computer looks after this task. When the main program needs the data, it takes it from the disc. This input of data is off line—remote from the main processor and not under its control.

Spooled output also saves the time of the main CPU. Instead of sending the results straight to a printer, it saves them on disc (or tape). Once more, a separate small machine will look after the transfer to printout. Figure 5.5 shows these two types of spooling.

The staff running a batching computer use a **job control language** (JCL) to give the OS the details it needs. The resulting job control program first lists the jobs to do. For each one it then gives user name and account number, and the details of the discs (and/or tapes) to use for programs and spooled data. The staff will also use the JCL to communicate with the OS for other reasons, such as to obtain status reports and summary logs.

A few decades ago, batching was the only way to use a system for a number of jobs. Thus school and college computing students would key their programs and data off line, using a card punch; once a week the batch of packs of cards would go off to a mainframe for running. A while later the printouts would come back.

Interactive computing is where a user enters data into a running program and gets results at once, on screen and/or on a printer. While it's fine for a cheap small micro to look after a single interactive user, this would be amazingly inefficient in the case of minis and mainframes. These therefore provide **multi-access** to (**timesharing** between) tens, hundreds or even thousands of people at once. Each person works at a terminal (Section 3.5) on line to the CPU. An on-line device is connected to and controlled by the CPU; people often describe **multi-user systems** as on line.

The OS of a multi-access machine is complex; it must ensure each user on line feels as if there's no one else working with it. One way of doing this is to give each user a small slice of time in turn if called on to do so. Figure 5.6 shows how the OS scans (polls) the terminal lines in turn.

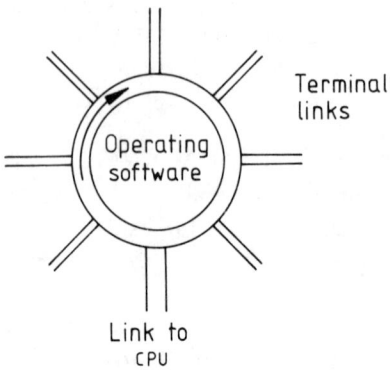

Figure 5.6   *Multi-access involves the OS polling each terminal line in turn and giving a time slice to each one that needs service*

When it finds a line for which output data or from which input data is waiting, it gives the system a slice of time to the task concerned. In most cases this is no more than a hundredth of a second: quite enough for a lot of processing if necessary.

Time sharing works on the basis of interrupts. That's just the same as with the batch time sharing between programs in a multiprogramming system. In this case, though, the sharing is on demand and the slices are fixed.

Users of a multi-access system would start to feel unhappy if response times were longer than a few seconds. They'd then know they weren't getting a computer all to themselves.

Figure 5.5   *Spooling input and output data saves a batch processing computer a lot of CPU time*

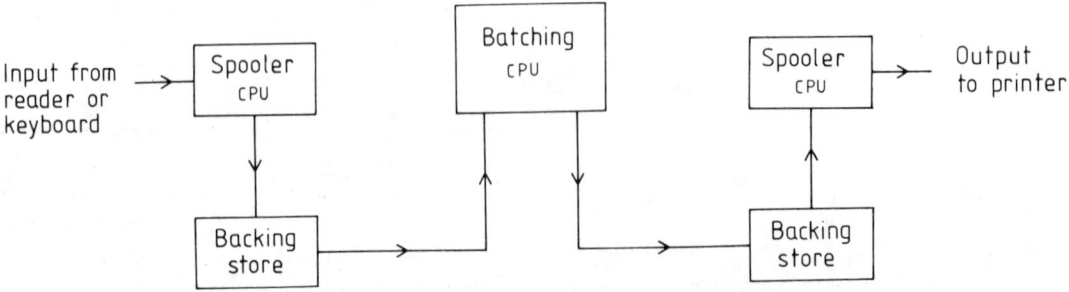

Up to a few seconds' response is no real problem for most human users (for example, users of viewdata systems such as Prestel and those for health care staff and travel agents).

Users of SEAQ and airline booking viewdata, however, expect almost instant updating of the data available. If lots of people are trading in a given stock, its price and availability can change from second to second. Again, you don't want to risk two travel agents both booking the last seat on the next plane from Birmingham to Glasgow. Some people call systems that give such speedy response 'real-time'. While they aren't truly so (see below), the OS must ensure

- very rapid updating,
- no access to a page being updated, and
- refreshing of each page accessed (sending the updated version to each person looking at it).

There are cases, however, where truly instant response is crucial. Such cases are where the computer's output must affect the input. Many control systems are in this group—control of processes in automated chemical plants and nuclear power stations, robots, vehicles, and weapons, for instance. (Don't include traffic-light and flood control in this list, for here a few seconds' delay is not a problem. Such systems use interrupts anyway.)

There are two ways to handle these instant response needs. One is to dedicate a computer to each such task. Thus a robot has its own computer; aircraft will have several, plus reserves. Often the computers concerned will be analog rather than digital; analog systems are single-purpose, so are much faster than general-purpose digital units. They are good with sensors too.

The second approach is when one computer has to handle the needs of several instant response lines. To do this we set up a **real-time system**; each line has its own 'front end' processor and, as with the aircraft, there are reserves. The OS has a waiting game to play. A multiprocessing real-time package like this is clearly very costly in that all its power is much underused. All the same, the cost of delayed response to a sensor output change in a chemical plant or aircraft could be far greater.

Multiprocessing is becoming common outside the real-time field; it arose from spooling systems. The main processor can concentrate better on 'real' processing if other processors specialise in peripheral tasks and running the OS. Indeed, machines with a number of main processors working in parallel are starting to appear. People designed the transputer for work in this category. Parallel processing computers are very fast and powerful, but give new tasks to the OS.

5.4 Mind your language

In Section 5.1 we met the concept of the layered nature of IT software. The operating software lives in the layer (in practice, several layers) in closest contact with the hardware; that's because its task in essence is to control the hardware. As a result, OS is normally machine-specific, supplied with the computer on purchase.

As I noted above, CP/M and MS-DOS are particularly common suites of OS for micros. The former, which stands for control program for microcomputers, is the older. (It became a major standard for the 8-bit micros that were the norm a few years ago and as such was fairly universal.) However, because OS must be machine-specific, and because each micro must differ from the rest in detail, there are many versions of CP/M and MS-DOS. All should appear the same to the users as far as concerns messages and procedures; all too should be able to work with the full range of higher layer software designed to be compatible with them. Sadly these ideals aren't always borne out in practice—possible individual variations between computer models may mean books aren't fully correct in their descriptions and so-called compatible applications software may not work properly.

The existence of non-standard varieties of so-called standard software makes systems development far more tricky than it could and should be. While it would be wrong to insist on full compatibility—for that would stifle progress—it's a real pity the end user suffers so much.

Those comments apply just as much to the next higher layer in the software ladder, the layer that carries program language software. Many applications programs don't access the OS directly; rather they depend on a language program to convert them into a form the OS can work with.

It's possible—and in computing's early days it was essential—to write computer programs in binary digital (bit) form so the system can at once follow each instruction. To program like that is very hard: it needs full knowledge of how each part of the hardware works and must take account of the transfer and processing of every single chunk of data. The rows of so-called machine code 0s and 1s are impossible to follow and a horror to check; think how tricky it would be to instruct computers with hundreds of lines of code like those in Figure 5.7.

Figure 5.7 *Once all computer programming had to be done with binary words like these*

As computers should make life easier for programmers as much as for any other user, over the decades people have devised better and better software for computers to translate clear instructions into the binary form they need. The translating programs go by the name of program language software, or **programming languages**. Their job is to change

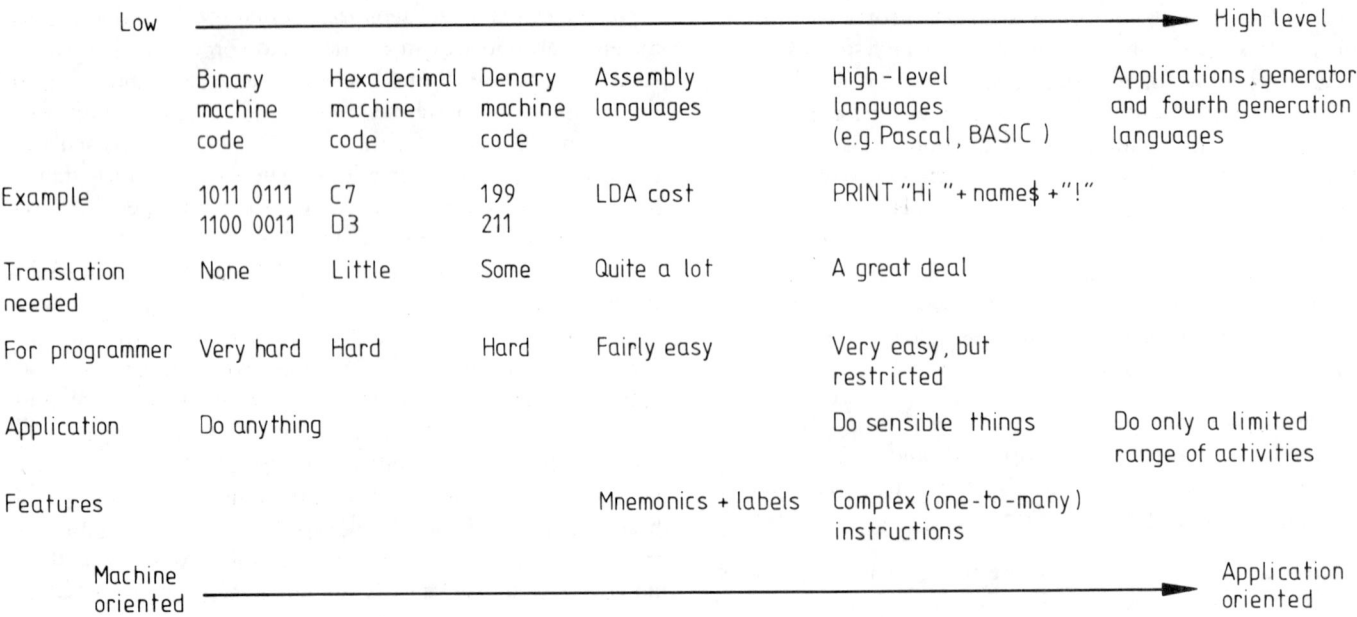

	Binary machine code	Hexadecimal machine code	Denary machine code	Assembly languages	High-level languages (e.g. Pascal, BASIC)	Applications, generators and fourth generation languages
Low ———→ **High level**						
Example	1011 0111 1100 0011	C7 D3	199 211	LDA cost	PRINT "Hi "+ name\$ +"!"	
Translation needed	None	Little	Some	Quite a lot	A great deal	
For programmer	Very hard	Hard	Hard	Fairly easy	Very easy, but restricted	
Application	Do anything				Do sensible things	Do only a limited range of activities
Features				Mnemonics + labels	Complex (one-to-many) instructions	
Machine oriented ———→ **Application oriented**						

Figure 5.8 *There's a spectrum of program languages*

Bottom	M a i n s t o r e			Top
Operating software	Assembler	Source program	Object program	Room for data

Figure 5.9 *An assembler translates an assembly language source program into a binary machine code object program*

each instruction received into the right sequence of 0s and 1s the system will be able to follow.

Figure 5.8 shows the spectrum of program languages—from binary machine code like that in Figure 5.7 to the high-level types (Section 5.5). After sample instructions, I set out the main characteristics (which I expand on later as appropriate), and their pros and cons from the programmer's points of view.

First we'll look at assembly languages (mentioned in Section 3.3). Each instruction starts with a keyword, a mnemonic opcode for what to do. (Mnemonic means easy to remember.) Examples are **LDA** (load a copy into the accumulator); **BIZ** (branch if accumulator contains zero); **PHA** (push accumulator contents onto stack); **HLT** (stop). Most instructions concern data storage cells and registers, so with them there's an address part (operand) after the opcode. The address part doesn't have to be a number: we can label a data item and leave the translator to worry about where each item is. An example is **LDA cost**.

We can also label instructions to mark where a branch is to: **BIN end** would tell the system to jump to the instruction labelled **end** if the accumulator contains a negative number. Most assembly languages also allow you to put a remark, or comment, after the instruction to remind you later what it's for. An assembly language instruction can therefore have four 'fields'—for instruction label, mnemonic opcode, data

item label, and comment. An assembly code instruction using all four fields would be

printer   LDA   result   prepare for printing

To the programmer, the advantages of assembly coding over machine coding are

- the mnemonic opcodes are easy to use,
- you can label data items,
- you can label program sections,
- you can add comments, and
- the labels make the program re-locatable.

To enter your assembly code into the computer, you need a program called a **text editor**. This is a special kind of word processor, although you can often use ordinary word processors. Your entered instructions go into main store. They're held as 0s and 1s, but not as binary machine code instructions. To convert this 'source code' into binary machine code, you next run a program called an **assembler**. This translates the source program into a usable form, the object program that the computer can then run. After assembly, the main store is laid out as in Figure 5.9; once the object code's checked, there's no further need for the editor, assembler and source code—you can therefore delete these from the main store, and save the object code alone for future use.

The assembler works through the source code. It takes note of any special instructions from the programmer. These directives provide background information to the assembler. It converts each mnemonic to the corresponding machine code byte; it also builds up a list of the labels it can't yet translate into cell addresses; it ignores the comments. The assembler then passes again through the code; now it can translate the labels it had to store before. The object program is now ready for testing.

In two ways I made this account of assembly coding a bit too simple. First, note that though there's strictly a one-to-one relation between source code instructions and the machine code instructions produced by assembly, some systems have a feature called macros. A **macro** is a single instruction the assembler recognises as standing for a series of instructions; it therefore replaces the macro with the set of machine code instructions.

The second point concerns addressing modes. There are many ways to refer to data items as well as using the item itself (so-called immediate addressing, as in **LDA 15**) or a label (symbolic addressing, e.g. **LDA vatrate**). Here are some addressing modes, where *n* is the operand (address part):

- **direct**—*n* is the address of the data
- **indirect**—cell *n* stores the address of the data
- **relative**—the address of the data is *n* places from the cell that contains the instruction
- **indexed**—the address of the data is *n* places from the cell whose address is in a special 'index' register

5.5 Higher levels

A **high-level program language**—such as BASIC, Logo, or Pascal—is much closer to a human language than assembly code is. All the same, we're still a long way from having computers 'understand' natural human language instructions. A human language has a large vocabulary (English, one of the richest, has over a million words); it also has a complex syntax (grammatical structure) with, moreover, lots of exceptions and special cases; there's also a great deal of ambiguity in practice—you can't always be sure of the meaning of a sentence, even if its structure is correct, without knowing the context.

A high-level program language, while like a human language (in most cases English), has a very small vocabulary of keywords, and a small and very rigid set of syntax rules; there can be no room for ambiguity as processors can't know about context.

All the same, instructions using such systems are complex. The translator may need to convert one into hundreds of machine code instructions—there's no longer a one-to-one relation between a source instruction and the machine code

form. Also, a high-level language is (supposed to be) system-independent; that is, problem-oriented rather than machine-oriented. A high-level program should be easy to **port** (transfer) to a different machine, as only the translating system is machine-specific.

Alas, things aren't always so simple in practice. Most high-level languages, like most human ones, have a number of dialects that make porting hard if not impossible. As I noted before, this aids progress, but leads to all sorts of problems.

People have produced hundreds of programming languages over the years to meet the specific needs of different markets or the specific ideas of different programmers. You may have heard of COBOL (common in commerce), FORTRAN (fine for formulas, in mathematical contexts), Pascal (for learning to program), and Logo (for programming by logical thinking). By far the most common programming language for micros at the moment is BASIC; indeed BASIC is the only program language supplied as standard in most cases. It was originally devised to help people learn to program; as a result it was made (and is) easy to grasp and use, and offers a selection of good features for many contexts. Most people with the need and the interest find that in a few hours they can gain the essentials of BASIC, enough to let them then rapidly pick up the other skills and concepts they may want.

We can describe any high-level language by its features. The features concern its

- block structures (divisions, procedures)
- data types
- data structures
- methods of assignment of values to data items
- input and output control (including graphics and sound)
- branching (decision-making) methods
- loop structures
- provision of iteration (letting the system home in on a value)
- provision of recursion (letting a procedure call itself)
- number handling features
- string handling features
- file handling features
- error handling features
- method of translation from source program to object code
- style, e.g. applicative (functional), declarative, or imperative

We've looked at most of the main features already, or shall do so in Chapter 7. Here therefore I'll just give notes on branching and loops and on translation methods.

The simplest program has a purely linear sequence from start to end; the system carries out each instruction in turn. As a computer works so fast, it's rarely of much value to use such a simple structure except to meet the simplest needs. Branching and looping let the system follow different paths

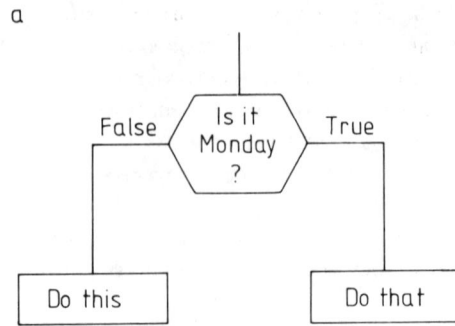
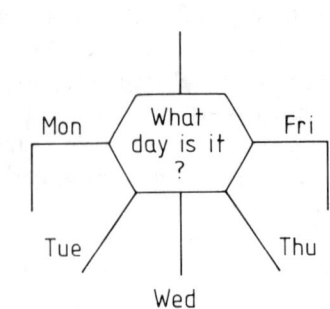

Figure 5.10 *Branching requires several possible paths after a decision*

through the program that depend on circumstances—they introduce decision making (the essence of most real problems).

A program branches if, after a decision, it can follow one of several paths. Figure 5.10a shows the simplest case, binary branching; Figure 5.10b is the more general case.

Here are some ways to code these, starting with the simplest:

```
IF day$="Monday" THEN GOSUB monday
```

```
IF day$="Monday" THEN PROC monday
ELSE PROC nonday
```

```
IF day$="Monday"
  monday
ELSE
  nonday
ENDIF
```

And for the multi-choice case:

```
IF day$="Monday" THEN GOSUB monday
IF day$="Tuesday" THEN GOSUB tuesday
```
etc.

```
IF day$="Monday" PROC monday
ELSE IF day$="Tuesday" PROC tuesday
```
etc.

```
SELECT day$
ON day$="Monday"
  monday
ON day$="Tuesday"
  tuesday

. . .
END SELECT
```

Those are all instructions that relate to dialects of BASIC (and there are plenty more ways of doing the tasks!). They will give you a flavour of the dialect problem that makes it so hard to port high-level programs between machines. The point I really want to make, though, is that the different structures offered by a language make a great difference to its ease of use and power. All high-level systems offer one or more forms of decision making to allow branching.

Most also have a blocking structure, as shown by the calls to closed subroutines with **GOSUB**, or to procedures with **PROC** or just the procedure name. (A **procedure** is an advanced type of closed subroutine.) To be able to label chunks of code for calling on when needed from elsewhere is a very important feature of high-level languages; it's much more advanced here than in assembly work. We'll come back to procedures in Chapter 7.

A loop is a chunk of the program through which the system may pass more than once; it is a **subroutine** (a block of code with a single purpose) but it's not kept apart from the rest—an open subroutine rather than a closed one. I'll give examples from BASIC, though all high-level languages offer the same type of thing.

Perhaps the most common need is to loop through the subroutine a fixed number of times. In BASIC the **FOR .../NEXT ...** structure offers this:

```
FOR record=1 TO 100
  READ name$
  PRINT name$
NEXT record
```

Often, though, the number of times to loop isn't always the same. **REPEAT/UNTIL ...** will run through the subroutine at least once, until the condition coded after **UNTIL** becomes true:

```
REPEAT
  READ name$
  PRINT name$
UNTIL name$='zzz'
```

This structure is also of great value in control:

```
REPEAT
  READ speedsensor
  INCREMENT motorspeed
UNTIL speedsensor=setspeed
```

The problem with **REPEAT/UNTIL ...** is the system will always pass through the loop at least once. The third looping structure (and the rarest!) gets over this problem. I'll give another control example.

```
WHILE temp<settemp
  INCREMENT heater
ENDWHILE
```

Figure 5.11 shows these three possible looping structures in picture form. It clearly shows that looping involves decision making just as much as the more obvious 'if' structures mentioned earlier.

All the examples make it clear that a high-level program instruction must translate to many machine-level opcodes and addresses. We no longer worry about data transfers to and from main store cells and registers (including the accumulator): we need know nothing about the structure and action of the hardware. The translator will handle all that. Even with a simple instruction like **PRINT name$**, it must

- find the address of the cell holding the first byte of the string (using its label table),
- find the length of the string (Figure 4.3), and
- copy the string byte by byte all the way through the system to the screen output.

There are two major types of high-level program translator: the **interpreter**, which translates and carries out each instruction when it comes to it; and the **compiler**, which translates the whole program before you can run it. A compiler works in much the same way as an assembler; its output is machine-level object code, so you can erase the source code, editor, and compiler from main store. This makes the program run more quickly, but means program writing and testing can't be interactive.

With an interpreter, you can interact with the system as you work on your program: you can try out instructions as direct commands; you can try out chunks of the program; you can print out values when testing; you can run, edit, run again.

However, an interpreter is really much less efficient and makes the program run much more slowly. That's because it translates each instruction before it can carry it out. Inside a loop it must translate each subroutine instruction on each pass. Most non-interactive programs are therefore compiled. Indeed, though BASIC is essentially an interpreted language, you can get BASIC compilers for most machines.

As I've mentioned, there are hundreds of high-level languages. Here are brief notes on the major ones, given in alphabetical order.

Ada (Ada Lovelace, who is sometimes described as the first programmer, worked with Charles Babbage), developed in 1980 from ALGOL and Pascal by the US military—very good for real-time work, growing in interest to commerce

ALGOL (ALGOrithmic Language), 1960, mainly used with students; very good for designing solutions to problems in science and engineering; compiled

BASIC (Beginners' All-purpose Symbolic Instruction Code), a general purpose system first published in 1964 for teaching, but now widely used and available in hundreds of dialects; numbers all instructions, though modern dialects offer much structure; interactive, so usually interpreted

COBOL (COmmon Business Oriented Language), still the main business program language (though first published in 1960), being good for file handling and input/output control; a COBOL program has four divisions—**identifi-**

Figure 5.11 *There are three possible looping structures*

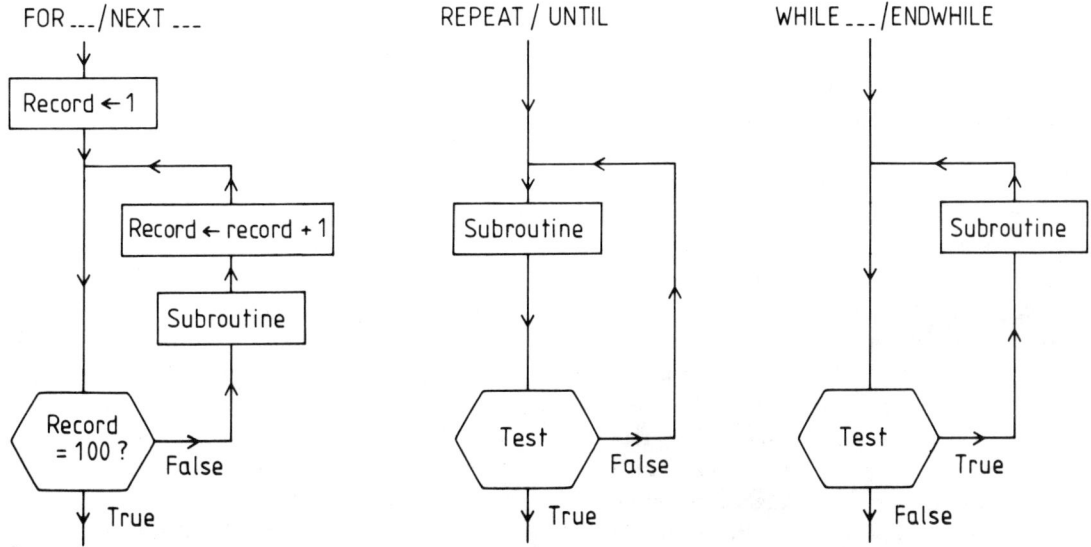

cation (describing the program), **environment** (describing the hardware system and data files), **data** (describing the data structures in detail), and **procedure** (listing the actual instructions); instructions appear very much like English sentences, so the system has a high memory demand; compiled

Forth (Fo(u)rth generation language), very compact procedural stack-based language (Section 4.3), widely used for real-time control; semi-compiled

FORTRAN (FORmula TRANslator), the first high-level language—IBM 1950s but updated since; very good for mathematical work (thus science and engineering), poor otherwise; procedure-based but poor in structure; compiled

Logo (designed for logical thinking), widely thought to be for youngsters to draw pictures and control robots with, but in fact a very powerful procedural list processing language; interpreted

Modula-2, a polished and extended Pascal, the module being its new concept; general purpose; compiled

Pascal (after Blaise Pascal, a 17th-century natural philosopher who developed calculating machines), a general purpose teaching language first published in 1971; compact and highly structured, with all declarations first; compiled

PROLOG (for PROgramming in LOGic), a compact interpreted language for machine intelligence work

The software involved with machine intelligence (Case study 9 and Section 9.1) lets the system draw conclusions and/or use 'fuzzy' (flexible) logic. To some people, this software is a layer of the onion outside that of the high-level program languages. I view it as just a rather thicker alternative layer. The same applies to the software used for content-free applications like word processing, spreadsheets and data base handling.

In any case, though, a program or machine intelligence language lies between the OS and the user's special purpose applications software and data. However, I must make clear that almost all computer users need know even less about program languages than about operating software. Programming knowledge is essential only if you want to write applications software or to tailor other people's to your own specific purpose.

People devise applications programs, the outermost layer of the software onion, with a particular task in mind; also (in theory, if not always in practice) they do so with a particular range of contexts in mind. Much (but not all) applications software depends on particular program languages; thus, a lot of the programs designed to run on home and school micros are written in BASIC. Don't forget, though, the point made about language versions. Just as OS like CP/M differs to some degree or other with each system it works on, so does language software. This is specially true of BASIC, the language of personal computers, for progress in the features offered by these machines has been astounding. For instance, we've moved in half a decade from monochrome upper case text as the only output to text using large character sets, with full colour, high-quality graphics and multi-voice sound.

There are two reasons why this applies to BASIC so much more than to other program languages. The first is obvious—its universal availability. The second is less so—BASIC is an interactive, interpreted, conversational context: most of the progress has been in making the interaction more effective and friendly.

Such work on the user interface is particularly important where someone not a computer expert works interactively with a system. The user **interface** is the link between user and system—nowadays normally keyboard and screen. A user-friendly interface is one where users always know what to do and how and why to do it. They should never feel unsure, confused, threatened or embarrassed. Even at OS level, user-friendly software provides a clear, uncluttered layout and the right amount of help on screen and on call.

As the user of almost any system (batch or interactive) will get printouts, the design of these too should be friendly—clear and well laid out.

SELF-DEVELOPMENT QUESTIONS

See Pages 136–137 for notes on these questions.

S5.1   List the eight main tasks of a mainframe's operating software and write a paragraph on each.

S5.2   Discuss which of the eight main tasks of a mainframe's operating software don't apply in the case of a micro.

S5.3   Outline, with a sketch like Figure 5.3, how a scheduler would share the resources of a large mainframe between programs to

   a   work out the value of pi to a million places,
   b   find the pay due to each of a thousand staff and print out the payslips, and
   c   word process a lengthy report.

S5.4   How do you think the system would allocate interrupt priorities for the jobs listed in S5.3?

S5.5   Select five tasks from each of the two lists for a micro user (the last two lists in Section 5.2) and research how to carry them out on a machine to which you have access.

S5.6   If your school or college has a hard disc in use, produce a poster showing its directory structure.

S5.7   If your school or college has a hard disc in use, comment on how and how often data is backed up.

S5.8   Distinguish with care between multiprogramming, multi-access, and multiprocessing. Sketch the hardware layout of each style of working.

S5.9   Chat with someone who works with batching. Make brief notes, including regarding the job control language.

S5.10   Find out the contexts in which your school or

college computer uses spooling. Make brief notes.

S5.11 Show how time sharing differs in multiprogramming and multi-user contexts.

S5.12 Distinguish with care between machine coding and assembly coding; describe the use of any special software.

S5.13 Find out how to code a simple assembly program, and produce and test one.

S5.14 Most assemblers can work with ten or more addressing modes. If this interests you, find out about them and make brief notes.

S5.15 Write out in English a set of instructions so someone can decide whether to take an umbrella to work. Comment on how easy or hard it would be for a robot to follow these instructions.

S5.16 How would the BASIC instruction **INPUT age%** appear in assembler?

S5.17 There's nothing like **INPUT age%** in COBOL. Why not? Note other ways in which COBOL differs from BASIC.

S5.18 Write a program to add two given numbers and display the result in as many high-level languages as you can. Comment.

S5.19 Discuss the quality of the OS user interface of a system you know, and of that of several different applications programs.

EXAMINATION QUESTIONS

Q5.1 **a** Distinguish carefully between the three processing modes batch, on-line, and interactive.

(9)

 b Discuss the factors which influence the choice of processing mode for the following systems:

 i an enquiry system for a life assurance company

(3)

 ii an order processing system for a mail order company.

(London)

(AEB specimen paper) (4)

Q5.2 A particular operating system for a certain computer allows a single directory per floppy disc. A more developed operating system for the same computer allows tree structured directories.

 a Give one advantage and one disadvantage of the simpler operating system.

 b Describe two advantages of tree structured directories.

 c Describe two operating system commands that must be part of the more advanced system and not part of the simpler system.

 (London) (6)

Q5.3 In a computer system the central processing unit and peripheral devices are coordinated by the operating system. State two functions which an operating system might provide.

 (London) (1)

Q5.4 A particular multiprogramming system is to run jobs of two types: type A and type B. Jobs of type A make much use of the central processor but not much use of peripherals. Jobs of type B make significantly less use of the central processor and more use of peripherals. State, with reasons, to which of these two types of jobs the scheduler should assign the highest priority.

 (JMB) (3)

Q5.5 The computing department in a school was asked to investigate the use of a microcomputer to control the stage lighting. Their report pointed out that the program would have to be written in machine code. Why should the program have to be written in machine code?

 (JMB) (1)

Q5.6 **a** State briefly the main difference between a compiler and an interpreter.

[2]

 b Why is interpretation often more suited to small computers than compilation?

 (COSSEC) [2]

Q5.7 Microcomputers often store systems software in read only storage whereas large computers normally use backing store for this purpose. State one advantage of each of these methods for storing systems software.

 (COSSEC) [2]

Q5.8 A computer with a 12-bit word length has 72 machine code operations, eight registers, and four addressing modes. Draw a diagram to show a suitable format for machine code instructions.

 (COSSEC) [4]

Q5.9 **a** Explain what is meant by the term multi-programming and describe briefly how it works and why it is useful.

 b Two programs which run in a multiprogramming system both direct output to a line printer during their execution. There is only one printer available. Explain briefly how spooling makes it possible for the two programs to run concurrently. State the main reasons why such a system uses spooling.

 (COSSEC) [6]

Q5.10 A floppy disc unit connected to a single-user microcomputer system is used for the permanent storage of programs and data. What facilities would you expect the operating system of the computer to provide to enable users to maintain their disc files?

 (COSSEC) [8]

6 Filing cabinet

Figure 6.1 *Using computers to process fingerprint information is not straightforward* (Metropolitan Police)

Case study 6—The Police National Computer

There are over a hundred police forces in Britain. They're independent of each other, but IT links have brought them much closer together. The Police National Computer (PNC) is the most important of those links. The data base is on offer to over a thousand terminals—this is a multi-user package.

The data base consists of three main files—the criminal names index (with some five million records), the vehicle index (well over twenty million records), and the suspect vehicles index. (There's also a fingerprint index, but the system here is too new for all forces yet to have direct access to it.)

Andrea Harbinger is a Sergeant in an East Midlands police force. Tonight she is on patrol on the M1 motorway, parked at the side of the road. Suddenly a white sports car races by at very high speed. Andrea and her partner try to note the number and a brief description, but the car is going so fast they don't do very well. They decide to investigate.

As Andrea accelerates in pursuit, her partner radios their control centre. The best they can do for the car number is A (or B) 123 SOB (or SDB), but at least they have the make and colour. The officer on duty enters the details into her terminal link to the PNC.

The system finds no matching record in the index of suspect vehicles. This file contains details of registration and chassis numbers of stolen vehicles and of others in which the police have some interest. (It also holds records of heavy equipment, such as construction industry and mining machines, and of boat engines.) People can search either by registration number or by chassis number. In this case the staff use the former method, but the system comes up with no vehicle with a registration number like that reported.

The search now moves to the main vehicle index. This contains details of all registered vehicles—owner (and address), numbers and description. The details come from the Driving and Vehicle Licence Centre computer at Swansea. [Should they?] The partial car number and the brief description are enough to identify the speeding car—and the owner, who, it turns out, bought it just a couple of weeks ago. Another quick check on the PNC—this time of the name index—shows that the owner is disqualified because of a recent drink-driving offence. The station informs Andrea at once.

Thus, only half a minute after the report went in from Andrea's car, she learns she's right to be zooming down the motorway. She can't yet see the car she's chasing, so she asks the control centre to warn the next patrol down the road. The driver of that police car should have no trouble stopping the speedster—and will have all the details needed to question the driver.

Andrea enjoys dealing with IT. So much of traditional police work is boring slog—the PNC is a great advance as it gets enquiries dealt with fast and cuts paper work.

So too do the local police force's own systems. These allow the staff to handle such tasks as

- keeping track automatically of all the force's cars
- analysing crimes to detect patterns
- ensuring they deal quickly with enquiries and emergency calls
- looking after automatic burglar alarm calls
- sharing jobs out fairly

She's keen too to explore the automation of motorway patrol work. One new system she's hoping to use is a car-mounted unit which takes photos of speeding cars, showing their number plates, and giving date, time and speed. They've tried one a bit like this that sits on motorway bridges, but she doesn't think it's so good as it isn't on line to a control centre, so doesn't allow rapid response.

Introduction

The massive data base of the PNC was the hero of that tale, but without the radiophone—an important field of modern IT—the suspect would have got away. IT is *not* just about computers. Computing isn't just about hardware, software and data either. I raised a little question for you to think about in that case study—should the DVLC computer pass data to the PNC? It's easy to do so (why?)—but is it right? Indeed should *any* Government IT system share data on citizens with others?

We'll turn in Chapter 10 to such matters, but really you should bear them in mind throughout the course. Questions like those become crucial when we deal with powerful electronic data bases of personal information. Data bases, and the files they include, are the subject of this chapter.

A file is any chunk of data with a name in main or backing store. Here we shall think only of data files (those with a single information topic) in backing store; text files, program files, spooled files, and scratch (temporary) files are separate.

Objectives

When you have worked through this chapter, you should be able to

1 outline the use of the three main data files in the Police National Computer
2 list local police uses of IT
3 describe the structure of a hierarchical data base
4 define 'key field' and comment on its use
5 compare fixed and variable length records and fields
6 outline the steps involved in file creation
7 note methods of data compaction (compression)
8 discuss the tasks of file searching and sorting
9 comment on file size, growth, activity and volatility
10 compare the physical arrangement of serial, sequential, indexed sequential, and direct access files
11 discuss simple hashing algorithms
12 describe the grandparent/parent/child approach to data security
13 outline how to merge two data files
14 compare, with examples of data items concerned, data validation and verification
15 describe the use and value of check digits
16 list and discuss methods of data security

6.1 Files

A file is a very important data structure; it's of most value where the amount of data is very large and/or where the data items are mixed in type. To input data items, process them, and output them involves the CPU and main store (except where spooling techniques are concerned—Section 5.3). A file of any great size must live in backing store, however, and much of this chapter deals with how that's done.

Often, as in the case of the PNC, a file is one of a number that form a data bank (or base). Each file holds a set of data for a given purpose. A firm's data bank may include, for instance, files of details of staff, customers, suppliers, and stock items. Each file consists of a number of records. A record is the set of data about one entity (person or stock item, say) in a file.

The actual data lives in a number of fields in the record. A field is storage space for one attribute (data item, such as a phone number or staff code) for an entity. Figure 6.2 shows the hierarchical nature of such a data bank. Alongside the tree I give examples from a library card index.

The concept of a **key field** appears in the figure. In most cases we define each record by its key field; in most cases, then, if you want a file put in order on the basis of the key field, it's wise to give each record a unique value for the purpose. Examples are the accession number of a library book, your national insurance number, the item number held in a bar code, a standard book number, your bank account number, a car's registration number. Key codes don't have to be real numbers (as the examples show); however, use of numbers cuts down processing time.

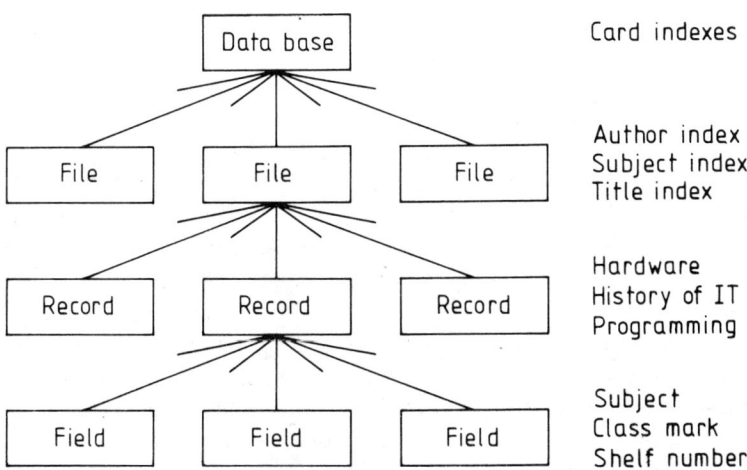

Card indexes

Author index
Subject index
Title index

Hardware
History of IT
Programming

Subject
Class mark
Shelf number

Figure 6.2 *A data base of files has a hierarchical structure*

Sometimes you can't give a unique key to each record. There'd then have to be a hierarchy of key fields. For instance, it's not worth the trouble to give a number to each student in a college (though some places do). The primary key would then be surname; where more than one person has the same surname, you'd also use the given name; birth date could be a third key in this hierarchy.

In any event, the key may change with purpose. For each book in a library, the staff may wish to produce three index cards, to be put in sets of drawers in order of accession number (for office use), author name (for the author index), and class code (for the subject file). Each card would carry the same data items, but in a different order and in a different layout. What a lot of work, to prepare and sort three sets of cards! What a lot of space is taken up! Holding the book data as a computer file means you need just to change the key field, sort on the basis of the new key—and print out the new version you want. (Of course it's even better to use the data bank itself, with access to records on screen rather than on cards.)

Libraries have long been an obvious field of computerisation, therefore. A record of a book needs typing only once now. You can then sort the book file records in three ways, to produce accession number, author, and subject files. After that you can leave the three files in the data base for people to search as required. You can also print them out onto cards for a traditional index or (more common now) onto microform for use with microform readers (Section 3.5).

Let's think again about the user interface as far as concerns record output. Say you're in a library and search the author file for details of the book in front of you now. You'll expect to find a card, microform display, or computer screen looking something like Figure 6.3—the order of items

and the layout are crucial aspects of user-friendly output.

As far as concerns data storage, there's a lot of wasted space there, though. In a backing store file (like all stored data structures, it is linear, not two-dimensional), the data would be as in Figure 6.4: as compact (compressed) as possible to save precious space. Saving space isn't good for its own sake alone—it also leads to time savings in various ways.

There I used variable length fields, so each needs an end of field marker. This is a special character—one that wouldn't otherwise appear—that the system can look out for. Fixed length fields need no markers and are simpler to process; on the other hand, they lead to a lot of wasted space. (All this also applies to variable and fixed length records.)

It's the programmer's job to instruct the system how to read in the data of the record, check it's the one needed, and display it as in Figure 6.3. Searching a file for a given record involves loading records block by block into main store (Section 3.4) and checking till a match appears. Then the data items from the various fields of that record would go neatly laid out onto the screen. The programmer would add the titles, messages, punctuation marks, colour codes, special symbols (for copyright, pound sign and such) and other extra bits and bobs—there's no point storing those on the tape or disc in every record.

Some of the code concerned might look like this:

```
OPEN authors
REPEAT
  READ authors: name1$, name2$, dob$,
    title$, class, . . .
  IF name1$ = "DEESON" AND name2$ =
"ERIC"
    ND dob$ = "1942" THEN display . . .
  . . .
UNTIL EOF OR notmore [end of file or search]
CLOSE authors

PROCdisplay
  CLS
  PRINT' 'Author: "+name1$+", "+name2$
  . . .
more [ask if user wants search to go on]
```

Transfers between main and backing store are the essence of file handling software. Indeed the work involved is much like that based on paper files in a filing cabinet—except you don't have to get off your chair. There are various possible

Figure 6.3 *For user-friendliness, a record should appear clearly laid out on screen*

```
DEESON, Eric                        001.5
1942 –
Computing and Information Technology

Basil Blackwell
1988

pp x ii + 164                      £ 6.95

ISBN  0  631  90168  X

                              Acc 9876
```

Figure 6.4 *In a file, the data is compact and in linear sequence*

Name	Fore name	Birth	Title	Class	Publisher	Date
Deeson	Eric	1942	Computing and Information Technology	001.5	Basil Blackwell	1988 etc.
field 1	2	3	4	5	6	7

tasks—creating a new file, searching a file for data, processing the data in a file, and updating the contents. In each case, you need to open the file first, and to close it when you're done with it.

Physically, creation involves no more than opening the new file, giving it a name (and perhaps directory—Section 5.3), feeding in the data, and closing it. It's wise first, however, to plan the structure, especially if you're using fixed length fields, and to work out how best to compact the data.

I mentioned above very simple ways to compact data. Using codes in at least some fields may save huge amounts of space (and, therefore, access time later). Thus you can store gender as 1 bit (0 for male, 1 for female), the last two characters of the year as a 6-bit integer, paid/unpaid code as one bit, and so on. That would mean bit-wise processing, but those three ideas reduce four or more bytes to one: a big saving when the file consists of many thousand records.

Searching a file for given data (interrogating it) is its main use; it's therefore a task you must make as efficient as possible. Searching is much quicker if the records are in key field order and the system can go direct to the right area.

Look again at the fragment of code above for searching an author file for 'DEESON'. If there were no matching records, or only one right at the end of the file, the system would have to check every single record. On the other hand, if the records were in alphabetical order of author surname, the search routine could check quickly till it came to the Ds, check through the Ds properly, and then stop. Even better would be to use an index, with a sequential (or ordered) or a direct access file. Then the search could start at just the right area.

Indexed sequential and direct access files (Section 6.2) are a method of arranging the data physically in backing store. As you can use them only with disc, planning a new file must take into account the physical storage methods you have.

From the above it may be clear that sorting records into a new order is, after searching, a second major aspect of file processing. There are various methods of handling the task, all beyond the scope of this book. All are tedious too—sorting a big file is a job for overnight. We've met the example of sorting a library book file three ways: not an easy task.

Planning should also take account of the file's likely size and rate of growth. These will affect its physical layout in backing store. They will also affect its logical structure: in terms of record size, number and size of fields, compaction, and so on. Other file characteristics the planner should bear in mind are likely activity and volatility.

A file's activity is measured by the hit rate. If in a normal day's working you process (match or change) 200 records in a 1000-record file, the hit rate (activity) is 20%. Don't confuse this with the file's volatility; this measures the rate at which you delete old records and insert new ones. An unpaid bills file would be volatile but not very active; a library book file would be active but not so volatile; a file of last year's insurance policy holders would be fairly inactive and static (not at all volatile).

Before turning to methods of file updating (changing the contents) and maintenance (looking after it in other ways), we need to explore physical structure a bit more.

6.2 Physical files

The logical structure of a hierarchical file is its layout in terms of records and fields (Figure 6.2). Here our concern is with its physical layout in the backing store.

In Section 3.4 we looked at some relevant aspects of magnetic tape and disc; in particular, recall that both store data in blocks, chunks of fixed length. The main reason for wanting fixed length records follows from this—it's far simpler to process a file if you know that, for instance, each block (physical record) contains room for ten logical records.

We describe the different physical files on the basis of how to access their records. The simplest case is the serial (access) file. Here the records follow each other in no special order. A file of the day's transactions for a firm would be like this. The transactions (orders and payments, perhaps) would go into the file in the order of receipt. A serial file will normally be on tape. To find a given record, you would need to work through the file from the start. However, it's not normal to search a serial file: it's too much trouble.

Tape is also often the home of sequential files. Again the records need serial access from the start of the file, but this time they're in key field order. A sorted serial file is therefore sequential; searching it for a given record takes only half as long on average.

If a system is fully tape-based, it can work only with serial and sequential files. As we saw in Section 3.4, the data that tape stores is so tightly packed, there'd be no way to go direct to a given record, even if you knew where it was; anyway, tapes stretch.

Disc-based systems can also work with serial and sequential files. However, discs offer two other types.

The indexed sequential file, as its name implies, appears in sequence on the disc and comes with an index (or more than one). The concept is just the same as with a book, except each index entry would now contain just one address (as the file is sequenced). The index references are to key field values, the key field being the one on which the file is sorted.

There are various methods of indexing; they depend on file size, growth rate and activity (Section 6.1). A large file may have a hierarchical index. Here the first index would be to the disc pack; stored on each disc pack would be a cylinder index; and each cylinder would have a sector index. See Figure 6.5. Note that an index entry is a pointer—an index cell stores the address of the data referred to.

The **direct access** (sometimes called **random access**) file

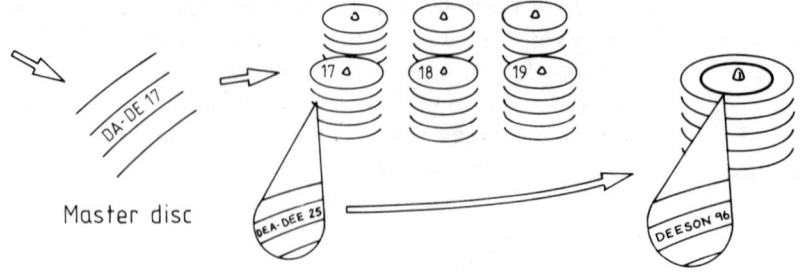

Master disc

Figure 6.5   *A very large file needs a hierarchical index*

also works with pointers. This time, though, the records aren't sequenced in backing store, so sequential file handling isn't possible. Also there's no point in having an index. Instead a hashing algorithm works out the address for each record. Here's a simple example.

Say the file, stored on one surface of a disc, may contain up to 10 000 records of car parts. Each part has a unique number, and the part number is the key. The records are of fixed length, there being ten to a block (disc surface sector). The block holding each record is the part number divided by 10—that's the simplest hashing algorithm. Thus part 3210 would be in track 32 sector 1; so would be records 3211–3219.

As soon as the system knows the part number it could send the disc head to track 32, and get it to copy the content of sector 1 to main store. It would then take only a moment longer to look at the details of record 0 (the first one).

A file like that described would happen also to be sequenced. However, if there are only 5000 car parts, with numbers in the range 0–9999, the records wouldn't be serial. (Some record spaces would be empty.)

In practice, hashing algorithms are a lot more complex—and more efficient—than just dividing by 10. However, they must depend on the physical file and not on its logical structure. This means it may well happen that more records are assigned to a block than there's room for. Some technique of block overflow handling must therefore exist. Then if the system fails to find a match for a given record, it will search the overflow area.

If overflow is likely to be quite common, the planner must set up a series of overflow blocks. This isn't efficient, as search time could then be quite lengthy: the system may have to search several blocks. If overflow isn't common, it's usual to put the extra record in the first free place after the correct block.

The strength of direct access is not only in the speed of interrogation (searching). If the data in a record needs changing, the new record can replace the old one in a very short space of time. Frequent backup is essential in such cases. File back-up is part of file maintenance.

6.3   File maintenance

Keeping a master file up to date is a major aspect of file maintenance. A **master file** is the one you'd use for reference. While some of the data in it is static (unchanging),

it's likely you'd need to amend some every so often. If it's not very volatile, it won't need much updating—so you'd just work with a straight backup copy (duplicate).

A very volatile file needs updating daily, or even more often, in order to keep the records accessed correct. Merging the latest transactions with the master file is an important example.

A firm's transactions often include the day's new orders from, and payments made by, the clients. As these reach the office, the staff build up a transaction file. As we saw in Section 6.2, this will likely be a serial file on tape. During the day the staff will interrogate the master file for their work—but they'll know the details obtained won't all be quite up to date.

To prepare a new master file for the next day is a job for the night shift. At the end of Day 1, we have the master file produced the night before, and Day 1's transaction file. The master file is, let's say, indexed sequential in form, sorted on client code number; to merge the serial transaction file with it, the system must first sort that on the basis of the same key field. Please refer to Figure 6.6, where I assume all files are on tape.

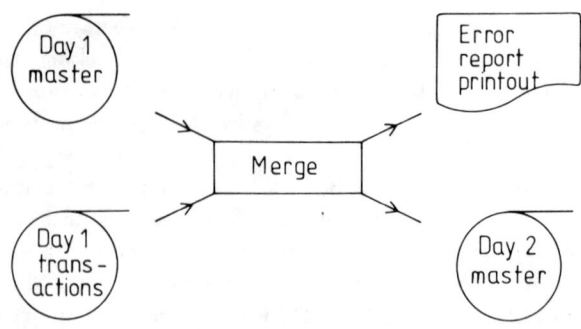

Figure 6.6   *The system merges a sorted (sequential) transaction file with the sequential master file to produce a new master*

Merging involves starting with the two sequential files rewound. Here's the algorithm (where I ignore the blocking factor):

```
repeat
  load next transaction record
  extract key field
  repeat
    load next old master record
    extract key field
    if key fields don't match
```

```
   copy old master record to new
     master file
   endif
 until key fields match
 process old master record
 copy new master record to new master
   file
until end of transaction file
repeat
   copy next master record to new master
     file
until end of old master file
```

Figure 6.6 also shows a second output from the merge process. This is the error report, a list of transactions which didn't match with any master records. Perhaps keying errors weren't trapped by the validation or verification systems (Section 6.4), or maybe there's some other problem. Staff will go through the error report the next day to produce valid transactions and add them to the day's transaction file.

After the merge you may back up the new master in case of accidents to it. This is an aspect of data security (of which more later). A second method, rather than making a straight copy, is the grandparent/parent/child approach. (The words are less sexist than the usual grandfather/father/son!) Figure 6.7 explains this, using the terms we've just worked with.

The master in use today is the child of last night's merge. The parent in that process is yesterday's master, in turn the product of merging the day before yesterday's master (grandparent) and transaction files.

For security, the firm will store the parent with yesterday's transaction file in a safe place (such as a bank). Then if there's a fire in the computer room, they can re-merge, with the loss only of today's transaction file. For further security, the firm may store the grandparent with the day before yesterday's transaction file in a second safe place. All these old files may also be of use if an error turns up.

Updating a file (using a transaction file or otherwise) involves three main tasks. You may wish to delete a record (client bankrupt, book stolen, patient died); add a new one (new customer, book, or patient); or amend a record. To amend a record means changing one or more field contents (insert new address, correct error in book title, note discharge from hospital). If the record's variable in length, you can also add a new field (new order, spare class mark, result of blood test). There's no point in having a data bank with out-of-date data.

6.4 Data security

Aspects of data security came up in the last section. **Security** involves making sure the data in store is correct, safe from loss, and open to access only by authorised people. Data integrity concerns the first of these—having data correct.

Keeping data correct concerns file maintenance, as just discussed. The processes of data validation and verification help ensure it's correct when first keyed in. Data entry is a danger area, for human errors are far more common than other kinds.

Validation is a software process that checks each input data item to see if it's valid. Some that aren't valid are

- a null string book title (no characters)
- date 30 Feb
- patient's year of birth 1842
- 50 000 aircraft ordered
- British post-code like 17B D9S
- 50 000 units of gas used at home in a quarter

Input checking procedures (**'mugtraps'**) in the data entry software should deal with all these, so that all data items keyed are valid. This requires great care in programming.

However, a data item can be valid but still wrong:

- Boggls for Bloggs
- 12 Feb for 21 Feb
- 1924 for 1942
- £5.67 for £50.67

Verification involves having two people enter the same data in turn. It's not likely both will make the same error, so the system looks out for data items that differ. Thus the second keyboard user verifies the entries of the first.

Figure 6.7 *The grandparent/parent/child approach is a method of data security*

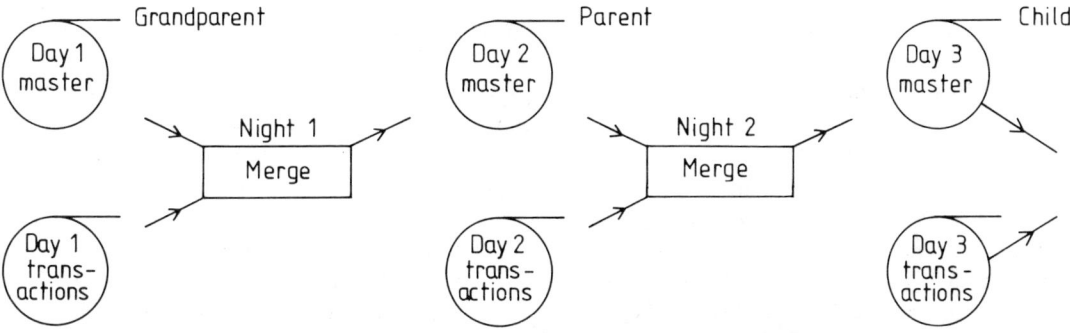

Verification doubles the amount of human work. Machine reading of data (Section 3.6) is one way to reduce this. A second involves check digits.

Check digits are much like parity bits (Section 3.4). They are one or more extra characters (*not* always digits) put at the end of a string or number to allow validation. Here's an example.

A firm's stock item numbers range from 1001 to 9999. In the stock list each number appears with five digits. To obtain the fifth—the check digit—add the four main digits, and keep adding the digits of the result till only one remains. For stock item 1234, for instance, the digits sum to 10, and those in turn sum to 1; the stock number becomes 12341. In the same way, 4567 becomes 45674.

Now, each time someone types a stock number in, the software sums the first four digits. If the result doesn't equal the check digit, this validation routine will issue a warning. Check digits are common as they reduce the need for verification. The International Standard Book Number (ISBN) is the best known case. In practice the algorithm that gives the check digit is more complex than the one I used as a sample. That's because mine wouldn't pick up the most common typing error—transposition, putting two characters in the reverse order. Thus my algorithm wouldn't report 21341 typed instead of 12341.

The second aspect of keeping data secure is to protect it from loss. This means using grandparent/parent/child when files are often merged. It also means using fireproof safes, quality data transfer links, and rules and check systems for the staff. The data librarian looking after thousands of tapes and disc packs will run the system just like a real library, maybe using a micro. Each time a tape goes out for use, the staff note who took it, when, and for what purpose.

This leads to the third aspect of data security. This is making sure only authorised people can access the data. Keys on terminals, passwords, and access logs are all methods used here. For instance, most staff can't enter the DP rooms, while when members of the computing team leave the firm, they'll get no notice and can do no more than clear their desks with someone watching. No staff can access parts of the data base which don't concern their work, and not all will be able to amend records. There's more on this in Section 10.2.

All this applies as much to personal data as to commercial data. However, we'll leave the protection of personal data to Section 10.3.

SELF-DEVELOPMENT QUESTIONS

See Page 137 for notes on these questions.

S6.1   Describe the hierarchical Police National Computer data base.

S6.2   Devise a story, like that in the case study, that involves the three open access PNC files.

S6.3   Visit a police station that works with IT and make notes on (a) the PNC, (b) local uses of computers, and (c) the handling of automatic burglar alarm calls.

S6.4   Prepare your own version of the layout of a record in Figure 6.3 with, as example, your book, record, stamp or other collection, or stock control in the science or IT department.

S6.5   Make notes on the key fields used with *all* the files of S6.4.

S6.6   Work out in detail the pros and cons of fixed length records and fields.

S6.7   Work out other examples of data compaction than those in Section 6.1.

S6.8   Write a case study essay on library computerisation. Include as many different uses of IT as you can.

S6.9   Explain with care the advantages of an electronic data base over the corresponding paper one, using either a library or an office for examples.

S6.10   How would you sort a dropped bundle of library index cards into alphabetical order of authors? Now make notes on how computers sort records.

S6.11   Outline the arrangement of logical records in a serial access file on tape, and in sequential, indexed sequential and direct access files on disc. Discuss the pros and cons.

S6.12   Write an essay to describe how a computerised mail order firm would handle its transactions. Start with a list of possible transaction types.

S6.13   Extend the algorithm in Section 6.3 to allow it to produce error reports (as in Figure 6.6).

S6.14   Outline mugtrapping (input checking) procedures to handle the validity problems in the first list in Section 6.4.

S6.15   List ten examples of valid, but incorrect, data. Describe how verification would be likely to pick up the errors.

S6.16   Write notes on the use of check 'digits' in the International Standard Book Number (ISBN) system.

S6.17   Report fully on the security of data in your school or college. Make any recommendations you think you should.

EXAMINATION QUESTIONS

Q6.1   A motorist is stopped for a minor traffic offence and a enquiry of central police records provides erroneous information that the motorist deserted from the Army eight years earlier. Explain how the error may have occurred, and suggest one control that would have prevented the error.
(AEB specimen paper)   (3)

Q6.2   In order to overcome equipment shortages in schools, the computer centre of the local education authority have decided to introduce an equipment loan service to link with an existing repair and maintenance facility. The system makes the following services available:

- schools may borrow equipment in an emergency caused by the breakdown of their own standard equipment;
- schools have access to specialised hardware (e.g. colour printers, robots, interactive video, etc.) which the authority cannot afford to provide to all schools;
- school equipment is maintained on a routine schedule and repaired as required;
- the local authority computer centre maintains accurate records of the overall situation.

The early analysis of the proposed system's requirements indicated that the use of a data base system presents the best approach.

Describe with the aid of a relevant example in each case:

a the advantages of the data base approach compared with the system involving the use of separate files,

(4)

b how the data can be kept accurate and consistent,

(3)

c how the factual information about breakdowns can be obtained,

(6)

d how unauthorised access to the data may be prevented in a data base environment.

(AEB specimen paper) (3)

Q6.3 From time to time certain parts of a computer system may fail. If on one such occasion the disc controller fails causing a file to be corrupted with the loss of a morning's transactions, discuss the steps that could have been taken beforehand to minimise the possibility of vital information being lost.

(AEB specimen paper) (4)

Q6.4 A typical line of output produced by an applications package used to control the stock in a warehouse is

061286 door hardwood Repton 75.50

Describe three possible valid interpretations of the first field.

(London) (4)

Q6.5 The data capture process for a particular computerised stock control system begins when a standard form is filled in at the stock issue counter. These forms are received and batched by data control. The data is then keyed to floppy disc for processing. Give examples of the types of error likely to occur.

(London) (4)

Q6.6 Distinguish between the *integrity* and the *security* of data.

(London) (4)

Q6.7 Explain how verification and validation might occur at the various stages of using an application package to process a given batch of data.

(London) (7)

Q6.8 A particular index-sequentially organised file is subdivided into blocks. It has a single one-level index. The index has one entry for each block recording the highest key allocated to that block. There is no overflow. The index has already been read into immediate access memory. Give an algorithm, either in words or with the help of a diagram, which, given the key, will efficiently retrieve one record from this file.

(JMB) (4)

Q6.9 To ensure that data which is processed by a computer is feasible, data validation will take place. One method of data validation is by means of check digits. Describe in detail how check digits are used to validate data.

(JMB) (3)

Q6.10 State *one* example where check digits would not be a good method of data validation. For this example, state what method could be used, and explain why this method would be suitable.

(JMB) (3)

Q6.11 A student constructed the following algorithm to update a master file (m/f) with amendments held on a transaction file (t/f) where the records on both files are in ascending key order. The student assumed that all necessary insertions and deletions had already taken place on a previous run.

```
eomf: = false
while eomf = false do
  read (t/f) record
  repeat
    read (m/f) record
    if end of m/f then
      eomf: = true
    else
      if t/f key > m/f key then
        write old m/f record to
        new m/f
      endif
    endif
  until eomf = true or t/f key < =
  m/f key
  if eomf = false then
    update m/f record
    write to new m/f
  endif
endwhile
end
```

By dry running this algorithm using the following data:

transaction file key 2 4 7 12
master file key 1 2 3 4 6 12 13 14 999

(the record with key 999 is a dummy record used to indicate the end of the master file),

a determine which situations the student has not catered for in the algorithm,

(4)

b produce a corrected version of the algorithm to provide for these situations.

(JMB)   (5)

Q6.12 What is a linked list? Describe in detail how you would implement such a list when it is to be stored on a file on disc.

(JMB)   (6)

Q6.13 A football club has a ground, whose accommodation includes 10 000 numbered seats. Each year, in advance of the season, the club sells 3000 season tickets, each of which confers the right to a particular seat at matches. During the season the general public can buy tickets for any of the next three matches and, at peak times, three ticket selling stations are used.

It is proposed to computerise the sale of tickets, printing each ticket only after it is sold.

a Suggest hardware for each station and describe the operation of such a system as seen by a customer.

(5)

b What files are necessary and what information will they hold?

(4)

c Which types of file should these be and when will they be first created?

(4)

d What prevents the ticket for the same seat being sold simultaneously by two or more stations?

(2)

e How can the transaction time be reduced in such a system?

(2)

f What benefits might be expected from such a system?

(JMB)   (3)

Q6.14 Describe briefly the design of a rates data base. What are the problems which can occur when trying to access a rate payer by name? How are the difficulties overcome?

(COSSEC)   [10]

Q6.15 A large multi-access computer system provides on-line disc storage for programs and data. What precautions should be taken to protect users' files in the event of either a hardware or software malfunction which results in the accidental destruction of some or all of the disc files? Describe how the users' files could be reconstructed if such a malfunction did occur.

(COSSEC)   [10]

Q6.16 A library computer system makes use of two files held on disc, the book file and the transaction file. During the day the book file is used to provide information for library staff and users about the books and their availability, while the transaction file is built up, consisting of the details of books borrowed and returned and new books acquired by the library that day. At night the transaction file is used to update the book file.

Making any assumptions you think fit, describe the structures for these two files. What precautions should be taken to minimise the danger of losing either of the files?

Describe in outline the processing involved in the night run. During this processing, why should the updating file be held on a different disc from the main file if possible?

(COSSEC)   (25)

7 Program development

Figure 7.1 *Desktop (personal) publishing is a superb extension of word processing* (T.V.E.I. (Technical Vocational Education Initiative))

Figure 7.2 *Traditional publishing involves a lot of time and cost; it can also lead to errors*

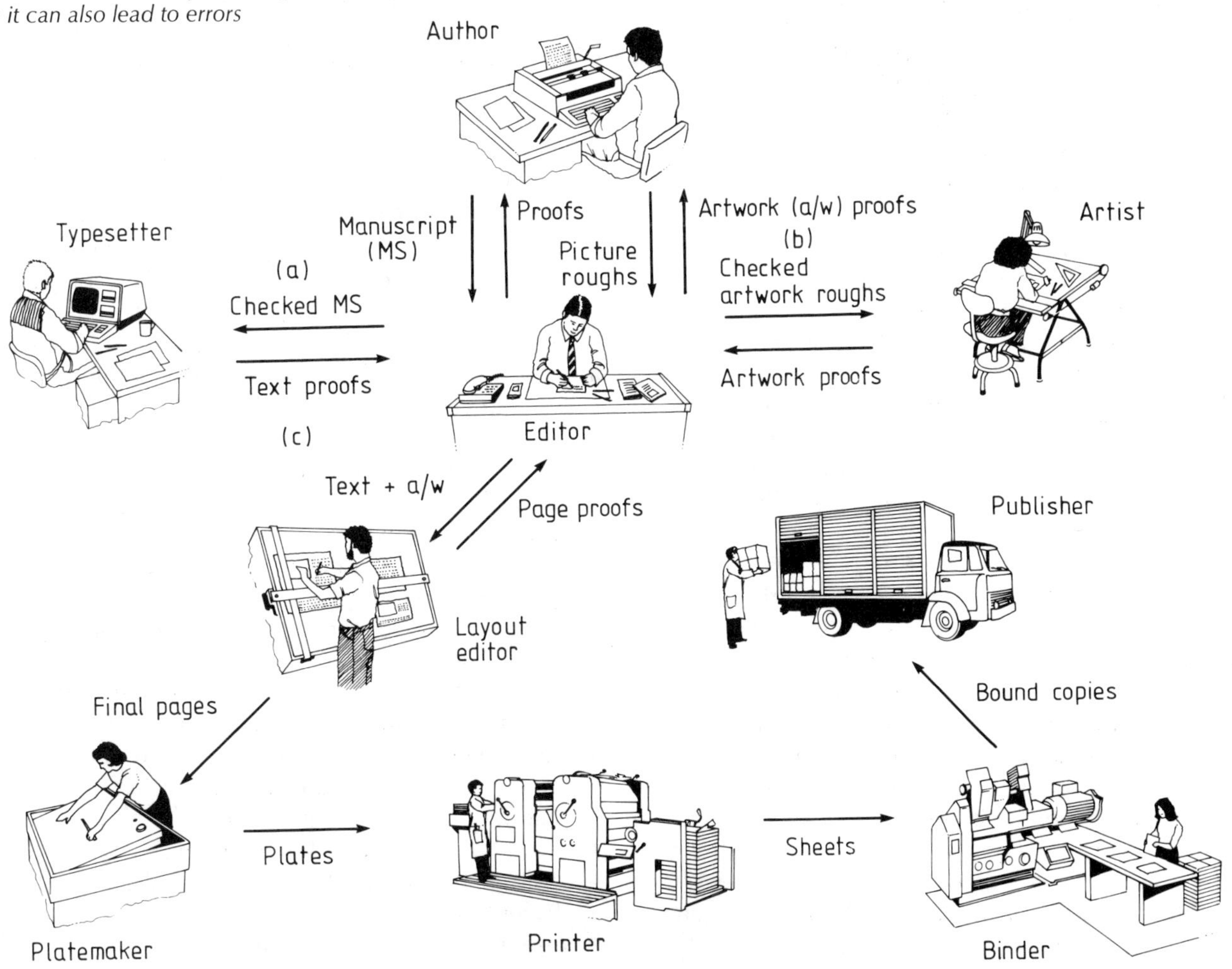

Case study 7—Esther gets personal

Esther Boswell, partner in CompAid, a small computer consultancy firm, is very excited. A few months ago, they bought a desktop publishing (DTP) package to run on their little network, and Esther has just finished using it to produce quite a major report. While it took her a lot of time to get to know the new software—she practised with small tasks—she's highly pleased at how well her first real product has come out.

Desktop publishing is so called as it brings to one person's work surface all the tasks of publishing. The tasks are those of author, editor, graphic artist and layout staff. Traditionally each such person works alone and calls on special skills. While DTP software doesn't mean those skills are no longer of value, it does make it very easy for one person to produce fair work. (It also makes it very

Author

Typesetter

Manuscript (MS)

(a)

Checked MS

Text proofs

(c)

Proofs

Picture roughs

Artwork (a/w) proofs
(b)
Checked artwork roughs

Artwork proofs

Artist

Editor

Text + a/w

Page proofs

Layout editor

Publisher

Final pages

Bound copies

Plates

Sheets

Platemaker

Printer

Binder

easy for one person to bungle all the skills and come up with awful results.)

Figure 7.2 shows the flow of work in traditional publishing. The flows all take time; they also lead to heavy costs and extra errors, for often people type much the same text two or three times.

When you publish a document such as a report, you make it ready for a print shop and then distribute the printed and bound copies to the public. Only very large firms have their own print shops—CompAid doesn't, and what Esther did was produce top quality copies of the report's pages. Their local printer is now photographing these into the form needed for printing; they will produce and bind the copies, and return them (with the bill) to CompAid in a few days.

Esther's report is in fact on the subject of DTP, for many of their clients have lately been asking about it. It's only a little introduction—sixteen sides of A5 (text and lots of illustrations) and a coloured cover. Esther's job was to

- write the text (acting as author),
- check it (the editor's role),
- lay it out into paged sections with the illustrations (layout and graphics),
- check it all again (this time more than usual with the help of her partner Keith Starsky), and
- dump a copy of the document page by page to the printer.

The first two jobs are standard for a word processor. CompAid's DTP software suite *PageAnt* includes a word processor. All the same, while this is fairly good, it doesn't work in the same way as the one Esther's used to. To prepare the text, therefore, Esther used her usual word processor and spooled the output onto disc in a form *PageAnt* could handle. Being able to do this was one of the reasons Esther and Keith chose this package from the many on the market.

After the text, the second element of a report is the graphic illustrations. As we have seen, there are different kinds of graphics. In this case, there was a need for photos, a couple of business graphics (bar charts and such, Figure 2.13), and half a dozen line diagrams. The last two types were easy to deal with.

To produce the charts, Esther again used one of CompAid's old programs—a spreadsheet (in fact part of their integrated business software package). She typed in and checked the numbers, then once more spooled the data to disc so *PageAnt* could deal with it. *PageAnt* hasn't a true spreadsheet—just a module of cells able to receive string and numeric data from elsewhere. However, *PageAnt*'s graphics module is very good. Esther scanned the sixteen graph types shown in picture form on screen, and chose the few she thought best for the purpose; she then had the software put her data into those forms and made her final choice. After that, *PageAnt* saved the

graphics data ready for later.

That was all very quick and pleasant. The DTP suite's two-dimensional design module was also quite good enough for Esther to spend no more than half an hour on each of her line diagrams. Again, she saved these to disc ready for the page layout stage.

CompAid doesn't (yet) have the hardware to deal with photos, however. What they would use is a scanner. This (Section 3.5) is much like a modern copier. However, instead of building a copy of the scanned image up on paper, it sends it to the computer to build it up on screen. There, you can edit the picture before saving the final version. Still, Esther can't do that—all she can do is keep safe the photos she wants, and leave numbered spaces for them in the pages. The print shop will then put the photos into the gaps.

After about a week's work, then, Esther had on disc the word processed text of the report and the images of the charts and line diagrams. Next she had to lay out the material—text, graphics and spaces for photos—onto the sixteen pages, doing this one at a time on screen.

This page layout stage of DTP usage needs careful planning and a good eye for appearance (balance of items, amount of white space, and such). A report like Esther's is quite complex: it's not like a book, with continuous text and a picture here and there. Esther's pages break into two columns, and she needed a lot of care to ensure a clear layout and an easy-to-follow sequence.

In fact she took a rough printout of the text the right width and set to with scissors and paste to try different effects. 'Cut and paste' traditionally describes the work of a layout artist; DTP software cuts out cut and paste, but Esther hasn't yet had enough practice. She therefore plans her pages with fingers as well as eyes before going back to the keyboard. At the keyboard, she creates each page of the report in turn, while still treating it as a whole. Here's a list of some of the things she can do, not in any special order. She can

- change text fonts (typefaces), styles, and sizes throughout the document or in any part of it
- set blocks of text into almost any number of columns
- adjust character and line spacing and margin sizes, and do so very finely
- change the size, format (shape), and placing of any illustration
- add banners, boxing, and special designs (such as the bullets which mark each item of this list, and logos)
- use foreign alphabet material and other special characters (for scientific writing, for instance), including ones she can design herself
- have the system check her spelling
- call up the on-line thesaurus—a collection of words by meaning
- use automatic hyphenation

- set text with proportional spacing and with various forms of justification
- produce contents and index lists if needed
- insert rules—straight lines—to help break pages into smaller chunks
- insert boxes, with all kinds of edge, and with angled or curved corners, to keep separate material separate
- call on a library of icons and logos, including ones she designs herself

A full list would be much longer, but I hope this gives you the flavour of a DTP (personal) publishing package.

Once Esther had worked through the pages of the document on screen, and checked draft printouts till she was happy, she printed final master copies out for the print shop. A modern page printer (Section 3.5) is best for this purpose—but these are quite costly machines and CompAid can't afford one yet. What Esther therefore did was print the pages of her report as A4 sheets. The print shop can reduce these to A5 (half size), at a stroke doubling resolution and clarity. Esther checked the effect with the reducing feature on the office copier—the results pleased her very much. Indeed she thinks her pages are lovely in all ways—hence her excitement.

Software like this has many uses. Some which Esther and Keith feel may be of interest to CompAid in the future are to produce:

- advertisements
- agendas
- briefing notes
- brochures
- certificates
- circuit diagrams with notes
- circulars

- financial statements
- forms
- graphic memo sheets
- greeting cards
- a house magazine for their clients
- instructions
- letter heads
- literature
- mail shots
- manuals
- maps (simple ones anyway)
- menus
- minutes
- news sheets
- notices
- plans
- posters
- price lists
- printed stationery
- questionnaires
- reports
- specifications
- staff lists
- training units
- visiting cards

This kind of software isn't just for long documents, like reports and book(let)s, with text and illustrations. Indeed, DTP is an advanced form of word processor, so has something to offer to *any* sort of document. It isn't hard to learn and to use, and can produce high quality output very quickly. Keith is thinking of getting such a package for his home micro; he plans to use it to help his children's school with a magazine.

Introduction

Let me repeat a message from that case study—'It is very easy for a person to bungle ... and come up with awful results.' There are dangers in leaping into a use of IT without knowing what's involved. Thinking and planning are crucial.

Consider setting up a personnel file, the kind of task discussed in the last chapter. It's a big task—at least, there is a lot of data to type in. However, if the file structure doesn't fully match the needs of the file's users, that work could well be a waste. Before you set up the file, you need to analyse with care the present and likely future needs of the system. This is **systems analysis** (Section 9.2).

Just the same applies to program development, the subject of this chapter. Nowadays, with easy access to computers and interactive program languages like BASIC, it's tempting to sit down with an idea and to keep on keying till the program works. Although it may work, it's not likely to be a good one—it *should* be fully correct, versatile, friendly, easy to amend in future. If you wish or need to design programs, make them good ones . . . .

Objectives

When you have worked through this chapter, you should be able to

1 outline the features of desktop publishing (DTP) software
2 describe how to use a DTP program to produce a well laid out document of text and graphics
3 show how planning helps effective IT use
4 state the nature of programming and the concept and advantages of top–down development

5 state what makes a program efficient

6 discuss in detail the steps of program development

7 compare algorithms in English, pseudocode, flowchart, and structure chart form

8 list the aims of program testing and approaches to it

9 list and compare the different types of error

10 explain the need for, and list the contents of, user and programmer documentation

7.1   What programming is about

This book is not a programming text, but this course involves something of the theory of software development. Here, as elsewhere, there are good habits and bad habits. If you want or need to learn programming, getting into good habits early on will make you glad later. Then your work, fun, or profit-making programming will be less work, more fun, and—who knows?—more profitable.

Programming involves the design of an ordered set of instructions, in a form the computer can follow, to carry out some given task. Crucial concepts in program development —*not* the same as programming (coding) itself—are planning, using top–down development, the aim being software that is efficient and friendly.

The essence of good habits in programming is planning. Indeed good programmers plan their planning. The worst thing to do when you get a program idea—trivial or world-shattering—is to sit at the keyboard and start typing. If you do that, you'll get into an awful mess. Even if the result seems to work, it won't be very efficient—it may have bugs in it (dreaded hidden errors that may lurk for months before springing out at the user); and it won't impress the folk who look at it as much as it should.

Efficiency in programming means having a product which

- works as you plan in all contexts,
- works at the right speed,
- uses as little memory as possible, and

- looks good to all who see it.

The essence of program design is an approach called **top–down development**. This means breaking your initial idea into smaller and more detailed chunks—concepts—till, at last, each one is a unit that's easy to handle. In practice we use the word '**module**' for each of those final units.

Coding is (fairly) simple when you've the idea in fragments before you. Each fragment—concept or module—can then transfer to a module of the program. People often call such a chunk of code a routine, or **subroutine**, or **procedure**. Module will do for any such chunk at any stage, and you should note that a **procedure** is strictly an advanced type of closed subroutine with special features. The sketch in Figure 7.3 shows what the planning part of top–down programming entails. You see what I mean? The original broad concept fragments into a lot of small chunks, mind-sized ones for easy brain-storming. The picture's a hierarchical one, a bit like the structure of our lungs—and for much the same reason: efficiency of processing.

Maybe the programs you're now writing are short. While you don't have to work out such a detailed set of modules for them, it's good to view your program not just as a whole, but also as a number of separate parts. Each part has its own aim; you'll code each part separately, and you'll test each part separately. Then the whole thing is much more likely to be neat, efficient, and bug-free.

If that sounds tough, take heart from the experience of professional programmers—the average rate of coding a major software product is about 15 instructions a day. (A 'major' software project, by the way, may have a million of them.)

7.2   Top–down development

Top–down development entails developing an idea, stage by stage, in a logical kind of way, so when you come to the coding itself, there's little problem. Here are the steps

Figure 7.3   *Top–down planning is the essence of programming*

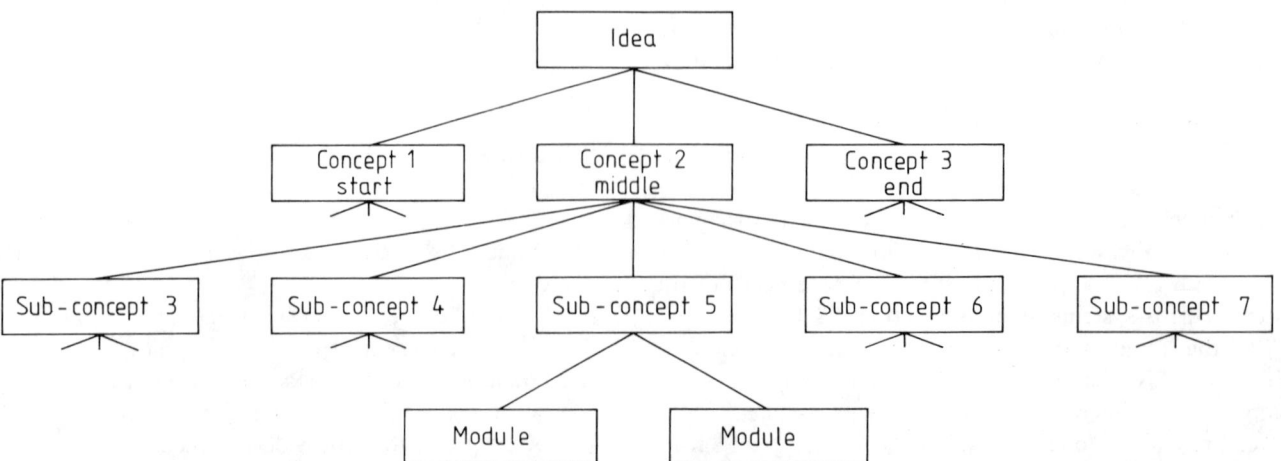

involved:

- Have an idea for a program to deal with a problem that a computer can best handle.
- Work out, from the user's point of view, what the program should do—in other words, define the problem.
- Work out, from a programmer's point of view, how the software should do it—define the solution. This involves producing an algorithm. An **algorithm** is a solution to a problem, in the form of an ordered set of logical steps. It may appear as a series of plain-language instructions, as a mix of program language terms and English (pseudocode), or in picture form (a flowchart or structure chart).
- Code the program section by section, with each section relating to a step in the algorithm. As you go along, test and document.
- Complete testing and documentation.

In computing, flowcharts and structure charts relate subroutines and outline their action. It's as important that a programmer, systems analyst (Section 9.2), or software engineer can devise and read a chart, as that an electrician or electrical engineer can handle circuit diagrams. Indeed, the concepts are very much the same: in both cases the diagram shows quickly and efficiently what's involved, and is simpler to check than the structure it stands for. Compare the circuit diagram in Figure 7.4 with the actual circuit beside it—which is better for showing a reader who knows the rules what the circuit's about?

As far as concerns flowcharts, a number of different standards exist; the variations are mainly in advanced use. I'll give here one set of rules and the symbols (Figure 7.5) that go with them.

a A flowchart should have only one start and (preferably no more than) one end. Symbols—START and END

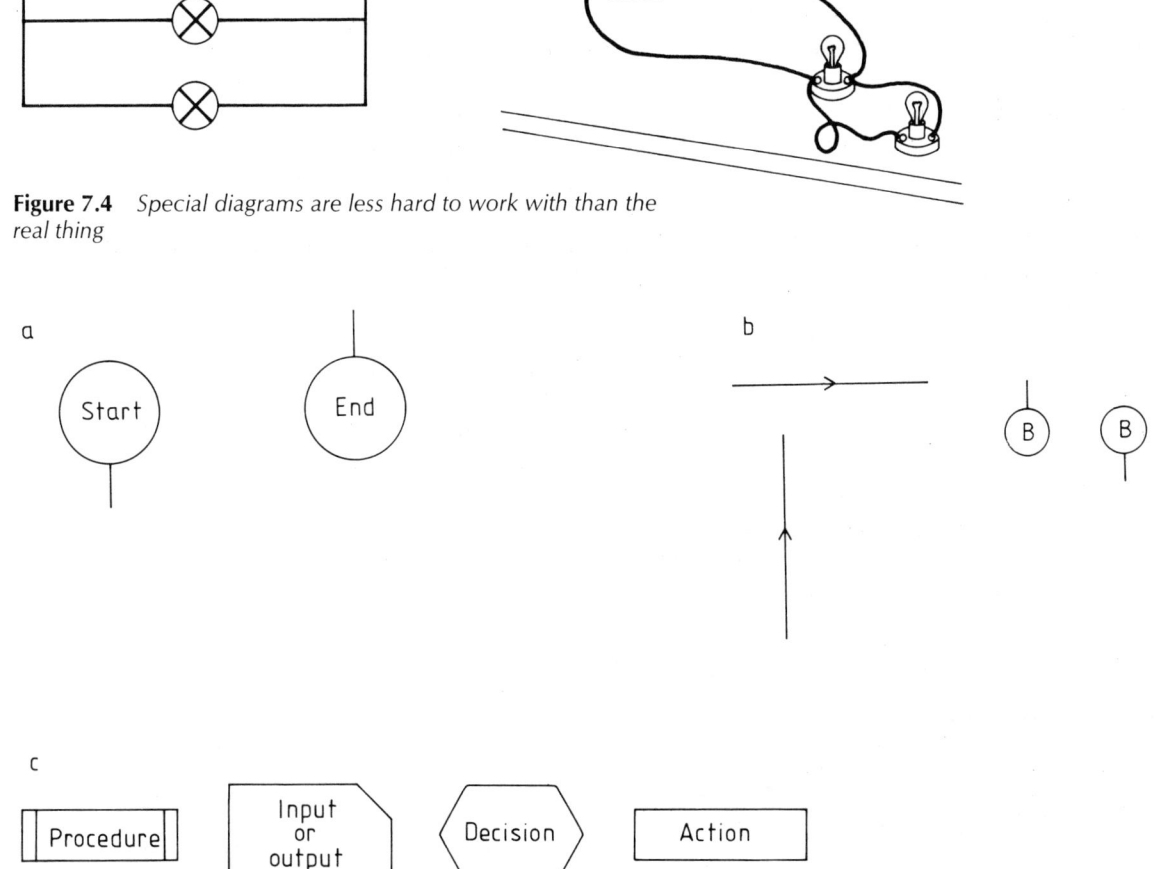

Figure 7.4 *Special diagrams are less hard to work with than the real thing*

Figure 7.5 *Flowcharts, based on a range of symbols, involve a few clear rules*

boxes

b Program flow is from START at the top to END at the bottom. Normal horizontal flow is to the right. Symbols —flow lines between the boxes concerned, with arrows *at least* where the flow is not in the normal directions and connector boxes if a chart covers more than one sheet

c Each stage of the algorithm leads to a box in the flowchart. Symbols—PROCEDURE, INPUT, OUTPUT, DECISION, ACTION (say, an assignment)

In the past—just a few years back—programmers had to develop flowcharts in great detail before starting to code any of the program itself. This was because computer keyboard time was so costly. Then there were at least two stages of flowchart development. First one would write an outline flowchart, showing the very broad progress of the project in not more than a few sheets. Then a more detailed flowchart would set out almost instruction by instruction what the program had to do.

Most people now feel there's rarely need for detailed flowcharts. The program itself should be very well laid out (structured), and quite clear to the casual glance. All the same, you may need a detailed flowchart for an unusually tricky procedure.

Indeed the standard flowchart doesn't at all well serve the modern demand for program structure. Its main use now is to show systems (Section 9.2) rather than programs. In the latter context, the **structure** (hierarchy) **chart** (Figure 7.6) is of more value. Here are the rules and symbols for that.

a The chart is **hierarchical**, set out in levels from top to bottom. At the top level is the program box; below that, from left to right, the main stages. Below, as far down as is needed, comes more and more detail. Symbols: ACTION, PROCEDURE, DECISION, LOOP, with lines linking boxes at adjacent levels

b To read a structure chart, start top left and move all round it anti-clockwise.

The algorithm produced in program development does not, however, need to be in diagram form (flowchart or structure chart). Most people find those easiest to work with—but some prefer to set out the steps involved in words. There are two ways to do this. The first is to use simple clear English sentences; you may often use this method to describe how to solve a problem in real life. ('First do this; second, do that; if you find such and such, then go back to step 2'; and so on.)

The other verbal form of algorithm uses what we call **pseudocode**. 'Pseudo' roughly means pretend. The basis of an algorithm set out in pseudocode is structures and terms that relate to what's done with the better program languages, like Pascal and modern structured BASICs. It has no step numbers, makes much use of 'repeat ... until', 'while ... endwhile', and 'if ... else ... endif' (Section 5.5), and shows the levels of hierarchy by indentation. English terms and statements prevent a pseudocode algorithm from having too much detail.

There are no fixed rules to distinguish pseudocode from algorithms set out in clear English. I've used pseudocode several times in this book—look, for instance, at the file merging algorithm in Section 6.3.

Here then are the stages of program development:

Stage 1 Have a brilliant idea ...
    THEN break it into concepts (modules).
Stage 2 Sketch the outline chart ...
    Each box relates to a module.
Stage 3a Code the program section by section ...
    Each subroutine relates to a box in the chart.
Stage 3b Test each section when it is done.
    Then each section should be all right.
Stage 4 Test the whole fully.
    Ensure it works as designed.
Stage 5 Try it out in practice.
    Let real users comment on how friendly the software is
Stage 6 Complete the documentation (Section 7.4).

7.3   Program testing

Testing concerns whether the program works as it should. Here are the questions to ask.

- Does the program carry out its design task?
- Does it do so efficiently, quickly, and (in the case of numerical work) to the correct levels of accuracy and

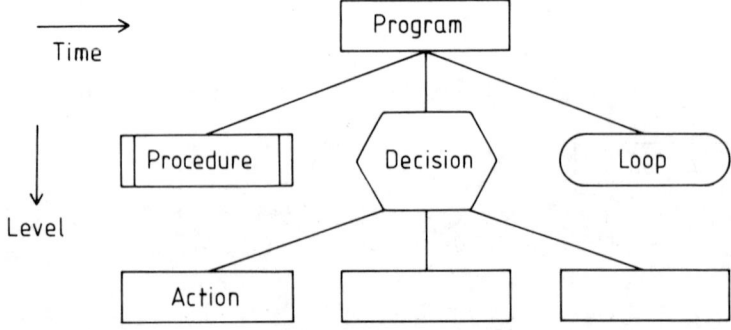

Figure 7.6   *A structure chart is hierarchical*

precision?

- Does it handle all conceivable cases?
- Can it cope with all conceivable inputs?
- Is it user-friendly?

Testing is therefore much more than just seeing if the program runs and gives results. It's as important to plan your testing process as to plan the program itself. You need to seek out and destroy various kinds of error (**bug**).

The story goes that in the very early days of electronic computing, rather less than half a century ago, computer breakdowns were often traced to the undercover work of insects making their homes among the nice warm circuits. Alas, users of modern computers no longer have that excuse for program failures. Coffee on the keyboard is *our* main hardware threat. Still, the use of the word bug, to mean a hard-to-find cause of system malfunction, remains.

Keying errors are fairly simple to find (though with major projects verification—Section 6.4—is usual). A keying error may lead to a **syntax error** report (diagnostic message)—the translator program tells you it can't follow an instruction as it isn't in the right form. For instance, typing PRONT name $ in BASIC rather than **PRINT name$** includes two syntax errors. Keying a message string wrongly won't lead to the system's reporting a syntax error, however (it can't); you need to check all output with great care to pick this up, therefore.

A second major class of errors picked up during translation concerns labels. For instance, the program calls a procedure that doesn't exist; you have given two procedures the same name; a label refers to more than one data item or structure; an expression involves mixed data types (such as adding an integer to a real); there's confusion between local and global labels. (A local label concerns data in one part of a program; a global applies throughout.)

Thus translation (assembly, compilation, or interpretation) leads to error reports. These diagnostics, in most systems, show the nature of the error (by code or by name) and where the system found the error. Note, though, that where the system found an error may not be where the error really is. A simple case is the report given by some BASICs of **NEXT without FOR in line . . .**; this shows that you earlier left out the start of a **FOR** loop (Section 5.4).

A program in use may sometimes halt (**crash**) as a result of a run-time error. A run-time error causes an interrupt (Section 5.2) from which the system should not recover. It depends on how it reacts to certain types of input data. Thus if a numeric input is 0 and the program divides a value by it, it will crash (due to overflow). The same may happen if the program is to add strings, and the result becomes too long for it to handle.

Testing for possible errors like these is much harder. The programmer must run the software a number of times with a well-planned series of input data sets. Thus, in the case of numeric data, you should try very large and very small values, positive and negative, and zero, as well as too few

and too many. Clear user instructions and mugtrapping—coding inputs for validity (Section 6.4)—are the answers to many of the problems that may arise here.

You should also identify critical values. Slight variations in these lead to major changes in the course of the program. Here, however, it's not enough to run the program with planned data sets and see if it crashes. There may be errors in the program logic. These will give answers—but some will be wrong. Thus, you must check your test run results by hand. Simple logical errors of this kind are putting * in a numeric expression rather than + or taking the left end of a string rather than the right.

Logical errors may also make the program flow wrongly if they appear in decision instructions. Putting **IF this < that THEN . . .** instead of **IF that < this THEN . . .** will cause the program to branch wrongly—and again give the wrong output.

Finding the cause of wrong output can be far from easy. If the error's in the design rather than in the code, careful dry running of the algorithm will show it up. **Dry running** means working through it yourself, following each instruction as if you are the computer, and writing down in a 'trace table' the values of all variables at each stage of the run.

The system may also be able to 'trace' the program for you so you can compare with the dry run. Tracing gives output of the path followed through the code during a run. (Note the two meanings of trace in these two paragraphs.) Some systems offer even more automated error-seeking (debugging) routines than tracing and giving error reports (diagnostic messages).

Elsewhere in this book we've come across other types of error. These include failures with parity bits and check digits, interrupts from peripherals, and arithmetic errors (rounding, overflow, underflow). A good program detects and deals suitably with all these, too.

Aiming for user-friendliness (a good user interface) is also a crucial part of software design. As well as working correctly and efficiently, the program must appeal to the user in other ways: that person should always be at ease and never wonder what to do. (This is mainly—but not just—for interactive programs.)

The most important thing here concerns planning the screen layout and the messages on it. Each message should be short but clear, well laid out and not cramped (and properly spelled and punctuated). Use

- a minimum of capital letters
- high lighting methods such as inverse, italic, special symbols, underlines, and framing
- colour—but not too much
- sound—the same applies
- time delays to help break down a page
- blank lines between paragraphs
- full or partial screen clearing to erase old messages

Such techniques greatly help the user—unless you overdo

them. It's very poor practice to have fairly simple text in a dozen colours, half of them flashing crudely at you, and silly tunes playing at the same time.

The best way to test the user interface is to try the program out on other (honest) people and to think with care about how they react.

7.4   Documentation

A program published for others must provide adequate help on its function and use. This documentation doesn't need to be on paper: it can appear on screen (either always or by request) or in a text file on disc. However, on the whole, paper documentation is easier to work with (even if easier to lose). If there's no paper documentation at all (not even a sentence on the package cover), the program name must make its function clear.

Documentation is for the user. There are, however, two types of user, with two types of documentation. One type of user is the person who views the program as a piece of applications software. The other is for a programmer (the original one or a second) who may wish to extend or amend the program in the future. If there's a Deeson's Law of Programming it's that *no program is ever perfect*. (The same applies to textbooks.)

Here's what the first type of user needs to know about a program:

- name (*exactly* the same as that on the disc, with special attention paid to directory, symbols and spaces if used)
- aims—what the program tries to do
- environment—machine and program language
- outline—problem(s) dealt with and notes on how the program solves them
- disc address
- details of protection
- special peripheral requirements
- author name(s)
- date and version number
- source (where the idea came from in the first place) and other acknowledgements
- loading details
- input formats accepted (if not clear from screen messages)
- unacceptable inputs and other limitations
- outputs to be expected
- ideas and instructions for the various uses
- relevant references

User documentation must include as little technical language as possible: assume a person who's never worked with a computer before. There can be short cuts and technical sections for the 'experts', however. Clearly, final package testing should include letting others work with the draft documentation.

Documentation for a programmer (or examiner!), on the other hand, will be technical. The notes must make it easy for that person to follow how the program works and to change it without difficulty.

For this purpose, as you build up a program that's not trivial—more than a few lines—it's crucial to record what you're doing, how, and why. The simplest way to do that is to (a) keep all the papers that pile up on the way—charts, notes, ideas, screen layout drafts, listings, printout runs; and (b) include lots of comments (**REMark**s in BASIC) in the listing: when you save the program you save all those details too, to refer to in the future.

If a finished program's very long, the comments take up a lot of memory (and slow down running). In any case, they're not as useful as having detailed notes on paper. Those notes should form part of the paper documentation for use by others. You can, therefore, remove almost all comments from copies of long programs you intend for common use—but keep them in the master you reserve for future development.

Here are the details you need to include in this file.

- program and sub-program names
- full environment details
- disc address of each copy (including backups) of each version (for exam only)
- author name(s)
- date of each version
- details of protection
- outline structure chart
- detailed structure charts of main procedures
- list of labels used and what they stand for
- references to symbols
- list of procedures (subroutines) and their functions
- details of special coding techniques used, perhaps with detailed flowcharts
- full listing of the final program, with notes (for exam only)
- full details of testing, including dry runs, data sets used, and trace tables
- problems met and their solutions (for exam only)
- ideas for possible future development

The mention in both those lists of a program's disc address brings me to another form of documentation. This is library documentation, the records of the software held by a person or firm. The subject comes under software management, but it's convenient to include it here.

Any computer user soon builds up a number of program, text, and data files; these are on hard disc or on a set of floppies (or both where the hard disc backup is to floppy), or on tapes and/or chips. There may be hundreds or thousands of such files, so proper management is essential. Right from the start of using a computer you should get into the habit of storing and keeping records of your files and chip software. You should do so in such a way that will let you, and the other people involved, be completely satisfied even when the library contains several hundred items, including backup copies.

Use codes for medium—tapes (T), discs (D), and chips (C) and for file type and subject too. Thus DTP*n*M could be the master copy of the *n*th set of physics text files on disc. Mark the coded numbers clearly on label and on the case; felt-tipped pens are best. At the same time, record the main details of each file, with the same coded number, in an exercise book, card index, loose-leaf file, or data base. This is the work of the data librarian in a large DP unit (Section 9.3).

Many programmers also collect up useful subroutines. Being small files, these need even more care in documentation; the details must include the line numbers in the case of closed BASIC subroutines kept for plugging into new programs.

7.5 Further programming concepts

Programming as such is beyond the scope of this book. All the same, I'd like to close this chapter by setting out some standard algorithms you may need to know about.

There are two very common tasks in commercial data processing: searching a file for a given data item, and sorting a file into some useful order. I'll therefore concentrate on searching and sorting algorithms, and I'll use some ideas from Chapter 6 (on files) as well as some from this chapter.

For any given programming task, people have devised a number of different algorithms that offer one special feature or another. The aim is always to maximise efficiency (Section 7.1) in given circumstances. In the case of carrying out a search, it's common to use the mean search time as the main criterion of efficiency. This is the average time needed to find a target data item in a set of given length.

Search time depends on two things. The first is the search length—the mean number of comparisons to achieve a match; this in turn depends on the algorithm used. The second is the hardware/software system used, in particular *its* speed and efficiency at carrying out instructions. In general, then, search length is the main measure of a search algorithm's efficiency.

In the middle of Section 6.1 a simple search algorithm appeared, one for finding the details of all books by Eric Deeson in a library file. Here it is again.

```
OPEN authors
REPEAT
  READ authors: name1$, name2$, dob$,
    title$, . . .
  IF name1$ = "DEESON" AND name2$ =
"ERIC"
    AND dob$ = "1942" THEN display
UNTIL EOF OR notmore [end of file or of search]
CLOSE authors
```

That very simple algorithm is a linear (or sequential) search: it goes through the file record by record till it finds a match. In that example I allowed for the possibility of there being more than one match (more than one title by the author in question); a simpler (and more usual) case is if the targets are unique, with only one match possible (or none, of course). The linear algorithm would then be like this:

```
LET flag = 0
OPEN file
REPEAT
  READ file: field1$, field2$, . . .
  IF field5$ = target$ THEN display
    [field5$ is for example]
UNTIL EOF OR flag
CLOSE file
IF NOT flag THEN PRINT "No match found."
. . .
PROCEDURE display
  CLS
  PRINT field5$, field1$ . . .
    [suitably laid out]
  LET flag = 1
END PROCEDURE
```

Figure 7.7 gives the structure chart for this linear search.

How efficient is the linear search? What, in other words, is the search length—the mean number of comparisons to find a match? If you think of searching through an old pack of cards for, say, the Queen of Hearts, the answer should be clear: on average you'll have to check half the records before finding a match. In the case of the Queen of Hearts in a 52-card pack, the search length is 26. Running a linear search on 25 000 client records to obtain the details of a given customer has a search length of 12 500. Doubling the number of records in the file will cause the search length to double (and thus the search time for a given hardware/software system).

The linear (sequential) search is *not* very efficient. The problem is, the algorithm assumes the data items aren't in order. If they were known to be in order, the search could be much quicker. (Thus you'd find the Queen of Hearts in a new pack, where the cards are in order, very quickly.)

If the file used in the last algorithm were sorted in order on the fifth field (**field5$**, the field I chose to search on), for sure you wouldn't need to look at each record starting from the first to find a match.

How would you manually search a drawer of library index cards for a given author if you know the cards are in alphabetical order of author name? You may have your own method which isn't the same as that of someone else, but I don't think you'd start from the first card and look at each one till you find what you want.

The **binary search** algorithm (sometimes called **binary chop**) is very much more efficient than the linear search, as long as the records are in order in the search (key) field.

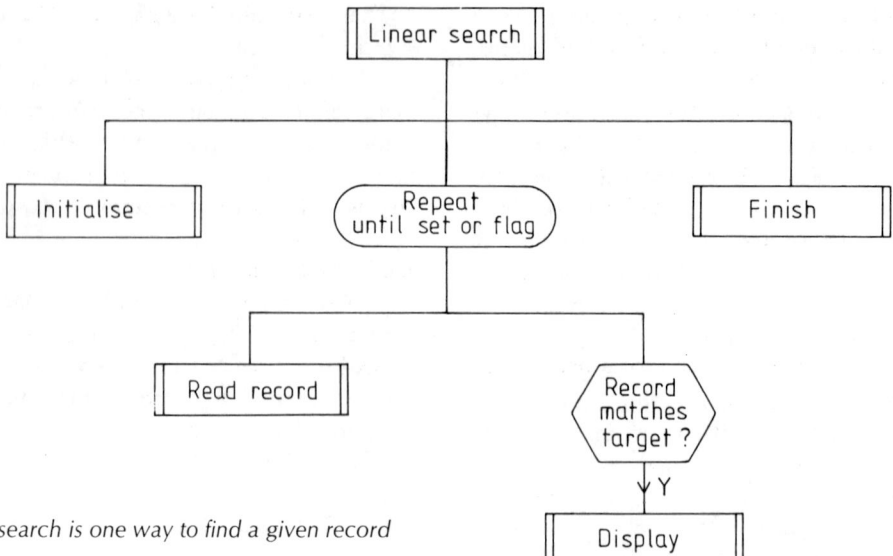

Figure 7.7   *The linear search is one way to find a given record in a file*

Here's how it works.

Go to the centre record of the set (the median).
If the key field value matches the target, display and stop.
If the key field value is greater than the target, search the lower half of the file, or
if the key field value is less than the target, search the upper half.

The search algorithm used in the last two steps can be binary too. In other words, this is a recursive technique— the algorithm calls itself until it finds a match (or until it finds there is no match).

The recursive nature of the binary search shows clearly in the structure chart of Figure 7.8. I leave it to you to extend the algorithm closer to real code if you need, but at least ensure (perhaps by working manually through a simple example) that you follow the method.

How efficient is the binary search? It should be clear that the search length is a lot less than that of the linear algorithm. Table 7.1, whose values you should quickly check, gives some sample data for the *maximum* number of comparisons needed in various cases.

Table 7.1

Number of items in set	Greatest number of comparisons
2	1 ($\log_2 2$)
4	2 ($\log_2 4$)
8	3 ($\log_2 8$)
16	4 ($\log_2 16$)
32	5 ($\log_2 32$)
64	6 ($\log_2 64$)

Figure 7.8   *The binary search, used on an ordered set of data items, is recursive, calling itself again and again until the search is over*

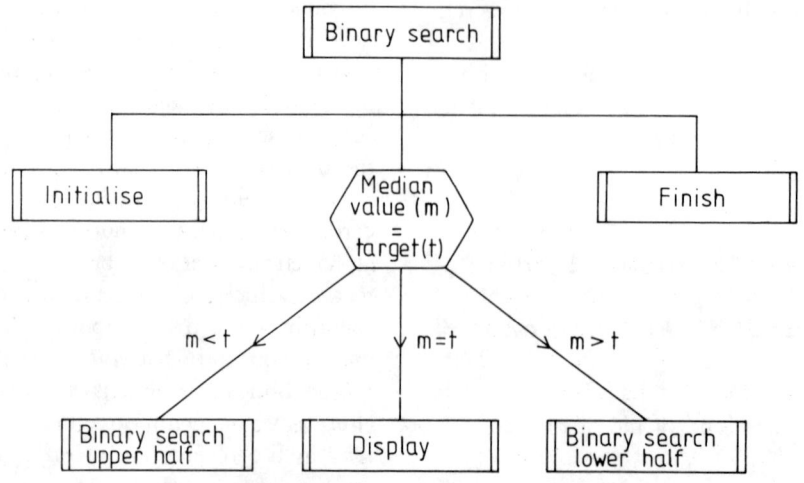

Thus to search a file of *n* records needs at most log$_2$*n* comparisons—the search length (the mean number of comparisons) is 0.5 log$_2$*n*. This time, doubling the number of data items increases the search length by 0.5, rather than doubling it.

The actual search time may not be so much less if the file has to be sorted first, for sorting is a lengthy, complex task. We'll now turn to some algorithms for sorting; again it will help you to try them on a simple data set (say, about ten letters or small integers).

First, though, think how you sort a set of items manually, a set of pieces of paper each with a number or a name on it, for instance. There are various methods, and they vary in efficiency. The usual criterion for efficiency here is the sort time—which is beyond the scope of this book as it depends on a number of factors, not least the original order of the set of records.

The insertion sort is the simplest algorithm, and is much like what most people do manually. Here's how to sort a set of items into ascending (e.g. alphabetical) order. Starting with the *second* item in the set and repeating to the end:

> compare the item with each before it; and
> insert it into the correct place.

To describe the algorithm in pseudocode, I'll use these terms. The number of records in the file (set) is *n*, and each record contains a number of fields, including the key field (the one we're actually sorting on). The record we're concerned with at the moment is **record(*x*)**, its key field value being **keyfield(*x*)**. We also need a pointer to keep track of where we are in the set of records below the current one—that gives us **record(*p*)**. Here's the algorithm then—follow it through.

```
LET x = 1
REPEAT
  LET x = x + 1
  LET p = 1
  REPEAT
    LET p = p + 1
  UNTIL keyfield(p) > keyfield(x) OR p
= x
  IF p < x THEN insert
UNTIL x = n
```

The **insert** procedure involves shifting the whole of record *x* to position *p*, and then moving all the records from *p* to *x* up one place. This is a time-consuming process, but of course you need something like it in any sort algorithm. It will involve using a temporary record's worth of storage.

The **bubble sort** is a popular approach (the name describes how each sorted item 'bubbles up' toward the lower or higher end of the set). The algorithm is a little more complex, in outline being as follows.

Starting with the second item in the set and repeating to the end (that is, making a pass through the set):

> compare the item with that below it;
> if the items are out of order, swap them and set a flag.

Repeat the whole process after resetting the flag until the flag is still unset at the end of a pass.

We've met the concept of a flag before, but this is the place to describe it in full.

A **flag** is a single-bit storage cell whose value can therefore be only 0 or 1. In use it is first reset to 0, but when any special event occurs, the software sets it to 1. Thus you can check the flag at any time; if it is waving (value 1) you know at once that that special event has happened. See how I use the flag in this pseudocode version of the bubble sort (where I also use the same terms as before).

```
REPEAT
  LET flag = 0
  LET x = 1
  REPEAT
    LET x = x + 1
    IF keyfield(x) < keyfield(x - 1)
THEN
      swap
  UNTIL x = n
UNTIL flag = 0
```

The **swap** procedure again involves using a temporary record—and also (this is crucial) must include setting the flag (making it wave). It will be something like this:

```
PROCEDURE swap
  LET record(temp) = record(x)
  LET record(x) = record(x - 1)
  LET record(x - 1) = record(temp)
  LET flag = 1
```

Both the insertion and bubble sorts are inefficient algorithms in that they involve lots of little swaps on each pass through the file. Various people have produced more efficient algorithms.

Whereas the sort times for insertion and bubble are roughly proportional to the square of the number of records (to *n*^{2}, in other words), much faster methods exist. Among these is the **quicksort**, whose sort time is approximately proportional to *n* log$_2$*n*. (The figures *are* approximate: recall that in practice efficiency depends significantly on—among other factors—the original order of the data items. Indeed, if the items happen to be in order already, the quicksort is far slower than the bubble.)

While quicksort may be fast, its algorithm is quite a complex one. It is recursive too—it calls on itself as does the binary search we looked at earlier. Quicksort involves splitting the set of records into two subsets—one each side of a 'reference record' that is in the correct place in the set—and then quicksorting each subset, and so on. Using the same terms as before, *l* and *u* to stand for records near the lower and upper ends of the set, and *r* for the 'reference record', quicksort goes like this:

```
LET r = 1: l = 1: u = n
REPEAT
 IF keyfield(n) < keyfield(l) THEN
swap
 IF r = l THEN LET n = n - 1 ELSE LET l =
   l + 1
UNTIL l = n
```

At the end of that (lengthy) pass, the set has the reference record in such a place in the set that its keyfield value is greater than those of all records below it and less than those of all the ones above it. It thus divides the original set into two subsets, each of which can now be quicksorted in turn. This goes on until all subsets are a single record.

While the algorithm is short when set out as above (and *swap* is just as before but without setting a flag), it's not easy to see how it works. Please try it, using a set of, say, ten small whole numbers on scraps of paper so you can follow it.

There are many algorithms around for tasks such as searching and sorting; their theory is a major field of study.

SELF-DEVELOPMENT QUESTIONS

See Page 137 for notes on these questions.

S7.1   Practise using a simple desktop publishing package. Why is it called desktop (or personal) publishing?

S7.2   Discuss this statement—Desktop publishing is a superb extension of word processing.

S7.3   Outline the need for planning in the use of a desktop publishing package, data base design, spreadsheet design, and one other IT system.

S7.4   An algorithm can be in English, pseudocode, flowchart or structure chart form. Produce an efficient algorithm of each type to do each of the following:

    a   output the times table for an input number,
    b   output ten input names in alphabetical order,
    c   show on screen the shape of one of three two-dimensional figures given in the user menu, and
    d   provide a ten-item multi-choice test, with user feedback and scoring, on a topic of your choice.

S7.5   Using the concepts in this chapter, produce one of the programs of S7.4.

S7.6   Give four examples of each type of error discussed at the end of Section 7.2. How may testing uncover each?

S7.7   Write a structured essay on structured program design.

S7.8   Study the user documentation of four different application programs and comment in the light of Section 7.3. The programs should range from simple to complex.

S7.9   Choose the simplest program studied for S7.8 and attempt to produce a file of program documentation for it.

S7.10   Discuss the software library documentation of your school or college.

EXAMINATION QUESTIONS

Q7.1   **a**   Write brief notes on each of the following processes which are carried out when developing a program:

    i   program design,
        (5)
    ii   program documentation.
        (6)

    b   Describe how you would test a program which is designed to read from a keyboard, in a random order, a number of transaction records each with several fields, to update a master file with these records causing several master file records to be modified.

(AEB specimen paper)   (5)

Q7.2   When a piece of software is being developed, certain errors may occur before and during program execution. State THREE types of possible error together with suitable examples.
(London)   (6)

Q7.3   The following is a top-level design of an algorithm for determining whether a given word string is palindromic, i.e. it reads the same both forwards and backwards. For example, the word 'TIPPIT' is palindromic.

    1 State the objectives of the problem.
    2 Input the string, character by character, into the string array WORD$, determining the number of characters *n*, which are read in.
    3 Initialise the array index variables left and right.
    4 while ((left < = right) and WORD$(left) = WORD$(right))
    5   begin
    6   left = left + 1
    7   right = right - 1
    8   end
    9 end while
    10 if C1 then palindrome = true
    11 else palindrome = false
    12 if C2 then output 'Word is palindromic.'
    13 else output 'Word is not palindromic.'

NB WORD$(*i*) represents the *i*th character in the

string held in the array.

a Write out the expressions C1 and C2 in steps 10 and 12.

(5)

b Trace the word 'REPAPER' using a trace table with the following four column headings:

left   right   left<=right   WORD$(left)
=WORD$(right)

(10)

c Refine step 2 of the design as a separate module.
(London)   (5)

Q7.4 Consider the testing of a newly developed program which has a modular structure.

a Explain what is meant by a program module.
(3)

b Give the reasons why modules are usually tested separately.
(3)

c Describe how the modules may be tested separately.
(5)

d Even though the testing of all individual modules has been successful, the complete program may fail. Explain how this may occur.
(London)   (4)

Q7.5 What is meant by an application package?
(3)

In addition to programs, what would you expect to be provided within such a package?
(3)

What are the advantages and disadvantages of implementing an application package compared with the development of a set of programs within a user's own data processing department?
(London)   (7)

Q7.6 **a** Describe **two** advantages of being able to compile subroutines independently from the programs in which they are used.
(2)

b Explain how subroutine libraries can make the programmer's job easier.
(JMB)   (3)

Q7.7 The computing department in a school was asked to investigate the use of a microcomputer to control the stage lighting. List the steps that would be needed to develop the fully working system.
(JMB)   (3)

Q7.8 Explain the difference between translation errors and execution errors, and describe *three* different ways in which each type of error can occur.
(London)   (6)

Q7.9 Why are procedures (subroutines) a particularly useful feature of any programming language?
(COSSEC)   (6)

Q7.10 When a program that does not contain any syntax errors is run it may terminate with an execution error otherwise the results may not be what the user expected.

Describe the techniques that a programmer could use to locate the source of such errors. In what ways can the facilities provided by the programming language and operating system help the programmer?
(COSSEC)   (10)

Q7.11 A program that processes weekly payroll for a company requires the following data for each employee.

name
employee number
number of hours worked on Monday
number of hours worked on Tuesday
number of hours worked on Wednesday
number of hours worked on Thursday
number of hours worked on Friday
number of hours worked on Saturday
number of days absent due to illness
number of days absent due to holiday

a Which data item is most likely to include a check digit? Why?

b What additional checks can be carried out on the data as it is entered into the computer?

c Suggest and justify an appropriate method for entering the data into the computer for subsequent processing.

d State one advantage of storing this data on a computer file in fixed length records and one advantage of using variable length records.

e Draw a system diagram [flow chart] of the weekly payroll run. Comment on the content of any additional files that are required and backing store used.
(COSSEC)   (25)

Q7.12 A computer is to be programmed to play noughts and crosses against a human opponent. The human will indicate who is to move first. The computer will then display the 3 × 3 grid on a raster graphics (TV screen) device and update the display as each move is made. The human move will be invited and made by typing coordinates. The computer move will be made at random. The computer will declare the result of the game when this is possible.

a Describe how the main sections of the algorithm for this program would be related to one another. If any parts of the algorithm are not obvious, explain them in sufficient detail to enable a programmer to code them.
(9, 6)

b Describe the data which would need to be held

for this program. How would it be structured? How could you estimate the storage that would be occupied?

(4, 5, 3)

c   What programming language facilities could be required for this?

(3)

d   What test-cases would you use to try to ensure that the algorithm was reliable?

(Oxford)   (5)

Q7.13   Eight queens have been positioned at random on a chess board. Design an algorithm to test, in this configuration, which of them are vulnerable to attack from others.

(7)

Convert your algorithm to one to find a single configuration of eight mutually non-threatening queens.

(Oxford)   (3)

8 Networking

Figure 8.1 *The modern newspaper office is based on an extensive IT network* (Rex Features Ltd)

Case study 8—All the news

Adjai Robinson is an editor in the Belfast office of a national daily paper. His main job is to work on the news of the region. Each day his reporters word process their stories; most use work stations on the office network (though some transfer their text from their own computers through a phone line or local link).

The editors also have work stations. Adjai studies the stories he pulls on to his screen; he uses the modern equivalent of the red pencil to edit the texts as required.

Some of the stories he sees are of national interest, so he sends them to London. For this purpose they use a direct line rather than a phone link. The direct line costs a great deal. On the other hand, it offers high-speed data transfer with very few errors and therefore saves much time. In London, the national editors work on the texts again. They tell Belfast which stories they'll use, and which they haven't room for.

During all this time, Adjai and the others continue with their work. All day long, therefore, new stories are coming in, old ones are filling out, and London and Belfast are sending files to and fro. An editor's day is a long one.

As the evening wears on, the paper reaches layout stage in London. There the office becomes more and more hectic as copy time draws near. The editors lay out the final pages on their screens and transfer them to plates for printing. IT means there's no more 'stop press' news—new major stories that come in can quickly squeeze into the screen pages, and new plates can replace old ones at any time.

The direct line to Belfast comes into its own when London transfers each laid-out page from screen to plate. At that time, electronic copies of the paper—text, illustrations, and layout—cross the country to the editors waiting at Belfast (and elsewhere). They have page layout software and a printing press too. Thus they can now produce a regional version of the paper in an hour or so.

Adjai has four types of material he can slot in for this purpose—stories London turned down, those Belfast didn't bother to send along the wire, extra details of stories that got into the London edition, and new ones. About half a page is mainly for regional material—it contains at the moment stories from southeast England, and most of these can come out, or at least drop to a few lines. To squeeze extra material into other pages means Adjai has to edit layout, cut text, and remove pictures, to make space for what he wants.

He finds this work a challenge and much enjoys it. He edits his pages—the first two or three of the paper—fast and firmly, while colleagues do much the same with their sections (sport, social, comment and so on). It takes the group of editors about an hour to finish making up the Belfast edition on their network screens. Even now, though, a new big story can break—and that means extra work to fit in and more data humming down the line to London.

By now London has only a few staff on duty, for the paper is coming off the printing press. Still, with direct links to Belfast, other British regional centres, and New York, Paris and Tokyo, there's plenty to do.

All round the world people are working on this same newspaper. Each regional office has its own local computer network, but the high-speed links between them mean the paper has a global data network, too. Wide area networks like this in fact first appeared in the newspaper industry. Readers demand up-to-date news; this is a good way to give them that.

Introduction

A **network**—local area (LAN), medium area (MAN), or wide area (WAN)—is a set of linked computers that can exchange data and share support. The concept is an important one in information technology where, for instance, phone networks have been growing for decades. In this chapter we'll start with computer networks, but also broaden the study to other areas of IT.

Objectives

When you have worked through this chapter, you should be able to

1 compare networks (distributed processing systems) with other multi-user computer systems
2 discuss how a large newspaper can use networks that differ in scale
3 outline the history of computer hardware and systems and their impact
4 compare star (cluster), bus, ring and hybrid networks
5 outline the functions of network operating software and of network versions of applications packages
6 outline the hierarchy of computer links, from micros sharing a printer, through local and medium (metropolitan) area networks, to wide area networks
7 state the nature of a gateway
8 sketch the layout of a public phone network
9 compare the techniques of analog and digital telephony and list advantages of the latter
10 outline the nature and use of optical fibre
11 outline the nature of the telex network and note the historical basis for its problems
12 list new and possible telex unit features
13 outline the nature and use of teletex
14 compare teletex with telex and with electronic mail
15 outline the nature and use of fax
16 list the features of a modern fax machine
17 describe uses of the circuit switched public data network
18 describe packet switching
19 outline the concept of electronic funds transfer at the point of sale and the use in this context of the smart card
20 describe the layout of the cellular mobile phone network
21 list some likely features of the integrated services data network

8.1   Distance no object

A computer network allows people to communicate with each other electronically in various ways; they can also share data and such items as costly output units. A network is therefore clearly a multi-user system in style. Unlike with true multi-usage, however, each person on the network has a computer which offers more than even an intelligent terminal.

The so-called first generation of electronic digital machines (forty or fifty years ago) fairly soon took up the multi-user concept. Those machines, based on the valve as the signal switching unit, were very costly, large and unreliable. They needed a great deal of power, their own purpose-designed rooms, and a highly trained operating staff. At first, normal mortals couldn't use them as they involved too much rare skill—technical knowledge, the concepts of programming in machine code, and so on. However, as systems became more user-friendly and standard software packages started to appear, the individual user's terminal became possible. So the early computer developed into what we would now call a mainframe. Figure 8.2 shows the basic layout.

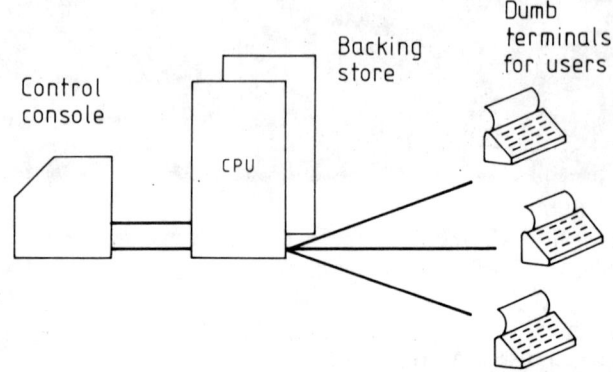

Figure 8.2   *The terminal was the first step to a computer system able to handle the needs of a number of remote users*

In those days, backing store often involved punched paper tape and/or cards; these were based on data storage techniques dating back to the eighteenth century. Punched media better suit batch processing (Section 5.3) rather than interactive work. The first terminals were simple communications devices that owed much to telegraphy; they had just a keyboard for data input and a slow printer for output. As with telegraphy's other main offspring—telex (Section 8.4)—the machines were heavy and slow and didn't offer graphics or lower case letters.

With a terminal, however, one could at least interact with a running program—keying in data when needed, and seeing results appear on the local printer. Even so, batch processing remained the norm with those mainframe computers—the expertise needed to work with them remained high, and the running costs of the hardware were too great to allow very much inherently slow interaction.

The invention of the transistor in the late 1940s led to the second generation of computers. A transistor, built from a tiny piece of semiconductor, could do the work of a valve, but was much smaller, cheaper to make and use, and more robust. With the transistor came the electronics industry as we know it now, and the start of its great progress in personal radio, audio, and video, as well as in computing. Computer systems became much cheaper, more compact, and more reliable, and they gained processing power and speed.

Control started to pass from the specialist engineer to the professional user, and the mini-computer appeared. Laboratories, smaller firms and departments could afford and use a mini—it also needed fewer (if any) specialist operating staff and environmental controls, and it really opened the way to interactive computer use. Figure 8.2 can still show such a system—but now people could manage without the operator's central control console, and by this time backing storage involved magnetic media (tape, drum, and then disc) instead of punched paper. Terminals started to lose their tape punches and readers and to have longer and longer links to the processor.

Then, in the 1960s, the electronic engineers learned to pack a number of transistors and other circuit elements in the surface of tiny scraps of semiconductor—the **chip** (integrated circuit) appeared. The trend toward miniaturisation appeared firmly as the way ahead, with tens, then hundreds, then thousands, of electronic elements packed into a silicon chip a few millimetres square. Again the radio, video and audio markets gained great benefit, and so did the computing industry; this came to the third generation of hardware as a result.

The new hardware—very cheap, compact and reliable—led to the concept of the **micro**. This transportable single-user machine, also called the personal computer, brought computing into millions of people's lives; appeared to imply the death of non-interactive processing; encouraged the rapid development of high-level program languages and friendly off-the-shelf applications software; and started the move toward the modern robot.

As more and more electronic circuit elements crammed on to each chip—the number is now far over a million—the price of a computer system halved each year, and the number of users doubled. Both those trends are now tailing off as we approach a level of market saturation that's likely to last several years. However, the tailing off saw the concept of networking appear, and a new type of multi-user computing environment arrived.

That quick historical survey doesn't really show the importance of user demand as a pressure in development. People have long seen that IT could offer them a lot in their own fields, and called for new styles and features that the hardware researchers tried to meet. Software development plays a major part in the story too; after all, software relates to actual usage much more than hardware and has often been the main force in the acceptance of new hardware. Now, more money goes on software development than on hardware research.

Figure 8.2 shows a **shared logic** (or shared processing) computer system. The mainframe or mini with its terminals has a single central processing unit. Each terminal is **dumb**—it has no processing power of its own, so is just a means to allow a human user to interact with the computer itself at the same time as others. The central processor

shares its time between the terminals on line at any given moment; it looks after all their needs as well as it can.

The best modern mainframe system can handle hundreds or even thousands of terminals at once, and those terminals are now intelligent—they have their own processors to share the load to an extent. All the same, during busy times at least, there can well be several seconds' delay between a terminal's input of data to the system and the response. As a micro system doesn't have this problem—it has only one user's needs to cater for—the movement away from shared logic to stand-alone units is easy to understand. Figure 8.3 shows the typical computer usage of the first half of the 1980s.

Figure 8.3 *The cheap micro led to a stand-alone personal computer on nearly every desk in some situations*

Having a **stand-alone** micro to yourself is great. You've full and sole responsibility for all aspects of its use—maintenance, operations, housekeeping, as well as actually running the applications software you want. All the system's data is *your* data; all the peripherals are yours, too. Rolled in to one body, you're operations staff, data preparation manager, technician, librarian, and user. Your system's output depends on the software *you* put in, and the peripherals you can afford to invest in. Your system's efficiency depends on *your* knowledge and on your attitudes.

Hmm. Maybe your own personal stand-alone micro is *not* the best result of fifty years of progress. IT should release people from irrelevant problems and cares, and let them get on with what they can best do. Should a personnel manager have to learn data processing skills, or a teacher to program? Should the boss have to become word processor expert and filing clerk too?

Those second thoughts spread fast after the cheap stand-alone micro hit the desks of the early 1980s. Certainly this new system offered much of value compared with the use of a terminal to a remote mainframe or mini. Yet the terminal user still had access to huge volumes of data, to processing power and speed that leave micros standing, to high quality peripherals, and (often) to aid from expert staff when problems arose.

The network concept shows that shared processing doesn't have to mean the delays of time sharing and cumbersome logging on procedures. With a network, shared processing can be for the benefit of all users, and shared data and shared high-cost peripherals lead to great savings of time, money and effort. Note though that a network isn't really a simple shared processing system: the work stations each have much intelligence of their own—**distributed processing** is a better term.

A **network** is a group of micros—work stations—linked to central hardware and software. The work stations are intelligent—full feature machines with their own powerful processors and memory and (often) backing store; they're not dumb communications terminals with no more than an input and an output device. Thus the person at the work station has on the desk top a system that can be almost as autonomous as desired.

On the other hand, there are those network links. As required, the system can copy software and data from the central unit to any work station. As required, any user can call on a more powerful information crunching central processor or a superb quality printer. As required, data as well as messages can shuffle between the stations.

So, in principle, the network offers the best of the two worlds of individual freedom and shared costly resources (including information). The integration of software explored in Section 2.4 is matched by hardware integration.

The networks of the late 1980s are far from perfect; all the same, they promise a real move toward the cost-effective and enjoyable liberation of the individual user's individual skills.

Figure 8.4 shows the three main network structures—the **star** (or cluster) that looks much like hanging terminals on to a mainframe or mini (Figure 8.2); the **bus**, which offers great saving in cable; and the **ring**, in effect a bus with the ends joined. Each style has its advantages and disadvantages and its own approach to handling data transfers between the individual stations. The ability to survive hardware faults is

relevant, too, with the bus being the most vulnerable as far as concerns cable faults.

Perhaps the biggest question concerns the ease of expansion, the ease of bringing new micros into the net. Rings and buses aren't as easy as stars to add new work stations to, and it's therefore common to install these with spare connectors to allow later growth without a lot of work. In the same way as people plan a modern office from the start to allow a truly flexible phone system, one should build in network cabling that offers a great variety of future uses.

In practice, though, many networks don't fall neatly into the categories of star, bus and ring. The hybrid of Figure 8.5, with special switching units called nodes, is such a layout; it's most likely to appear when people join two networks.

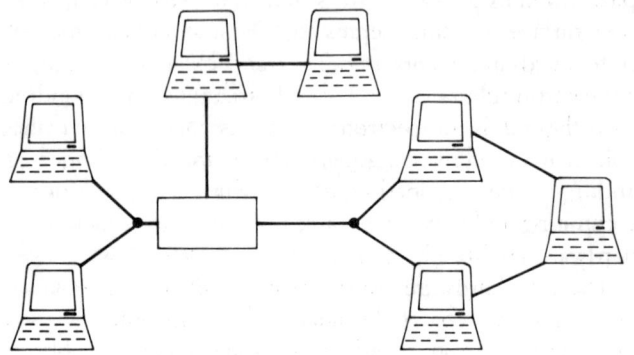

Figure 8.5   *In practice, it's not often that you can describe a network as a simple star, bus or ring*

8.2   Distributed processing

There may seem to be no problem in sharing access through a network—a distributed processing system—to common software and data. Each user can load the software desired and work on it, calling up, adding, and changing data as needed. Yet things can't be quite so simple. Maybe two people decide to edit the same draft report using word processor software at the same time. A simple system couldn't stop that, nor could it merge the two edited versions. As a result, there'll be either two differently edited copies of the report, or one which includes only one person's work.

The same sort of problem could arise with the sharing of accounts information. One clerk could access the figures for September and start sorting them, while a second could be just about to change some aspect. Sharing data between linked independent micros can lead to disaster.

Because of this, network operating software (OS) can't be the same as single-user systems software; the applications programs would need to be in new versions too.

Typical network applications programs come in two levels. The main accounts package, for instance, stays with the main network processor, while each work station involved with accounting has a local (front end) version. The

Figure 8.4   *There are various ways to arrange a network*

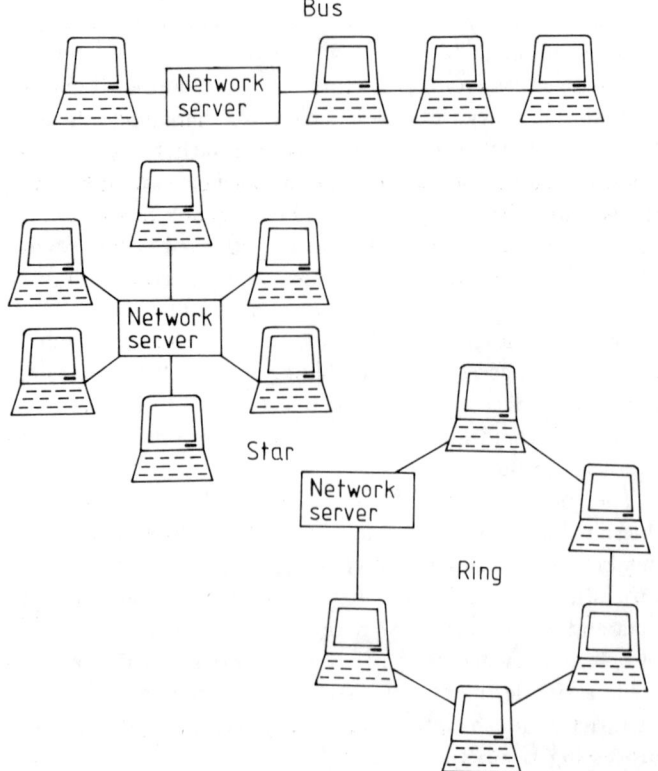

front end displays a menu of allowed actions and can check entered data for validity and so on. Only when an approved user approves entered data does it pass to the main program for merging with the main file. As the main program can do only one task at a time, there's now no chance of clashes.

As well as handling joint access to shared data and shared resources, the network operating system will need to offer a level of security. It needs some kind of password system (a secure logging-on procedure) to prevent unauthorised access to network data. This may have to be on several levels, with some people allowed only to scan certain files and others able to change almost anything. There's more on this in Section 10.2.

In the same way as there's a great range of network layouts (Figures 8.4 and 8.5), there's a range of OS power and style. A network can be, at the one extreme, a set of powerful micros with little central processing, or, at the other, a sophisticated central unit with work stations of fairly low intelligence (or low autonomy).

As yet, network operation is far from perfect. It involves sharing, so is likely sometimes to involve delay. The central backing store is probably always a fixed hard disc pack (a **Winchester** unit)—compact, cheap, very fast in action, and able to store huge quantities of data. All the same, if one user runs a program that involves many data transfers to and from disc, the others will find their work slowing down when they too need disc access. High volumes of data transfer can also cause problems in bus and ring networks. Though the cable can carry a lot of data (perhaps millions of bits per second), transfer is serial, with only one packet able to pass each point at a time. Thus the cable can clog up (overflow), so data due to pass one node may have to wait a few seconds for a gap.

I'll close this section with a summary of the hierarchy of network links. At the lowest level, you can join several micros so they share a printer. Some of the stations may have their own individual low-cost printers too; that's at a higher level than if they don't. Figure 8.6 shows this higher level—a typical star (or cluster) with a manual switching unit to tell the central printer which machine to work with. The big advantage of this follows the facts that a good printer

isn't cheap and few users need to print out often. A printer for each micro is wasteful, therefore.

The next step up is to share software and data by using a common disc drive, almost always a hard (Winchester) disc unit. Again, each micro can have its own drive (for floppies or even for a hard disc); rather than a manual control, software in the central file server handles and interleaves the individual accesses to the central disc. This is because, unlike the case of the shared printer, disc data transfers rarely last more than a few seconds. Figure 8.7 shows this first true network, again with a star (cluster) approach. A simple cluster like that can support a dozen or two stations with little problem of delays; the top limit is often 32. The stations don't need all to be the same type, by the way—you can (if you need) mix 8-bit with 16-bit processors and even, perhaps, include a sprinkling of comparatively dumb terminals.

At the next level up, we expect a basic bus or ring structure rather than a star; a much greater upper limit on the number of users at a time; and significantly increased speed. Various standards apply here, such as the Ethernet (which can support over a thousand users).

Those systems often go under the name of **local area network** (LAN). Here in whatever way the individual work stations and shared central resources link logically in the area concerned, the links involve cable with routing which is at least semi-permanent. This defines a local area network, even if the cabling is of such high quality that it can carry data as fast as 100 million bits a second; even if the system includes several mainframes; even if the number of simultaneous users is well into four figures; and even if the distance between two extreme stations is several kilometres. It's a rare office that reaches those limits, though such great LANs are common on campus.

In the case of such a large LAN, making the data transfer links to the central processor(s) and the shared peripherals can be a problem. One solution is to bundle the data into uniform packets at various PADs (**packet assembly and disassembly** points). Figure 8.15 shows what happens here; it's in the section on packet switching in a public phone or data network, but the concepts are much the same. Phone

Figure 8.6 *Sharing a printer between several micros is a simple form of networking*

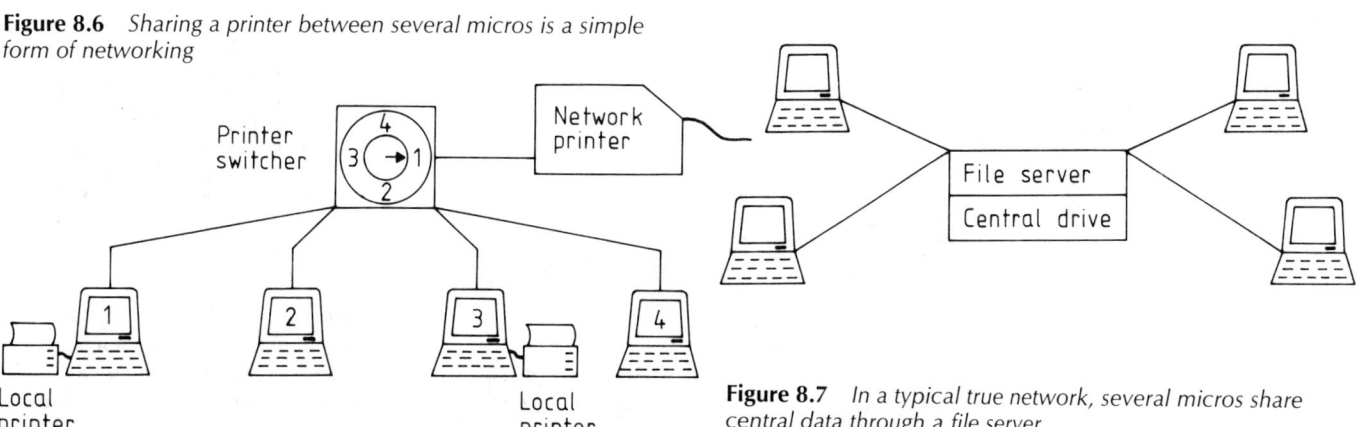

Figure 8.7 *In a typical true network, several micros share central data through a file server*

systems also give a clue to the second method of cutting down the problems of handling the traffic on a large LAN—you can set up a **private branch exchange** (PBX) and look on the various work stations and shared resources as phone extensions.

There's also a great need to share information (and even resources) with computer users on other, distant (remote) sites. It's often too costly to set up a cable to extend a LAN over more than a few kilometres (and anyway, for technical reasons, that doesn't work well at the moment). To allow distant users to share information we must therefore call on telecommunications. This is the use of radio, microwave, light or electric current links, through space, metal cables or optical fibres. Such channels of communication exist already, in particular in the public phone system.

Allowing data transfers between computer users in this way isn't hard; we've explored it in the context of Prestel in particular. The phrase **wide area network** (WAN) covers the approach and, as its use grows rapidly, the term is coming into common usage. In between the LAN and the WAN is the MAN—**medium** (or **metropolitan**) **area network**. Here the links can be rather greater than a few kilometres, so need special techniques. There's a network like this in the City of London, round the SEAQ system (Case study 5).

A **gateway** is a common type of WAN link; it can, in theory at least, join any two types of system. A gateway has to be able to convert data in transit—between different data transfer rates, different packet makeups and sizes, different security systems, different addressing methods, different ways of handling errors, and so on. A gateway allows access from one remote computer system to a second; you may have come across it with Prestel (for example, by its gateways into NERIS and the British Rail computer).

8.3   On the phone

With a history spanning over a century, the telephone is one of the oldest methods of electronic information transfer. During most of that lifetime, however, other than the invention of the concept itself, there was only one truly major advance. This was the development of phone networks based on exchanges (switching centres). Prior to that step, phone communication between two people could take place only through a special (**dedicated**) link from handset to handset. It took several years to move away from that, despite experience with the rather similar telegraphy technique. Figure 8.8 shows how the modern system connects two handsets in two countries. A link may be metal wire, glass fibre (optical cable), or a radio (wireless) channel.

The exchanges—switching centres—have other functions than making links. Each exchange line carries a meter for billing purposes, and electronics also ensures roughly equal signal strength in the two directions.

A second factor to do with signal strength is the need for repeaters every few tens of kilometres along a trunk line. The resistance of a wire to the passage of electrical signals is the reason; the effect is that a line longer than a certain distance so much weakens (attenuates) an input signal that it can't be picked up at the output. A repeater is an amplifier; it boosts a weak input signal to a strength adequate for the next stage in the journey. A repeater needs its own power supply.

The modern digital phone network improves matters in this regard. Phone users may suffer from 'wrong numbers', 'crossed lines', bad lines, delays in operator service, being cut off, and so on. Things have improved greatly in recent years; the main cause of the improvement is the change from analog signal transfer to digital. Figure 8.9 (a repeat of Figure 1.11) shows how analog signals differ from digital.

Figure 8.9   *An analog signal is wavy; a digital one is pulsed*

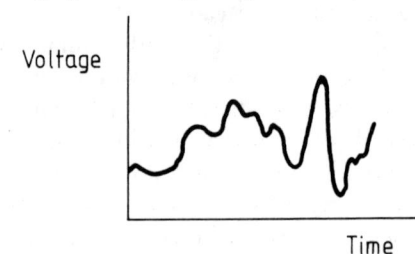

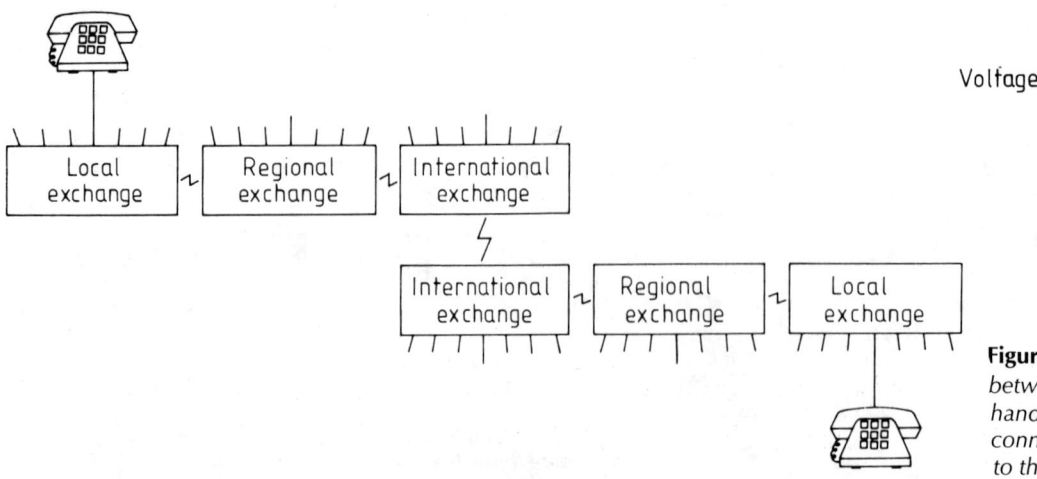

Figure 8.8   *To allow communication between two individual phone handsets, a number of switched connections produce a link from one to the other*

Sound waves—not pulses—carry speech, so speech is an analog signal. There's a lot of sense, therefore, in using an analog system for the electronic transfer of speech. The simple microphone in the phone handset converts the input sound waves (analog) to a wavy electric current (digital). This passes through the system of Figure 8.8, amplified by repeaters every so often. At the receiving end the speaker (earpiece) in the handset converts the wavy electric current back to an analog sound wave.

The quality of the sound from the speaker depends on factors that include the quality of the speaker itself and that of the microphone. Both these are of ancient design. They can't handle signals with much fidelity, nor pass high frequencies (those of high-pitched sounds) very well. Because of these limits the analog phone network doesn't itself need to be high quality—so it isn't. A major result of low quality in the system is line noise—the hisses, clicks and buzzes caused by a large variety of types of interference.

Digital transfer—passing the signals in pulses rather than as wave forms—has many advantages. It's faster and can deal better with high frequencies; interference is reduced and line noise can be cut out; the lines are cheaper yet can carry far more traffic; and automation can increase. Also, the regenerators (equivalent of repeaters) can be much further apart.

The new cables aren't made of lots of metal wires, but are bundles of hair-thin strands of very pure glass fibre. These cost much the same as copper cables, but the signals pass through them as light rather than as electric current; this feature, as much as going digital itself, is the cause of the huge potential improvements mentioned in the last paragraph —a light signal is of much higher frequency than an electric one, so can carry a lot more data.

Within a few years Britain's digital networks will be complete—all the digital exchanges and the optical fibre trunk lines will be working. Analog elements will remain for much longer, though—bringing an optical fibre line to every handset in the country is not yet worth the cost.

Analog equipment, like the standard phone handset, will work just as well as before. However, only digital equipment will be able to give its users all the potential advantages. As digital equipment includes communicating computers, fax machines and teletex units, many people will gain a great deal. In particular, data transfer rates can greatly increase, while data transfer costs fall.

8.4 Other IT networks

There are other systems of electronic information transfer organised in the same kind of way as the phone network; some indeed use it directly. I've already mentioned three—telex, fax, and electronic mail.

Telex grew out of the telegraph system; this appeared long before electronic telephony became a fact in the 1870s.

The need for the telegraph was for sending messages associated with the growing rail network of the early nineteenth century. The laborious and slow method of information transfer used was open to much error— messages were keyed manually character by character using Morse code or similar. This code involved sending short and long pulses of current through the telegraph wire, with the transmitter's Morse key (a sort of simple switch) held closed for short or long periods.

A major advance was the development of the Baudot code at the start of this century. The sender could now use a sort of typewriter keyboard; each different key-press automatically generated a 5-bit combination (word) of current pulses or pulse absences—1 and 0 respectively. At the receiving end a special output unit could reproduce the message, either by punching holes in coded patterns in a paper tape, or by putting readable characters directly on to a paper tape.

Though the Baudot system was a great advance, it caused the later telex network to lose a lot of potential. This is because 5 bits allow no more than thirty-two different words (codes). Many are for special effects like ringing a bell at the receiving end—so a telegram could consist of only upper case (capital) letters, the ten digits and a few common symbols and punctuation marks.

The next big step in telegraphy came in the 1930s—the concept of a public (rather than private as before) switched network, to which anyone could subscribe. Now, instead of there needing to be dedicated lines between each pair of telegraph users, systems like those in Figure 8.8 appeared. This is **telex** ('telegraph exchange'), a switched network quite separate from that used for telephony. Automatic transmission of messages using pre-punched paper tape came, too, as did the tele-typewriter, with output on sheet paper rather than tape.

Using a special telex terminal, a user keys messages for transfer. Perhaps they're stored on punched paper tape. At sending time, you dial the number of the receiver and switch the unit to transmit. The terminal at the other end will acknowledge that it's ready, take the call, print out the message, and perhaps also prepare a punched tape. Telex receipt is automatic, as long as the called terminal is on line; there's much less automation at the sending end.

Lately there've been a number of improvements—new exchanges, new lines, new terminal equipment, and new features. Telex in the 1990s may offer

- more automation at the sending end
- a kind of exchange-based answering machine, in which you send a message to the exchange and that message goes to anyone who calls your number
- the ability to use the terminal keyboard keys rather than a rotary dial for calling out
- itemised billing, where the bills show the details and cost of each telex sent
- itemised logging, showing the date and time of each telex sent as well as the called terminal's code
- detailed reports of problems on the line if a telex can't

get through
- a full character set rather than the limited range of the 5-bit Baudot code
- word processor style working, so you can prepare material off line, edit as desired, and send it to fast backing store for later transfer
- priority ratings
- multi-addressing—you can code a given message with several recipients' numbers to have it sent to each automatically
- coded addressing
- automated repeat of the calling and despatch process if the message doesn't get through first time
- chat mode—keeping the line between two terminals open, so messages can pass to and fro in turn

However, telex faces more and more competition from alternative systems of electronic information transfer. Whether telex can (or should) survive in a world with so many more friendly alternatives is a question I cannot address here; the situation will become clearer within a few years.

For almost a decade now, **teletex**—a special new form of **electronic mail** (email)—has offered much better features than telex. However, only Canada, Sweden and West Germany have proper systems running at the time of writing (early 1988). Teletex is an international standard for information transfer between electronic equipment using the phone network. Both aspects at once make teletex far cheaper than telex. There's no more need for special terminals, as any computer or word processor (or even electronic typewriter) can use the system if its communications software is teletex-compatible. And there's the whole phone network there to pass signals: telex has some two million users world-wide, but there are hundreds of millions of phone lines.

Teletex has two other big features in its favour. The first is that data transfer is like that of micros—in units of 8 rather than 5 bits; a message can include a very large range of characters. Second, data transfer can reach fifty words a second—telex can't do much more than one.

The phone and telex networks are linked by Interstream, so teletex (and other email) users can send messages to telex terminals and vice versa. The speed of information transfer has to be that of telex, though—one word a second, you

recall. Also, the costs of Interstream are high—not just because of the slow message speed, but because telex access and line charges go on top of what may well be long distance phone charges.

The crucial thing about teletex is that it *is* standard. Also, many features that are options in a modern telex terminal are the norm for teletex equipment. Here I think of the various forms of detailed message logging, automatic re-try, and the ability to receive teletex messages while using the machine off line as you prepare out-going ones.

You may recognise that teletex is much like electronic mail in function; its strength is that, unlike email, teletex has a world-wide standard. On the other hand, as I say, it's not yet widespread.

Facsimile transfer—called **fax** for short—is another fairly ancient technology that's now growing fast. The first relevant invention dates back to about 1850, but useful systems have been working only since the 1930s. Like telex and teletex, fax requires special hardware linked permanently to a switched communications line. Unlike telex, though, it uses the standard phone circuits, thus adding flexibility, increasing the potential user base, and cutting running costs.

Using fax is much like photocopying, except the copy comes out at a machine somewhere else in the world. There's been great growth in this market in recent years—standardisation, reduced costs, increased effectiveness, and improved features combine to increase the number of users.

Figure 8.10 outlines the concept. At the sending end is a document reader; a light beam scans the original, in effect treating it as hundreds of rows of tiny cells which may be either light or dark. The light reflected from each cell becomes part of a digital electric signal. This passes through the phone network to the receiver, which constructs an image of the original dot pattern on a sheet of paper.

As with telex, the two special machines must be on line at the same time. This means the sender has to make the connection as required; it also implies a fax machine should have its own phone exchange line so it can receive incoming calls.

The strength of fax is that it can transfer copies of almost any kind of document. The system can handle anything you can photocopy (though as yet output quality isn't nearly as good)—diagrams, graphs, signatures and other handwritten material, newspaper cuttings, computer printout, and so on.

Figure 8.10   *Facsimile transmission requires an open line between the sending and the receiving machines*

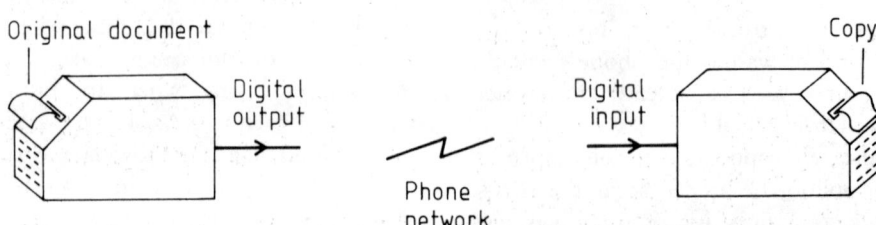

Historically, the major uses have been the transfer of newspaper pictures—and more recently whole newspapers—and weather charts. A modern fax link can transfer an A4 copy in much less than a minute—even as little as a few seconds.

To connect a computer to the analog phone network requires a modem; it's just the same with a fax machine. Figure 8.11 shows the function of a modem.

The features a fax machine may offer include

- the ability to reduce an original from A3 size, say, to A4 (for such material as computer printouts and architectural drawings)
- the ability to enlarge all or part of an original before transfer
- the ability to increase the resolution of scanning
- scanning and printing on a three-point scale—white, grey, black
- automatic dialling
- automatic re-try
- logging
- saving the signal from a scanned document to disc for later use

Figure 8.12 shows modern telex and fax machines. There are also portable fax machines, of special value to travelling staff; these can plug into a phone socket anywhere, or be used with the cellular (mobile) radio phone system.

8.5 To the future

Figure 8.13 shows the various telecommunications techniques described in this chapter. Now I'd like to tie them together.

A few decades ago, the public phone network and that used for telex were quite separate. Now links are growing between them (e.g. Interstream, as mentioned above), and the former handles more and more types of traffic. The end result of these current trends should be a single network with interfaces (sometimes called gateways) between the various functions.

Britain is working towards that single telephony system, able to carry both voice traffic and data without problem. It is called the **integrated services data network** (ISDN). The ISDN will be part of a world-wide common carrier (see Figure 8.14).

Not all such information is carried by electric currents. Much modern digital transfer is by electromagnetic radiation in optical fibres or through microwave links, while radio plays a part, too (particularly in the context of mobile and other wireless phones). Indeed, the amateur radio system has developed excellent techniques for digital data transfer; maybe this will also gain gateways to the public phone network in due course.

The **circuit switched public data network** (CSPDN) is specially for major users of digital information transfer. For each data transfer, the system sets up a circuit just as with telephony; at each end, however, is a unit of digital hardware rather than a person. There are many growth areas for CSPDN. As well as teletex communication between computers, there are the rapidly expanding needs of

Figure 8.11 *To convert electronic signals from digital to analog or analog to digital requires a modem*

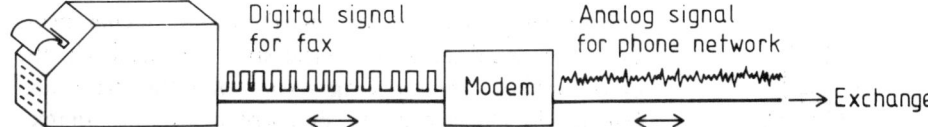

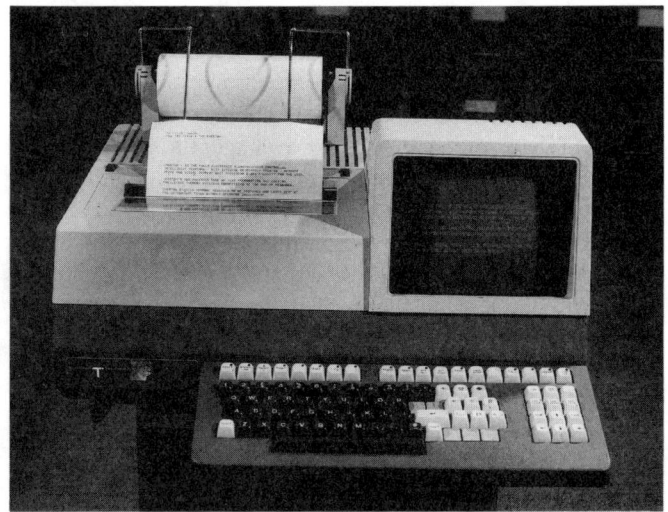

Figure 8.12 *Modern telex and fax units*

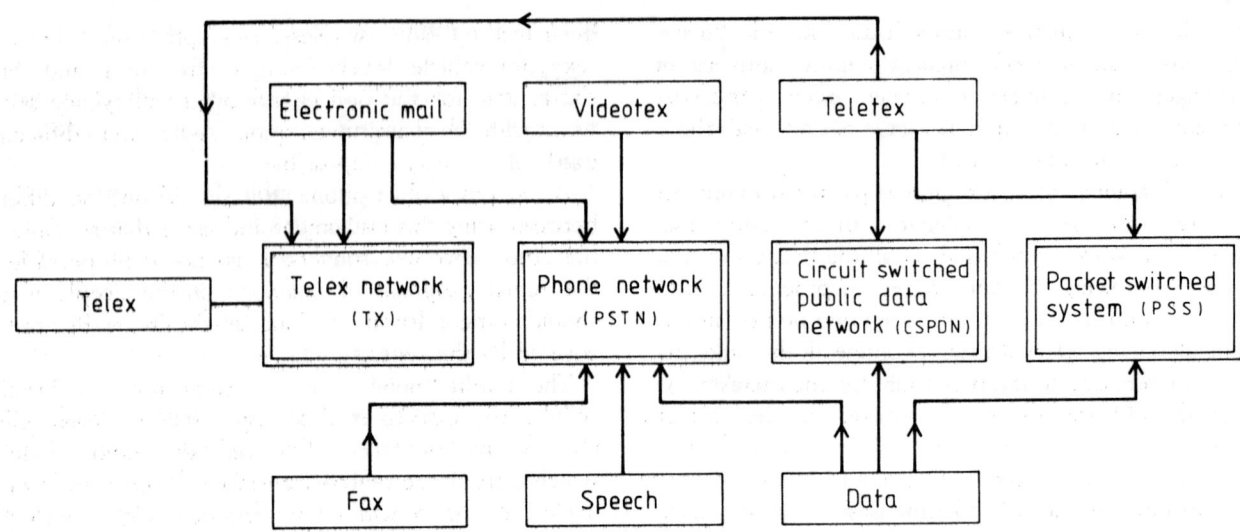

Figure 8.13   *There are various public cable-based telecommunications systems*

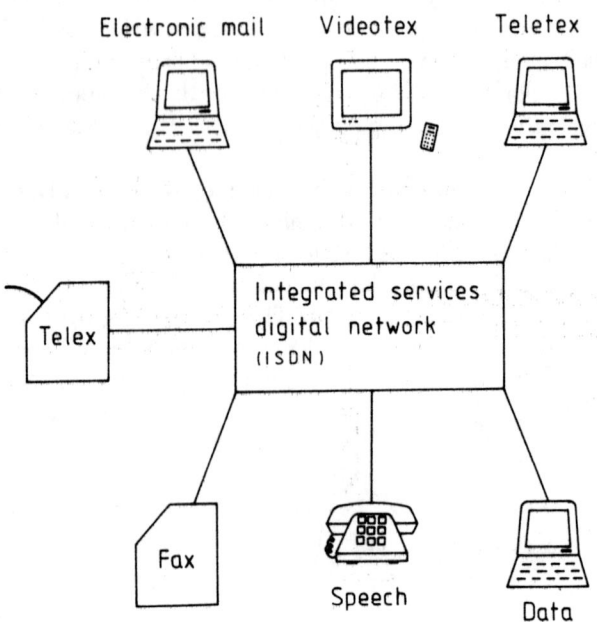

Figure 8.14   *Eventually an integrated services data network will carry all voice and digital signals*

electronic funds transfer (EFT), credit card authorisations, and computer booking traffic to handle. Here are some examples.

Automatic tellers (ATMs) are the electronic terminals fitted to the High Street walls of many banks and building societies. These are terminals in that they can link to distant main frame computers. The terminal's own (local) processing power can deal with verifying the **personal identification number** (PIN) typed in with that on the cash or credit card and with issuing bank notes. However, services such as showing the balance in the user's account or ordering a statement or cheque book need data transfer. The terminal will then call for a line to the central computer to allow the exchange to take place.

Electronic funds transfer (EFT) is also growing fast. In several parts of the country, by 'swiping' your plastics card through an EFT terminal rather like an ATM, you can obtain fuel from unstaffed petrol stations, or purchase rail tickets. In some areas, retail outlets are using the same kind of system. Here the shopper inserts the card—a debit rather than a credit card—and keys in the PIN. The terminal links to the till at the **point of sale** (POS) and to the bank's computer; without effort and with little paper, the till total transfers from the shopper's account to that of the trader. **Electronic funds transfer at the point of sale** is EFTPOS.

If the shopper's card is a **'smart'** one, with a chip inside as well as a magnetic or optical stripe on the back, the card can keep an on-going record of transactions and balance for later printout or display. In this context, though, the important thing is the use of the CSPDN to transfer the data that represents cash between the till terminal and the banks' computers.

Computerised booking—telebooking—is very important in the daily work of specialist companies such as travel and theatre agents. Again the CSPDN provides the crucial links. When someone visits a travel agent to book a flight, it's likely now that the agent can key in the relevant information and questions and confirm the best available booking at once. To do that requires a CSPDN link to the airline's computer, which stores and keeps up to date the current status of all flights.

Where the transfer is basically one way, however, or involves much less data, it's a lot cheaper to use a **packet switching service** (PSS, or **packet switched public data network**, PSPDN). This breaks down the stream of data to uniform compressed chunks; each such packet gains a header with the recipient's address code and the packet number, plus a tail of check digits. Computer software in the exchanges from moment to moment decides the best route for each packet, and interleaves the packets with those that carry data from other sources.

Figure 8.15 compares the circuit and packet switching of data transfer, though I've simplified it in the latter case. What I've done in the sketch is show all the packets from a given source following the same route. In practice, there's always a good number of routes between two points, and as the traffic along any one will vary in volume all the time, the system computers decide the best route for each packet. At the far end, software re-joins the packets in the correct order.

There's long been a need for communication between people who move round a lot. In the past, the needs have been met by radio (wireless telegraphy)—in military contexts, for vehicle drivers (taxis, trains, buses) and ship-to-shore, and for the police and other emergency services. Links with the conventional phone system were difficult and costly, if not nearly impossible.

A modern mobile phone user should find no difference between using this instrument and using that at home or in the office. Two-way conversations should be possible, and the actual geographical positions of the people involved shouldn't be relevant (as long as they're within the area covered by the system).

The public mobile phone system used in Britain is cellular: the areas covered consist of separate small cells. As the user moves from cell to cell, the radio phone link switches from one central transmitter/receiver to a second; the call continues without interruption. Figure 8.16 shows

Figure 8.15 *High-volume two-way data transfer is best by a circuit switched network; packet switching allows efficient small one-way transfers*

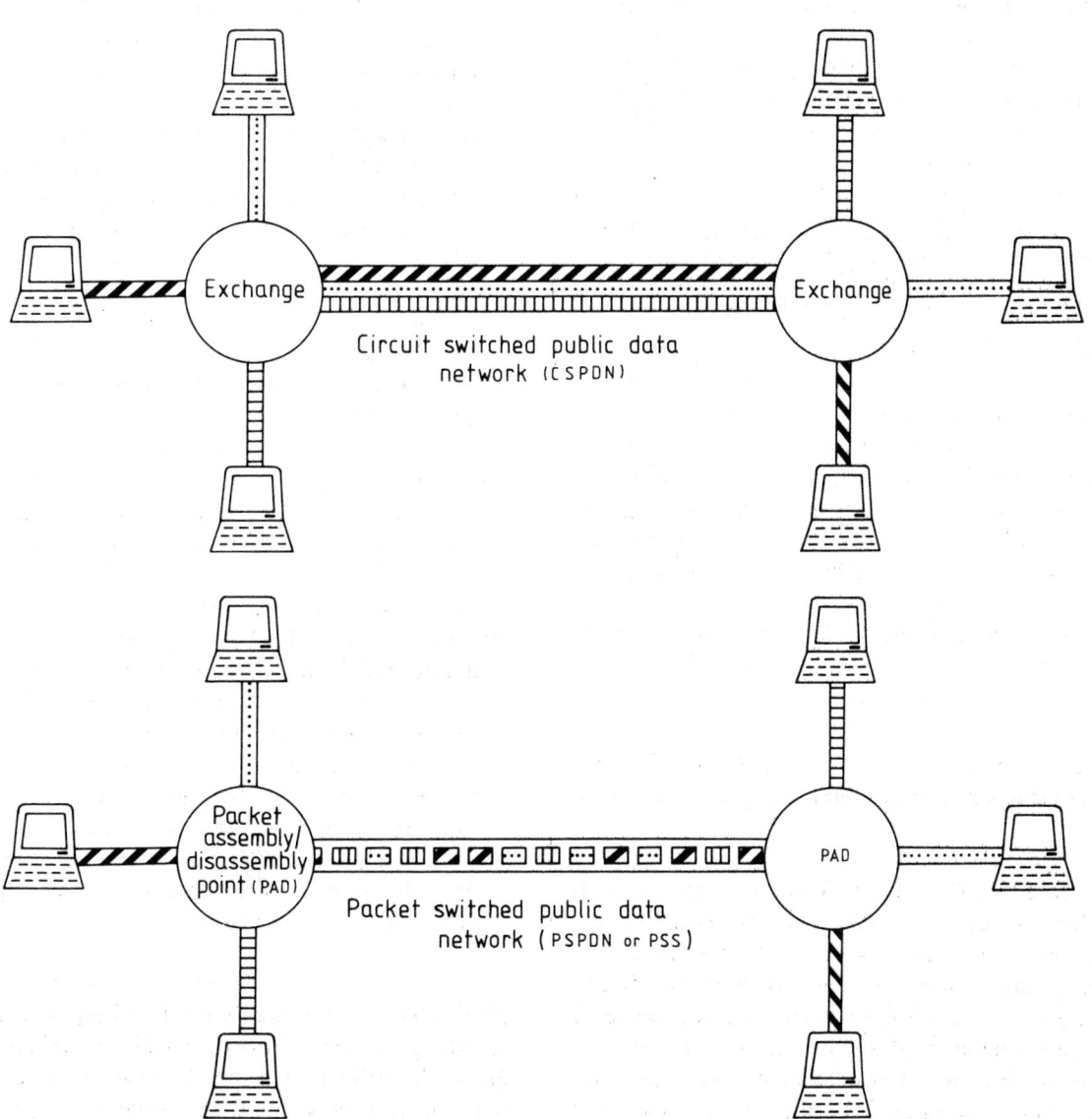

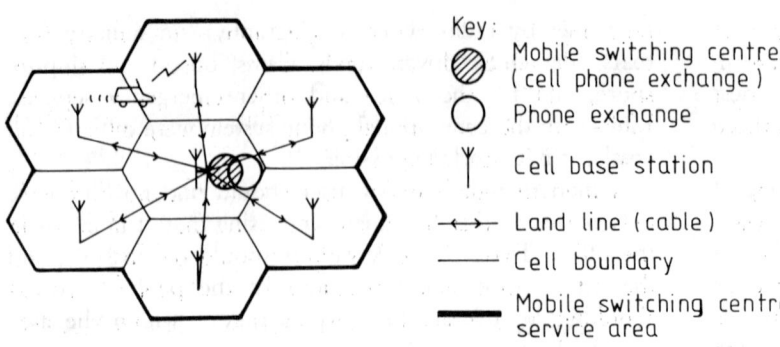

Key:

◉ Mobile switching centre (cell phone exchange)

○ Phone exchange

Y Cell base station

←→ Land line (cable)

—— Cell boundary

▬▬ Mobile switching centre service area

Figure 8.16 *Mobile phone users move between small cells served by separate aerials*

the arrangement. The base station at the centre of each cell in a group, with its separate radio transmitter/receiver and aerial, connects to a (fixed) mobile switching centre (MSC). This links to a standard phone exchange, so calls can pass between mobile and other subscribers.

Still, maybe the days of the mobile executive with mobile phone, computer modem and fax unit are numbered. IT may extend the home to a workplace at the centre of a web of modern communications. With telecommuting it's possible for you to stay indoors and use a terminal to link to whatever computer systems you may need. Teleconferring is the equivalent within the phone system. Using a teleconference link, more than two remote people can join a phone call at once. A computer conference is much the same—with a number of people contributing to a developing series of related typed messages. (There's also the video conference, in which more than two people link by video phone.)

The high-quality integrated digital phone network of the near future is sure to play a major role in this move away from excessive travel. Which systems—telecommuting, teleconferring, mobile phones, videophones and videoconferring —become prime factors in that trend remains to be seen. Still, the single high-volume digital cable system of the future—the **integrated services data network** (ISDN)—can carry all such signals cheaply and reliably. Fed by signals—voice, video and data—from local sources and from other networks (including by satellite links), ISDN has the power to produce the global village. This is a view of the future in which all work, living and leisure units are part of a great web of two way communications media. We'll return to this theme at the start of Chapter 10.

SELF-DEVELOPMENT QUESTIONS

See Page 137 for notes on these questions.

S8.1   Sketch the computer layout described in the case study and comment on how it aids efficiency.

S8.2   Read up the history of computing. Write an essay on the generations of hardware. Relate these to mainframe, mini and micro.

S8.3   Discuss the pros and cons of having your own micro rather than a work station on a larger system.

S8.4   Compare star (cluster), bus, ring and hybrid networks. If your school or college has one network or more, sketch the layout(s) and identify the type(s).

S8.5   Compare such a local area network with other links between computers in your school or college.

S8.6   Compare such a local area network with a wide area network such as Prestel. Include some notes on gateways.

S8.7   Research the pros and cons of the digital phone network over the older analog system. Write a full essay on the subject.

S8.8   Visit a local firm and explore and discuss its use of telex.

S8.9   Find out more about telex, teletex, and electronic mail, and compare them.

S8.10 Visit a local firm and explore and discuss its use of fax.

S8.11 Compare your school or college phone system to a multi-user computer.

S8.12 List the features of a modern local phone system based on a private branch exchange. Compare them with those of a key system. How many features are in common use in practice?

S8.13 Design a phone system and handset(s) to suit the needs of your home.

S8.14 List the types and features of modern phone ancillary equipment—answering machines, voicebank, loggers, for instance.

S8.15 Find out more about CSPDN, PSS and ISDN; compare them and assess their likely impact on daily life.

S8.16 Discuss with a user the pros and cons of the cellular mobile phone system.

S8.17 If EFTPOS is in use in your area, study it fully.

S8.18 What services would you like to have from an integrated services data network based on an optical cable link to all buildings?

S8.19 Would you like to telecommute?

EXAMINATION QUESTIONS

Q8.1   Explain the meaning of distributed processing. Explain briefly how distributed processing could bring advantages for either:

a the computerisation of the PAYE tax system, or

b the compilation of local editions of a large national daily newspaper

(AEB specimen paper) (6)

Q8.2 A preserved railway line runs from Ayton to Deeborough ten miles away with intermediate stations at Beeford and Seaham. The railway company are exploring the possibility of having a network of local terminals, one at each of the four stations, so that bookings can be made and recorded on a central computer. This would enable central accounting details to be provided for each station on each day of operation. The further expansion would be a second terminal at each station to allow travellers to obtain details of the train service and fares.

a Describe the hardware which the railway company would need to provide at each station to enable this system to be implemented.

(2)

b Describe the input and output requirements of

(i) the booking system
(ii) the train information system.

(8)

c Outline the files which will be necessary to store the information required for producing the accounting details.

(4)

d When the total system is operational what benefits and disadvantages are there likely to be for

(i) the railway company
(ii) the travellers?

(London) (6)

Q8.3 **a** Show, with the aid of a diagram, how a simple microcomputer network can be organised. Explain the purpose of the various parts of the system, and describe in outline how the microcomputers can communicate with each other.

b A multi-access system, with several terminals connected to a single computer, is similar to a microcomputer network in that both allow several users to work concurrently on the same system. What are the particular advantages of each of these systems?

(COSSEC) [8]

Q8.4 Discuss the relative merits of using British Telecom services or a private line to connect to establishments

in general [for data transfer]. Include in your discussions the choice of line speed.

(Oxford) (6)

Q8.5 The head office of a building society has fifteen rooms on each of the four floors accommodating office staff involved in maintaining financial and other records for all its customers and clients. In addition the society has ninety-seven branch outlets all within a 20-mile radius of the head office.

a What is meant by the terms LAN and WAN?

(2,2)

b What would be the advantages to the building society of installing a LAN? Where would it be installed?

(3,2)

c What would be the advantages to the society of installing a WAN?

(2,2)

d What equipment would be required to give branch offices on-line access to centrally held data?

(3)

The building society has recently taken over a smaller society, which operates around a city some 60 miles' distance from the first building society's headquarters. It has a similar operation but with only two floors of central office and forty-three branch outlets. As a result, there is a requirement to transfer files of several millions of characters between the two head offices regularly during the day.

e Approximately how long will it take to transmit a 5-megabyte file at a transmission speed of 9600 bits per second?

(2)

f For what purposes would branch offices use on-line access?

(Oxford) (4)

Q8.6 An architects' business has offices in London and Paris, and regularly needs to exchange information on designs. Describe and explain *two* possible alternative ways of operating, and discuss their relative merits and costs.

(Oxford) (20)

Q8.7 Why are standards needed for protocols and interfaces between communicating devices?

(3)

Give two examples of areas where interface standards exist for devices in specific application areas.

(Oxford) (4)

9 Systems

Figure 9.1   *Some computers need a lot of people to look after them* (ICL)

Case study 9—Expert witness

The newest member of staff on the payroll of Solomon Solicitors is a computer. It's not a special one; in fact it's just the same model as most of the machines the firm uses already. Yet some of the partners are a bit afraid of it—and others rub their hands with glee at the thought of the extra money they'll earn with it. What makes the new micro special is the expert system package it runs. Expert systems come in the field of machine (or artificial) intelligence.

Solomon Solicitor's expert system is a data base of legal facts—details of law, and the verdicts and rulings of past court cases. It's not, however, a simple data base of the sort discussed in Section 2.3 (nor even one of the more modern and flexible relational data bases); rather, it's a knowledge base—a structured collection of relevant facts, relationships, opinions and probabilities. This knowledge base is set in software that allows the system to ask an enquirer the questions it needs to reach a conclusion about the point at issue.

Figure 9.2 is a sketch of such a knowledge-based expert system (KBES)—a set of hardware (a personal computer) with the knowledge base and the enquiry software held in store and backing store. Solomon's expert micro sits in the corner of one of the offices, and a number of the partners use it during the course of most days.

Solomon Solicitors purchased the complete expert system as a package. It was developed by a specialist company of knowledge engineers, and a number of law firms are trying it now. The knowledge engineers had the task of gathering the facts and opinions held by several expert lawyers round the country. They had to collate this material and store it in a form that best allows easy access.

In a simple query session one of the partners, working with a client, is using the system to find out the client's rights to unemployment payments. The client has lost her job, the reason stated being that she wasn't able to cope

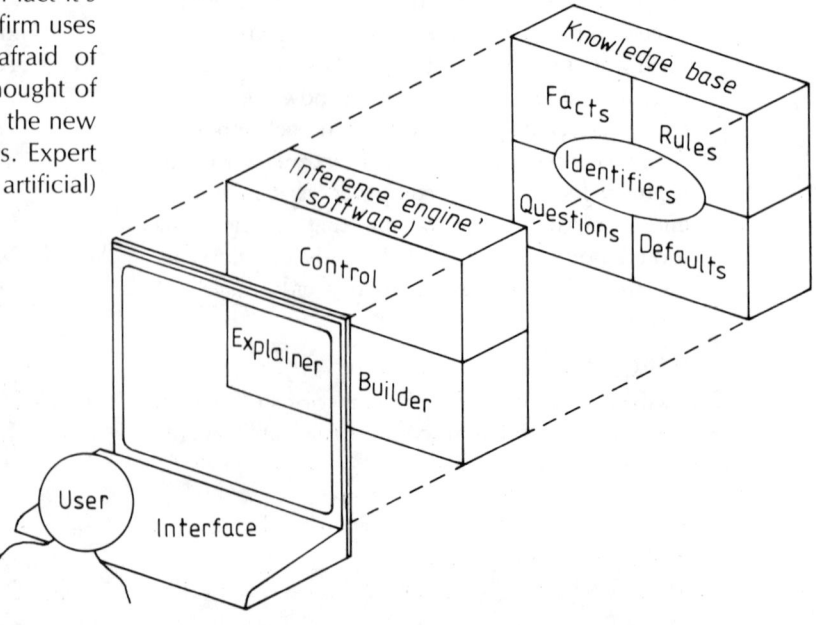

Figure 9.2   *A knowledge-based expert system is a computer with a data base of facts and relationships accessed through a query language*

with the tasks given her. She feels, however, that a personal problem with one of her bosses is the real reason.

During the session, the system asks more and more questions till it decides it knows all it needs about the case. It then gives its opinion—that the client would have a 75% chance of success if she sued for wrongful dismissal. If a court case came to that verdict, she would have the right to compensation—the system reckons £2500 would be a fair payment. She would also have the right to unemployment pay back-dated to the day she lost her job.

The lawyer now asks the micro to explain this judgment. From the printer comes a couple of sheets of paper. The notes refer to the clauses in the relevant laws and to past cases that have been much the same. (British verdicts are based not just on the law, but also on what past judges have thought was right.)

This session with the computer lasts just over an hour. No doubt the partner dealing with the case would have come to the same conclusion without the micro—but it would have taken quite a lot longer (and therefore would have cost much more in lawyers' time). Doing without the micro would also have meant a great deal of research through law books in the office and perhaps in a distant law library. Indeed, if the case had been really complex and the client had gone to a small law firm, it might have taken months and cost thousands of pounds to reach the same conclusion as the computer.

Solomon Solicitors know the expert system is not a god and can give opinions only on the basis of what it knows. All the same, the cases they've used it with have clearly shown this is a very useful short cut, and one that, while not perfect, seems on the whole to reach useful answers.

Introduction

What is intelligence? That lies behind the long asked question of if/when machines will be better than humans. Many people fear computers will eventually become so 'intelligent' that they'll take over the world. A more useful fear would concern human abuse of the huge powers already given us by IT, but it's still worth considering what we mean by computers being 'better' than people.

The first section of this chapter looks at the topic of machine intelligence. As well as expert systems, there are other relevant fields of interest, particularly work with natural (human) languages and with robotics. We'll then turn to more traditional uses of computers as we think about systems analysis and other computer-related jobs; systems analysts must now more and more decide whether machine intelligence can answer any of their clients' needs.

Objectives

When you have worked through this chapter, you should be able to

1 discuss what people mean by machine (artificial) intelligence and give examples of cases to which it may apply
2 outline the nature, development, structure and use of a knowledge-based expert system
3 describe briefly the use of an example expert system
4 state what 'system' and 'systems analysis' mean
5 outline the characteristics of a good systems analyst
6 describe the stages of setting up a new IT-based system and explain the system life cycle concept
7 apply the techniques of systems analysis, design and implementation to a simple case
8 show the hierarchical nature of a typical large data processing department, and outline the work of each person or group

9.1 Machine intelligence

So *are* computers likely to become better than people?

Computers are already better than people in many ways. Any computer can churn out invoices and circulars with fewer mistakes and at greater speed than any person. At least, it can do so once it's programmed and supplied with suitable data. Any computer can quickly crunch numbers of great size. At least, it can do so if someone's told it how. Any computer with a CD-ROM encyclopaedia on line is far better than you or I at finding a given item of information. At least, it's far quicker at showing on screen all paragraphs in which appears the phrase 'information technology', for instance. Quicker it may be at all such tasks, but discriminating it isn't—human users of a paper encyclopaedia may be slower at finding something, but at least they can reject references that aren't of value to them. Similar comments apply to all uses of computers—they can do tasks of varied kinds very well, but in a blind, unthinking, uncomprehending way. How we can do the same kinds of tasks, with insight and inspiration and a feel for relevance and short cuts, isn't open to analysis; it's an aspect of our intelligence.

People have defined human intelligence in many ways. I like to think of it as shown when someone does something for which there are no clear and obvious rules. Stringing words together to make a memorable poem; struggling to make sense of someone's handwriting; throwing out a quick view in a debate; using leftovers to make a lovely meal; knowing what to do in a crisis; sketching a landscape; planning a novel test in physics—none of these involve set procedures, and none are predictable in detail or clear as to method: all show intelligence.

A machine can't do any of those things. That's because a machine can do no more than follow the precise instructions given it—and the instructions *must* be precise. Yet the world is now full of talk of **machine intelligence**. If it has **artificial intelligence** (AI) a machine should clearly be able to do more than follow precise rules; it should rather act with 'fuzzy' logic and thus carry out tasks in a more 'human' way.

Most computers in use so far follow so called algorithms, precise (but restricted) sets of instructions and rules. The goal of workers in machine intelligence is to replace algorithms by **heuristics**—rules of thumb rather than of logic. 'If it's getting cloudy, I'll take a coat when I go out' is a heuristic. When these people reach that goal, computers *will* be able to carry out tasks in a more human way. For instance, they'll be able to react to natural language rather than the current baby talk we need to use; they'll be able to play games such as chess with a kind of insight, rather than by using immense number crunching power to assess all moves; they'll be able to solve problems, rather than just long sums: they'll appear to reason, rather than act blindly.

To do such things, the computer must be programmed with those heuristics rather than with the precise rules of the 1980s; it must also draw on a data base of facts and relationships; and it must be able to extend its data base, to 'learn by experience'.

An artificially intelligent computer with a knowledge data base is called a **knowledge-based expert system** (KBES or expert system for short). People who set up such systems are **knowledge engineers**.

Useful expert systems of this kind already exist in a number of areas of interest; people use them, for instance, in teaching and training, and in branches of medicine, architecture, engineering, and business, as well as law. In each case, the knowledge engineers obtain from human experts the facts, rules and heuristics for the data base. They would put in probabilities too, so the output can include possible solutions to the stated problem in order of likelihood. When that's been done, the computer carries an expert system. This means that when you enter a statement of a problem within its field in the right form, the system should be able to come up with reasonable solutions.

So an expert system is a data base of facts and relationships from which the software can make deductions rather as a human could. The content of the data base isn't just objective information, therefore—it forms a body of knowledge. If the data base is big enough and properly engineered, an expert system can approach or even surpass the standard of any single human expert. That means being able to solve well-stated problems correctly and in an apparently human way. Expert systems therefore meet one criterion of intelligence.

If you set the data base up right, and if you correctly state the problem, an expert system should actually give better solutions than any one human could. This is because it carries, and correctly works with, the knowledge of a number of experts in the field. But it doesn't have insight or show inspiration—computers aren't truly intelligent, and giving them an expert system doesn't make them so.

As expert systems become more common, people will more and more discuss this question of machine intelligence. However, there are other aspects of machine behaviour that raise the same question.

The ability to work fully with natural (human) language is a very important one, especially if speech input and output are being used rather than keyboard and screen. If a computer can be given a good grasp of natural language vocabulary, rules and heuristics, it should, for instance, be able to translate between human languages with no more error than could a human. In practice this is a hugely hard task. People could also use it for the automatic monitoring of suspects' telephone lines, a *Nineteen eighty-four* outcome that would be much less welcome. Thus, for a computer to work with human language means more than being able to converse with a user in a natural way.

Artificial speech leads us to artificial vision. Called pattern recognition, this is another important area of research that could produce to claims of machine intelligence. In turn it leads us to robotics; the future will bring machines that really can replace people in many areas of manufacturing. Able to see and to decide what to do on the basis of what they see, future robots will be much more flexible than those we have now.

But will they be intelligent? Perhaps we need to ask how much intelligence the replaced humans had to bring to bear on their work. Does drudgery *need* intelligence?

The Turing test is reckoned to be a good way to decide if a machine is smart or not. First proposed by Alan Turing forty years ago, a system would pass this test if someone interacting with it couldn't tell if it was a machine or a human. Figure 9.3 shows how to set up a Turing test for a computer. The user faces an input and an output device. As no current machine has good enough speech recognition and voice synthesis, these would have to be a keyboard and a screen or printer. Behind those is the machine under

Figure 9.3   *To pass the Turing test, a machine would have to behave just like a human*

test—or a second person, also with keyboard and screen. The machine would pass the test if it could persuade the user that it's the human—that is, if users couldn't tell whether they were conversing with machine or person.

The reasoning behind the Turing test is that we define a machine as being intelligent if what it does would be called intelligent in a living creature. The Turing test would pass a machine only if it showed human-level intelligence, so is very hard. On the other hand, it's not easy to devise a test to show if a machine has the intelligence of, for instance, a dog. There's a spectrum of intelligence in living things, that of creatures in the range from simple one cell life-forms, through plants, insects, and higher animals, to humans.

People described computers of the late 1970s as having the intelligence of earwigs; I'm not aware, though, if there was any scientific basis for that claim. We assess the intelligence of non-human life forms on the basis of behaviour rather than on that of conversational ability. We could try to measure machine intelligence with robots by finding out how well they interact with a changing environment, and how well they learn. A robot 'mouse' that can learn the best route through a maze has a degree of intelligence, therefore. It wouldn't be as smart as a mouse in all situations; only so as regards that task.

Because of this, adding a useful vision system to a robot is as important in the field of machine intelligence as is adding the power of speech input/output to a personal computer. Neither is a hardware challenge, but both require much storage, complex programs, and great processing power to show worthwhile success. Thus machine intelligence much above the earwig level requires main store with many megabytes of RAM, very sophisticated software for the analysis of inputs and the synthesis of outputs, and high-speed working. A current robot challenge—to design and build a machine to play table tennis—is indeed a challenge.

9.2 Systems analysis

Many people in the computing and IT industries feel systems analysts have the most exciting and rewarding lives. A really good systems analyst can have an excellent career and be very well paid indeed for the trouble. All the same, **systems analysis** requires very hard work and very hard thinking.

The job involves first looking with great care at the needs of an organisation (say, a firm), and at how they're meeting those needs at the moment (if they are). The next step is to decide if the current system for dealing with those needs is the best one. Here the word 'system' does *not* mean a computer system (a complete set of hardware, software, and liveware used to carry out a task). The word is more general: the complete set of people, procedures, and aids used to carry out the task. It's this kind of system a systems analyst analyses.

Having analysed the firm's needs and its current system,

and decided the latter isn't the best way to meet the former, the analyst tries to design a more suitable system. Again, this need *not* be an IT-based one; however, it normally is because many of a client firm's tasks concern information handling. In any event, the aim is to work out how to meet the firm's present and likely future needs most effectively: successfully, reliably, and cheaply.

Lastly, it's likely the systems analyst will watch over the introduction of the new system (that is, if the firm agrees to go ahead). After that there may be an on-going remote supervision role.

Most big firms have a systems analyst or two of their own; indeed some have large systems analysis departments. The latter may include more junior organisation and methods (O & M) staff as well as graduate analysts. A small firm, on the other hand, will call in this kind of expertise from outside when needed. As a result, many systems analysts and some O & M people are consultants—they work on their own or as a partner in a specialist group. Many computer bureaux can supply systems analysis expertise. A bureau is a specialist firm that rents out computer time, staff and expertise. It may well also run training courses using its own experts.

In any case, the people concerned need a deep, wide and always up-to-date knowledge and experience of IT.

In a given contract, the systems analyst is likely to work through all or most of these stages:

- defining the problem in outline and then in depth
- carrying out a feasibility study
- fact finding
- systems analysis itself
- new system design
- new system implementation
- system maintenance

People call this set of stages a system's life cycle. The name implies a circular process. This is as it should be—circumstances change (inside a firm, in its areas of interest, and in IT), so any system needs constant review.

Having defined what's to be done, the analyst carries out a feasibility study. This means getting enough information about the client to decide whether full study and analysis are likely to be worth while. It may well be that the current system is close enough to the best to make any change a matter of pointless expense and upset.

Fact finding is most important. This is carrying out a highly detailed review of the work being done at the moment and the system (methods) involved. The analyst's golden rule is to know clearly the context of the problem being looked at. The philosophy of fact finding includes

- finding out the hierarchical structure of the client firm and working within it (handling people well is crucial, especially where they may fear there's change on the way)

- having an open mind at all times (people's views of their work may not be correct)
- being flexible in the methods used (no two firms are the same)
- finding out who the experts are (they may be low down on the ladder)
- being prepared to rely on hunches to some extent (having a feel for one's work is of great value)

The main methods used in the fact finding stage are

- collecting relevant papers
- interviewing staff, and maybe some of the firm's clients
- quiet observation
- questionnaires

The work cannot be rushed: fact finding for a major project may take several analysts a couple of years. This is why large firms have their own full-time analysts—all the time they study what's going on and how it may be improved.

Quite often a new system is needed for some procedure that doesn't yet exist. For instance, a chain of shops may wish to extend to mail order. In this case the analyst will work mainly with the people who are planning the change and try to find out what they want to achieve. Even so, a great deal of the above kind of fact finding is needed.

Once the hundreds or thousands of facts have been collected and sorted out, the next step is to analyse the problem and the system and produce a summary report. Often the analyst may set this out in a flowchart (graphic) form—as always, a picture tends to be easier to study and work with than a lot of text; it's often much more compact, as well. The report shows the information flows into, through, and out of the system. (As in other contexts, information may well include money.) It also outlines the analyst's proposals for change (if any), and gives some idea of cost and time scale.

The analyst's report goes to the firm's management for consideration. They must decide whether they agree with the content and whether they wish to go ahead with the outlined proposals.

Once the client has agreed to proceed, the analyst will define and design the new system—the processes to do the job. Now is the stage at which the analyst looks hard at different ways of meeting the needs found. Now is the stage to compare the various solutions that involve IT, as well as those that don't. If the best solution found doesn't involve IT—which, to repeat, is not rare—then the rest of the analyst's work on that contract isn't relevant here.

This stage of systems analysis involves working out the best solution. How exactly can new information technology help? What are the precise computing needs? How should the hardware link into a local network or with systems elsewhere? What programs will carry out the tasks involved? How much can the IT systems that the client already has be used?

It's likely that the analyst will use a flowchart to describe the planned system. This is a system flowchart rather than one for a program (Section 7.2); Figure 9.4 shows some of the main extra symbols that may appear. Note that a flowchart is the most appropriate graphic here—an information-handling system is a sequential one; thus a structure chart is of less value.

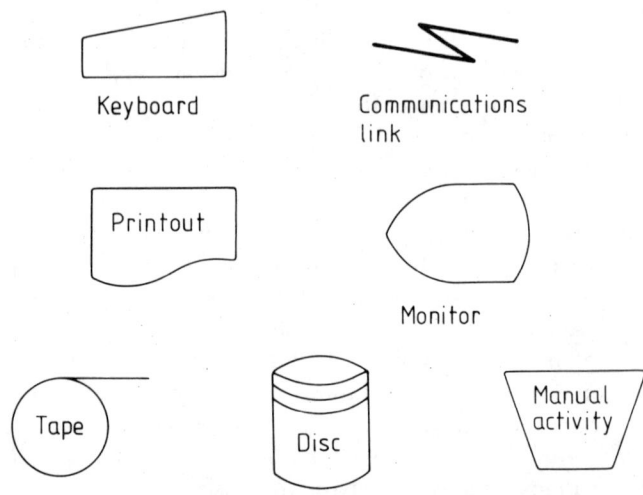

Figure 9.4   *A system flowchart involves a number of extra symbols*

If there's software on the market that can do the needed work, this will help determine what central processor should be bought in. That's because as yet no software runs on all computers; the current big problem of incompatibility, while getting smaller, will remain into the next century.

If no current software fits the user's needs, the analyst will call on a programmer to tailor something to suit, or even invite a programming team to produce a software suite from scratch. A big firm with its own systems analysts will likely have this expertise on tap too. Even if that's the case, the analyst will need to gain management approval at this stage; software development can cost more than hardware purchase.

The analyst will devise a broad structure chart or flowchart for the programmers, with notes on the files to be used (nature, content, type, structure), and on input and output data types and hardware. When those concerned have agreed the details, the programmers can get on with the job.

In designing the hardware/software system, the analyst always keeps in mind the following questions.

- Who are the users—and therefore how simple can we make the system?
- How easy is it to obtain the information needed to feed the system?
- How many different tasks can we carry out without making the system too complex?

All the while the analyst will have kept management

informed of progress, and when the hardware has been chosen it's time to get full approval to go ahead with purchase (or rental) and installation. The analyst must be able to provide detailed costings; to write good, clear, short reports; and to discuss them fully with non-experts as well as with experts.

Once the hardware and software are approved, the analyst schedules introduction. This needs close work with all the people concerned with usage—that includes the cleaning, security, and catering staff as well perhaps as architects, builders, designers, and suppliers.

At the same time the analyst will start to prepare detailed documentation for the actual users. Again it's crucial to be able to communicate effectively, this time not just with management and other professionals.

It's also the analyst's responsibility to prepare detailed test data and plans to check out the completed system, and to arrange the tests. Once this is done it's time to prepare a final schedule to put the new system into full operation, and to assist the users to prepare for it.

During the actual implementation of the new computer system, the analyst will have to deal at once with anything that goes wrong. This isn't easy, as there'll be a stage of parallel running—with the old system still in use while people check and then test the new one with real data. The analyst may well have a training role at this time too.

That may all make it sound as if systems analysts are super-human. Don't forget that in practice a team, perhaps a large one, will handle a big project, and will work closely with management. O & M staff may help with the less demanding parts of the work. All the same, an analyst must be

- an expert in hardware, software, management, and finance
- highly literate and able with numbers
- imaginative
- a good listener and communicator
- a good seller of ideas
- patient and tactful
- very attentive to detail

9.3 Liveware

A micro, and even a small network, may have no specialist staff to look after it, other than the users themselves; a technician or engineer may drop by every so often. A mainframe, on the other hand, can give employment to a large number of people. It may help to think of these people in two groups—users and others; however, the structure of a typical computing department in a big firm is as shown, hierarchically, in Figure 9.5.

The usual name for this part of a firm is the data processing department. **Data processing** (DP) has long been

Figure 9.5 *A large computer system provides work for many people*

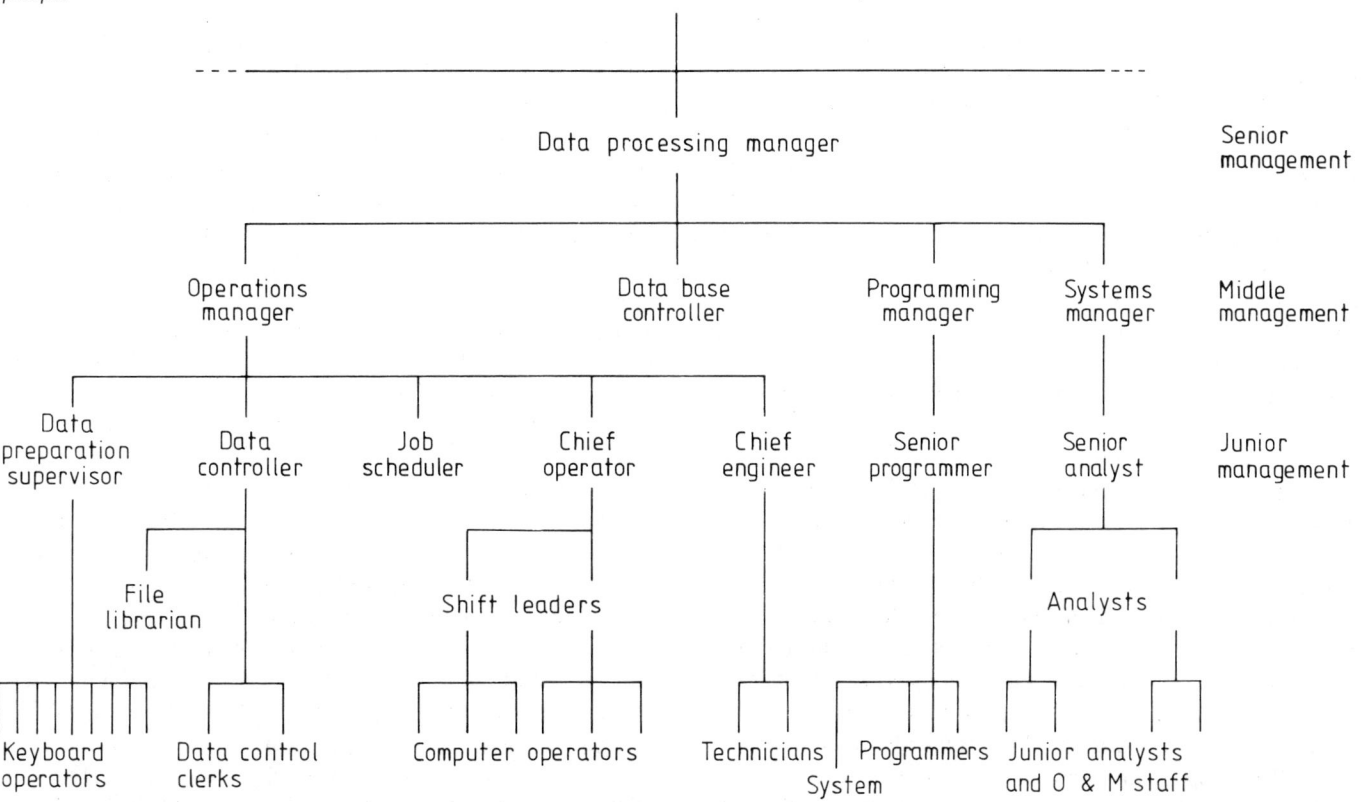

the name for the handling of business information—its input, storage, processing, transfer and output. When modern IT came to assist, the term electronic data processing (EDP) appeared. Now, though, people assume DP involves IT.

The DP manager not only looks after the whole department, but is part of the firm's senior or middle management team. Management expertise *is* crucial. So too is IT knowledge—thus many DP managers have a systems analysis background.

Below the DP manager come the people responsible for operations, data base control, systems, and programming. They look after their section of the department's work on a day-to-day basis, and consult as required with the others and with the DP manager on short-term needs and long-term planning.

The data base controller is a type of systems analyst (and in a smaller department may work in that section rather than separately). It's this person's task to ensure that at all times the data base (the firm's structured set of data) meets all design and anticipated needs and works as an integrated whole. There is an important planning role here, and the data base controller will often need to work closely with the system analysis staff.

While it's important for the system analysts always to try to keep up to date with the industry's hardware and software developments, in a large organisation one or more staff may have just this specific role. In such cases, in other words, there may well be a research and development team; the members work full time at exploring new types of software and new hardware units. In most cases these people would come in the systems section.

Section 9.2 looked at system analysis in detail, and also mentioned how the people concerned would liaise with the programming staff. The programmers have two areas of work—maintaining the existing software, and developing new programs; for this latter task their work would link closely with that of the system analysts. I touched on software maintenance before; in essence it consists of

- adding new procedures and removing old ones as the firm's needs change
- linking programs together in new ways for the same reason
- dealing with bugs as these arise
- increasing the efficiency of the programs
- enabling the software to work with new peripherals

They may also have a role in system security (Section 10.2).

Under the operations manager come all the people that we could call the system's real handlers. The manager is an administrator, who needs good knowledge of the system and its daily workings—the task here is to ensure that all jobs receive the right priority and are handled correctly and on time. The job scheduler assists in this particular aspect.

In a large DP department it's a huge task to control the data on a day-to-day basis. The file librarian (who may have assistants to help) is in charge of the large collection of program and data discs and tapes. For reasons of efficiency and security, a data library runs much like a book library—it involves a well-designed system for the issue of discs and tapes to the operators and their return when they're finished with. The librarian will also ensure that people always back up programs and data properly, and will have an important role in system security.

The operations staff are the only people who have much contact with the computer itself. Working in the computer room, to which few other people will have access, it's their job to keep the system running smoothly and to provide the peripherals with their needs from moment to moment. There will be people whose job is simply to ensure that the right discs and tapes are on the right drives at the right times, while others feed paper to the printers, put in new ribbons, and so on.

A large computer department, with hardware worth more than a million pounds, must work 24 hours a day. This is to make it cost-effective. It's normal, therefore, for there to be three shifts of operating staff; the shift leader of each group will sit at the main console and communicate with the computer. This person has to give the system its instructions —using job control language—and to react to messages from the processor about completed jobs and problems that arise.

All the work of the DP department depends on the transactions entered each day by the data preparation staff; they're a big section of the real users. A large firm may have hundreds of people entering data each day, either in the same building as the computer, or scattered round the country. These are keyboard operators, efficient typists whose work involves getting data into the system from source documents (like forms, invoices, and questionnaires) and their phone calls.

It would not be efficient for the central processor to look after the needs of so many input units; if it does it may have little time left for real processing. Thus it's normal for the keyboard operators to work off line using a separate key to store (for instance, key to disc) approach. This involves a separate computer, maybe a mini, which works full time collating the input data into one or more transaction files. As described in Section 6.3, a major task of the night shift staff will be to merge the previous day's transaction files with the master files, and produce child masters for people to work with the next day.

There are of course other computer users within a firm of any size—secretarial staff and typists using word processors, people working with accounts software and other business programs, and all the staff searching for information. Many of these people may well use stand-alone micros or one or more networks not linked full time to the main computer.

The DP manager will have responsibility for all IT equipment used within the firm; however, apart from dealing with problems and providing advice, the DP staff will have little day-to-day contact with these other users.

The work of systems analysts is important in all stages of the so-called system life cycle. That phrase describes the development and implementation of a new system for carrying out a task or set of tasks. It also implies, by using the word 'cycle', that development and implementation never finish, that the systems analyst's job is rather like painting the Forth Bridge: when you get to the end, you have to start again.

We've looked at the stages of a system life cycle in this section, and Table 9.1 below shows them in graphic form. This doesn't differ much in outline from the list at the start of the section, but now I show the cyclic aspect as well. I also include the analyst's skills (listed above) at some of the most appropriate points.

Table 9.1

Life cycle stage	Systems analyst's skills
Use current system	
* Recognise (potential) problem	Management expertise
Define problem	
Carry out feasibility study (including fact finding)	Patience and tact Communications
Report	Literacy Salesmanship Management expertise
Design new system	IT expertise Imagination Attention to detail
Implement new system	IT expertise
Document new system	Literacy
Test new system	IT expertise
Supervise parallel running and training	Management expertise Patience and tact
Phase out old system	Ditto
Maintain system	IT expertise
Back to *	

The system life cycle view applies throughout the spectrum of systems development. (And, I repeat, it applies whether or not new information technology is part of the solution to the problem identified.) At one extreme, it applies to thinking about getting a personal computer at home to word process formal letters and party invitations and for playing games, or to bringing IT to the rescue of the manager of a corner shop who finds stock control and tax records too much to cope with manually. At the other extreme, just the same ideas are involved in setting up a new automated assembly line costing tens of millions of pounds or converting the news room of a large broadcasting company to a computer network.

The level of expertise required of the person(s) who act as systems analysts in these extreme cases will of course differ greatly (as will the cost of using the expertise)—but the principles are just the same.

A highly experienced and highly successful freelance systems analyst may earn £50 000 or more a year, an income matched in the IT field only by that of top sales staff. You can see why many people working in computing therefore dream of fighting their way on to and up the systems analysis ladder.

SELF-DEVELOPMENT QUESTIONS

See Page 137 for notes on these questions.

S9.1 Can a client sue a legal expert system if it gives the wrong ruling as the most likely?

S9.2 An expert system in the field of expert systems could design a better expert system than itself. Could this go on to produce a perfect expert system? If so, would it 'rule the world'?

S9.3 If you can, use an expert system to reach a conclusion about a simple question in the subject area it handles.

S9.4 If you have a knowledge-based expert system shell in your school or college, work with a couple of friends on the same course as yourself to produce a small but valid expert system on a topic of your choice.

S9.5 Try to obtain access to Prolog (the best version is *Simple*) or another so-called artificial intelligence language and work through some simple tasks. You should build up a small knowledge base and query it.

S9.6 The authors of many BASIC programs claim these let a micro show intelligence. Work with one such program and assess how well it fares on the Turing test. If you don't agree that it's in any way intelligent, why is it claimed to be?

S9.7 If you can work with a maze-running robot mouse, do so, and assess how intelligent it is. Otherwise attempt to design a suitable program for a floor turtle or other mobile robot.

S9.8 I noted in the case study that some Solomon Solicitors partners much welcome the expert system, while others are rather afraid of it. Join a group of students to enact a partners' meeting. Choose either a meeting at which one person proposes getting the system, or one a few months after it arrives, at which the firm tries to assess its worth.

S9.9 Use the final paragraph in Section 9.1 as the basis for an outline assessment of the hardware and software needs of one or more of these systems:

a   to decode a spoken instruction in the form of a natural English sentence

b   to produce a natural-sounding response to a natural language question

c   to take a given book from a shelf of books

d   to play table tennis

S9.10   Word process a little 'handbook' for a systems analyst, 1500–2500 words in length.

S9.11   Choose a department or section of your school or college (one you know well, if you can) that uses one or two computers. Analyse the system and report on its effectiveness to the person in charge.

S9.12   In the same way choose an area that doesn't use computers. Design a suitable system within an agreed budget and report.

S9.13   Explain why a good systems analyst must have the nature and skills listed at the end of Section 9.2.

S9.14   Draw a set of systems flowcharts for the school or college library. There should be a chart each for the accessioning, loan, and return of an item. Can you amend the charts to show how the library handles (a) reservations, and (b) overdue items?

S9.15   Carry out a feasibility study and prepare a report for one of the following small-scale systems:

a   the use of a personal computer in the home of a family with one or two professional parents (e.g. teacher, doctor, lawyer, architect);

b   the use of a micro to ease the administrative pressures on the owner of a small corner shop.

EXAMINATION QUESTIONS

Q9.1   An applications package for a computer system is to replace a manual system. A stage in the testing of the package is to run the two systems together, in parallel, using the same live data. What, in your opinion, are the aims of this stage of the testing?
(London)   (5)

Q9.2   Give *three* characteristics of a system that would lead you to believe that it may be suitable for computer implementation.
(JMB)   (3)

Q9.3   Give *three* features of a problem that make it likely that an applications package already exists for implementing its solution.
(JMB)   (3)

Q9.4   A language for programming in logic has two parts,

a   a data base of rules or facts, and

b   a set of definitions for relationships.

Here are some facts:

(RDY Male)	(RDY Father-of E4)
(E4 Male)	(RDY Father-of G)
(G Male)	(RDY Father-of R3)
(R3 Male)	(E4 Father-of E5)
(E5 Male)	(E4 Father-of R)
(R Male)	(E4 Father-of L)
(A Male)	(H8 Father-of M1)
(H8 Male)	(H8 Father-of L1)
(E6 Male)	(H8 Father-of E6)
(L Female)	(L Mother-of A)
(L1 Female)	(L Mother-of H8)
(M1 Female)	

Here are some definitions of relationships:

(X Son-of Y): (Y Father-of X), (X Male)
(X Son-of Y): (Y Mother-of X), (X Male)
(X Male-line-descendent Y): (X Son-of Y)
(X Male-line-descendent Y): (X Son-of Z), (Z Male-line-descendent Y)

Thus, for example, (R3 Son-of RDY) and (E5 Male-line-descendent RDY).
Suggest definitions for

Brother-of   (3)
Ancestor-of   (3)
Uncle-of   (2)

In each case apply your definitions to the data base above and give all incidences of your relationships.
Draw the family tree.
(Oxford)   (2)

10 Computers and you

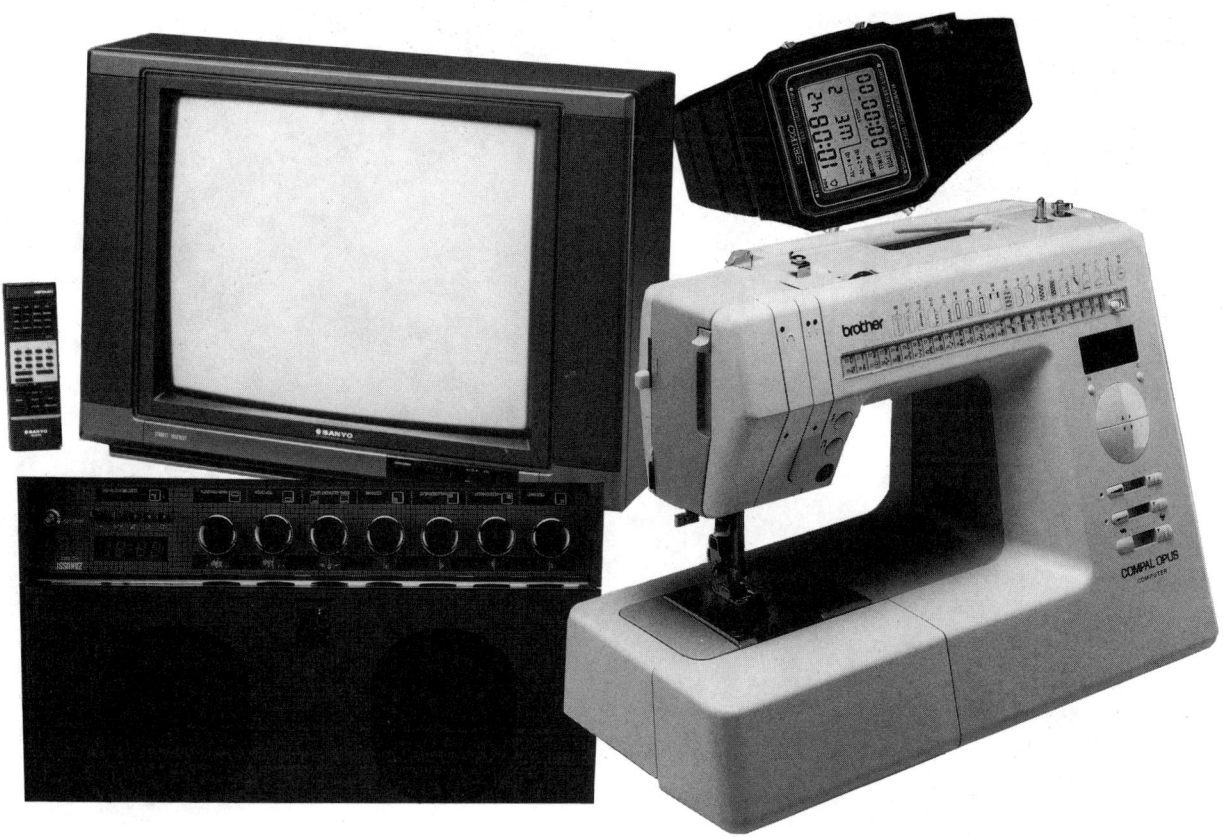

Figure 10.1 *Many home items contain computers, or at least special purpose microprocessors, even if not all are obvious*

(Zanussi; Seiko; Brother)

Case study 10—Home sweet home, 2001?

Perhaps your home in a decade or so may be like this! Let's say you're married with a couple of small children. You and/or your partner may have a job, but even if not, where you live is almost sure to have a lot of IT systems. Some will work alone; some will link to others in the home and outside. Some are like those you had at home when you were at school; others are new.

In your childhood home you very likely had a TV set. Since then TV has gone on growing in sophistication, flexibility and importance. The TV set in your 2001 home offers high definition, with the pictures built up of well over a thousand lines rather than the 625 of your youth. The screen area may thus be as much as four times larger—but the set will be flat rather than deep like those of the 1980s, so you can fix it to a wall like a picture.

The TV signals come to the set (at least if you live in a town or a city) by cable rather than through an aerial. All the area's houses and other buildings link to a web of underground lines like the electric power network. Instead of having a TV licence you pay the cable operator charges that depend on usage (in the same way as your parents paid for using the phone). The cable operator provides fifteen viewing channels—the six national channels, output from the local community TV services, and programmes from other countries that it picks up on its satellite dish aerial.

When you switch the set on, the screen divides into twelve or more windows, each showing the picture for one channel. It's easy now, therefore, to choose what to view. However, when you've chosen one channel to watch, you can still keep a little picture of a second in the top left corner of the display if you wish. Thus you can sit down to one programme while waiting for the news to start on the second channel.

Some programmes are interactive. The signal-carrying power of the cable is enough to let you send messages 'up

Figure 10.2   *The developments in video starting to come into homes in the 1980s were all based on microprocessors*

stream' to the cable operator. Thus, at the end of each part of a debate you can vote on the topic discussed. At the crucial stage of a film you can say which ending you'd like to see. The Government may even sometimes seek your views on matters of policy.

There are other sources of signals than the cable. When your video cassette machine broke down a couple of years ago, you replaced it with a video disc recorder which you can use in much the same way. You can buy or hire video discs to play at home—but each one, about the size of an LP, contains many hours of video material. You can record on to your own video discs—taking programmes received down the cable or signals from your own video camera.

That cable can carry your home video material up stream to the operator too. You and a group of friends may produce a TV programme to go out on a community channel. There's also the equivalent of the radio phone-in programme, to which you can contribute your views with a picture of you talking, or clips from your home-made videos on matters that may interest others.

Figure 10.2 shows late 1980s versions of some of the systems mentioned above—but all the systems mentioned above existed then, even if only as prototypes in some cases.

By 2001 the phone system has become much more versatile. Your house is only a few years old; its builders linked it to the area's cable without question, and the cable carries voice phone signals as well as video. You've a couple of phone handsets which you carry round the house and garden; radio keeps each in touch with the living room unit that links to the cable. These wireless phone extensions are a lot more convenient than the units most people used in the 1980s; indeed one might be a cell phone (Section 8.4) you use in the car or in the streets anywhere in Europe.

Each phone handset has a microprocessor and main store too. This intelligence lets you call any one of a hundred frequently used numbers with a couple of key-presses; it lets you re-call any of the last five numbers you tried; it keeps on trying till it gets through if it meets the engaged tone; it lets you join in a conference with several other phone users at a time. A flat display the size of a passport photo shows the time, the number, length and cost of each call; and other information.

Like video, the phone signals pass through the cable network. The high capacity of this means that wide-band (large frequency range) phone communication is very cheap. As a result, many people now have video phones—each person using one sees the other's face while hearing the voice. For most, these are only a gimmick; all the same, there are more serious uses—though the image is only black and white (monochrome) and, because of the slow frame transfer rate (just a couple of frames a second), it doesn't show movement well.

Even so, the video phone system is good enough to transmit an image of a piece of paper—so you can show such things as maps, pictures, and letters to people you speak to on the phone. You can even attach a printer to some new models, so a key-press gives you a paper copy of the screen image for later study. While by now every office uses fax (Section 8.4), it's still rare in the home—maybe by the time your children are in their teens the video phone printer link will provide just as good a service.

By then too, perhaps most video phones will handle colour pictures. That will make it even easier for you to produce home videos and to send your own material along the cable into the community TV 'phone-in' programmes mentioned above.

The cell phone concept has also come a long way since the mid-1980s. When it started, it fast became highly popular—as a result, many people who wanted to join the scheme couldn't, and the costs all stayed too high. Now the problems are mostly overcome and the whole of Europe is one great cell net, with many millions of private cell phones in use. Phones are common in public transport as well—taxis, trains, buses, planes; the old public call box system has changed dramatically as a result, much to the dismay of the vandals.

Even when you were at school, the phone system was growing fast as a carrier of data as well as of voice signals. Now every cable operator offers all subscribers both a whole video channel for teletext and Picture Prestel.

Teletext—one-way videotex—has been very popular since it first appeared in the 1980s. Then, however, it was tied to radio broadcasting rather than cable, and only a tiny part of each TV channel was set aside for data. That meant each channel could offer no more than a couple of hundred pages of data—while users still had to face quite long waits to receive what they wanted.

By giving a whole video channel to teletext, the operators can broadcast data at several hundred frames a second. They now offer a full service of news, weather and sports reports, plus such features as the arrivals and departures screens of the nearby main rail stations and airports.

Viewdata is still of importance to many people, though, and it has many million users in Britain. Viewdata has two advantages over teletext—it's two-way (interactive), and, as it sends pages only on demand, it can offer millions of them. Picture Prestel is better than 1980s Prestel in having far better graphics (far higher resolution). Now, for instance, if you want to move house, you can look at pictures of suitable homes in the part of the country you want; when you plan your holiday, you can study views of hotels, beaches, and tourist traps; when you teleshop, you can study the goods you may buy.

Some people still access cable teletext and viewdata on their wall-mounted TV sets using small remote-control keypads. This approach isn't very good for such purposes as sending electronic mail messages; *you* use the home computer, therefore. However, before we turn to your 2001 home computer, look at Figure 10.3 to see pictures of some late 1980s systems in the area of phone communication that led to the above techniques. These too were all based on microprocessors.

The typical home computer of 2001 looks nothing like what you used at home and/or school when you were young. Figure 1.13 still describes it, of course, but you can't see it to check that statement: the hardware is all built into the house. The central processor and main store are in a cupboard upstairs; the main input units are a microphone in each room, with speakers for output; you don't touch backing store very much so the drives are in the walls in living room, kitchen and spare room.

2001 is the title of a popular old science fiction story. The tale featured just such a computer, called Hal. Hal was built in, but it was much more intelligent than your home computer is. Both systems have a fair grasp of human language, and of voice input and output. Hal was described as being very smart in the sense of being able to draw conclusions from input data and to learn—your system may be quite clever, but it's nowhere near as good.

All the same, your computer can respond to a wide range of spoken commands, as long as it's a member of your family speaking them and you don't gabble. It works 24 hours a day, ready at all times to do what it's told as far as concerns running the house, the IT systems, and itself.

The unit automatically

- controls heating, cooling, lighting
- opens and closes doors, curtains and windows
- handles fire, intruder and other security needs
- deals with incoming and outgoing video, voice phone, and data phone signals
- reports the meter readings for water, gas, phone, power, TV

Figure 10.3   *The new phone systems of the late 1980s were just the start of a hugely important telecommunications revolution (Telefocus)*

- guards the outside door locks

Some people's home computers handle even more complex robotic tasks, like watering plants and feeding pets, but you don't want *all* your work done for you, do you?

At any time, you or one of the others in the family can tell the computer to do such things as

- check the car for fuel and service needs (if the car's plugged in so its computer can communicate with the home system),
- get a friend on the phone,
- display frames on screen from teletext or viewdata,
- load a certain compact disc into the player so you can listen to music in bed,
- look up something in an encyclopaedia video disc,
- and so on.

The operating software of such a computer is quite complex, but doesn't differ significantly from that of a 1980s school or office network. The main backing store is a compact disc (CD-ROM); this holds all the main programs and data you're likely to need, but you can use any of the drives to load in a new disc for some special purpose if you need. Your cable operator also offers a telesoftware service anyway—so you can download new programs and data as required, and put them on disc for later use.

Your home computer isn't as good as some modern office machines at understanding spoken English. You therefore need a keyboard sometimes—for example, for text processing; getting messages ready for electronic mail; adding new records to your various data bases; and perhaps for tasks related to your job. Maybe when the children are a bit older, they too will need to use a keyboard sometimes as they work on learning software.

Computers and you 125

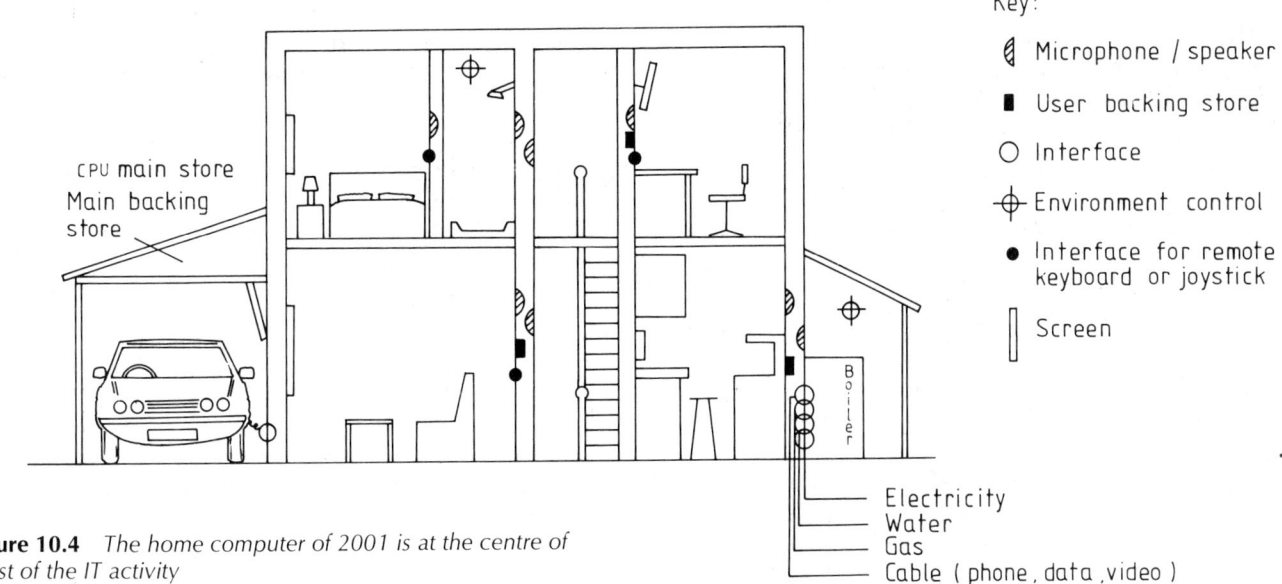

Key:
- Microphone / speaker
- User backing store
- Interface
- Environment control
- Interface for remote keyboard or joystick
- Screen

CPU main store
Main backing store

Electricity
Water
Gas
Cable (phone , data , video)

Figure 10.4 *The home computer of 2001 is at the centre of most of the IT activity*

Now, though, their games and simple learning software need input only from the infra-red signal from a joystick or mouse.

There isn't the space here to say more about all the different things your 2001 home computer can do. The system is complex, for in a sense it's the IT control centre at your address—as the outline system chart of Figure 10.4 shows.

Introduction

There isn't the space here, either, to take this case study further. Teleshopping and telecommuting are two big areas of home IT in 2001 that you must think about for yourself.

The above story may sound rather like science fiction—and in a sense it is. Yet I've described nothing there that isn't likely to be in at least some First World homes by 2001, and there's absolutely no reason for the central home computer system I described not to be common and cheap.

However, the crucial development is not actually the computer—it's the cable network that must be in place to take our homes into the new IT world of the twenty-first century. Many people hope that by 2001 large parts of Britain will have cable networks as described, but at the time of writing it's not certain whether the plans will be agreed soon enough.

When they are, Britain will start moving toward a society very different from any in the past. That society will become part of the 'global village'—when all people in the developed countries can access masses of information quickly and very cheaply. The global village concept sees us all linked together in a web of computer-aided information access that makes distance lose its meaning—it should be as easy to communicate (voice, video, data) with someone in Beijing, Buenos Aires or Bucharest as with someone in the next street. Whether you'll want to is a different matter, but the ability to do so has profound implications, both for people's world views and for world peace.

IT also has its dangers. While Hal in the novel *2001* is a good model of the home computer, Big Brother in *Nineteen eighty-four* abuses the power of the cable network and the central computer data base. In this chapter we must touch on such matters too. After all, Hal went mad . . .

Objectives

When you have worked through this chapter, you should be able to

1 describe some likely near-future developments in TV
2 outline the nature of a cable network and comment on the services it could provide
3 list likely near-future developments in the fields of compact and video discs
4 list likely near-future developments in video and mobile phones
5 list likely near-future developments of teletext and viewdata
6 list likely near-future developments in home computer technology
7 discuss the pros and cons of aspects of new IT as regards society and the individual
8 outline the optimistic and pessimistic views of the impact of IT on employment
9 state examples of computer-based crime
10 outline and assess typical security precautions

11 state who is, and who is not, a data user in the context of the British Data Protection Act

12 outline the code of practice of a data user

13 state the rights of data subjects in respect of personal data held on them by data users

10.1   IT moves on

As much of this chapter so far has us looking forward, we can fairly go on in the same vein a little longer. Where is IT taking us?

IT's concern is the storage, access, processing and transfer of information fast and cheaply, and in a way from which all concerned can gain most.

In the global village future, all people have cheap, effective access to the information they need and want. Various scenarios could let that happen; all depend on world-wide availability of the right hardware, the right software, and cheap means of high-volume information storage and transfer. Cable and satellite links can provide that last feature, and progress in hardware will continue its amazing pace. As far as storage is concerned, floppy magnetic discs are moving to capacities as high as 100 MB; hard discs, **digital audio tape** (DAT), and compact and video discs will show an increase in storage density of the same order. Within a decade computer users could have as much information locally on line as they may wish.

Continued miniaturisation, with its spin-off of increased reliability and reduced costs, is also significant. (This is so even in such areas as electric motors—some now fit on to the chips that carry their control circuits, so are just a tenth of a millimetre across.) Super-conductivity may reduce to nearly nothing the electric power demands of hardware units and network links, while bio-electronics brings people and machines much closer together.

As far as concerns programs, we can expect highly integrated software in artificially intelligent systems, plus multi-processing, the ability to handle large quantities of data at speed using a number of programs in a number of processors at the same time.

While most of these developments will first affect large organisations, they'll rapidly spread to the small firm, to education and training, and to the home.

Thus a scenario near one end of the spectrum sees a global satellite and cable network linking each work, living and leisure unit. In the unit—office, school, shop, home, pub—is an adequate supply of intelligent work stations. Current progress in machine intelligence and true concurrent processing could lead to those being non-local, in the sense described in the case study. Talking with a computer tucked away out of sight may give people problems, however. Anyway, talking may not always be the best way to get information into and out of a computer: think of noise and security problems.

There'll always be a need for visual displays, to let you study (for example) tables of information, views of products or places, and data in text, table or graphic form. The large flat wall unit will show broadcast and recorded TV, the face of the person across the world with whom you're holding a phone call, frames from any of many videotex data bases (teletext and viewdata), documents and pictures from microform and video disc archives, restful scenes from your library of pet landscape photos, and computer-generated graphics to match your mood with a kind of living wall paper. The software driving the display would of course offer windows (a split-screen feature, in other words) in all these contexts, so you could keep an eye on, or work with, information from various sources at once. That cable system has a lot to carry . . .

Near the other end of the scale is a scenario in which each unit is fairly self-sufficient in information. There'd be much the same hardware, but in most cases users would work with information on the unit's own bank of chips and discs. The social view behind this particular scenario involves the idea of the village in a true sense—one where people relate to each other in a tight local community rather than in the world as a whole.

Current thinking seems to lean toward a unification of global communications—and thus some easing in their use—rather than a fragmentation. But can IT really reduce the stresses that seem to come with the current style of living and working?

One way that could reduce those stresses at work is a much increased degree of telecommuting. In this view, the need for local and long-distance business travel falls as information transfer—communication—becomes faster and cheaper. In the case of many jobs, working from home or from a base down the street is no problem if there's a global cable network. The video phone and its potential for video-conferences should reduce the urge for face-to-face meetings. Better expert systems, universal and fast electronic mail, interactive video, electronic and desktop publishing, fax—better versions of most things we've looked at indeed should all reduce the need for travel.

There are many possible IT-based views of the future. On the way there, hardware, software, machine intelligence and telecommunications links will all continue to improve, cheapen and spread—almost regardless of the social system. What happens depends on how people decide to use what's on offer rather than on changed technology as such. Choice therefore concerns how to give all the people involved a fuller life—less drudgery, less boredom, more freedom to do their own thing in their own way. This should be so wherever we end up on that spectrum of IT futures. Living with IT shouldn't mean just coping with it, but using it as a positive aid to dealing with your needs in society.

10.2   IT and social change

In Question S9.8, I invited you to explore why some of the

solicitors in Case study 9 were afraid of the firm's new knowledge-based expert system package. Without doubt, it's a fact that many people, well educated or less so, show real fear or express concern about the current 'information revolution'. On the other hand, many welcome new information technology; they do so on the grounds that it can extend and free the power of the human brain—in the same way as machines extend and free the power of human muscle.

It isn't hard to take that analogy further. If you do so, you may think of people's fears and society's problems when the major industrial revolution got under way in the late eighteenth century. The times were marked by much concern about machines taking work from humans—just as now so many worry about loss of employment as a result of computers and robots.

It's crucial to realise that point of view makes a lot of difference. If IT helps a firm become more efficient, this may be a Good Thing—for a large number of people, both in the firm and outside it. That will be so even if the number of staff employed falls; there's much sense in taking productivity—output per person—as a measure of efficiency. All the same, the staff members who lose their jobs as a direct result of IT won't feel quite the same.

Properly applied, IT has the power to make many kinds of organisation more efficient, and thus to improve society as a whole. Most of us would agree that an improved society is one whose members lead longer and more pleasant lives: have more money, more goods, more leisure, less hassle, less pain, less drudgery. However, as society improves in these ways, it shouldn't do so by the careless sacrifice of individuals. It's important for progress to be humane.

Humane progress is more likely if the members of society are aware of what's going on. I say this not from a feeling that those who are aware exploit those who aren't. It's because I believe that a society whose individuals can discuss the nature of life and its trends, and can come to terms with (even if not effect) change, is better than one where this isn't the case. For sure, information technology has done much in its own public relations cause, but it's a pity that people involved in different aspects of its work find it hard to explain to the rest what they're doing. Computer jargon is a real barrier to the communication and discussion we need.

The basic argument for the introduction or extension of IT in society even at the cost of jobs is this. Without IT the firms and organisations concerned—and I include individuals and their homes—would become less efficient. In that case they'd become less able to survive. In other words, there may be even greater job losses and even more misery if firms and people don't computerise and automate.

The argument then goes on that an organisation using IT can grow, as a result of the increase in demand for its cheaper goods and services that follows improved efficiency. Then it can employ more staff, have them work shorter hours, pay them more, and *still* provide more goods more cheaply to the rest of society.

Lastly, as the firms, their staff and their customers pay more tax as a result of the above, society will better be able to support its dependants—the unemployed, the young, the retired, the sick.

There are two sides to many other related arguments. For instance, some people feel that for workers to have computers or robots to help would reduce morale, because they would have less responsibility. On the other hand, there are those who say that having such help will free us (that is, our time and energy) for more interesting tasks, in particular for planning. There's some truth in the latter view, but it does expect us to be fairly well educated, and also to have a positive attitude to change. We may need to be re-trained, for instance; indeed, by the next century some people may find themselves re-trained three or four times during their working lives.

Most of the comments made so far in this section applied just as much to the Industrial Revolution as they apply to the present spread of information technology. The most important social effect of the former was not the feared fall in employment (indeed the opposite was the case); it was the major change in the structure of society that followed.

Within a few decades, Britain changed from a society in which almost all the population lived and worked on the land to an industrial system with most of the people living in towns and working in offices and factories. Will the present 'revolution' have any such sweeping effect on society as a whole?

This question is just as significant as that of employment. I'll say little about it, but give you just a few pointers to think about and discuss.

It is a bit too simple to claim that we're seeing a major shift from employment in industry to employment in information-related work and the service industries. In particular, it may make you feel society is turning into one of parasites, one whose members don't truly contribute. It's also easy to infer from that statement that production will fall, and therefore that society will become poorer. That is not the case.

Britain became extremely rich in the nineteenth century because machines helped people create wealth. It's now possible for society to gain further in wealth by letting computers and robots help people. I implied as much when we looked at the effects of IT on employment. In the same way as the Industrial Revolution led to farms, ships, mines, and factories (and very many other organisations) being able to run with greater efficiency but only a handful of people, so will the IT revolution give us much more of the same. There can be continued growth in a country's wealth; the only important thing to ensure, surely, is that all receive a fair share of that wealth, even if they're not owners or in work.

In this chapter we've already looked forward to a possible future half a lifetime away in which a First World country like Britain has reached social equilibrium following the upheaval of the information revolution. That picture is one in which every home, work place, and public area links to an IT network (the cable system) making information very cheap, easy to access, and easy to share.

I raised the concept of telecommuting, in which very many people work from home, using IT links as needed. Should telecommuting become the norm—as some people think it could—a major reason for the existence of towns and cities would vanish: the main modern function of towns and cities is as work centres with residential suburbs.

Perhaps, then, the information revolution might reverse the result of the Industrial Revolution, and return the population to a much more even spread over the land. This may remove urban problems—heavy traffic, noise, dirt, the troubles of the inner cities; on the other hand, it could also lead to a fragmentation of society that not all would welcome. Yes, again there are opposing points of view. Some people fear the home's becoming an IT cocoon from which most people would never venture; others note the tremendous growth in leisure pursuits in recent decades and expect that to continue.

Perhaps there's little any one person can do about any of the trends discussed here. To repeat, being aware of what's going on is what matters. So is being prepared to form reasoned views of what life should be like, to make them public, and even to campaign for them. There are, however, other causes for concern about which more can be done. These include computer-related crime and IT abuse in a concrete sense. In this context, security concerns setting up safeguards to protect data (in the widest sense) from being copied, erased, or changed with criminal intent.

We should define 'computer crime' as criminal acts which couldn't happen without computers. Yet people often blame IT for many crimes which have long existed, just because the criminals now use computers to help them. Currently, computer criminals in the strict sense tend to be clever, fairly young, professional people who at least start with the simple aim of beating a security system—meeting a challenge, in other words. They then may take unfair advantage of the system once they've cracked it. The security system in question may be in their own place of work or elsewhere; if the former is the case there may also be a feeling of getting revenge for some real or imagined insult or lack of promotion. The challenge aspect of computer crime is enforced by the fairly common practice of not taking a criminal to court once caught; this seems to be on the grounds that the publicity could cause loss of confidence in the firm concerned. Indeed, once found out, quite a few of these poachers turn gamekeeper, by taking up work in computer security.

There are two main classes of computer crime. The first involves theft of electronic money; the second is theft of electronic information. In either case, the approach would be to divert the money or the information from where it should be to where the criminal can access it. Moving a penny from each of a bank's accounts to the criminal's own account, and hacking into a supposedly secure data base (as in the film *War games*) are examples of these two classes.

Keeping a system—hardware, software, and data base—secure involves trying to set up methods by which only authorised people can access it; it's also providing checks to detect and prevent abuse. Allowing only a few people to enter the computer area, providing it with a separate power supply, setting up multi-layer levels of passwords (especially for remote users), and ensuring no one person has access to too large a section—all these are methods of improving security. However, no computer system can be totally secure from abuse, especially abuse by someone who knows it well.

Firms whose computers store highly sensitive information will also try to ensure they fully check in advance all who have access. They'll then perhaps issue them with electronic key-cards so they can enter only certain rooms, and special keys to switch on their terminals, as well as having them use passwords.

Part of the function of the **operating software** will be to keep a record of who logs on, when, at what terminal, and for how long, as well as the software and/or data they access. There'll be security guards in and round the building, and certain staff will have at all times the right to look at what each member of staff is doing. Data printed out on paper would go to a shredder rather than just be thrown away when it was no longer needed, and highly complex algorithms would code (**encrypt**) data before transfer to a remote terminal.

All these methods are costly; indeed in some organisations security may now come near the top of the budget of running costs. Even so, as I say, no system is perfect yet. The computer industry is after all a young one; it may be some decades before we can feel that electronic data is truly safe.

10.3   IT and the individual

It's particularly important in a free society to protect data about individuals. The use of computers to store and process personal data has grown rapidly; it's very likely that details about *you* are to be found in various computers round the country. When you were born or came to this country, full details had to be provided, by law, to the state; each time you obtain medical advice or treatment, notes go into your personal files; many records exist of your progress through the educational system; social security, income tax, part-time jobs may all lead to information being stored about you. More and more of that information goes into computers rather than staying on paper; it's surely important to try to keep what's held secure from abuse. Doing this involves keeping data private.

Abuse is applying the stored data for a purpose it's not designed for, in particular to damage the rights of the individuals concerned. Blackmail comes to mind; so do making up mailing lists for junk letters, and building up profiles of householders so sales staff can approach them with highly personalised offers.

The British Data Protection Act, which became law in 1984, is an attempt to set up systems to protect personal data. Government passed the law as a result of feared abuse of the immense processing and storage power of computers (and also to meet international demands). The administration of the Act is in the hands of the Data Protection Registrar; it's the duty of data users to register if their work falls within its scope.

For the purpose of the Act, data users are individual people, firms, or other organisations who hold personal data and process it automatically for themselves or for clients, or who allow others to use their hardware, especially backing store, for the purpose. Thus, many computer bureaux are data users.

A data subject, on the other hand, is a person about whom a computer system holds details. The Act defines personal data as 'information about a living individual, including expressions of opinion about him or her, but excluding any indication of the intentions of the data user in respect of that individual'.

With certain exceptions, you should register as a data user—fill in the lengthy form and send it off with a fee—if you hold personal data in such a way that you have the power to process it automatically.

The main exceptions are (broadly speaking)

- data held by an individual for personal, family, household or hobby reasons
- data held by the police and by the state for the purpose of national security
- data held in payroll and accounts files and used for no other purpose
- details about the members of small clubs
- data used just for research and to prepare statistics

Otherwise, a data user must register name and proper address, the data held, the reason it's held, where it comes from, and what they intend to do with it (and that includes where and to whom it might go). Data users must also follow a code of practice, and ensure their staff follow the rules. They must

- collect and process personal data fairly and lawfully
- hold personal data only for registered lawful purposes
- disclose data only to registered recipients and approved countries
- ensure the data held is adequate, relevant, accurate and up to date
- delete personal data when it's no longer needed
- use appropriate security measures
- allow data subjects to have access

The first of those principles means that data obtained by deceit isn't lawful. It is against the law to collect personal data if you pretend to carry out a market survey when your true intentions are different, for instance.

It's also worth giving a little more detail about the last principle—the one which gives data subjects the right to examine records held about them. Here's what the law says:

An individual shall be entitled

a at reasonable intervals and without undue delay and expense

   (i) to be informed by any data user whether he holds personal data of which that individual is the subject, and

   (ii) to have access to any such data held by a data user; and

b where appropriate, to have such data corrected or erased.

To most members of the public, therefore, letting this happen is the most important job of the Data Registrar. Major libraries hold complete lists of registered data users—all members of the public can look to see who might hold information about them. They may then write to any data user to ask if they're in that user's files, and (paying a reasonable fee if requested) obtain copies of the personal details held.

Since the Act became law in 1984 there've been many areas of uncertainty; some remain. In order to clarify those queries, the Data Protection Registrar has set up test cases in the courts. However, some people feel the law isn't strong enough, and that there are too many exemptions; on the other hand, many data users find it very complex to work with. In practice, it's not easy for data subjects to find out what's on record in their names.

You are for sure a data subject. You may also be, or become, a data user as defined by the Act. For instance, using a home computer you may run a small business, or for a computer project at school or college you may set up a data base holding personal information. You'd be wise to find out whether your usage of personal data should be registered or not.

SELF-DEVELOPMENT QUESTIONS

See Page 137 for notes on these questions.

S10.1   List the features you'd like in a TV set. Try to outline the hardware and software needs to achieve each one.

S10.2   Write a short account of the current state of play as regards the proposed British national cable network concept. Investigate the costs involved and how a working system could be funded.

S10.3   List the services a cable network of the type described in the case study could provide. Assess the likely value of each to a typical family.

S10.4   Research European satellite TV systems.

S10.5   Make a 5-minute TV programme. The type and subject can be your choice, but here are some ideas:

a group discussion (e.g. on the good and bad aspects of new IT); a documentary (e.g. about life in one street or block of flats); a little play (e.g. about how schooling could be made of more use); a newscast (e.g. on recent happy events in your friends' lives); an advertising film (e.g. about a new course at your school or college)

Carry out a survey of how viewers felt about your programme. Assess the likely value of video films produced at home for community TV.

S10.6 Find out about current uses of read-only compact and video discs and about likely future uses of such discs on which you can record.

S10.7 How useful would a video phone be to your family?

S10.9 How intelligent is the home computer in the case study likely to be, in practice?

S10.10 Write a short essay about trends in car computers.

S10.11 Would you like to live in an IT-based 'global village'?

S10.12 How easy would it be for a Government to run a country *Nineteen eighty-four*-style?

S10.13 'To communicate (voice, video, data) with someone in Beijing, Buenos Aires or Bucharest ... has profound implications for a world view and for world peace.' Discuss this quotation from the introduction to Chapter 10.

S10.14 How much could the IT-based home of 2001 affect formal schooling? In what other ways may IT affect formal schooling? What barriers may make the changes to formal schooling come about more slowly than they could?

S10.15 Survey the use of IT in your school or college in an attempt to decide the levels of security needed. If you find a department in which you feel security is not adequate, make and explain recommendations. Be diplomatic.

S10.16 Obtain permission to look at a file of personal data held in your school or college. Study it and its usage in the light of the Data Protection Act. Is the file registered? Should it be?

S10.17 Say a firm holds personal data about you as a result of a twelve-month magazine subscription you took out a couple of years ago. Should they hold that data? How could someone abuse it?

S10.18 What is 'hacking'? Is it wrong?

EXAMINATION QUESTIONS

Q10.1 A certain hospital has a large computer system providing many interactive VDUs which are used in the wards, consulting rooms and by the hospital administration. Discuss the steps that may be taken to maintain the confidentiality of information in such a system.
(AEB Specimen paper)   (4)

Q10.2 Why is it desirable to have legislation to control the use and the storage of personal data on a computer? List the main provisions that you would expect to find in such legislation.
(London)   (7)

Q10.3 The Personnel Manager of a particular company is considering whether it is feasible to transfer the personal information about all employees of the company to the central computer. Currently this information is held on paper files.

The Personnel Manager is very much concerned with the integrity and the security of the information should it be held on the computer. He is aware that there are some legal requirements with regard to computer data which refers to living persons.

The Personnel Manager decides to consult the Data Processing Manager. The Data Processing Manager believes that the management of the central computer system is such that the Personnel Manager need have no worries if the decision was made to hold personal data. The Data Processing Manager agrees to produce a report to detail the methods which could be used to ensure the integrity and security of data.

Construct an outline of the Data Processing Manager's report to the Personnel Manager. (Remember that the Personnel Manager may well consult other technical experts when evaluating the report.)

The outline should include consideration of the physical security of the data, management of the data and general legal requirements.
(London)   (16)

Q10.4 **a** Explain the difference between the terms 'privacy of information' and 'security of information'.
                                                  (2)

b Outline *two* methods of attempting to achieve each of

i   privacy,
ii security.
                                                  (4)

c Briefly describe *two* developments of computing which might increase public concern about privacy of information.
                                                  (4)

d Briefly discuss *two* provisions of the Data Protection Act which are aimed at alleviating public concern.
(JMB)   (6)

Q10.5 **a** Discuss briefly the developments in computing

that have led to the widespread use of computers in homes, in offices and factories.

b What developments are likely to occur in computer technology in the foreseeable future? How might such developments change the way computers are used?

(COSSEC) [10]

Q10.6 The Data Protection Act was introduced in 1984. The Act requires the setting up of a Data Protection Register, run by a government appointed registrar. Why was such an act considered to be necessary?

(4)

The Act deals with two distinct classes of person/organisation: 'Data Users' and 'Data Subjects'. What is a Data User and what is a Data Subject?

(2,2)

It would ease the job of processing queries if the Data Registrar were to hold a list of every data subject for every data user. Why will this not be done?

(Oxford) (4)

Appendix A
Extra questions

I've put these examination questions here mostly because they cover more than one major chapter area, or are specialised. They include some exercises based on case studies, to give you a flavour of this kind of work if necessary; of course, you won't be able to answer them properly without access to the case studies concerned.

QA.1
  a Explain what is meant by the term 'relational data base'. (5)

  b Describe the following features of data base systems:
sharing of data; (5)
differing views of data; (5)
security of data.

(London) (5)

QA.2 The bits of a byte are numbered so that the least significant is identified by digit 0 and the most significant by digit 7. Write down the mask and the logical operation required to achieve each of the following.

  a Make bits 2, 3, 5 and 6 equal to 1 leaving the other bits unaltered.

  b Form the complement of bits 4, 5 and 6 leaving the other bits unaltered.

(JMB) (4)

QA.3 In the Kingston-upon-Hull Borough Council Vaccination and Immunisation Scheme, describe how a vaccination appointment is made, what is recorded when it is kept, and what action is taken if it is not kept. What part does the computer play in these activities?
(COSSEC case study) [10]

QA.4 A file consists of 100 fixed length records. Each record includes a field for part number, and the file is kept in ascending order of part number, from record 1 to 100. Any record may be read directly by use of its record number.

  a Describe in detail an efficient method for finding the record which corresponds to a given part number, or reporting that there is no such record.

  b **i** What is the maximum number of records which may need to be read in a search using your method, for a record which is present in the file?

    ii What, approximately, is the average number of records which may need to be read in a search using your method, for a record which is present in the file?

(COSSEC) [10]

QA.5 The school appoints an additional secretary. Discuss the relative merits of:

  a acquiring a stand-alone word processor (3)

  b expanding the system to allow multi-access (3)

The LEA wishes the school, as part of its computerisation program, to transmit, at the end of each year, the final marks obtained by each school leaver in every subject in the school's own examinations. This should be replaced by the GCSE or A-level grade where appropriate. How would this data be organised and transmitted, and why would a dedicated line connecting the school to the LEA be inappropriate? (6)

The school is left a sum of money by a former pupil, to be spent on the use of modern technology. You do not know how much money is involved, but are invited to suggest ways in which this could be applied. Discuss briefly two approaches, which should not be mutually exclusive.
(Oxford) (6,6)

QA.6 You have been given the task of redesigning a fast-food outlet (such as a drive-in Euroburger Bar). It is suggested to you that you might use simulation.

  a What factors would influence whether or not you would employ a simulation? (3)

  b If you decide to simulate the enterprise in some fashion, comment on some of the factors that you would include in your simulation.
(Oxford) (5)

QA.7 A domestic clothes-washer needs to take in cold water, pass it through a detergent tray to collect the detergent, heat the water and maintain it at a set temperature whilst agitating the clothes, pump out the water to the drain, rinse the clothes twice with agitation in fresh cold water, and finally spin-dry the clothes. A microcomputer is to be used to control this process.

a What properties of the system must the micro-computer sense during heating, washing and pumping?

(3)

Explain briefly how the sensed values are made available to the processor in the micro-computer.

(4)

b What physical mechanisms would the computer need to control in order to drive the machine?

(6)

c Give either a structured description, or a flow diagram, for an algorithm that would enable a programmer to write the necessary program to drive the machine through a washing cycle, without further instruction.

(Oxford) (8)

QA.8 A program is to be produced to store a set of announcements, and display them repeatedly in order. There are to be facilities for removing the oldest announcement and for adding a new one to the end of the list. The program will use library subroutines for adding an item to a linked list, and for removing one.

a Explain how the data for this program could be structured, as a linked list. Describe the algorithm for making use of the data-structure.

(5,6)

b Explain what would happen to the source code provided by the programmer as the program was compiled, linked, loaded and run.

(7)

c Describe a suitable set of parameters for communication between the main program and the subroutine to add an item to a linked list.

(Oxford) (4)

QA.9 A tunnel is to be driven through soft rock under a strait. The problems include:

(i) supplying fresh cutting gear and tunnel lining materials and removing worn parts,
(ii) removing excavated material and disposing of it,
(iii) transporting operators to and from the work-face and supplying ventilation and other facilities to them,
(iv) dealing with the possibility of flooding,
(v) monitoring the progress and accuracy of the course of the tunnel.

a Explain how computer simulation could be applied to each of these problems, stating clearly what further data you require to exercise the model.

(15)

b How, if at all, would such simulations be helpful? When should they be carried out?

(6,3)

c How effective could such simulations be expected to be as predictors of actual events in the tunneling operation?

(3)

d What computing facilities would be required for effective operation of the simulations and presentation of their results?

(Oxford) (3)

Appendix B
Notes on questions

These are necessarily very brief. The questions themselves, and/or the marks given for them, should inform you how long your answers should be. All the same, though the notes are brief (specially in the case of later chapters, where I hope you'll need less help!), don't use them as guides to your answers—rather, check them when you've done the work. Note that your exam board may have published notes on, and/or marking schemes for, their sample questions.

Self-development questions

Chapter 1

S1.1   Banking is one of the industries which have most taken IT on board. Your research should have turned up plenty of internal uses as well as ones that directly affect customers. Staffing levels and efficiency, security, speed of handling transfers, customer comfort, costs of transfers, ease of obtaining information—these are some areas you should explore. Are there areas of bank operations which have not yet gained benefit from IT?

S1.2   An interesting question I hope you raised is how much people use all the facilities available. If they don't—why not?

S1.3   The Post Office is starting to offer IT to counter staff. How much difference do you think it will make?

S1.4   There are four ways to find a frame you need on Prestel—working through from the main menu, finding the frame number from the printed directory, working with the on-line directories, or using a star command like ***greece**. Compare these as you gain familiarity with Prestel and its many services. How would you improve Prestel?

S1.5   Figure 1.13 describes a calculator too, doesn't it? Check (and understand and learn) the definition of a computer in Section 1.3. Look at, and use if you can, pocket and lap computers like the Psion Organiser and the Cambridge Z88. They look like calculators —are they? (North Americans call calculators computers, by the way. Would my definition have to change if we did the same?)

S1.6   This is mainly chapter research. However, how many different peripherals can you find out about? —there are dozens . . .

S1.7   This question is related to S1.6, but is more

practical.

S1.8   Note the word 'available'. You should be able to explain why that word is significant.

S1.9   We'll look at networks in more detail in Chapters 3 and 8; basic ideas are worthwhile at this stage.

S1.10 The best test of your success here is whether your notes (as well as being clear, error-free and neatly laid out) can in fact help someone with no experience of micros. Try it.

S1.11 A word processor should offer ease of text entry, editing, saving in backing store for the future, loading from backing store, and printing. Do you think this enough to persuade a typist to change to modern IT?

S1.12 The basis for this answer is in the chapter; for more than the basis try Chapter 8, other books, or audio-visual packages.

S1.13 That money is information is an important view as we move into an information-based society. Whether you think information is money, on the other hand, may depend on your political stance.

Chapter 2

S2.1   Check how we define IT (Section 1.1) and information. At the heart of a robot, for instance, is a processor and store; there are inputs and outputs. The only special question (one of philosophy) is whether the inputs and outputs are of information or data.

S2.2   There are also plenty of useful articles, books, and videos on the subject.

S2.3   This task involves systems analysis. What are the inputs and outputs? In what ways must the outputs affect the inputs (in a feedback loop)? Note that process control (the name for this field) assumes the process is continuous rather than batched. A batched process would need robots, and would be more complex.

S2.4   Refer to the glossary and to Section 10.2 if you wish.

S2.5   As in S2.3, work on inputs, outputs and feedback.

S2.6   Work on inputs, outputs and feedback here, too.

S2.7   Work on inputs, outputs and feedback is needed here, too, with autonomy being measured by lack of need of *human* control in this case. (Check the glossary for the usual IT meaning.)

S2.9   Most general purpose CAD programs can cope with any of these. There are special software packs for the first three at least; try the science, domestic science, and technology staff.

S2.10   At the time of writing the *Ecodisc* is the best known in education. However, some large petrol and motorway service stations have a Shell system with maps of Britain.

S2.11   Note that there's a legal aspect to this. Thus in France an electronic document (contract or invoice, for instance) isn't valid unless confirmed on paper.

S2.12   Tasks you think of may include looking up someone's address using an intercom unit to make a query, and filing a letter.

S2.13   Many libraries use microform (film or fiche). You may also find it in a large discount chain store or on a car spare parts counter.

S2.14   Whichever one you choose, think a little about the rest—spreadsheets have very many uses.

S2.15   The techniques of communication by graphs are important. This is partly because people so often abuse them to create a false view (of what they're selling for instance).

S2.18   A Filofax costs almost as much as the electronic versions (such as the Psion Organiser), though some organiser programs for cheap micros are not so dear.

S2.19   You may be able to write such a program yourself. However, if you fancy a challenge, how about doing so for a micro with a modem so the system calls the number of the person you type in?

S2.20   This is a project idea for people who have to know how to program. Others may find it just as good to design a paper-based approach. In both cases, the task is one of systems analysis. Systems analysis does *not* have to lead to electronic systems.

S2.21   More systems analysis. Section 9.2 has much on this.

S2.22   In the words of an ICL poster—'Will your children's children go to school?'

S2.23   The most important task is to put yourself in the place of the type of learner at whom each program is aimed. Does the documentation clearly describe the market, though?

Chapter 3

S3.1   Please refer to the notes above for S1.4.

S3.2   The major difference is that viewdata is interactive (two-way) while teletext is non-interactive (one-way). Serial and direct access, size of data bases, and charging differences follow from this. Can you find out (a) about other public access viewdata bases, and (b) how teletext may develop in the future with cable systems (or if we could use a whole TV channel for it)? See Case study 10.

S3.3   Work through the services offered and compare with more traditional means of obtaining them. Then consider traditional services you don't get with home and office banking.

S3.4   What are the functions of cash (think widely!)? Can you come up with ways IT could replace each one? Think too, about social effects.

S3.5   Scrolling viewdata often bears the name 'electronic mail', though this is rarely its sole function, so the name is bad. The other functions are mainly internal and external data base access.

S3.6   For some micros, you may be able to find books with very full details (such as those for service staff).

S3.8   Respectively (and very briefly)—

Get a byte from the input (buffer) and store it in cell 4000

Store a copy of the content of cell 4000 in the accumulator

Take the content of cell 4001 from that of the accumulator, and leave the result there

Jump to cell 3020 for the next instruction if the accumulator value is negative

S3.9   Here's one answer. (Can you find others?)

3001	INP 4001
3002	INP 4002
3003	LDA 4001
3004	SUB 4002
3005	BIN 3008
3006	OUP 4001
3007	HLT 0
3008	OUP 4002
3009	HLT 0

S3.10   The three (or four) levels are registers (cache), main store, backing store. Some people would add virtual storage somehow between main and backing store.

S3.11   The chapter gives very basic notes only—you need library research.

S3.12   Here, too, you need library research.

S3.13   With the data in the chapter (Section 3.5): **a** 100 B/mm; **b** about 4 : 6; **c** 825 K/s; 3 K/s; **d** about six minutes.

S3.14   Typically you need about 95, these often being coded 32–127. Codes 0–31 are generally kept for output device control (beep, clear screen and such); 128–255 may hold special characters (other fonts, other alphabets, graphic blocks, etc). In decimal (denary) ASCII, *my* name is 69 114 105 99 32 68 101 101 115 111 110. (Note the 32—for a space—in there.)

S3.15   You should recognise, describe, and know the purpose of—spindle hole, index hole, collar, read/write hole, sleeve, write-protect notch, label and envelope. Why not cut open a dud disc?

S3.16   Use a CD-ROM with a micro if you can, and compare it with audio CD.

S3.17   Include the optical (laser) stripe card and CD-ROM

as well as video disc (and the use of this with interactive video).

S3.19   Look through advertisements in computer magazines.

S3.20   The biggest disadvantage is noise—outside noise confusing the system, and your talking annoying others. Think of a bus full of people talking with their pocket micros!

S3.22   Library research again.

S3.23   This also will involve library research, including advertisements.

S3.24   This is a practical exercise.

S3.26   The systems used in Britain, EAN (European Article Numbering), and in North America UPC (Universal Product Code) are both sadly complex.

S3.28   Include in your notes the automation aspects, and what you think the various interfaces are.

Chapter 4

S4.1   There may be problems of security, so be extra sweet!

S4.2   Plenty of print and video material exists to help here.

S4.3   This may be too costly—at the time of writing, Healthdata is on a London phone line. However, your school may have the disc version—not up to date and not complete, but a good basis for your answer.

S4.4   **a** 0111, 0011 0001, 1111 1001; **b** 7, 31, F9. Note the links between binary and hex.

S4.5   **a** OD, 5A, 99; **b** 13, 90, 153. The note to S4.4b applies here.

S4.6   Do this to the extent your teacher suggests. Binary sums are not in all syllabuses.

S4.7   The denary answers are 77, 69, 129.

S4.8   1011.01, 0111 1011.101, 1010.0000 01

S4.12   The pair of denary 8-bit integers 42 21, the 16-bit value 10773, the ASCII character ')' followed by the 'disable VDU' control code (Acorn BBC version, but there are others), a double-precision positive sign and magnitude number, etc., etc. See also Q4.5.

S4.13   Do this only if you need to program. An example is a program to ask the user for name, age in years, and height in metres.

S4.14   Try a real control program if you can.

S4.15   Weather data?

S4.16   An example would be weather data for several places. Any array goes in main store as a linear set of data items in a block of cells; dimensioning it will (a) reserve the right amount of space, and (b) allow easy (direct) access to the individual elements.

S4.17   There are several books on Forth, and versions of the language for many micros.

S4.18   You'll need a string array; one-word strings will suffice.

S4.19   There are many such programs for use in school and college.

S4.20   Compare with S4.18.

S4.21   Developing an essay plan in a word processor is very much worth while. Indeed, some word processors have extra features to help here. A linked list isn't the best way, therefore, but I think it remains a good question!

S4.22   As noted in the text, you'll need an extra head pointer and an extra tail pointer for each item.

S4.23   I can only repeat my comments for S4.21.

S4.24   In-order traversal needs practice.

S4.26   Adding an extra data item just means following the rules for entry. To delete one, you'll have to sort out the pointers.

Chapter 5

S5.2   Practise some tasks with a micro's operating software —you never know when you may have to use them in earnest.

S5.3   **a** is low priority but uses a great deal of processing and (maybe) some backing store. **b** will involve taking data from an input file (disc or tape), a little processing, and storing the results in an output file (also on disc or tape), for later spooling to a printer. **c** needs very little processing but a slow yet steady sequence of input/output control; it has the highest priority. In general, jobs making much use of the processor should have lower priority than those that mainly involve data transfers; this is because the processor works so much faster.

S5.4   See S5.3 as well.

S5.5   See also S5.2.

S5.9   Job control programs are quite interesting, and not hard to follow once you see the basic principles.

S5.10   The best kind of spooling is when you use the computer for other tasks while it's going on. Alas, not all micros allow this.

S5.11   Both styles of computer use involve time-sharing (slicing), but . . .

S5.12   The special software mentioned may include editor, linker, loader, debugger.

S5.13   This isn't easy with some school and college micros. Maybe you have access to a home micro that allows it.

S5.14   The ones in the chapter are the most important.

S5.15   Refer, if you wish, to the material in Chapter 9 on machine intelligence.

S5.16   A one-to-many instruction.

S5.17   In this context the major difference is that Cobol wasn't designed to be interactive. The chapter gives others you should look at.

S5.18   Is the task much harder (for the computer) in some cases? High-level languages are aimed at different needs.

S5.19   There are two main principles, it seems to me: a

computer should make the user's life easier and better than that without; the user should never be unsure what to do.

Chapter 6

S6.1   You should be able to produce a good answer from what's in the chapter. However, the police have issued a booklet on the system, and a number of articles describe it.

S6.2   Note that the fingerprint file isn't yet (at the end of 1987) on line to most police forces.

S6.7   This needs lateral thinking—there's hardly a limit to what you can do. Thus you could use FredWmDeesn for Frederick William Deeson, Bham for Birmingham, 12345678 for the phone number 01-234 5678, or 52E7 for 520 000 000. (Many systems do this last automatically, using standard form for large and small numbers.) Bitwise compression, mentioned in Section 6.1, can give even greater savings of space (at the cost of extra processing).

S6.10   Can you devise a more efficient manual method than in your answer? Say you often drop packs of sorted index cards . . . .

S6.12   Have you included administration transactions, such as those to do with staff payments, the canteen, or banking cheques?

S6.13   Don't forget, the master file is sequential.

S6.14   In the first case, this pseudocode algorithm would do:

```
repeat
  get title
  if titlelength = 0 then display
    message
until titlelength > 0
```

S6.16   The system used, called modulo-11 weighting, is complex but very effective.

S6.17   See also Sections 10.2 and 10.3.

Chapter 7

S7.1   Why not a school or college or community magazine, or a really good publicity booklet about courses on offer?

S7.2   Start with a definition of word (text) processing.

S7.4   Omit this if it's not part of your course—or (better) choose much simpler tasks.

S7.5   The same applies.

S7.8   I suspect you may find very few examples of first class documentation.

S7.10   As with audio and video tapes, this may not be as good as it could be (for the best of reasons). Can you help out?

Chapter 8

S8.1   The main thing is the use of a LAN *and* a WAN.

S8.3   The major pros of a micro are personal access and personal control; cons include increased hassle and increased cost.

S8.4   You should consider such matters as reliability and cost, as well as the actual layout.

S8.10   If you're at a large college, you may find a fax system in use.

S8.11   Your school or college is almost sure to have a phone network. There are many kinds, however, with different degrees of intelligence, as opposed to human control.

S8.13   Systems analysis—Section 9.2—is what's involved here. Systems analysis is *not* just about using computers.

S8.18   See also Chapter 10 (the case study, for instance).

S8.19   See also Chapter 10 (Section 10.2, for instance).

Chapter 9

S9.3   While people have set up very few expert systems just for teaching or training, teachers and trainers use 'real' ones more and more to help the learners learn.

S9.4   A number of teachers reckon that helping learners set up a knowledge base in an expert system shell is a very good way for them to learn the field concerned.

S9.5   Prolog is likely to remain for a while the most common 'machine intelligence' system in education (though it's not very common, yet at least). You can hardly call it easy to use, but it shows the principles well. See also Q9.4. (Micro)Codil is better in many ways; it's worth a try if you can get hold of a copy.

S9.6   Programs in this group include *Eliza, Animal*, generators of 'poetry', and systems that can play games (ranging from noughts and crosses to chess). I don't think most of these show as much smartness as an earwig.

S9.7   The crucial aspect of this approach is learning about the environment.

S9.8   More on this in Chapter 10.

S9.9   The crucial word is 'outline'!

S9.11   Don't forget that diplomacy is a crucial skill for an analyst.

S9.12   The same applies.

Chapter 10

S10.1   Why not be really open-ended, with plans based on careful thinking about the early part of this chapter?

S10.2   Cable systems already exist in some parts of Britain. Can you obtain an up-to-date list, and then try to make some contacts?

S10.3   See the notes for S10.1.

S10.5   It can take many hours to prepare a 5-minute film.

S10.12   Your answer should also cover how easy it would be for a people used to freedom to accept such a state.

S10.14   To repeat a question from earlier in the book— 'Will your children's children go to school?'

Examination questions

Chapter 1

Q1.1   **a** It is essential that you practise word processing as much as you can; see S1.11 above for the basic principles. However, here you will need to detail different forms of text editing, including block operations, merging, and search and replace.

   b There are few areas of human activity where word processing cannot help. In questions like this avoid the obvious office answer. Think about the work of school or college, a hospital, a travel agent, an author, for instance—or what about your own future career area?

Q1.2   You should enjoy reading something of the history of IT; try your libraries and/or the reading list at the end of this book.

Chapter 2

Q2.1   A spreadsheet, used in 'what if?' mode, is the answer. You *could* use a program based on an array (Section 4.3), but it would be slow and far less effective.

Q2.2   Figure 2.9 is a good model. To it you should be able to add most of the main types of business software discussed in this chapter. You won't be able to give much detail in the time allowed, though.

Q2.3   You may need to refer to Chapter 3 in the case of the hardware side.

Chapter 3

Q3.1   In your answer, try to distinguish between the non-interactive nature of teletext (e.g. Ceefax) and the interactive nature of viewdata (e.g. Prestel and Telecom Gold).

Q3.2   This name for main store makes the answer clear.

Q3.3   This question concerns machine-readable media— like autoteller cards and bar-coded library tickets.

Q3.5   4,0
0,470
1,900
4,1
1,500
. . .
4,0
5,0

There are many other answers you can have. I've used two new codes—4 to control the pen (0 up; 1 down), and 5 to send the pen back home (to 0,0).

Q3.8   **a** Lower arm till in range, then close claw till it grips, then raise arm.

   b No object grabbed.

   c 1100.

Q3.9   Systems software is the set of programs that runs a computer. In ROM it generally works faster, but you can't change it. Also, if these programs are in backing store, you can just load and use the parts you want.

Q3.11   **a** This needs you to discuss analog to digital conversion.

   b
```
repeat
   rotate drum
   blow fan
   if T < TMAX use heater
   if T > TMAX switch off heater
until H < HMIN
start timer
repeat
   rotate drum
   blow fan
until TIME > 600 seconds
```

There are other ways, as usual. I assume there's a check that all the parts are working (otherwise switch the whole thing off), but the above routine will handle you putting in hot and/or dry clothes.

Q3.12   **a** Deal with this question stage by stage, in part as in the last question.

   b The main problem with the system as described will be that it reacts to every single passing wheel. This will cause timing confusion and maybe accidents. We need timers and delays for proper use, as well perhaps as several sensors at some distance each side.

   c This may make the system better, but it will also lead to greater cost and danger of damage or breakdown.

Q3.13   You won't need modems as a system like this will have its own digital cabling. At each junction, however, you'll have something like that described for Q3.12, with fail-safe techniques there and in the central unit.

Chapter 4

Q4.2   Each of the three data items would be in binary in practice. The first is an integer, almost sure to live in a special register; the second is likely to be a 5-

byte sequence with 2 bytes for day and year and 1 for month, stored in the disc directory; the third is a string of fixed length, also in the directory. Most computers reading a disc directory will copy all the data to a reserved block of main store.

Q4.3   **c** Chapters 6 and 7 give more detail on file structure and algorithms respectively.

Q4.4   See also S4.12.

Chapter 5

Q5.1   **b** The two modes would likely be on-line interactive and batch (assuming all orders come to the same place).

Q5.2   **c** Two extra commands would come from: make new sub-directory, change directory, delete sub-directory, and list the files in a given sub-directory.

Q5.4   B jobs should have higher priority as far as concerns interrupts. This doesn't mean they're more important.

Q5.6   **b** The main point here concerns the *usage* of the small (personal) micro, not any special hardware or software limitation.

Q5.8   The system needs 7 bits for the opcode, 3 for the register, and 2 for the address mode, leaving the other fields to go in extra words. In fact there are spare bits, as there is overlap between these functions—or you can provide overlap to make the system more efficient.

Q5.9   **b** Note that *true* concurrent processing is parallel multiprocessing rather than multiprogramming. People often use the word loosely.

Chapter 6

Q6.1   There are several possible causes, and therefore various solutions you could mention. The causes range from there being two people with the same name to deliberate tampering with the stored data.

Q6.4   Date of entry, part number, location in warehouse.

Q6.5   Various types of human error turn up here. Mishearing dictated words, bad writing and tiredness are among them.

Q6.7   The main stages concern data input. However, many systems will also validate the results of data processing, and almost all will use a check digit (e.g. parity bit) technique on transferred bytes.

Q6.10   It isn't often easy to use check digits with strings—the algorithm is tougher, and anyway the extra character would change the meaning, causing confusion. Another case is of variable data entered interactively (see, for instance, Q7.11). Verification is better here (so is using machine-readable input data).

Q6.11   Compare with the algorithm in Section 6.3 and

Figure 6.6.

Q6.12   As long as you recall that a pointer is an address, and that you can address a disc as well as main store, this should be straight forward.

Chapter 7

Q7.1   **b** It may help to work with the algorithms of Q6.13 and the above notes on that.

Q7.3   **a** C1: left>right C2: palindrome = true.

Q7.4   **c** A bar to the separate testing of a single program module (closed subroutine) is that in most cases it will depend on others called before. There are various ways round this in the case of modern procedures. If you can't use any of those, run a version of the program with the new module but leaving out all the others that can't possibly affect it. The answer to **d** relates to these points.

Q7.9   As well as being essential in a top–down approach to program design and development, closed subroutines **a** allow the program to carry out a given task a number of times while being coded only once; and **b** allow the programmer to build up a closed subroutine library.

Q7.11   Much of this relates to Chapter 6. However, Section 9.2 may help with **e**.

Chapter 8

Q8.1   **a** doesn't really differ so much from **b**—and **b** is close to the case study. If you did the question as asked, you probably chose **b**; why not now think about **a**?

Q8.2   **a** Don't forget the ticket printers.

Q8.4   This question isn't meant to give you the chance to slate British Telecom—it concerns the pros and cons of your own communications line compared to joining in a public network. (Line speed means the highest rate of error-free data transfer.)

Q8.5   **e** Somewhat over an hour. Maybe you'd like to think again about Q8.4 and the line speed point? 9600 bits/s (about 9600 baud) is faster than most public phone lines can cope with.

Q8.6   The two ways that involve new IT are the transfer by phone of graphics data files (taken from the CAD software, or by scanner from paper), and the use of fax. Note, though, that few fax machines can cope with sheets much larger than A4. More conventional schemes are public mail and a courier service.

Q8.7   Why are standards needed for information transfer between communicating humans?

Chapter 9

Q9.1   The main aim of parallel running is to get the new

system working fully without danger to data. Bugs need finding; staff need training; system problems need solving.

Q9.2   Crucial aspects to bring in are the volume of input data and the routine nature of the processing.

Q9.4   In the case of a fact, read the word 'is' between subject and attribute. In the case of a relationship, put 'is' between the subject and the relationship, read the colon as 'if', and any comma as 'and' . The first definition needed is

$$\text{(X Brother-of Y):(X Male), (Z Father-of X),}$$
$$\text{(Z Father-of Y)}$$

This means X (is a) brother-of Y (if) X (is) male

(and) Z (is) father-of X (and) Z (is) father-of Y.

Chapter 10

Q10.1   'Confidentiality' means security from unauthorised access. You should note why we need this, as well as how to obtain it.

Q10.2   You should not just state what Britain's act provides for—are there other things you feel the law should address?

Q10.3   A report is not an essay—it needs much more detailed structure.

Q10.4   c   The two most obvious are cheap micros and cheap modem links. There are others.

Appendix C
Resources for learning

Working wisely with this book should be more than enough to get you comfortably through the written papers (at least) in your exam. However, I can't claim that it's enough to make you really with it in the IT sense (though I've tried . . .). Reading a text and doing questions is not the best way to learn. Here are some other resources for learning in these areas (but I shan't try to cover computer software).

By far the most useful extra resource for learning is other people—your teacher, other IT staff at your school or college, your friends and family, other past and present IT students, and people you know who have IT-related work. Thoughtful discussion, based on a certain number of facts, is a great way to extend your knowledge and enrich your view.

As TV is the area of IT that has had more effect on the people of Britain than any other, use it to help you on this course. There are many programmes you'll find of value—including those in series such as *Horizon* and *Tomorrow's world* and the output of the Open College and the Open University. If you can afford to build up a video library on IT and computing, do so—you're allowed to copy TV programmes for the purpose of your studies. There are, in any event, many video films published on IT and computing, some of which are quite good. (They tend, however, to date fast, and some are *very* boring.) See if your school or college library or resource centre has any; there may also be useful slide-sets and audio tapes.

There's plenty of science and technology material in the other media, too, at least at the more highbrow end. Radio 3 and Radio 4 have some useful talks, discussions, and history programmes, while the quality daily and Sunday newspapers have relevant material in most issues. If you're able to obtain papers when their owners have finished with them, it's a good idea to build up a cuttings collection. Organise this, perhaps, on the basis of the chapters in this book; think of setting up a computer data base to help you search and sort it.

Such a collection will grow very fast if you can add material from magazines such as *New Scientist* and the computer industry papers and magazines. Very many of the latter are free to people in the business: although that doesn't include students, you may be able to find someone who gets the papers and doesn't want to keep them.

Talking of books in these areas is no easy task—there are thousands of them, and they vary greatly in price and quality. Browse in local libraries and book shops; you'll surely find one or two volumes that are relevant, interesting, and up to date. Being relevant, interesting and/or up to date is how I'd describe most of the titles on the list that follows.

Although it's a personal selection—and I must emphasise that point—I think it a solid and useful basis for study of information technology and computing.

Computer studies for GCSE Mark Bindley (Blackwell 1986)
  A superb textbook coverage of the field for the more able learners, able to give you an excellent background
Computers at work Peter Bishop (Arnold 1986)
  A good, thought-provoking account of IT in practice, suited to the more able GCSE candidate—so you'll find it of use
Faster than thought Lord Bowden (Pitman 1971)
  OK, not up to date and not easy to find—but a gem for those who'd like to read some real IT history
Understanding computer science Ray Bradley (Hutchinson 1987)
  An excellent advanced level text despite some out-dated aspects
Careers in computing and IT Eric Deeson (Kogan Page 1987)
  A brief survey, with plenty of case studies, and also relevant to Chapter 9
Managing with IT Eric Deeson (Kogan Page 1987)
  A thorough (and, I think, readable) introduction to business IT and computing, aimed at management but with students very much in mind
Handbook of new office technology John Derrick & Philip Oppenheim (Kogan Page 1986)
  An extremely thorough and down-to-earth survey of the whole IT field in practice
Using computers D.G. Dologite (Addison-Wesley 1987)
  A well-designed and beautifully presented North American college introduction to business computing
Telecommunications Ericsson (Chartwell-Bratt 1986 onward)
  Judging by the first two titles (on telephone networks), this series will be of great value
The microelectronics revolution Tom Forester (ed.) (Blackwell 1980)
  Still, despite its age, perhaps the best survey of the social aspects of IT
Computer science C.S. French (DPP 1984)
  A cheap concise advanced level text—hard to read, but useful for reference
Expert systems Paul Harmon & David King (Wiley 1985)
  One of the clearest surveys of the subject
Business computer systems R.W. Hudson & R.P. Batten (McGraw Hill-1986)
  A splendid introduction, aimed at business students but of value to all

Structured program design Gwyn Jones (Hodder 1985)
Not structured enough for me, but far better than most—so worth a look if you have to write programs

CD ROM Steve Lambert & Suzanne Ropiequet (Microsoft 1986)
As CD-ROM typifies an important growing area of IT, this book—thorough and readable—is a useful one

Computers Larry & Nancy Long (Addison-Wesley 1986)
A gorgeous North American college text, superbly illustrated, and very useful for this course

Dictionary of computing and new IT A.J. Meadows et al. (Kogan Page 1984)
A compact and accurate glossary, though rather dry

Glossary of computing terms British Computer Society (Cambridge 1987)
A very compact glossary, used by many examination boards despite some controversial entries

Inside information Jacquetta Megarry (BBC 1985)
A compact but wide-ranging and well-illustrated introduction to IT at AS level (part of a course which also involves software, audio visual, and a computer-based exam)

Learning and teaching with computers Tim O'Shea & John Self (Harvester 1983)
A thoughtful, though sometimes blinkered, survey, with pleasing concern for the potential of machine intelligence to learning

The robot book Richard Pawson (Windward 1985)
Excellent in parts

Educational computing Eileen Scanlon & Tim O'Shea (Wiley 1987)
A well-chosen and wide-ranging set of papers on this important field

Microcomputers in education John Self (Harvester 1986)
A hard-hitting attack on most work so far

Robots and robotology R.H. Warring (Lutterworth 1983)
Rather dry but very clear

Note, too, that many Open University course texts are well designed, relevant and easy to read.

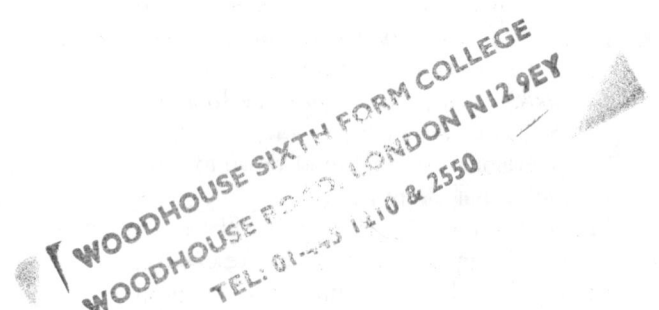

Appendix D
Objectives

The lists of objectives for each chapter are brought together here. This is to let you have a check list you may refer to quickly. You may make a copy of this appendix so you can (a) cross out, with your teacher's help, the items not in your syllabus; and (b) tick off the others as you learn about them, writing by each the numbers of the pages in your notes that cover them.

Chapter 1

When you have worked through this chapter, you should be able to

1 state what information technology is and explain its importance
2 discuss briefly the significance of information technology to the financial world
3 describe briefly some of the uses of Prestel
4 comment on the benefits of information technology to public and private transport
5 define 'computer' and explain the terms used in your definition
6 state the difference between analog and digital signals
7 define 'computer program' and explain why people need programs
8 state, with examples, the difference between data and information
9 draw a block diagram of a standard computer, showing the directions of data flow; explain the function of and need for each block; and give examples of each type of peripheral
10 define 'bit' and 'byte' and discuss the use of bytes as a measure of computer memory size
11 distinguish between ROM and RAM
12 discuss the nature and uses of a mainframe, mini-computer, micro-computer and network
13 define 'hardware', 'software' and 'firmware'
14 discuss the basics of internal and external computer communications
15 describe the features and use of a typical word processor

Chapter 2

When you have worked through this chapter, you should be able to
1 give an account of the principles of robotics using

automated pallets and static general purpose arms as examples
2 discuss the nature and advantages of automation
3 state what feedback is, and discuss examples
4 write simple control program outlines
5 give examples to show why people prefer a robot to a human worker
6 describe how a typical user works with a computer-aided design (CAD) package and the hardware that might be involved
7 distinguish between paint software, business graphics, and CAD
8 outline how advanced CAD software can simulate the testing of a design
9 state the principles of computer-aided design and manufacture (CADCAM)
10 state the nature of an office and outline typical information flows
11 compare traditional and electronic methods of office information handling
12 discuss the five main business software programs and list five others
13 describe how to use a spreadsheet
14 describe how to use a business graphics program
15 list the advantages and disadvantages of integrated business software and give examples of its use
16 describe the use of a critical path analysis program (scheduler)
17 outline the value and use of electronic organisers (hardware or software)
18 outline the value and use of a stock control package
19 outline the value and use of accounts software
20 outline the value and use of payroll programs
21 list the main uses of IT in education
22 list uses of business software by tutors and learners
23 outline the value and use of computer-managed learning (CML)
24 discuss examples of computer-aided learning (CAL) software and place them on a spectrum of 'intelligence'
25 outline the value and use of CAL authoring systems

Chapter 3

When you have worked through this chapter, you should be able to

1 list ten or more uses of Prestel, describe several in detail,

and comment on their advantages compared to traditional methods of handling the same tasks

2 discuss the significance of IT in the current financial world and in the future

3 list the parts of a computer's central processor and explain their functions

4 distinguish between ROM and RAM, and note typical sizes

5 comment on a central processor as an electric circuit

6 explain the difference between an integrated circuit and a chip

7 draw and explain a simple sketch of the structure of a computer processor

8 state what a register is, and explain two examples

9 outline what happens during a computer's fetch–execute–reset cycle

10 note the nature and advantages of a RISC machine

11 distinguish between an instruction's opcode and address part

12 describe how a processor carries out simple assembly language instructions

13 state the three main levels of computer memory and briefly explain the working of each

14 outline the nature of bubble and CCD memory and compare these to traditional microelectronic devices

15 describe the nature and value of cache storage

16 list several input and output devices and describe their action and use

17 discuss the nature and value of a WIMP (desktop) environment

18 compare dumb and intelligent terminals

19 write brief notes on character, line and page printers

20 compare bed and drum plotters

21 discuss the value of computer output on microform (COM)

22 comment on speech recognition and synthesis

23 compare optical mark reading and optical character reading

24 compare magnetic and optical stripe cards

25 discuss the use of bar codes in shops and libraries

26 outline the nature of fax

27 list some sensors and describe the use of one

28 explain the need for analog-to-digital and digital-to-analog converters

29 describe briefly the concept of automation, with an example

30 list the functions of a peripheral interface

31 compare serial and parallel data transfer

Chapter 4

When you have worked through this chapter, you should be able to

1 list the main uses of IT in health care

2 give an account of local and remote patient monitoring

3 outline some ways modern technology can help the disabled

4 define binary and hexadecimal systems and convert numbers between binary and denary and binary and hex (both ways)

5 add, subtract, multiply and divide binary numbers, including use of the binary point

6 obtain the 2s complement of a number and use it in subtraction

7 explain and use the sign and magnitude method of floating point number representation, and work with it in fixed word length contexts

8 state the nature and cause of rounding error, overflow and underflow

9 state the need for programmers to work with different data types

10 give examples of three common data types and list three less common ones

11 explain, with examples, the need for special data structures for processing

12 give examples of the use of linear lists and multi-dimensional arrays

13 explain, with an example, the nature and use of a last in, first out stack

14 explain, with an example, the nature and use of a first in, first out queue

15 explain, with an example, the nature and use of a linked list

16 state, with examples, what a pointer is and does

17 define a tree and the terms node, parent, child, leaf, root, sub-tree

18 enter random string or numeric data into a small binary tree and access it in order

Chapter 5

When you have worked through this chapter, you should be able to

1 describe the Stock Exchange Automated Quotations system, SEAQ, and comment on its features

2 discuss the layered nature of a computer's software

3 list and explain the main general tasks of a mainframe's operating software (OS)

4 describe multi-programming, multi-usage, multi-processing, batching systems, and real-time working, with examples of use, and note the main OS functions in each case

5 give examples of interrupts and outline the process of interrupt handling

6 list some tasks a micro user faces that a mini or mainframe's OS would handle

7 state what disc formatting entails

8 describe, with an example, a hierarchical (tree) directory

layout and its use

9 state the need for backing up data and outline methods of doing it
10 list other disc management tasks
11 discuss the nature and advantages of spooling
12 state what a job control language is, and note some uses
13 distinguish between multi-programming and multi-user time sharing
14 outline the nature of machine code programming
15 show, and discuss, the spectrum of program languages
16 state, with examples, the use of the four fields of an assembly language instruction
17 state the functions and usage of editor and assembler programs and of directives and macros
18 outline the main addressing modes
19 compare high-level program language to human language
20 compare high- and assembly-level program language
21 list the features that describe a high-level program language, and comment
22 compare methods of program control branching and looping
23 compare compilation and interpretation
24 show some knowledge of several major high-level languages
25 comment on user interface quality

Chapter 6

When you have worked through this chapter, you should be able to

1 outline the use of the three main data files in the Police National Computer
2 list local police uses of IT
3 describe the structure of a hierarchical data base
4 define 'key field' and comment on its use
5 compare fixed and variable length records and fields
6 outline the steps involved in file creation
7 note methods of data compaction (compression)
8 discuss the tasks of file searching and sorting
9 comment on file size, growth, activity and volatility
10 compare the physical arrangement of serial, sequential, indexed sequential, and direct access files
11 discuss simple hashing algorithms
12 describe the grandparent/parent/child approach to data security
13 outline how to merge two data files
14 compare, with examples of data items concerned, data validation and verification
15 describe the use and value of check digits
16 list and discuss methods of data security

Chapter 7

When you have worked through this chapter, you should be able to

1 outline the features of desktop publishing (DTP) software
2 describe how to use a DTP program to produce a well laid out document of text and graphics
3 show how planning helps effective IT use
4 state the nature of programming and the concept and advantages of top–down development
5 state what makes a program efficient
6 discuss in detail the steps of program development
7 compare algorithms in English, pseudocode, flowchart, and structure chart form
8 list the aims of program testing and approaches to it
9 list and compare the different types of error
10 explain the need for, and list the contents of, user and programmer documentation

Chapter 8

When you have worked through this chapter, you should be able to

1 compare networks (distributed processing systems) with other multi-user computer systems
2 discuss how a large newspaper can use networks that differ in scale
3 outline the history of computer hardware and systems and their impact
4 compare star (cluster), bus, ring and hybrid networks
5 outline the functions of network operating software and of network versions of applications packages
6 outline the hierarchy of computer links, from micros sharing a printer, through local and medium (metropolitan) area networks, to wide area networks
7 state the nature of a gateway
8 sketch the layout of a public phone network
9 compare the techniques of analog and digital telephony and list advantages of the latter
10 outline the nature and use of optical fibre
11 outline the nature of the telex network and note the historical basis for its problems
12 list new and possible telex unit features
13 outline the nature and use of teletex
14 compare teletex with telex and with electronic mail
15 outline the nature and use of fax
16 list the features of a modern fax machine
17 describe uses of the circuit switched public data network

18 describe packet switching
19 outline the concept of electronic funds transfer at the point of sale and the use in this context of the smart card
20 describe the layout of the cellular mobile phone network
21 list some likely features of the integrated services data network

Chapter 9

When you have worked through this chapter, you should be able to

1 discuss what people mean by machine (artificial) intelligence and give examples of cases to which it may apply
2 outline the nature, development, structure and use of a knowledge-based expert system
3 describe briefly the use of an example expert system
4 state what 'system' and 'systems analysis' mean
5 outline the characteristics of a good systems analyst
6 describe the stages of setting up a new IT-based system and explain the system life cycle concept
7 apply the techniques of systems analysis, design and implementation to a simple case
8 show the hierarchical nature of a typical large data processing department, and outline the work of each person or group

Chapter 10

When you have worked through this chapter, you should be able to

1 describe some likely near-future developments in TV
2 outline the nature of a cable network and comment on the services it could provide
3 list likely near-future developments in the fields of compact and video discs
4 list likely near-future developments in video and mobile phones
5 list likely near-future developments of teletext and viewdata
6 list likely near-future developments in home computer technology
7 discuss the pros and cons of aspects of new IT as regards society and the individual
8 outline the optimistic and pessimistic views of the impact of IT on employment
9 state examples of computer-based crime
10 outline and assess typical security precautions
11 state who is, and who is not, a data user in the context of the British Data Protection Act
12 outline the code of practice of a data user
13 state the rights of data subjects in respect of personal data held on them by data users

Appendix E
Glossary

Here I give brief notes on the main technical terms used in the book. The entries are for initial reference only—this isn't an encyclopaedia. However, the material should provide enough information to help you in your reading and to understand more detailed explanations elsewhere. Please also refer to the index and, in general, to the *Glossary of computing terms* (Appendix C) if your board uses it.

access The retrieval of information from whatever stores it—e.g. a chip, a disc (*see also* **direct access**) or a video tape. Access time is how long a system takes to find a given packet of data. As a verb the word means to get access to.

Access to a system may be open to all who can work it; on the other hand, there may be control by formalities like subscriptions, logging-on procedures, passwords and so on.

accounts An important area of business computing, where software greatly helps the keeping of accurate and up-to-date financial records.

accumulator A major processor register that stores data items during processing, holding one operand for an operation and then the result.

accuracy A measure of how close a result is to the correct value.

acoustic coupler This type of modem cradles a phone handset, and links to a computer through a cable. The coupler turns computer output into sound signals and vice versa. Its data transfer rate is not as high as that of a standard modem, and it can be unreliable in that it can pick up noise from outside; all the same, it's cheap, easy to carry, and more flexible in use.

activity Sometimes called **hit rate,** a measure of how much a file is used—the fraction of records accessed in a period.

ADC Analog-to-digital converter.

address This number, label or code identifies a particular cell in a computer memory or sector on a disc. The various styles include **direct, indirect, absolute, indexed** and **relative. Address generation** is getting an address from other data, e.g. a record's address on a disc from its key field value. The word can also be a verb: a processor addresses a particular area when it directly reads information from it or writes to it.

aerial A structure that picks up or sends out long electromagnetic (radio) waves.

AI Machine (artificial) intelligence.

algorithm The solution to a problem in the form of a logical series of steps, in English, in pseudocode, or as a chart (or a proof that no solution is possible).

ALU Arithmetic and logic unit.

ASCII American Standard Code for Information Interchange.

analog Real-world measures (e.g. time, acidity, pressure, weight) that vary smoothly in value rather than being stepped (digital).

analog computer A machine in which data transfer, storage and processing are analog.

analog-to-digital converter (ADC) Part of an interface or modem, with an analog input and a proportional digital output.

analysis This involves working out the structure and action of a system in terms of its parts. The aim may be to make the structure simpler and the action more efficient.

animation Showing a sequence of separate pictures, e.g. video frames or computer graphics, so quickly they appear to the viewer to show motion.

APG Applications program generator.

applications program Software that applies a computer to a real world problem, e.g. handling accounts or driving a robot.

applications program generator (APG) A fourth-generation language system that allows a user to define the broad details of a program (e.g. input/output and files) and then produces the program code for the task.

applicative program language Functional program language.

architecture The logical (effective) layout of a circuit, device, system, or network.

archive Data held to meet long-term needs, perhaps for reference, and not often needing access.

arithmetic and logic unit (ALU) Where a processor carries out (binary) arithmetic processes and logical comparisons.

array A data structure, equivalent to a list or table, with a single label, each of whose elements has its own subscript(s).

artificial intelligence (AI) Machine intelligence.

ASCII The American Standard Code for Information Interchange, generally accepted for coding control signals and characters for storage, processing, and transfer.

assembly language Low-level program languages of this sort use coded versions of English words to give instructions to a processor and labels to refer to data items and addresses. An assembler program automatically translates these into machine code. Assembly language is harder for humans to work with than high-level program languages as it works at a machine level rather than with problems.

assignment Giving a value to a data item (by label),

directly, during input, or by reading data in main store or in a file.

ATM   Automatic teller machine.

attenuate   To weaken, as of a signal in a data transfer channel.

attributes   The properties of a data entity described by the values of the fields of its record in a data base.

audio   Concerned with sound waves in the audible frequency range (roughly 20 Hz to 20 000 Hz), electric signals in the same range, and equipment to handle them.

authoring language   High-level language for speeding up and easing the job of writing textual applications software. Authoring (or author) languages may also have special editing facilities and software tools to let people who aren't professional programmers write their own software—for example, for training—they then may be called **authoring systems.** People often use modern authoring software for the control of presentation systems that include video tape or disc.

automatic teller machine (ATM; autoteller)   A bank's intelligent cash dispenser terminal which links as required to the central mainframe.

automation   Putting processes and machines under the control of software rather than of people.

autonomy   The freedom of a device or system from central computer control.

auxiliary store   Backing store.

background   A processor can divide its attention between several jobs held in store at the same time. The simplest form of this time sharing is where the system works on one job (say, a spreadsheet) in the foreground, while a second (such as printing some text) takes place during the small gaps in this job that is, in the background.

backing store   Large-scale external memory, based on tape or disc for instance, that supports a system's main store.

backup   Backup hardware stays in reserve in case crucial items break down. In the same way, people keep backup software in case of loss of, or damage to, the originals. To back up a disc is to copy all its contents.

bandwidth   A measure of the data-carrying ability of a communication channel, the unit being the hertz (Hz).

bar code   A machine-readable data code with light/dark stripe patterns for numbers.

barrel printer   A type of line printer whose characters lie over the surface of a fast-turning drum.

BASIC   Beginners' All-purpose Symbolic Instruction Code—a very common high-level program language that has many dialects.

batch processing   Non-interactive computing where the computer works in turn through a set (batch) of programs and the data provided in advance for them.

baud   A rate of data transfer of about a bit a second.

BCD   Binary coded decimal.

binary coded decimal (BCD)   A method of data handling where the system converts each digit in a decimal number to binary. *See also* **EBCDIC.**

binary number   A binary number consists only of the digits 0 and 1, perhaps with a binary point. Place values are powers of 2: 1 2 4 8 . . . (and after the point) ½ ¼ ⅛ . . .

binary search (chop)   A way to search a sequenced list for an item—repeat: find the centre and choose the half that should contain the item, until the item's found or known not to be there.

binary system   A method of counting with only two digits (0 and 1) instead of the ten (0 to 9) of denary.

binary tree   A branching data structure in which no parent can have more than two children.

bio-electronics   Microelectronics using organic materials and with possible biological links in mind.

bit   A binary digit, 0 or 1.

block   The smallest unit in a backing store medium you can address or transfer. The medium's blocking factor gives the number of logical records a block (physical record) can hold. A block is also a structural element of a program.

board   A circuit and set of chips on a printed circuit board which, when added to a hardware device, provides extra features.

Boolean   The logic used in microelectronics is much like the mathematical system devised by George Boole in the nineteenth century. A Boolean data item can have only two values—true or false.

boot   You can make programs load and run automatically on switch on, so the system boots itself—'pulls itself up by its bootstraps'.

branch   To pass through a program, data structure, or course by a route that depends on circumstances, rather than being fixed (linear); also the link between parent and child nodes in a tree.

British Telecom Gold (BTG)   The major British scrolling interactive viewdata base, with a strong electronic mail aspect.

broadcast videotex   Teletext.

bubble store   The chips here have a magnetic surface; moving domains in the surface can stand for 0s and 1s. Bubble storage is cheap and non-volatile, but rare.

bucket   A group of data blocks treated as a unit during processing.

buffer   A store for a block of data in transfer, in particular between peripheral and centre. *See also* **double buffering.**

bug   A mistake in a system or program, removed by debugging.

bulletin board   A communal electronic notice board that allows people to log on and exchange news, views, for sale notices, and wants.

bus   A high-volume channel through which data passes with the bits of each word in parallel.

byte   A byte, typically a group of 8 bits, can represent any keyboard character or control code. An 8-bit processor handles information in bytes (still sometimes called **octets**); machines with more power deal with data in pairs of bytes or even larger groups.

cable   This describes video distributed by wire rather than broadcast by radio waves. In areas with poor reception, a cable operator may erect a high performance aerial and distribute the signal by cable. A cable network in an area may offer a whole new approach to many kinds of electronic information transfer.

cache   High-speed data storage between a processor's registers and the main store.

CAD   Computer-aided design/drawing.

CADCAM   Computer-aided design and manufacture.

CAL   Computer-aided learning.

CAM   Computer-aided manufacture.

card   (a) (Printed circuit) board; (b) an out-dated storage medium, the data being held as patterns of punched holes made by a card punch and read by a card reader.

carousel   A system that cycles again and again through a series of routines, pictures or viewdata frames.

catalogue   Where a disc carries the list of its files (also called **directory**). *Compare with* **index.**

Cauzin strip   Data printed in robust and compact form on paper for reading by a special input device.

CCD   Charge-coupled device.

CD   Compact disc—**CD-I** is compact disc interactive; **CD-ROM** is compact disc read-only memory.

Ceefax   The teletext service of the British Broadcasting Corporation.

cell   A particular item in an array—e.g., a main storage unit, a data site in a spreadsheet, a unit (pixel) of the picture on a screen.

central processing unit (CPU)   Processor.

chain printer   A line printer with the characters held on the surface of a chain or belt.

channel   A path for data transfer—whatever connects a data source to a receiver. A single complete channel may consist of several transfer links and several units of hardware.

character   Any number, letter, symbol or control code for a keyboard, screen or printer, or in a file, the group of all those a system can handle being its character set.

character printer   One which in effect prints a character at a time.

charge-coupled device (CCD)   Basis of a new form of data storage, the bits being held as tiny lumps of electric charge in the surface of the device.

chat mode   The design of electronic mail and telex systems allows the sender to transfer a message to someone who may not be available till later. However, if both are on line at the same time, they may also communicate in chat mode. This is a sort of typed-out phone conversation in which each sees each other's words on screen and can type in the reply at once.

check bit/digit   A character (in most cases a bit or denary digit) added to the end of a data item to aid validation (checking).

check sum   A data item (in most cases a number) added to the end of a data block to aid checking after transfer.

chief operator   The person in charge of the daily operations of a computer suite.

child   (a) The current master in a grandparent/parent/child file backup approach; (b) a lower level node linked to a node in a tree.

chip   A tiny piece of material that can contain complex electronic circuits.

CIM   Computer-integrated manufacture.

circular list   Ring list.

clock   A chip in the control unit of a processor whose function is to send out pulses at a regular rate.

closed subroutine   Part of a program with a single function, kept apart from and called by the main program; a procedure.

closed user group (CUG)   A group of subscribers to Prestel (for instance) who have access to the public pages and to private pages as well.

CML   Computer-managed learning.

co-axial cable (co-ax)   Wire with a sleeve of braided metal screening to prevent interference with the signal it carries, as with the wire that connects a TV aerial to the set.

COBOL   COmmon Business Oriented Language—a high-level program language widely used in business.

code   To write out a computer program—the chunks of program that result are code.

Codes are also a way to compress data so they take up less space in a channel or a store.

COM   Computer output on microform.

command mode   A style of system use in which you control the action by typing in commands (direct instructions) or command codes, rather than choosing from a menu.

comment   A note from the programmer in a program listing, stored with the listing but ignored by the computer.

commission   To set up a new system or package.

communications software   Programs that let you transfer messages and data files over a distance, often using a phone link.

compact disc (CD)   This 12 cm disc, designed to store high-quality audio signals, can also carry hundreds of megabytes of digital data. In the latter case, this leads to **CD-ROM** (CD read-only memory), a method for putting very large amounts of data on line to a computer in read-only form.

Another field is **CD-I** (compact disc interactive); this has an approach rather like that of interactive video.

compaction   Making data items and structures take up as little storage space as possible.

compatibility   A measure of how much you can feed data from one system straight to a second.

compile   To translate, with a compiler, the whole of a high-level language source program into a machine code object program.

compression   Compaction.

computer   A modern high-speed, stored program, digital electronic data processor.

computer output on microform (COM)   Rather than going to screen, the output forms a set of tiny images on film which, which processed, is viewed as microfilm or fiche.

computer-aided design (CAD)   A software package to help design work by giving good graphics, a library of standard sub-designs, analysis, and simulation.

computer-aided drawing (draughting) (CAD)   A simple version of computer-aided design.

computer-aided learning (CAL)   The use of IT directly to assist a learner's progress.

computer-aided manufacture (CAM)   The integrated control of machine tools and assembly lines.

computer-integrated manufacture (CIM)   The use of IT in the factory, including robotics and automated testing.

computer-managed learning (CML)   A style of learning of software in which the system keeps records of learners' progress, and may also attempt to guide each one to further work.

concept keyboard   An input device that is of value to people who find a standard keyboard an obstacle. Instead of having to type out words letter by letter, you press the part of the surface that bears a picture or symbol for a given concept. The board accepts a variety of overlays, so you can work it with different software.

concurrent   Literally, this means occurring at the same time. Multiprogramming makes a number of programs seem to run in parallel, by letting them take turns at the processor. Multiprocessing is true concurrent processing: a number of processors linked together in parallel (as in a transputer) can really do different things at the same time.

configuration   A particular combination of equipment and software that makes up a working system. To configure a device or system is to set it up or modify it to meet some individual set of needs.

connectivity   The degree to which a computer system can link with others to form a network.

console   The terminal in a mainframe computer room at which a system's chief operator or shift leader works to monitor and control the flow of jobs.

constant   A data item whose value doesn't change during a program run.

consultant   An expert (in theory) in some aspect of IT, who should have no ties to any particular system or supplier, and should therefore be able to give you valid impartial aid and advice.

consumables   Anything you need a regular supply of, like printer paper and fuses.

continuous stationery   Paper in continuous form, roll or fan fold, instead of in separate sheets.

control code   A byte with the function of causing something to happen in a peripheral (e.g. clear a screen or buzz a buzzer).

control unit   The section of a processor which looks after the operation of the system, by ordering and decoding

instructions and overseeing the action of the other units.

convergence   The coming together of previously separate technologies by making use of the same basic principles (e.g. digital coding of information) and sometimes even the same hardware (like video receiver/monitors and compact disc or video disc players).

co-processor   A second processor, slave to the main one in a system, that specialises in certain tasks (e.g. mathematical work or data base management).

core store   Main store.

corporate communication   Meeting the information needs inside a group—such as by putting up notices, sending out circulars or a house magazine, or publishing the occasional video tape for the staff.

corruption   Unwanted changes to data in store or during transfer, a result of software errors, interference, or attenuation.

CPA   Critical path analysis.

CP/M   Control program for micros, a widely used standard operating software package for 8-bit systems, now also available for 16-bit hardware.

CPU   Processor.

crash   When a program stops when it's not at the end, we say it's crashed. Good software design should prevent this. A **head** (or **disc**) **crash** is when the read/write head of a drive touches a disc surface and causes damage and loss of data.

critical path analysis (CPA)   A technique, now often used with the aid of a computer, to schedule the tasks involved in, and the resources needed by, a project.

cursor   A symbol on a screen that shows where you are—perhaps a square blob or underline mark, often flashing.

cut and paste   The technique of joining chunks of text and pictures together to make a camera-ready copy of a page for printing, now much aided by desktop publishing software on computers.

cycle time   The delay between calling up a teletext page and when it appears on screen, caused by the time taken for the magazine to cycle through all its pages.

cylinder   The set of all tracks with the same number in a disc pack—that is, that the head unit can access without moving.

DAC   Digital-to-analog converter.

daisy wheel   The central part in a high-quality (but slow) character printer—a wheel without a rim with the characters at the ends of the spokes (petals).

DAT   Digital audio tape.

data   Generally, this is coded information—that is, it has no obvious meaning, even if it is in the form of letters or numbers you can read. Some people take it to mean information after a system has prepared it for processing, storage, or transfer.

data bank   A collection—usually a large one—of data held in a computer, the term sometimes being used to mean

data base.

data base   A collection of information organised systematically on the basis of the relationships between the data items concerned, so as to make processing, searching and sorting easy. **Data base management systems** (DBMS) are computer programs for designing a data base and allowing its use, normally by more than one person. A **hierarchical data base** is a tree-like data structure (files, records, fields); a **relational data base** allows many more useful links between data items; a distributed data base is shared between processors.

data capture   (a) The process by which a computer automatically uses sensors to obtain data from the environment; (b) the process by which people obtain information, e.g. on a data capture form, so they can feed it into a computer with few errors.

data control   Looking after the flow of (programs and) data into and out of a large computer system.

data entry   Keying data into a system, especially a large data base, from source documents (e.g. data capture forms) or the phone, for instance, normally using a key-to-disc technique.

data item   A single piece of data.

data processing (DP)   Loosely, the handling of information, usually referring in practice to the batch processing by computer of large volumes of prepared data, such as gas bills or pay slips.

data protection   Procedures and laws designed to ensure the privacy and security of stored personal data.

data structure   A set of data items with a single name and function.

data type   Character, string, integer, real (number), or Boolean, each type having its own set of properties and being processed in its own way.

DDE   Direct data entry.

debug   To remove mistakes (bugs), a **debugger** being a special program to help with this.

declaration   The block of statements that programs in some languages must open with to get things, especially main storage areas, ready.

declarative program language   A non-procedural system in which a program describes the result (as a set of equations) rather than how to obtain it, important in mathematics, science, engineering and so on.

dedicated   Specially designed for, or limited to, a particular function, instead of being user-reprogrammable (general purpose).

default   The value or behaviour a system assumes unless otherwise instructed.

denary   The correct name for the base 10 counting system (decimal).

desktop publishing (DTP)   With desktop publishing (or page layout) software you can use a compact in-house computer system to produce pages of well laid-out text and graphics ready for printing.

device   A hardware unit with a single clear function, a

device driver   being a utility program or routine for working it.

diagnostic   A message output by a translator or operating program, to state the nature and site of a software error.

dialect   A variant of a standard program language.

digital   Anything that can be counted as separate numbers, the opposite of analog—a digital signal is step-like, while an analog one is wavy.

digital audio tape (DAT)   Magnetic tape on which you can store analog sound signals in digital form, and therefore with very high quality and potential for computer backing store.

digital optical disc   A video disc that carries its data in digital rather than analog form, so has potential in computer backing storage.

digital-to-analog converter (DAC)   A device, e.g. in an interface or modem, with a digital input and a proportional analog output.

digitiser   Any device able to give a digital output from some form of analog input is a digitiser. People use the term most often for graphics pads, for scanners, and for systems that convert a video signal so a computer can process it.

dimension   The size of an array as given by the number of subscripts each element needs.

direct access   Also called **random access**, this describes how you go straight to any part of a computer memory, storage disc or video disc, without having to work through from the start. *Compare with* **serial access.**

direct broadcast by satellite   Using a satellite to relay the signals sent to it so anyone with a suitable aerial in a large area can pick them up.

direct connect modem   A modem that links directly to the telephone network, unlike an acoustic coupler.

direct data entry (DDE)   When input data passes straight to backing store, as opposed to being batched off line with a key-to-store system.

directive   An instruction to the assembler in an assembly code source program (not for translation).

directory   Catalogue.

disable   The opposite of enable—to prevent from operating (sometimes it's useful to disable a key, like a computer's BREAK key, or a device, e.g. a printer if you don't need printout).

disc   A flat circular sheet of material used to store information; it may be hard (rigid) or flexible (floppy). Discs for computer data storage are magnetic; compact and video discs are non-magnetic.

disc drive   A device that retrieves (reads) information from and records (writes) it to a disc.

disc pack   A set of hard discs with a single spindle, addressed by cylinder, surface, sector.

distributed processing   The arrangement of a network.

documentation   The instructions and manuals needed to get the best from a system.

dot matrix   A character printer whose output consists of a series of vertical dot patterns formed by pins striking ink from the ribbon onto the paper.

double buffering Reading blocks from tape or disc into two buffers alternately, with the contents of one buffer being processed while the other's filling with a new block.

double precision Using twice as many bytes as usual to store a number, so giving it twice the normal precision (number of significant figures).

download Transfer of data from one computer to a smaller one, e.g. from a mainframe to a terminal or from a network to a work station.

DP (data processing) Most large firms have DP departments with DP managers in charge.

drum An outdated magnetic backing storage device—a cylinder coated on the outside. (b) A **drum printer** is a barrel printer. (c) In a **drum plotter** the paper moves back and forth while the pen moves to and fro.

dry run A test that carries out, in order, the steps of an algorithm or program to find errors.

DTP Desktop publishing.

dumb Describes a device with no processing power or storage of its own. *Compare* **intelligent.**

dump To copy a file or a block of computer memory somewhere else, such as to a printer (thus a **screen dump** is a printout version of the screen display) or to backing store.

EAN European Article Number, a major bar coding system.

EBCDIC Extended binary coded decimal interchange code—BCD with extra codes for characters other than digits.

edit To improve, cut or re-arrange material, such as text, programs or video tape, an **editor** being a device or program to help.

EDP Electronic data processing—another name for DP.

EFT Electronic funds transfer.

EFTPOS Electronic funds transfer at the point of sale.

electronic document storage (EDS) Holding copies of documents (pure text or with graphics) in a form a computer can access, as on some kind of disc.

electronic funds transfer (EFT) The transfer of data that stands for cash, e.g. between banks or between banks and clients.

electronic funds transfer at the point of sale (EFTPOS) The transfer of data that stands for cash between a shop, its bank, and the customer's bank, perhaps using smart cards at the point of sale.

electronic mail (email) A method of transferring data between remote computers using cable, telephone lines, broadcast waves or satellites; along the line the data is stored in a host computer for later access by the recipient. (Confusingly and wrongly, some people also use the phrase to describe scrolling interactive videotex (viewdata) systems like BTG and The Times Network System.)

electronic office An office where there's much use of IT.

electronic publishing Preparing and storing documents (pure text or with graphics) so other people can access them by computer, e.g. on disc or through a communications link.

electronics The technology of systems that involve small electric currents.

element A single data item in an array.

email Electronic mail.

encryption Coding data before storage or transfer to make wrongful access pointless.

environment The hardware and software system a program needs to run.

enquiry language A high-level language designed for interrogating (asking questions of) a data base, in particular that of an expert system.

enter To put instructions or data into a computer.

ergonomics The study of the relationship between the design of equipment and systems and the user's comfort and efficiency.

error A bug in a program; there are various kinds of bugs that programmers and users must watch out for.

execute The stage when a processor actually carries out the instructions in a program.

expert system Software that builds up expertise in making judgements from input evidence and thus displays a form of machine intelligence. Some expert systems can converse with humans in a relatively natural way, and some can explain and justify their line of reasoning. So far, the most successful expert systems tend to operate in a restricted field of knowledge; we call these knowledge-based expert systems.

external device Peripheral.

even parity A parity system where the number of 1s in each byte plus parity bit is even.

fatal error An error that causes a program to crash.

fax Facsimile transfer (or telegraphy), in which a machine scans the entire content of a sheet of paper (including diagrams, letterhead, signature and so on), codes it and sends it to a compatible remote machine for printing.

feasibility study A stage in systems analysis during which one compares possible solutions to needs.

feedback The transfer of information from the output of a device or system to the input so as to control its action.

fetch–execute–reset The cycle of actions in a processor that allows the system to carry out a single machine code instruction.

fibre optics The use of thin flexible strands of very pure glass to carry information on light signals.

field (a) The space for a single data item (attribute, such as age or code number) in each record of a data base; (b) the image produced by a single scan of a TV-type display.

FIFO First in, first out.

fifth generation The imminent style of computer use, with very large scale integration of electronics, parallel processing, human–machine communication by speech, and software giving freer use of natural language than at present.

file A data structure with a single name—a set of instructions (program), text (document), or other data (part of a data base)—in a computer's main or backing store.

file maintenance Keeping the data in a file up to date and backed up.

firmware Intermediate between software and hardware, firmware carries instructions semi-permanently, usually in the form of ROM chips.

first in, first out (FIFO) Describes the action of a queue.

fixed point number A number in which (in binary) the binary point is always in the same place.

flag A 1-bit data item, whose two values show the two possible states of some aspect of a system.

flat bed A plotter on the flat surface of which the paper is fixed while the pen moves up and down and to and fro over it. *Compare* **drum.**

floating point number A number given (in binary) as, for instance, a value between 0.5_{10} and 1 (mantissa) and an integral power of two (exponent).

floppy *See* **disc.**

flowchart A method of showing an algorithm or the sequence of actions in a system using boxes joined with arrowed lines.

format (a) The layout, headings, spacing, and margins of a piece of text; (b) the arrangement of data in a file, on a disc, or on a screen; (c) the physical size and colour standard (among other things) of a video tape or disc. (d) To format a disc is to prepare it to receive information in the form suited to your system.

Forth A semi-compiled high-level program language whose instructions act on the contents of a stack.

FORTRAN Formula Translator—a high-level program language of use in science, mathematics and engineering.

fourth generation The current (1970s and 1980s) style of computing, with integrated circuit electronics, large main stores, connectivity (support for networking), data base management, and applications program generation software.

front end The interface between a hardware and/or software system and its user.

functional program language Also called **applicative**, this is a type of declarative language whose programs define the desired results in terms of equations and functions that may be recursive.

fuzzy Applied to the 'rules of logic' involved in some styles of 'intelligent' software that involves flexibility in coming to conclusions.

gate A logic device that has the effect of controlling the flow of data through it.

gateway A link that allows certain network or viewdata users access to other networks or computers and their data.

GIGO Short for garbage in, garbage out—a well-known cliché about (ab)using computers.

global Describes a variable used throughout a program. *Compare* **local.**

grandparent The oldest master file in a grandparent–parent–child sequence of file updating.

graphics These are pictures a processor can draw on screen or print on to paper. The higher the resolution of the output device (graphics display, printer, or plotter), the better the picture. Business graphics software lets you quickly build up high-quality graphs and charts. *See also* **computer-aided design.**

graphics pad A form of digitiser, an input device on which you trace a shape that appears on screen and is coded in digital form for the computer to process, store and output.

handshake The exchange of check signals before a data transfer between a peripheral and the processor.

hard copy Printout.

hard disc A high-speed, high-density backing store medium that can hold much more information than a floppy, but if fixed in the computer (as is common), isn't easy to back up.

hard interrupt An interrupt signal from a peripheral.

hardware The equipment that makes up an IT system, as opposed to the software that drives it.

hash algorithm An address generation routine—to process a record's key field value to obtain its storage address in a direct access file.

hex(adecimal) Base 16 counting.

heuristics The fuzzy rules of thumb that guide certain machine intelligence systems.

hierarchy An arrangement in which there are several levels, with higher levels more general than lower ones. Trees are hierarchical data structures. Hierarchical data bases like Prestel are tree like in their logical design.

high-level (program) language A language like BASIC or COBOL, in which instructions use English-like words, labels, and advanced structures, for translation by compiler or interpreter into machine code, and in which programming relates to problems rather than to machine-level activities.

high-resolution graphics Computer-generated pictures with a lot of detail, which can, for instance, show smooth curves.

hit rate Activity.

host The central storage computer in an electronic mail or viewdata network.

hybrid A mix of types—a **hybrid computer** has analog and digital parts; a **hybrid network** is more complex than a simple star, bus or ring.

hypertext A form of three-dimensional word processor that allows links between words and phrases, and perhaps graphics, in the various levels.

IBG   Inter-block gap.

IC   Integrated circuit (chip).

icon   A picture or graphic symbol for a particular function; for instance, choosing at a rubbish bin icon lets you delete a file.

immediate access store   Main store.

impact printer   One which involves actual contact between a moving part and the paper.

imperative program language   A procedural language, one whose programs define the method of reaching the desired results as a series of operations in order. *Compare* **declarative.**

implementation   Carrying out (as of a program idea or a system design).

index   (a) A list of key field ranges and addresses on a disc that gives direct access to the records of an indexed or indexed sequential file; (b) A base address in store.

information   That which adds to human knowledge, data with meaning (or, to some, structure).

information provider   An individual or organisation providing data for a data base, usually in the context of viewdata systems, but in general an electronic publisher.

information retrieval   An IT application in which you can access the content of a large information store at any time.

information technology (IT)   This includes modern methods of collecting, handling, storing, and passing information, as text, graphics or sound.

The UNESCO definition is—the scientific, technological and engineering disciplines and the management techniques used in information handling and processing; their applications; computers and their interaction with people and machines; and associated social, economic and cultural matters.

inkjet   The mechanism of a compact, fast, quiet printer which sprays tiny drops of ink onto the paper.

in-order traverse   A way of passing through the data items of a tree to output them in order.

input   To feed data into a system (also a noun meaning what's fed in), with an input device (e.g. keyboard) having the function of aiding this.

instruction   A single request for a system to do something, in a program (statement) or directly (command)—the system's instruction set is all the instructions it can follow.

integer   A whole number. *Compare* **real.**

integrated circuit (IC)   Chip.

integrated software   Programs designed as a suite so you can feed data from one automatically into a second.

intelligence   The ability to react appropriately to unpredictable events, and/or to follow fuzzy rather than clear rules, perhaps with insight and/or inspiration, plus the ability to learn. *See also* **machine intelligence.**

intelligent   Smart, describes a peripheral (e.g. terminal) with its own (local) processing power and store.

interactive   Interactive communication is two-way—what one side does depends on the response just received from the other, and vice versa. Interactive (conversational) computing is the opposite of batch processing. Viewdata is interactive videotex.

interactive video (IV)   This communications medium combines features of computing with those of video presentation. Instead of viewing a video programme in linear sequence, software helps you choose your own route(s) through.

interactive videotex   Viewdata.

inter-block gap (IBG)   The gap between two data blocks on a tape or disc.

interface   The join between two things. To interface two devices is to do what's needed to let them transfer data. Computer interfaces often involve software as well as chips (e.g. buffers, DACs and ADCs), plugs and cables.

interrogate   To ask a data base for information.

inventory software   An advanced type of stock control software with some accounts features.

interpreter   A translating program that translates and carries out high-level language program instructions only when it comes to them, rather than changing a program as a whole into machine code (as does a compiler).

interrupt   A signal telling the processor to stop what it's doing and handle something else.

IT   Information technology.

IV   Interactive video.

JCL   Job control language. *See* **job.**

job   A single program task, especially in a batch processing system where **job control language (JCL)** programs are how the operator or programmer tells the system what to do.

joystick   A computer input device with a short lever you can move freely in any direction, often used in place of a keyboard with computer software and interactive video, and also called a **paddle.**

K   Kilobyte, or (as a prefix) 1024.

KBES   Knowledge-based expert system.

key   A button switch on a keyboard or a keypad; a field through which you search a file or data base for specific records; a string used to decode encrypted data.

key system   A form of local phone network whose users can each take on some of the roles of switchboard operator and whose handsets offer a wide range of features.

key to store   A method of data entry to off-line backing store (e.g. disc or tape) that doesn't need the attention of the main computer. *Compare* **direct data entry.**

keyword   You can search some data bases by keywords that unlock their contents; the system knows each item by a number of keywords that show what it's about. In a high-level program language, keywords are reserved instruction words that relate to low-level operations.

kilobyte (K)   A thousand bytes (actually 2^{10} or 1024); as a byte is able to store one character, 1 K can carry about 150 words of text.

knowledge engineering   Building up a knowledge-based expert system—at least the data base of facts and rules, but also perhaps the means of access to it.

label   The name of a data item, structure, or sub-program.

LAN   Local area network.

laser   A device to produce a high-energy beam of radiation (often light) with important uses in IT: laser printers are fast, quality page printers; some bar-code readers, scanners, robot vision units, and video disc systems use lasers.

laser disc   An optical video disc (though some people also use the term for compact disc too).

last in, first out (LIFO)   Describes the action of a stack.

layout   The structure and appearance of material on paper or on screen, for instance.

LCD   Liquid crystal display: liquid crystals don't give out light, but can switch from opaque to transparent using little power to provide a legible display in suitable light; LCDs are common in lap-held computers as well as in calculators and watches.

leaf   A tree's terminal node (one with no children).

LED   Light emitting diode—an element of a display that gives out light when passing an electric current. Such displays are brighter than LCDs, but use more power.

library   The set of discs or tapes used by a DP section (the responsibility of the data librarian), of programs and subprograms used by a programmer, or of stored designs in CAD.

LIFO   Last in, first out.

light pen   A pointing device, with a photocell in the head, with which you can select from choices on a screen, or (sometimes) draw shapes directly on it; another type acts as a bar code reader.

line printer   A printer that in effect constructs a line of output at a time.

line speed   The rate of data transfer in a channel, often measured in baud (bits per second, roughly).

linked list   A linear data structure into which, at any point, you can insert extra items, and from which you can delete them, each item carrying a pointer to the next in the logical sequence.

list   A one-dimensional array or other linear data structure.

liveware   Jargon denoting the people who run a computer system.

load   To copy data from backing store into main store.

local   (a) Describes short full-time links between the parts of an IT system that are in effect permanently on line. (b) A local label is for a data item used in only part of a program.

local area network (LAN)   A method of linking a set of nearby computers and peripherals.

local processing   The use by a peripheral, terminal or networked microcomputer of its own processing power and storage rather than that in the centre of the system.

log   A continuous timed record of what's happened: for example, a phone log is a record of all calls made, with details of time, extension used, and destination; a computer log is a printout from the operating software of jobs done, problems met, accesses tried, and actions taken.

log on   To start work with a remote computer or network station, perhaps including proving you have the right to do so.

logical record   A record in a file viewed as a set of fields rather than by how it's stored.

loop   A high-level program structure which lets a sub-routine act a given number of times or until some condition changes.

low-level program languages   Machine code and assembler.

Logo   A list-processing style of high-level program language, designed for the encouragement of logical thinking in learners but also able to be used for highly sophisticated tasks.

M   Megabyte.

machine code   The language of binary numbers in which a processor works (or, to some, the equivalent code in hexadecimal form or even assembler).

machine intelligence   Some programs are intelligent in that, if humans were to do the same work, you'd call them intelligent. For instance, a program may add to its 'knowledge' from previous runs; interpret the meaning of a question from its context; prove mathematical theorems; or diagnose diseases or electronic faults. *See also* **expert system.**

machine-readable   A suitable input device can transfer a copy of such data (e.g. bar code) to a computer.

macro   An instruction in assembly language that translates to a pre-written series of machine code actions, or the series to which the assembler translates it.

magnetic ink character reader (MICR)   A device for reading magnetic ink characters into main store.

magnetic media   Media on which a system can store data in the form of a magnetic record.

mailbox   Space in the memory of a computer reserved for messages for a user.

mail merge   This word processing facility inserts details from a file of names and addresses into the right places in standard letters.

main store   Where a system keeps instructions and data ready for immediate access.

mainframe   A large powerful computer able to handle the needs of many, often remote, users, and to work with various programs in the same time.

mark sensor/reader   An input device able to convert information held as marks on the source document to data.

master file   A file in a data bank currently available for access, rather than a backup copy or one for holding new transactions.

MB   Megabyte.

medium   The actual substance or item which stores data.

megabyte (M or MB)   A million (in fact 2^{20}, 1 048 576) bytes.

memory   Data store—a device (or a set of devices) able to store information temporarily or permanently. Internal (main) memory contains the instructions of the current program and working space for data. External (backing) memory stores larger volumes of information for less frequent access.

menu driven   A style of program which you control by choosing options from a menu, rather than typing in commands.

MICR   Magnetic ink character reader.

micro(computer)   A fairly small computer used by only one person at a time.

micro-   A millionth; for example, a microsecond is a millionth of a second.

microform   Microfilm or fiche, able to store pages of data as tiny images. A microform reader projects full-sized pages on a screen; it may also have a printer.

microprocessor   A computer processor on a single chip.

microviewdata   Local (or closed circuit) viewdata, even perhaps on a single micro.

mini(computer)   Cheaper and more compact than a mainframe, this is more likely than a micro to have several users at once.

mnemonic   An assembly language opcode, whose function is fairly easy to remember.

modem   A device that allows digital units like fax machines and computers to transfer data into and from an analog system, in particular the phone network. *See also* **acoustic coupler** *and* **direct connect modem.**

module   A self-contained unit you can readily add to or build on, computer hardware, phone systems and programs being modular.

monitor   (a) The part of operating software that watches the action of the rest; (b) a high-quality visual output unit with a steady clear display.

mouse   Input device which you roll round on a surface to control the movement of a pointer on screen; pressing buttons on the mouse causes actions.

MS-DOS   A type of operating software widely used with 16-bit hardware, including the IBM PC (in which it is called **PC-DOS**).

mugtrap   To provide a validity test for input data.

multi-access   Multi-user.

multiprocessing   Using a system with two or more processors working in parallel, sharing tasks and providing support for each other.

multiprogramming   A system which runs more than one program during a given period by time sharing, switching between them from moment to moment.

multitasking   Describes a concurrent system, one that can handle two or more programs at a time.

multi-user   A system that can handle the needs of more than one user at a time.

network   (a) System for linking IT units so they can communicate with each other and (in the case of computers) share facilities like disc drives and printers; (b) a complex data structure, rather like a tree but with extra links to show relationships between nodes not in a direct line.

neural   structured rather like a brain, with many links of different priority between the parts.

node   (a) A junction in a network; (b) space in a tree for a single data item.

noise   An unwanted signal that reduces or alters the proper one.

non-impact printer   One in which there's no direct contact of a moving part with the paper.

normalised   Describes numeric data put into standard form.

null   Empty. A **null string** has no characters; a **null pointer** points nowhere (so marks, for instance, the end of a data item or structure in store).

object program   A machine code program produced by an assembler or compiler and ready to run.

OCR   Optical character reader.

odd parity   The converse of even parity.

off line   Describes a hardware device not at the moment linked to and controlled by a computer but resting or carrying out its own processing locally.

OMR   Optical mark reader.

on line   Connected to and under the control of a working computer system, locally or remotely through a telecommunications link.

1s complement   The result of switching each 1 in a binary number to 0 and each 0 (including any implied at the left) to 1.

opcode   Operation code.

open subroutine   A block in a program with a single function, not kept apart from the main program. *Compare* **closed subroutine;** *see also* **macro.**

operand   The data item an opcode, mnemonic or keyword is to work on.

operating software (OS)   The program(s) in overall control of a computer system, without which the system would be useless.

operation code (opcode)   The assembler mnemonic that describes what operation the whole instruction is to carry out, or the machine code value it translates to.

operations manager   The person in charge of the day-to-day running of a large computer.

operator   A person with the task of keeping a large computer system working.

optical   To do with light. Light waves have very high frequencies compared with radio, so give far greater information carrying capacity; the optical fibres that can carry them have a major role in modern telecommunications. Compact discs and some video disc systems are optical as well—they depend on the effect on laser light.

optical character reader (OCR)   An input device able to recognise the shapes of characters which are also human readable.

optical mark reader (OMR) An input device for reading marks in given places on special forms.

optical fibre A thin flexible strand of highly pure glass with a high data transfer capacity.

optical publishing Publishing material in optical form, such as on video disc or compact disc.

organiser A type of computer or business software package with such features as diary, address book, and appointments data base.

output Any result produced by an IT system—usually text and/or graphics shown on screen and/or printed on paper if for human use, or signals to one or more device control units in the case of an automated system.

overflow A problem caused by something not fitting the space available (e.g. a result being larger than the system can handle, a direct access file record going to a full block, new data trying to enter a full queue, or a packet that can't squeeze into a busy data transfer channel).

package Program or suite complete with documentation (and perhaps hardware), designed for a particular application.

packet A chunk of data prepared for rapid transfer through a local or public network (e.g. BT's packet switching system).

packet switching system (PSS) A style of data transfer in a network in which a message is split into a number of packets, each supplied with details including address, the packets then moving by various paths to the destination where they are re-assembled.

paddle Joystick.

page printer A fast, quiet printer that in effect constructs for output a page at a time.

paper tape Much the same as card, but narrow and continuous.

parallel processing When two or more processors of roughly equal status share a task by working on parts at the same time, the same as multiprocessing.

parallel transfer When the bits of a byte pass along a bundle of lines together rather than serially along one.

parameter A label or value passed from a program when calling a closed subroutine or vice versa.

parent (a) A node with children, in a tree; (b) the old master file used to create the current one (the child).

parity A technique that lets a system check the validity of data in transfer by sending an extra check bit (parity bit) with each byte (*see* **even parity**) and checking at the other end.

Pascal A general purpose high-level program language that offers good data structure features, widely used with learners.

password A user's secret code to bar others from access to a system, the software perhaps giving different types of user access to different levels of information and action.

PCB Printed circuit board.

peripheral Any computer hardware item other than the processor—an input/output device or backing storage unit in particular.

personal computer A computer small or cheap enough for use mainly by one person.

personal identity number (PIN) The secret number a user of a card has to type into an autoteller or EFTPOS terminal.

physical file/record Described in terms of layout in the storage medium used rather than logically, in terms of hierarchy etc.

PIN Personal identity number.

pixel *See* **cell.**

plotter An output device for drawing graphics and lettering in which a computer directly controls the movement of one or more pens over the paper. *See* **drum** *and* **flat bed.**

point of sale (POS) The place where a shop transaction occurs (for example, a checkout).

pointer (a) The cell or disc address of a data item or structure held so the system can access it quickly; (b) a symbol on a WIMP screen under mouse control that lets you point at the icon for the task you want done.

pop To remove the data item at the open end of a stack.

port (a) A point of access of a peripheral to a processor; (b) to transfer a program from one system to a second.

portable (a) Easy to carry, like a small micro; (b) able to run on other systems, like a standard language program.

POS Point of sale.

precision Measures the number of significant figures in numeric data.

Prestel The major public paged viewdata system in Britain.

primary store Main store.

printed circuit board (PCB) A plastics sheet with printed metal wiring and sockets for chips and other circuit elements, a module in a hardware unit's overall design.

printout Hard copy output from a computer printer.

privacy Keeping data, especially personal and commercial data, out of the wrong hands.

private branch exchange (PBX) A local phone exchange (switching centre), installed on your own premises and run by your own staff.

procedural program language Imperative program language.

procedure An advanced type of closed subroutine, a named part of a program with a given task that's kept apart from the rest, but which can easily share data with it.

process control The automation of a process, involving feedback from the output to the input and a program that looks after the tasks involved.

processor The part of a computer that actually does the arithmetic and makes the decisions, sometimes called **central processing unit** (CPU), in a micro, often a microprocessor.

program   An ordered list of instructions for a system to follow to carry out a given task.

program language   System for giving special instructions to computers (which have to translate programs written using them into machine code before they can follow the instructions).

programmable   Describes a general purpose device or system which you can program for any of a range of tasks (as opposed to a dedicated one which you can't).

programmer   A person whose task is to produce instructions a computer can follow from an algorithm devised during systems analysis.

project scheduler   An advanced form of critical path analysis software package.

Prolog   A high-level programming language devised for developing expert systems.

protect   To use a method which cuts down the chances of losing data by mistake.

protocol   A set of widely agreed rules for, for instance, data transfer, to reduce problems of incompatibility.

pseudocode   A means of setting out an algorithm, in a form part way between natural English and a structured high-level program language.

PSS   Packet switching system.

publishing   Preparing material (pure text or with pictures) for others to access—on paper, on microform, on magnetic or other kind of disc (e.g. optical publishing), or within a viewdata system (electronic publishing).

pull down (or **pop up**) **menu**   WIMP computer displays show icons for the various facilities on offer. You place the pointer, and click the mouse button to pull down or pop up a menu. If the icon stands for shading, the menu would show the shading styles you can use.

punched card   *See* **card.**

push   To add a data item to the open end of a stack.

query language   A high-level language specially designed for asking questions of a data base.

queue   A linear data structure working with data items in first in, first out fashion.

RAM   A form of storage used in computers, the data in which you can change as well as access (*see* **read and write** *and compare* **ROM**); widely but incorrectly given as 'random access memory'.

random access   Direct access.

read   To retrieve a copy of data from backing store.

read and write   Describes anything you can both read from and write to, such as a note book, RAM and an unprotected disc.

read and write memory (RAM)   Storage space inside a computer for holding data while in use, whose contents are constantly over-written as different programs run, and may vanish when you switch off.

read-only   Describes anything you can read from but not write to, such as a text book, ROM, and a protected disc.

read-only memory (ROM)   The part of a system's main store for software in frequent use—it's not volatile and you can't write to it.

real   A number which can have a fractional part, rather than being an integer.

real-time   Of a system that reacts to each input it receives quickly enough to be able to affect the source of the input in say control or (pseudo real time) interactive work.

real time clock   Keeps a count of day, date and time for use with filing and/or display.

record   (a) In a file, the data on one entity (e.g. car part, client). (b) To record data is to store it for later use, recording density being a measure of how much the data packs onto the surface of the medium in use.

recursion   When a program subroutine calls itself with a reduced version of the problem concerned.

regenerator   A device in a digital data transfer line needed to restore the weak input signal for onward passage.

register   A small special purpose store (with no more than a few cells) in a processor for holding data during processing.

relational   Describes a data base management system that represents, in the form of linked tables, some of the more complex relationships that exist between the data items it stores.

re-locatable   Describes a machine code program without any reference to actual storage cell addresses, so it can go anywhere in store when run.

remote   (a) Not permanently on line; (b) non-local.

repeater   A device in an analog data transfer line designed to amplify the weak input signal for onward passage.

report   (a) A user-defined summary of, or extract from, information held in a data base, a **report generator** being a program to extract, sort, and collate information for the purpose; (b) computer output telling the user of problems met and perhaps actions taken during a job.

resident   Permanently fitted in a system—for example, held in ROM.

resolution   Measures the quality of printout and of computer displays and graphics, for instance—the higher the resolution, the finer the detail.

ring   (a) A linked list whose tail links to its head; (b) a network laid out in a loop.

robot   A machine you can program to do a variety of jobs automatically.

robust   Describes environment-proof hardware, software unlikely to crash, signals hard to corrupt.

ROM   Read-only memory.

root   The node on which a tree structure depends; the highest object in any hierarchy.

rounding   Reaching the best approximate value if a number is too precise (has too many significant figures) for a system to cope with, a **rounding error** being if the final answer is wrong as a result.

satellite In this field, artificial earth satellites are for the transfer of communication signals—they pick up, boost, and re-transmit them.

save To copy data from main to backing store.

scan To pass something in a regular way—e.g. a page cell by cell, and down row by row, perhaps to produce a digital version. A scanner is a digitiser used in this way.

scheduler The part of operating software which looks after the allocation of time in time sharing situations.

screen (a) Output device, such as a monitor or flat LCD; (b) a method of shading printed text and the effect produced.

screen dump The content of a screen display printed as a whole on paper.

scroll When output text is longer than a screen, the processor makes it seem to move for display 'page' by 'page'. Most systems can scroll up and down; some (such as spreadsheets) also need to scroll from side to side.

search To hunt through a data structure for specified data items. **Search time** is a measure of the speed of doing this.

secondary key A field in the records of a file that is used as a key instead of, or as well as, the normal one.

secondary store Backing store.

sector A physical unit (block or physical record) of disc storage. The size of a sector is a factor of the track length.

security Keeping data safe from loss and corruption.

semi-compilation The translation of a program in a language such as Forth, with a small interpreter as well as a compiler.

sensor Device that detects touch, temperature, sound, acidity or some other similar (analog) physical or chemical information, with a corresponding electrical output, thus able to allow computers and robots to react to their environment.

sequential In some order. A sequential file has the records in key field value order.

serial (a) For data transfer and access—the bits of a byte pass along a single line one after the other. *Compare* **parallel.** (b) As a physical file—the records come one after the other, but in no special order. *Compare* **sequential.**

server A hardware and software unit with the function of looking after the needs of a single peripheral—as a file server works with a disc drive.

shared logic Describes when a number of terminals share the same processor.

shell (a) The innermost layer of operating software, closest to the hardware; (b) a knowledge-based expert system without the knowledge; (c) a method of sorting data items.

signal Any energy transfer that carries information from place to place, such as a radio broadcast, speech in a telephone system, or computer data on its way to a peripheral.

silicon Produced from sand, the main semi-conductor at present used in chipmaking.

simulator System that accurately models something too large, costly, dangerous or difficult to work with direct, for training and research.

smart Intelligent.

smart card Like a credit card, with a small computer inside, used for instance in EFTPOS.

soft interrupt An interrupt from operating staff, a run-time error, or a timer.

software The programs and data used to drive a system (operating software) or to carry out a task (application or language software).

sort To order the items of a data file on the basis of current needs.

source document A piece of paper that contains information ready for input to a computer.

source program The set of instructions produced (in assembly or high-level language) before translation (assembly or compilation) to the machine code object program or for execution by an interpreter.

speech recognition Using software to allow computer input of spoken data and commands.

speech synthesis The production by software through a speaker of sounds like human speech.

spelling checker A program that checks the words of processed text against its list, and takes appropriate action about those it can't find.

spooling The transfer of data between main store and peripheral, or between peripherals, with little action from the central processor.

spreadsheet A business software package that displays a grid of entries (such as accounts) and lets you work on the relationships between them, showing at once the effects of changes.

stack A last in, first out linear data structure, one with only one open end.

stand alone A system used on its own—not part of a network, mainframe system, or telecommunications link.

standard A set of rules about hardware, software or communications that allows easier links between systems that follow it.

standard form Describes a denary number expressed as mantissa and exponent, the binary version being floating point form.

star Also called **cluster,** a simple layout (e.g. of network) whose links radiate from the centre.

stock control Business software able to handle changing stock levels and re-ordering.

store To hold data for later use, or the place where it's held. An IT system have three main levels of storage (internal registers, immediate access main store, and backing store, perhaps with cache between the first two).

store and forward The main form of public electronic mail service—a message doesn't go straight to the recipient but waits in the central (host) computer's store for later access.

stored program concept A major aspect of the modern computer: it can store in main memory the set of instructions it needs to carry out so that the system can branch and/or modify the instructions during a run.

streamer   A special tape and drive used to back up a fixed hard disc unit.

string   A sequence of any keyboard characters.

structure   The layout of (for example) system or program; a **structure chart** shows how the parts relate.

structured programming   Setting up programs in a top-down (or other logical) way so they work well and are easy to follow and change.

subroutine   A set of instructions in a program with a clear single task, being either inside the main program (open) or apart from it (closed).

subtree   The tree below a node of a larger tree.

syntax   The rules (grammar) of a language, a **syntax error** being when one such rule is broken.

synthesiser   Device that outputs artificial speech or music from electronic inputs.

system   A set of hardware and/or software and/or people, or a set of working procedures, to carry out a given task.

systems analysis   Analysing an information handling need and working out what systems would best meet it.

systems software   Software like the operating software and program languages a system needs for it to do anything useful.

super-conductivity   The property of certain materials that makes them show no resistance to electric current.

tape   Magnetically or optically coated plastics tape used for holding data—audio, video and computer—for access by a suitable drive.

telecommunications   Transfer and reception of information over a distance.

telecommuting   Working from home using IT links to other work places.

teleconference   A meeting between people linked by telecommunications: audio (using speech on phone lines), video (using pictures carried by cable), or computer (using electronic mail in a form of chat mode).

telesoftware   Programs and/or data copied between two computers at a distance, using phone lines or broadcast waves.

teletex   International standard system for transfer of text and data between terminals using the public phone network, a form of electronic mail.

teletext   Information broadcast in a radio (e.g. TV) signal displayed by sets with special decoders.

television (TV)   The transfer of video picture signals, usually with sound, to a screen—either broadcast (mainly by short radio waves) or by cable (mainly in local distribution and closed circuit TV systems).

telex   A world-wide public telegraph service that allows communication between special printers, by modern standards slow (about a word a second), costly and inflexible, but well established and widely available.

terminal   (a) Hardware combining input and output units to let the user communicate with a remote system; (b) leaf, a childless node in a tree.

test   To check a program or system for faults, using carefully thought out methods and data.

text editor   A program that lets you enter and edit assembly language source code or other text.

text processor   A better name for word processor.

time sharing   Letting a processor work on several jobs at once, by sharing its time in turn between them (perhaps with fixed length slices), as in multiprogramming and multi-user systems.

top–down   Describes planning something (such as a program) hierarchically, from the general concept to layers of more and more specific chunks.

touch screen   Lets you make choices by pointing with a finger (the sensors being of pressure or shadow), making the screen an input as well as an output device.

trace   (a) To dry-run an algorithm, giving most attention to data item values (putting them in a trace table); (b) to have a system output the details of its route through (part of) a program.

track   A linear (on a tape) or circular (on a disc) space for laying down data.

tracker ball   Much like an upside-down mouse, and with the same effect as a mouse or joystick.

transaction file   A file of a firm's transactions. Each new transaction record is added after the last; the file is thus in no useful order.

transducer   Sensor.

transputer   A computer on a chip designed for use in a multiprocessing system.

tree   A branching (hierarchical) data structure, each data site (node) having one parent (unless it's the root) and one or more children (unless it's a leaf).

Turing test   A test for machine intelligence, passed if the machine acts so like a human that an observer can't be sure which is which.

turtle   A small mobile robot used with learners.

2s complement   One more than the 1s complement of a binary value, used to represent negative numbers in a form compatible with addition/subtraction hardware.

underflow   A problem caused when a value is too small for a system to handle; also the case where you try to access an element from an empty data structure (such as a queue).

upgrade   The process of improving or adding to a hardware or software system.

user interface   The mode of interaction between a system and a user, and its associated hardware and software.

user friendly   Describes IT systems that are easy to learn and to use by people like those for whom they're designed.

utilities   Programs that let you do useful jobs like backing up discs and editing the contents of main store.

validation   Checking whether entered data is valid (feasible) or has correct parity or check digits.

variable   A data item referred to by a label and with a value that may change during the course of running a program.

VDU   Visual display unit.

vector   A 1D array (linear list).

verification   Having a second person type in a set of new data so the system can look for disagreement (which shows an error).

video   Describes hardware and systems working with very high frequency signals.

video conference   A 'meeting' between people in different places using video links (radio, cable or phone) to transfer speech, data and pictures.

video disc   A plastics, metal, or glass disc that can store and quickly access large numbers of moving or still video pictures plus sound, with great potential for computer data storage.

video phone   A phone that can transmit an image from a camera and put one received onto a screen, as well as handling speech in the normal way.

videotex   A method of receiving data from a distance and showing it on screen (and/or storing or printing it), using broadcast signals (teletext, one-way or broadcast videotex) or phone lines (viewdata, two-way or interactive videotex).

viewdata   The two-way transfer of data, mainly by phone line, so users not only can access information in large data bases but also can send messages and instructions.

virtual storage   A method of getting main store to hold larger programs or more data than normal, by loading into it just certain blocks from backing store.

visual display unit (VDU)   A device that displays computer output on a screen. Also used loosely to mean a combined screen and keyboard unit (work station or terminal).

voice recognition unit   A computer input device you can train to identify spoken words. *See also* **speech.**

volatile   Describes (a) computer storage whose contents vanish when you switch off; (b) a file whose users often add and delete records.

WIMP   Windows, icons, mouse and pointers (or pull down menus); a modern flexible and friendly type of user interface.

Winchester   A type of small sealed hard disc unit widely used with micros.

windows   The effect of splitting a display screen into sections, with each section able to hold data you can interact with and process.

word   A system's basic unit of data processing—a byte in the case of an 8-bit machine, a double byte with a 16-bit machine, and so on.

word processing   A system for entering, editing, laying out, printing and storing text, now coming close to desk top publishing.

work station   Where a user interacts with a network.

worksheet   A data base or data display set up in the form of a spreadsheet, with a row for each record and a column for each field.

write   To write to a disc (for instance) is to send data to it for storage. *See also* **read.**

WYSIWYG   What you see is what you get; a word processing or desktop publishing system whose display of text is somewhat like a printout would be.

xerography   A form of reproduction in which some page printers charge a drum electrically in the pattern of the original; the charge attracts a plastics dust (toner) which then bakes on to the paper.

Index